INTELLIGENCE AND INTERNATIONAL RELATIONS

1900–1945

EXETER STUDIES IN HISTORY

General Editor: Colin Jones, BA DPhil FRHistS

Editorial Committee

J. Barry, MA DPhil
D. C. Braund, MA PhD
M. Duffy, MA DPhil FRHistS

R. A. Higham, BA PhD
M. D. D. Newitt, BA PhD FRHistS

Publications

INTELLIGENCE
AND INTERNATIONAL RELATIONS
1900–1945

Edited by

Christopher Andrew and Jeremy Noakes

EXETER STUDIES IN HISTORY NO. 15

UNIVERSITY OF EXETER

© 1987   Department of History and Archaeology, University of Exeter

First published 1987 by the University of Exeter

ISBN 0 85989 243 3
ISSN 0260 8626

Exeter University Publications,
Hailey Wing,
Reed Hall,
Streatham Drive,
Exeter EX4 4QR

Typeset by AB Typesetting, Exeter
Printed and Bound by A. Wheaton & Co. Ltd., Exeter

Contents

Foreword

The contents of this volume arise out of the first Medlicott Symposium, held by the Department of History and Archaeology of the University of Exeter on 31 October and 1 November 1985. Professor Norton Medlicott was Professor of History and Head of Department at Exeter from 1946 to 1953, and to commemorate his association with Exeter, the Department organises occasional major international symposia in modern history. This first symposium was attended by several dozen university scholars and others who have first-hand experience of intelligence work. The Exeter Studies in History are pleased to publish the revised proceedings of what was undoubtedly a highly stimulating, successful and topical symposium, and one which constitutes a major contribution to what has been one of Professor Medlicott's own areas of specialism.

Colin Jones
General Editor
Exeter Studies in History

Exeter, January 1987

Abbreviations

AI	Air Intelligence
APS	Axis Planning Staff
BP	Bletchley Park
CID	Committee of Imperial Defence
CIGS	Chief of the Imperial General Staff
COS	Chiefs of Staff
DCI	Department of Criminal Intelligence of the (British) Government of India
DDI	Deputy Director of Intelligence (Air Ministry)
DDMI	Deputy Director of Intelligence (War Office)
DDMO & I	Deputy Director of Military Operations and Intelligence
DMO & I	Director of Military Operations and Intelligence
DNI	Director of Naval Intelligence
FCI	Industrial Intelligence in Foreign Countries Sub-Committee (of CID)
FHO	Fremde Heere Ost (German Army Intelligence in the East)
FO	Foreign Office
FOES	Future Operations (Enemy) Staff
FPC	Foreign Policy Committee
GAF	German Air Force
GC&CS	Government Code and Cypher School
IIC	Industrial Intelligence Centre
ISIC	Inter-Service Intelligence Committee
JIC	Joint Intelligence Committee
JIS	Joint Intelligence Staff
JPS	Joint Planning Staff
MEW	Ministry of Economic Warfare
MI	Military Intelligence
MI 1c	Predecessor of MI6
MI 3(b)	Military Intelligence's German Section
MI5	Security Service
MI6	Successor to MI 1c as military section of, later alternative designation for SIS

MOMP	Mid-ocean Meeting Point
NID	Naval Intelligence Department/Division
OB	Oberbefehlshaber (Commander-in-Chief)
OIC	Operational Intelligence Centre (in the Admiralty)
OKH	Oberkommando des Heeres (Army High Command)
OKW	Oberkommando der Wehrmacht (Armed Forces High Command)
OMP	Ocean Meeting Point
PG	Panzergrenadier
PR	Photographic Reconnaissance
PRO	Public Record Office
Sigint	Signals Intelligence
SIS	Secret Intelligence Service
SRC	Situation Report Centre
W/T	Wireless Telegraphy

Introduction:
Intelligence and International
Relations 1900–1945

CHRISTOPHER ANDREW

As recently as the beginning of the 1970s books on twentieth-century international relations commonly omitted intelligence altogether. Some still do. Over the last fifteen years, however, research on intelligence has helped to transform our understanding of the Second World War. There are, nonetheless, still major gaps in our knowledge of wartime intelligence (Soviet signals intelligence, for example, remains uncharted ground) and even larger gaps for the previous generation. This volume of essays cannot hope to cover the vast programme of research on intelligence and modern international relations which still remains. But it seeks to assess some of the progress made over the last decade and to advance the present frontiers of research in a number of significant directions.

My own article attempts an overview of the influence of secret intelligence on British foreign policy up to the Second World War and shows its capacity to confuse as well as to enlighten its consumers. Because of the lack of any adequate prewar system of intelligence co-ordination and assessment, Whitehall swallowed whole a series of intelligence plants on the eve and at the beginning of the Second World War. The permanent undersecretary at the Foreign Office, Sir Alexander Cadogan, confessed that even when he chose to credit accurate rather than misleading intelligence reports, 'It just happened that these were correct; we had no means of evaluating their reliability at the time of receipt'. Without major wartime improvements in intelligence assessment, much of the priceless 'Ultra' intelligence which began to come on stream just as Churchill became prime minister in May 1940 would have been wasted.

Despite the growing literature on signals intelligence (sigint) during the two World Wars, studies of the origins of the First World War frequently omit all reference to it. Russian cryptanalysts, however, succeeded before 1914 in decrypting, at least intermittently, the diplomatic traffic of all the great powers.[1] The French *cabinets noirs* also achieved some striking successes. Jean Stengers shows how an important episode in the 1914 July crisis—the failure of Maurice Paléologue, the French ambassador in St Petersburg, to pass on vital information to his government—has been misunderstood by historians because of their failure to take sigint into account. Paléologue feared that his telegrams to Paris would be intercepted by both the Russians and the Germans. His fears were well founded so far as the Russian codebreakers were concerned but mistaken as regards the Germans. Neither Paléologue nor the Quai d'Orsay realised that before 1914 the Germans had no diplomatic sigint at all.[2]

British intelligence during the period covered by this volume was at the centre of a growing imperial intelligence network which represents an important field for future research. The articles by Richard Popplewell, Peter Morris, Keith Jeffery and Alan Sharp cast new light on the confused early development of this network. Richard Popplewell shows how surveillance of the Indian diaspora in North America before the First World War gradually produced, despite many hesitations, some degree of intelligence cooperation between agencies in Canada, Britain and India. In the light of the alleged responsibility of Vancouver Sikhs for the Air India Boeing 747 disaster in 1985 it is instructive to learn that the Sikh community in Vancouver was under surveillance before the First World War and that, shortly after the outbreak of war, a Vancouver Sikh assassinated the officer in charge of the surveillance. The First World War produced a major expansion of Indian as well as British intelligence. In 1915 the Indian government set up an intelligence agency for the whole of the Pacific and Far East. Its head, David Petrie, went on to become director general of MI5 during the Second World War.

The wartime expansion of both British and Indian intelligence led inevitably to problems of demarcation between the two. One of the areas of greatest confusion was Mesopotamia where responsibility for intelligence gathering was divided between London and Simla. Peter Morris shows how intelligence confusion contributed to the disastrous Mesopotamian campaign of 1914–16 which ended in surrender to the Turks at Kut al-Amara—perhaps the greatest British military humiliation of the war. In March 1915 the War Office estimated the number of Turkish troops in Mesopotamia at 65,000; Simla put the figure, more realistically, at just over 20,000. Such confusion helps to explain why the British commander, General Sir John Nixon, failed to heed intelligence which might have persuaded him to halt his advance on Baghdad and so avoid disaster at Kut.

Keith Jeffery and Alan Sharp emphasise Lord Curzon's interest in sigint as foreign secretary from 1919 to 1924 and provide the first detailed analysis of its influence on his policy in the Middle East. Some of this sigint came from the newly established Government Code and Cypher School in London. A substantial contribution was also made by the British military sigint agency at Constantinople (later moved to Sarafand in Palestine) whose operations mark an important stage in the development of an imperial sigint network which since the Second World War has been largely incorporated in the UKUSA Security Agreement which divides the globe into spheres of cryptographic influence. Jeffery and Sharp demonstrate how the Foreign Office was fed with a regular diet of French, Greek and Turkish intercepts during negotiations for the peace settlement in the Middle East. From these intercepts Curzon learned much, not merely about the policies of other powers but also about the pro-Greek foreign policy independently pursued by the prime minister, Lloyd George.

Intelligence research has hitherto concentrated overwhelmingly on the West and the Soviet bloc. The study of Asian intelligence systems is still in its infancy. Research on the intelligence duel between Japan and the West, particularly in the West, has so far been strikingly one-sided. It is now notorious, for example, that Japanese codes were broken at frequent intervals by Western cryptanalysts from the Russo-Japanese to the Second World War. But little has been published on Japanese intelligence work against the West. Ian Nish and John Chapman go some way to redress the balance. Ian Nish shows that, despite her backwardness in sigint, Japan had developed worldwide intelligence interests before the First World War. Intelligence had, however, a smaller influence on her operations against Germany in 1914–18 than on the wars with China in 1894–5 and with Russia in 1904–5 or in the Siberian intervention of 1918–22. John Chapman emphasises the structural weaknesses of Japanese intelligence in the Second World War, despite substantial interwar advances. The Japanese navy had only a rudimentary version of the operational intelligence centres established in Britain, Germany and the United States. Intelligence coordination never approached the level achieved in Britain and the United States, and was probably even worse than in Germany. The Japanese high command both undervalued the contribution of intelligence to the conduct of the war and convinced itself that Japan knew more about her enemies than her enemies knew about Japan.

The history of French intelligence on the eve of the Second World War has been clouded by the exaggerated claims of some of its former chiefs. Anthony Adamthwaite gives a more sober and convincing assessment. Some of the French failings he reveals were strikingly similar to those in Britain during the final years of peace: poor coordination, exaggerated estimates of German military strength at the time of Munich, underestimation of both Soviet military potential and the likelihood of a Nazi-Soviet pact, the reporting of a series of false alarms of German attacks in the final months of peace. Even the celebrated case of the documents purloined from the safe of the British ambassador in Rome by the Italian secret police turns out to have a close parallel in the almost equally insecure safe of the French ambassador. No French intelligence chief, however, equalled the influence of the head of SIS, Admiral Sir Hugh 'Quex' Sinclair, who gained the ear of both the Foreign Office and the prime minister.

The most popular and successful area for intelligence research over the last decade has been the Second World War. The major work in the field is the monumental *British Intelligence in the Second World War* by a team of official historians led by Sir Harry Hinsley. Sir Harry's article in this volume emphasizes that sigint was 'incomparably more valuable' than other wartime intelligence sources. By 1943 Bletchley Park was reading 3,000 German 'Ultra' signals a day in addition to lower-grade German traffic and Italian and Japanese signals. But, contrary to common belief, the most valuable sigint from 1943 onwards came not from Enigma decrypts but from radio signals based on teleprinter impulses decrypted by Colossus, the world's first electronic computer (whose plans are still classified!). Sir Harry Hinsley attributes the Germans' failure to grasp that the ciphers were broken less to their own incompetence than to brilliantly successful British security measures to disguise the extent and the source of their intelligence. It is tempting to conclude that the high priority given to wartime sigint security reflected awareness of the damage done by poor interwar security—in particular the loss of the Soviet codes in 1927.

Sir Harry Hinsley's collaborator in the official history, Edward Thomas, analyses one of the key elements in wartime intelligence: the Joint Intelligence Committee (whose papers, like Colossus, are still classified). During the 1930s 'Muddle and mischance had brought a potentially effective machine into being. It would take the shocks of war to make that machine truly effective'. Though founded in 1936, the JIC did not become 'truly effective' until the creation of the Joint Intelligence Staff to service it in 1941. The JIS quickly became 'the corporate memory of the entire intelligence community'. Like other sections of the wartime intelligence it benefited greatly from a transfusion of highly intelligent civilian recruits. Its key members included a barrister, a history don and an advertising agent, thinly disguised as officers. The final JIS wartime appreciation, entitled 'Why the Germans lost the War', reasonably included among the list of Germany's major weaknesses the lack of a JIC.

Enormously valuable though Ultra was to the conduct of the war, its importance fluctuated very considerably. Ralph Bennett emphasizes its variable quality in the land battles of the Mediterranean theatre, where its content varied from month to month, sometimes even from day to day. The difficulties of plotting these fluctuations today are multiplied by Whitehall's eccentric refusal to declassify material which would make it possible to distinguish with certainty German army and airforce intercepts in the Public Record Office. Until army Enigma decrypts came on stream in the spring of 1942, Ultra revealed much about the movements of enemy shipping in the Mediterranean but little about what it was carrying. In particular it revealed nothing about the supply of tanks which was crucial to Rommel's North African campaigns. The serious British miscalculations which assisted Rommel's successes early in 1942 ceased once Bletchley Park began to decrypt the *Panzerlage* a few months later.

Like Sir Harry Hinsley, Edward Thomas and Ralph Bennett, the late Patrick Beesly had personal experience of Ultra in the Second World War. His article in this volume (completed shortly before his death) emphasises the importance of the precedent set by the Naval Intelligence Division in the First World War under its dynamic head, Admiral Sir Reginald 'Blinker' Hall, for naval intelligence in the Second. Captain (later Admiral) John Godfrey, who was appointed Director of Naval Intelligence in January 1939, acknowledged that 'When in doubt I often asked myself what Hall would have done'. Having compared German naval intercepts of the two world wars, Patrick Beesly concludes that 'one would, if one ignored the dates, be hard put to it to decide which period they belonged to, so similar in form and context are they—and in the type of information which they provided'. The chief difference was that in the Second World War, partly because of the Admiralty's ability to learn from the mistakes as well as the successes of the First, naval intelligence was much better used. Jürgen Rohwer reveals that the German naval sigint agency, the *x-B Dienst*, was also influenced by the First World War achievements of the sigint unit in the Admiralty, Room 40. He shows, however, that the *x-B Dienst* was steadily overtaken by Bletchley Park in both the scale and the speed of its operations. Ultra, he argues, had a decisive influence on the eventual Allied victory in the long drawn-out Battle of the Atlantic. But Bletchley Park's victory, though decisive, was not total. Rohwer demonstrates that, contrary to common belief, the *x-B Dienst* continued even after the Battle of the Atlantic to decrypt some British signals.

Germany's most glaring intelligence failures were probably on the Eastern rather than the Western Front. In the West she eventually fell victim to the massive deception of 'Operation Fortitude' which made possible the D-Day landings. In the East, German self-deception may have done more damage than Soviet deception.[3] Bernd Wegner shows how even after the expectations of a swift and easy victory which inspired Operation Barbarossa in June 1941 had been dissipated, the Germans continued to underestimate severely both Russian manpower and arms production. Hitler acknowledged, uncharacteristically, in the summer of 1942 that he had been completely wrong in his assessment of Soviet forces a year before. Even had he been supplied with correct figures for Soviet tank forces in 1941, he would—he admitted—have dismissed them out of hand. Hitler, however, made the same mistake in the summer of 1942. The knowledge that the Führer did not welcome pessimistic estimates of Soviet strength discouraged his advisers from supplying them. But Hitler in any case took his major decisions on the Eastern offensive in the summer of 1942 before receiving the main intelligence assessments about Soviet resources of men and matériel. Not the least important aspect of Churchill's superiority over Hitler as a war leader was his much greater grasp of the role and importance of intelligence.

Taken together, the articles in this volume illustrate some of the opportunities and the tribulations which intelligence presents to both the historian and the policy-maker. For the historian the study of intelligence offers a perspective of international relations, and sometimes of national politics, which until recently was usually ignored. But the extraordinary overclassification in Britain and elsewhere of even the most elderly intelligence archives with no conceivable bearing on contemporary national security presents obstacles to research which are more formidable than those in any other area of international relations. For the policy-maker good intelligence can sometimes, as Sir Horace Rumbold discovered, 'reveal the cards in his adversary's hands'.[4] Revelation of the cards in Hitler's hand shortened the Second World War. But for the statesman without the means to assess it or the judgement to use it wisely, intelligence is as likely to sow confusion as to shed light. Knowledge is power. Raw intelligence is not.

Notes

1. Christopher Andrew and Keith Neilson, 'Tsarist Codebreakers and British Codes', *Intelligence and National Security*, I (1986), no. 1.
2. Christopher Andrew, 'Déchiffrement et diplomatie: le cabinet noir du Quai d'Orsay sous la Troisième République', *Relations Internationales*, III (1976), no. 5.
3. See, however, the pioneering study by David M. Glantz, 'The Real Mask: The Nature and Legacy of Soviet Military Deception in World War II', forthcoming in *Intelligence and National Security*, II (1987), no. 3.
4. See below, p. 115.

Secret Intelligence and British Foreign Policy 1900–1939

CHRISTOPHER ANDREW

In studying the sources for British foreign policy in the twentieth century we need constantly to remember that we are dealing with a laundered archive. It is an archive laundered by honourable men in what they believed to be the national interest. But it is still a laundered archive.

Often the laundering does not matter very much. Sometimes, however, it matters a great deal. No-one, for example, would nowadays dream of writing a history of Anglo-Soviet relations during the decade after the Bolshevik Revolution without referring to the British interception of Soviet diplomatic traffic. But the many thousands of *Documents on British Foreign Policy* published by the Foreign Office for the 1920s contain not a single Soviet intercept. Not merely did the Foreign Office refuse to release interwar intercepts. It tried for many years to conceal even the fact that intercepts existed. In what it considers the interests of national security, Whitehall has sometimes been guilty of the worst kind of censorship—the censorship which hides its own existence. Those who consult the entry for 'Secret Service' in the Public Record Office index to the cabinet minutes for the period 1919 to 1921 will find simply a suspicious looking gap. Anyone who then consults the entry 'Scotland Yard' will find a cross-reference which gives the game away. It reads 'See Secret Service'—which is, of course, precisely what we are not supposed to see.[1]

The silent censorship of the archives has misled historians of international relations in a variety of ways. Histories of Anglo-French relations between the wars, for example, almost invariably fail to mention signals intelligence. We now know, however, that from the treaty of Versailles until 1935 *all* French diplomatic codes and ciphers were broken by the codebreakers of GC&CS, the Government Code and Cypher School.[2] Even though much of the diplomatic traffic to Paris went by diplomatic bag rather than by telegram, it follows that any historian of Anglo-French relations between the

9

wars requires access to the intercepted French telegrams supplied to the Foreign Office if he is fully to understand British policy to France. Her Majesty's Government, however, continues to believe that the release of these and similar telegrams would put national security at risk. So dangerous is the threat to national security from these telegrams that, we are told, it may *never* be possible to release them. Indeed, Her Majesty's Government goes even further. In the interests of national security it will not acknowledge that the telegrams exist at all.

There is thus a basic conflict of interest between the interests of historical research on the one hand and the interests of national security as defined by Her Majesty's Government on the other hand. A commonsense method of seeking to resolve that conflict was suggested in 1981 by the Committee on the Public Records chaired by the former ambassador in Moscow, Sir Duncan Wilson. The Wilson Committee proposed that a suitably experienced sub-committee of the Advisory Council on Public Records, possibly composed of privy counsellors already on the Council like Lord Denning, should advise on the release of intelligence and other sensitive files over thirty years old. That commonsense proposal was examined in 1982-3 by the Commons Select Committee on Education, Science and the Arts. Sadly, an election intervened before the Committee could draw up an official report. But the minutes of the Committee's meetings make a powerful case for the Wilson report.[3] The government has so far brushed most of that report aside.

The traditional attempt to enforce a total ban on the intelligence archive has, mercifully, begun to crumble. Since, however, Whitehall has so far declined to substitute any coherent policy for the traditional total ban, the historian of British foreign policy is faced with a series of bizarre contradictions as he attempts to make sense of the archives. As the cabinet secretary, Sir Robert Armstrong, told the Commons Select Committee in 1983, peacetime intelligence is officially considered much more secret than wartime intelligence—apparently without limit of time.[4] Thus while some wartime intercepts of the 1940s are available at the Public Record Office, peacetime intercepts of the 1920s are supposed to be withheld indefinitely. Different departments within Whitehall are nowadays apt to take different views about what needs to be kept secret. A remarkable recent case in point concerns the last article by the great wartime cryptanalyst, Gordon Welchman, 'From Polish Bomba to British Bombe: The Birth of Ultra'.[5] On 8 July 1985 the contents of the article were cleared for publication by the Defence, Press and Broadcasting Committee (better known as the 'D Notice' Committee) which advises on the publication of material with a possible bearing on national security. Four days later, on 12 July 1985, the director of GCHQ, Sir Peter Marychurch, wrote a personal letter to Gordon Welchman, alleging that the publicaton of the article would cause 'direct damage to security' and set 'a disastrous example to others'. Welchman's former colleague at Bletchley Park, Sir Stuart Milner-Barry, who later became undersecretary and ceremonial officer at the Treasury, has described Sir Peter Marychurch's letter as 'a prime example of the lengths to which GCHQ's paranoia about ancient secrets will carry them'.[6]

Sir Robert Armstrong's distinction between peacetime and wartime archives, like Sir Peter Marychurch's alarmism about ancient secrets of both war and peace, can be understood only within the long tradition of eccentricity which forms so important a theme in British intelligence history—or, to be more precise, in the history of government use of intelligence and the intelligence services. One of the main conclusions which emerges from a study of the accessible part of the intelligence record is the slowness of successive governments to make sensible use of intelligence and the intelligence services in the conduct of British foreign policy. They did not do so consistently until the Second World War, and the standards of the Second World War were not always maintained by postwar governments.

Assessing the influence of secret intelligence on British foreign policy before the First World War seems at first sight fairly simple. Though it received intelligence of various kinds from the Middle East and from the frontiers of empire, the Foreign Office received very little secret intelligence from the continent of Europe. Before 1914 it received no sigint at all. After the closure of its Decyphering Branch in 1844, the Foreign Office usually stuck to the principle later enunciated by the American Secretary of State, Henry Stimson, that 'Gentlemen do not read each other's mail'.[7] The Indian government had fewer scruples than the Foreign Office. Its concern with the Russian menace on the North-West Frontier led it to begin intercepting Russian communications in 1904. Over the next few years two Indian army officers, Major G. R. M. Church and Captain G. S. Palmer, had some success in breaking (probably relatively low-grade) Tsarist and Chinese codes and ciphers.[8] The Foreign Office failed to follow suit.

Fortunately Germany seems to have taken no advantage of British cryptographic innocence. The powers who had most success with prewar Britain's diplomatic codes and ciphers were, ironically, her wartime allies France and Russia. The Russians, indeed, were sometimes embarrassed by the ease with which they read British diplomatic traffic. Sir Charles Hardinge, the ambassador in St Petersburg, complained to the Foreign Office in June 1904 that he had just received 'a disagreeable shock'. A leading Russian statesman had impressed on him that he 'did not mind how much I reported in writing what he told me in conversation but he begged me on no account to telegraph as all our telegrams are known'. The Foreign Office was slow to take the hint. In 1916 the station chief for SIS (then known as MI1c) in Petrograd, Sir Samuel Hoare (later foreign secretary), was warned by a Russian intelligence officer to change his ciphers since his existing ones could be read as easily as a 'newspaper'.[9]

At least in Europe the prewar Foreign Office was almost as bereft of humint (human intelligence) as of sigint. Even the founding of the Secret Service Bureau in 1909 did little to improve the flow of political intelligence. Commander (later Captain Sir) Mansfield Cumming, the first head of its foreign department (the future SIS), was so short of money that he could not afford full-time agents. He relied instead on what were called 'casual agents': mostly men in the shipping or arms industries who were either based in Germany or regularly travelled round it, and used their business cover to engage in part-time intelligence work. Cumming supplemented their efforts by travelling around Germany himself dressed in disguises which are still classified and carrying a swordstick which remains in the family's possession. 'This business', Cumming told one of his agents, 'is really amusing. It's capital sport'. Most of the 'casual agents' disagreed. But capital sport or not, Cumming's expeditions and the efforts of his part-time spies provided little insight into German policy. Anxious to preserve its monopoly of political reporting, the Foreign Office preferred the Secret Service Bureau to confine itself to military and naval intelligence.[10] According to a secret post-war report:

> [Cumming's] organisation was merely military and naval, and its restricted energies were almost entirely directed against Germany. With the funds then available attempt could only be made to unravel a few technical problems, and for this purpose use had to be made of casual agents whose employment has by war experience been clearly demonstrated to be undesirable.[11]

But though Whitehall received little good intelligence about Germany's prewar policy it received a surprising amount of bad intelligence. Some of it came from freelance Brussels espionage agencies who produced forged documents with the same enthusiasm as White Russian forgers after the October Revolution. But the principal sources were patriotic British citizens, mostly excitable readers of spy novels who were convinced that they had identified German spies at large in Britain. Much of this spectacularly bad intelligence pointed to two false conclusions: first, that Germany was planning an invasion of the British Isles; and, secondly, that some hundreds, if not thousands, of German spies were at work in Britain preparing for this invasion and planning a large-scale campaign of sabotage and subversion to coincide with the outbreak of war.

War Office intelligence officers took these reports quite seriously. Lieutenant-Colonel (later Major-General Sir) James Edmonds, responsible for War Office counter-espionage and later official historian of the First World War, assured the Committee of Imperial Defence in 1909 that thanks to a massive campaign of German espionage, 'a German general landing a force in East Anglia would know more about the country than any British General, more about each town than its own British Mayor'. In support of this extraordinary proposition Edmonds assembled perhaps the most eccentric collection of evidence ever to have influenced modern British defence policy. He admitted that none of the cases of suspected espionage which he reported had been noticed by either the armed services or the police:

> The military authorities are entirely dependent for information on the subject on the enterprise of individual members of the public . . . It is only since certain newspapers have directed attention to the subject that many cases have come to notice.

This remarkable evidence, based on civilian reports of mostly non-existent spies, persuaded R. B. Haldane, the secretary of state for war, and a sub-committee of the Committee of Imperial Defence, that there was 'no doubt that an extensive system of German espionage exists in this country'. Their report led to the creation by Asquith's cabinet in 1909 of the Secret Service Bureau whose home and foreign departments later became, respectively, the counterespionage agency MI5 and the espionage agency usually known as SIS or MI6.[12]

Inaccurate and alarmist intelligence which wildly exaggerated both the scale and sinister intent of German espionage made a significant contribution to the worsening of Anglo-German relations. It impressed even two of Germany's main friends within the Asquith cabinet, Haldane and Churchill. Haldane, complained John Morley, the secretary of state for India, 'wearies his Cabinet colleagues by long harangues on the contribution of Germany to culture'. During the Great War he was hounded from office because of his allegedly pro-German sympathies. But in 1909 it was the Haldane sub-committee report which led to the foundation of the Secret Service Bureau.[13]

Churchill was slower than Haldane to become concerned by the German spy menace. His plans for labour exchanges and national insurance while President of the Board of Trade in 1909 were heavily influenced by German example. In cabinet debates during that year Churchill took the side of the so-called 'economists' against the navalists' demand for a rapid expansion of the fleet to meet the German menace. The crucial influence in persuading Churchill to take the German spy menace seriously was Vernon Kell, head of MI5 from its foundation in 1909 as the home department of the Secret Service Bureau until the Second World War. As both home secretary in 1910–11 and First Lord of the Admiralty in 1911–15 Churchill had 'a great deal to do' with Kell, and found him 'thoroughly trustworthy and competent'. He sometimes circulated Kell's alarmist reports to Sir Edward Grey, Lloyd George and other ministers. By the Agadir crisis of 1911 intelligence reports, particularly from Kell, had led Churchill to the erroneous conclusion that a large German spy ring in England was engaged in 'minute and scientific' military and naval espionage. 'No other country in the world', wrote Churchill, 'pays us such attention'.[14] The German espionage network was, he believed, also engaged in peacetime subversion and preparations for wartime sabotage. In the summer of 1911 Churchill told the cabinet that the great strike wave in the docks and on the railways was being financed by German gold.[15]

The First World War produced a vast increase in the flow of diplomatic as well as military and naval intelligence. What is striking, however, is how little attention the Foreign Office paid to it. The greatest intelligence advance of the War was, without doubt, the revival of British codebreaking after a gap of seventy years. Remarkably, the Foreign Office had nothing to do with that revival. The initiative came instead from the Director of Naval Intelligence, Admiral (later Sir) Reginald 'Blinker' Hall, who founded a diplomatic annexe to the wartime Admiralty sigint unit, Room 40, under his personal control in the summer of 1915. Hall decided on his own initiative what diplomatic intercepts he would show the Foreign Office or anyone else outside the Admiralty. Indeed he was perfectly capable of taking secret diplomatic initiatives without consulting the Foreign Office at all. During the Dardanelles campaign in 1915 he sent secret emissaries to Constantinople with authority to offer up to £4 million to secure the passage of the British Fleet.[16]

Before the Irish Easter Rising in 1916, Hall learned from decrypted telegrams exchanged between the German foreign ministry and its Washington embassy of plans to land both German arms and the Irish nationalist Sir Roger Casement on the west coast of Ireland. Though the intelligence came from diplomatic traffic, Hall failed to inform either the Foreign Office or the Irish government. Dublin Castle learned of it only accidentally through an indiscretion of the naval commander in Queenstown.

Hall's whole behaviour before and after the Easter Rising strongly suggests that he was anxious for the Rising to go ahead in order to force the government to respond with the repression he thought necessary—and that he deliberately suppressed intelligence which he feared might allow the Rising to be nipped in the bud.[17] Even over the celebrated Zimmerman telegram, which revealed German attempts early in 1917 to lure Mexico into the war against the United States, Hall continued to allow himself a remarkable freedom of action. On 20 February 1917 Hall uncharacteristically turned up at the Foreign Office and asked permission to show the newly decrypted telegram to the American Embassy. What he failed to mention, however, was that he had already done so on the previous day.[18]

Even within the Admiralty, Hall's empire was considered both too large and too independent. Captain (later Admiral Sir) William 'Bubbles' James, whom Hall put in charge of Room 40 for the final eighteen months of the war, found that the Naval Intelligence Department's 'very remarkable reputation was, unfortunately, tarnished in the opinion of a great many officers'. The employment by Hall of sometimes eccentric civilians in Room 40 and other parts of NID 'caused a great deal of adverse criticism by our brother officers':

> It is true that, if for the better prosecution of the war you collect such an imposing array of men of intellect, it is extremely difficult to groom and guide them as you do men of a lesser calibre and more normal temperament. . . .

The 'imposing array of men of intellect' recruited by Hall for Room 40, though they tried the patience of the Admiralty, were to form a vital precedent for recruitment to Bletchley Park in the Second World War. Without such men 'Ultra'—the most valuable intelligence in British history—would have been impossible. Hall's outsize, unconventional personality and the influence which sigint gave him ceased to be tolerated within the Admiralty once victory was won. Captain James concluded:

> An intense enthusiasm, a superimaginative intellect and a remarkable determination, which characterised Admiral Hall, cannot be given scope without some disadvantages arising.[19]

Hall's more tactful peacetime successor, Captain (later Admiral Sir) Hugh 'Quex' Sinclair, stepped on fewer toes in both the Admiralty and the Foreign Office during his two-year term as DNI (1919–21). In April 1919 Sinclair gained approval from the Foreign Office, War Office and Admiralty for the establishment under his 'general direction' of a new sigint agency from the post-war remnants of Room 40 and its smaller military counterpart, MI1b.

Because of the Foreign Office's lack of involvement in wartime sigint, the Admiralty was able to argue persuasively that, at least 'in the first instance', control of the agency should be vested in one of the service departments, who 'had far more experience of this work in the immediate past'. The new unit, christened after some discussion the Government Code and Cypher School (GC&CS), was authorised by the cabinet to start work on 1 November 1919 under Admiralty control. The Admiralty acknowledged, however, that 'in the future' it was 'immaterial' which ministry assumed responsibility for GC&CS. The preponderance of diplomatic rather than service traffic in the post-war signals decrypted quickly strengthened the claims of the Foreign Office. In 1921 responsibility for GC&CS passed from the Admiralty to the Foreign Office. Since, however, the Foreign Office was anxious to avoid the publicity attendant on the presentation of a supplementary estimate for GC&CS during the 1921/2 financial year, the Admiralty agreed to retain 'financial responsibility' until 1 April 1922.[20]

GC&CS provided the Foreign Office between the wars with an average of just over seventy 'flimsies' a week.[21] But though the number of 'flimsies' remained relatively constant, the intelligence they provided was probably more valuable in the aftermath of the First World War than in the run-up to the Second—chiefly because some at least of the code and cipher systems used by the major powers were then more vulnerable than they later became. This was particularly true of Russia. For a decade after the Bolshevik Revolution, Soviet diplomatic ciphers were perhaps the most vulnerable of all the major powers.[22] For several years after the First World War the 'flimsies' from GC&CS—especially the Soviet intercepts—circulated within the cabinet with a freedom which later became unthinkable. Churchill later claimed that as secretary for war and air in 1918–21 and as colonial secretary in 1921–2 he had 'read every one of these flimsies', and not merely those which concerned his own department. Though the evidence is fragmentary, other senior ministers also seem to have enjoyed access to as many intercepts as they wished. The evidence of Soviet 'duplicity' provided by the intercepts in 1920 was at the heart of heated cabinet debates over whether to proceed with the negotiatons which led up to the Anglo-Soviet trade agreement of March 1921. Both Churchill and the foreign secretary Lord Curzon studied the intercepts with almost obsessional interest. 'I attach more importance to them as a means of forming a true judgement of public policy in these spheres', wrote Churchill, 'than to any other sources of knowledge at the disposal of the State'.[23] Curzon agreed. 'The decyphered telegrams of foreign governments', he concluded, 'are without doubt the most valuable source of our secret information respecting their policy and actions'.[24]

Curzon's ability to use the intercepts as diplomatic trump cards was sometimes hampered by his deep sense of personal outrage at their contents. In his negotiations with both the French and the Russians, he was, in the words of the senior British diplomat, Sir Horace Rumbold, 'in the position of a man who is playing bridge and knows the cards in his adversary's hands'.[25] Having seen the cards, however, Curzon found it increasingly difficult to preserve a poker-face. He had long regarded the French as not the kind of people 'to go tiger-shooting with'. The evidence of French intrigue in the Middle East revealed by both GC&CS and military codebreakers in Constantinople led him to revise his opinion downwards. French intercepts convinced Curzon that Raymond Poincaré, French prime minister and foreign minister from 1922 to 1924, 'lied shamelessly'. By the Chanak crisis in September 1922 he could stand it no longer. The secret evidence of what he considered Poincaré's ill-faith and his inability to confront him with it helped to reduce Curzon to perhaps the most humiliating nervous collapse ever suffered by a British foreign secretary. At a meeting with Poincaré he burst into tears and was led from the room sobbing, 'I can't bear that horrid little man. I can't bear him'.[26] Until 1922 the French ambassador, the comte de Saint-Aulaire, had regarded Curzon, despite his excitable nature, as the outward epitome of British official decorum. In his meetings with Curzon during that year, however, he believed that the national stereotypes of 'the highly-strung Frenchman' and 'the phlegmatic Englishman' were neatly reversed.[27] During his final months in office Curzon became almost obsessed by the belief that the French were plotting against him. In October 1923 he claimed to have discovered from French intercepts a plot by Poincaré, Saint-Aulaire and the editor of the *Morning Post* to have him sacked as foreign secretary. During the few months which remained of Baldwin's first government, Curzon refused even to see the French ambassador and told Baldwin: 'This is the worst thing that I have come across in my public life'. It was not, of course, the worst thing—and the idea that Poincaré and Saint Aulaire could, with some help from the *Morning Post*, have him sacked is somewhat preposterous. But the fact that Curzon could denounce the contents of French telegrams as 'the worst thing' in his whole career is a striking example of his emotional difficulty in coping with wounding references to himself in diplomatic intercepts.[28]

The evidence of Soviet perfidy contained in Soviet intercepts provoked Curzon to express his outrage in a different form. The 'Curzon ultimatum' of May 1923 which warned the Soviet Union in no uncertain terms to mend its subversive ways was probably the most undiplomatic British diplomatic note of modern times. Not merely did Curzon quote intercepted Soviet telegrams—he taunted the Russians with the fact that their codes were broken. After some delay the new code and cipher systems introduced by the Russians after the Curzon ultimatum were also broken by GC&CS. British cryptanalysts finally lost the ability to decrypt Soviet diplomatic traffic after further, if less flamboyant, revelations of their successes by the government in May 1927. In order to justify their decision to break off Anglo-Soviet diplomatic relations the prime minister, Stanley Baldwin, the foreign secretary Austen Chamberlain, and the home secretary, Joynson Hicks, read out to the Commons subversive extracts from the Soviet intercepts.[29] Baldwin's indiscretion may actually have been even worse than *Hansard* suggested. In reading out an intercepted telegram from the Soviet chargé d'affaires in London to Moscow, Baldwin said at one point, according to *Hansard*, 'There is one word missing'.[30] But it seems possible that *Hansard* watered down what the prime minister actually said. The cryptanalysts of GC&CS were told that the prime minister had copies of its 'flimsies' at the despatch box, had used the cryptographic jargon 'One group corrupt', and had been visibly quoting from the original text of a GC&CS decrypt.[31] No wonder that Alastair Denniston, the operational head of GC&CS, wrote indignantly that Baldwin's government had 'compromise[d] our work beyond question'. Henceforth Soviet diplomatic traffic went by the virtually unbreakable 'one-time pad', and Britain had lost its most valuable interwar intelligence source.[32]

During the decade after the First World War SIS had less influence on British foreign policy than GC&CS. Though Cumming had been financed from the Foreign Office secret vote since the First World War, the Foreign Office only assumed complete responsibility for SIS in 1921. It was initially unenthusiastic about the decision to allow Cumming's station chiefs abroad to operate under semi-diplomatic cover as passport control officers attached to British embassies and legations. Some diplomats continued to regard intelligence as a dirty business which might soil diplomatic hands. Their fears seemed justified when in the autumn of 1921 SIS caused one major diplomatic embarrassment. During the early years after the Bolshevik Revolution SIS was taken in by a number of anti-Soviet forgeries and bogus intelligence reports much as it had fallen for some bogus German intelligence before the war. In a protest note to the Soviet government of September 1921 Curzon quoted several forged documents supplied by the SIS which were then exposed in the Soviet reply. Though refusing to acknowledge their embarrassing error in public, in private Curzon vented his considerable wrath on both his own advisers and SIS. 'I am positively appalled', he told them, '. . . at the entire history of this case'. SIS was required henceforth to submit all its intelligence 'to careful consideration both as regards reliability and value' and to grade its reports on a three-point scale (A1, A2, B) according to reliability. Readers of the reports were cautioned to consider them 'in conjunction with reports from official sources'. Thereafter Foreign Office confidence in the authenticity of SIS reports appears to have recovered. Even in the case of the highly controversial 'Zinoviev letter' of 15 September 1924 from Comintern to the British Party, used as anti-Labour propaganda during the October election campaign, the Foreign Office was fully satisfied by SIS evidence of authenticity. The Foreign Office was by now used to a regular (and usually reliable) diet of intercepted Comintern documents as well as Soviet diplomatic traffic and, like the intelligence services, claimed some expertise in detecting forgeries.[33]

Though the Foreign Office received regular SIS intelligence reports and read those concerning Soviet policy with particular attention, it held SIS itself at arm's length. It paid no attention to SIS recruitment, made litttle or no effort to protect SIS's exiguous budget from the postwar economy drive, and seems generally to have left 'Quex' Sinclair, who in 1923 succeeded Cumming as 'C' as well as becoming (non-operational) director of GC&CS, to decide his own priorities and operations. With a deserved reputation as 'a terrific anti-Bolshevik', Sinclair inevitably viewed the arrival of the first Labour government with some apprehension. His main anxiety probably concerned the future of GC&CS. Both Sinclair and the Foreign Office must surely have feared that the new cabinet might take Henry Stimson's view that 'Gentlemen do not read each other's mail', and abolish British sigint. So Labour ministers were not at first told that GC&CS did read other governments' mail. Winston Churchill discovered on returning to office in November 1924 that even Ramsay MacDonald, who was foreign secretary as well as prime minister, 'was himself long kept in ignorance of [intercepts] by the Foreign Office'. Before the advent of the Labour government copies of the most important intercepts had been made available to a number of senior ministers. Henceforth, save for intercepts which chiefly concerned the service ministries, they remained safely within the Foreign Office. That practice was maintained when the Conservatives returned to power.

Labour ministers were introduced slowly, and on the whole successfully, to the wicked world of secret intelligence. The cabinet Committee on Industrial Unrest declared itself 'impressed' by intelligence on Communist involvement in strikes in the docks and on the railways and of secret subsidies from Comintern. It agreed in May that 'responsible Trade Union leaders' should be shown some of this secret evidence 'informally and confidentially'. Ironically, in view of the furore caused later in the year by the Zinoviev letter, the intelligence which so impressed the government came largely from intercepted Communist and Comintern communcations. Even those ministers who retained ethical objections about the intelligence services generally preferred to wash their hands of the whole business rather than to campaign for their abolition. Arthur Ponsonby, MacDonald's undersecretary at the Foreign Office, who bore the main day-to-day responsibility for the Labour government's Russian policy, regarded all intelligence work as a dirty business but conceded that probably 'you have to do it'. Foreign Office officials refused to show Ponsonby any intercepts or SIS reports on the dubious grounds that he was only an undersecretary. So far from protesting, Ponsonby later admitted that he was glad it was so.[34]

Even Ramsay MacDonald preferred to keep SIS quite literally at arms length. When he wished to question the head of the SIS political section and Foreign Office liaison officer, Major Malcolm 'Woolly' Woollcombe, about the Zinoviev letter, he could not bring himself to conduct a face-to-face interview. Instead Woollcombe was placed in a room adjoining MacDonald's at the Foreign Office while the permanent undersecretary, Sir Eyre Crowe, positioned himself in the doorway between the two. The prime minister then addressed his questions to Crowe who relayed them to Woollcombe and reported the answers to MacDonald. At no point during these bizarre proceedings did Woollcombe catch sight of the prime minister.[35]

Even during the Baldwin governments which preceded and followed MacDonald's first ministry, personal contact between senior Foreign Office officials and leading officials of SIS and GC&CS was spasmodic. When J. D. Gregory, the head of the Northern Department (which, since its responsibilities included Russia, received more SIS intelligence than any other), was dismissed for currency speculation in 1928, he received a letter of sympathy from Sinclair. Gregory failed at first to realise who it was from. He later wrote to Sinclair:

> You and I never corresponded in any way, and I knew neither your writing nor your signature! . . . We have not had an enormous amount of work in common but I have invariably enjoyed your periodic visits and I have always regretted that our association has been so spasmodic.[36]

The involvement of intelligence officers, serving and retired, in publicising the Zinoviev letter during the election campaign of October 1924 left SIS with a difficult exercise in bridge-building before the advent of the second Labour government in June 1929. Sinclair tackled the exercise with some skill, recruiting to his headquarters staff at about the time of the 1929 elections the Labour politician and former Liberal MP, Lieutenant

Commander Reginald ('Reggie') Fletcher, who became head of SIS operations in Europe and the Near East in the early 1930s. In 1935 Fletcher left SIS to become Labour MP for Nuneaton and later, as Lord Winster, became a minister in the postwar Attlee government.[37]

MacDonald's two main foreign secretaries, Arthur Henderson in the Labour government of 1929–31 and Sir John Simon in the National Government of 1931–5, seem to have paid remarkably little attention to either SIS or GC&CS. Henderson's attitude was much the same as Ponsonby's in 1924. According to Sir Robert Vansittart, permanent undersecretary from 1930 to 1938, the teetotal Henderson 'rated Secret Service like hard liquor, because he knew, and wanted to know, nothing of it'. Vansittart had to wait until Henderson was in what he considered 'his best mood' before slipping the secret service estimates among his papers for signature. Henderson would 'pause, sign and sigh "You'll be the death of me one day Van"'.[38]

Sinclair's main priority during Henderson's and part of Simon's term as foreign secretary remained Soviet Russia. Despite the loss of the Soviet diplomatic codes in 1927 and the growing difficulty of intelligence operations within the increasingly hostile environment of Stalin's Russia, the successful interception of coded and uncoded Comintern communications together with reports from MI5 informers at British Communist Party headquarters provided continued evidence of Soviet subsidies channelled via Comintern to Communist and front organisations in Britain.[39] Ivan Maisky, who arrived in London as Russian ambassador in 1932, was regularly informed that these subsidies were closely monitored. Despite occasional alarms over Communist agitation in the armed forces, however, official concern at Soviet subversion was considerably lower in the early 1930s than a decade before. Simon told Maisky in 1935 that Soviet subsidies were 'a waste of money':

> . . . He thought it his duty to repeat in a very friendly but very emphatic fashion his conviction that the game was not worth the candle from the Soviet Government's point of view, and that from his own it was a petty and pointless irritant.[40]

Whitehall was further reassured during the Popular Front era of the mid-thirties by the first evidence of attempts by Comintern to persuade the Communist Party to moderate its propaganda in the interests of anti-Fascist unity. The Special Branch reported in 1935, for example, that Comintern had sent instructions for 'hostile criticism' of the Royal Family to be toned down:

> The leading members of the Communist Party in London are not at all pleased with these instructions, and they propose taking up the matter with the Communist

International. It is to be emphasised that the recent increase in the sales of the 'Daily Worker' and other communist literature is definitely attributed to 'MARO's' anti-royalist cartoons, and the satirical articles by various writers about the King and other members of the Royal Family, which have now become a common feature.[41]

By the mid-thirties the Soviet menace had slipped into fourth place in the SIS 'Order of Priority' behind the more important threats to British interests from Germany, Italy and Japan.[42] The main target of British foreign intelligence was now Nazi Germany. The rise of Adolf Hitler and the beginning of German rearmament together caused greater government interest in intelligence than at any time since the breach of Anglo-Soviet relations in May 1927. The shock caused by Hitler's misleading claim to Simon in March 1935 that the Luftwaffe had 'reached parity' with the RAF produced an immediate cabinet demand for more intelligence and some improvement in SIS's miserly budget. More German shocks over the next few years and the lesser shocks produced by Mussolini and Franco further increased Whitehall's appetite for secret intelligence. GC&CS had considerable success with Italian ciphers but its inability to master the German 'enigma' machine cipher until 1940 placed the main responsibility for Geman secret intelligence during the 1930s on SIS.[43]

There were also more personal reasons for the modest revival of SIS and GC&CS fortunes from the mid-thirties onwards and for the growing influence of Sinclair himself. Vansittart had a much greater passion for secret intelligence than any of his twentieth-century predecessors as permanent undersecretary, and was convinced of its importance in understanding Nazi policy. He dined regularly with Sinclair and encouraged his efforts to expand the SIS network, despite its exiguous funds, through the usually part-time, frequently unpaid, services of businessmen and others willing to work for Claude Dansey's 'Z Organisation'. Van also developed his own group of informants on German policy, known within Whitehall as his 'private detective agency'. Sinclair initially described Vansittart's replacement by Sir Alexander Cadogan in January 1938 as 'disastrous'. But though Cadogan never equalled his predecessor's enthusiasm for secret intelligence, he quickly came to regard Sinclair with affection as well as respect.[44]

Helped by his immense clubability and reputation as an epicure, Sinclair's influence in the higher reaches of Whitehall during the 1930s extended well beyond the Foreign Office. His surviving papers from the thirties consist largely of elaborate menu cards from private dinners, some hosted by himself, at the Savoy and other exclusive locations. Sinclair also treasured notes from appreciative guests such as Admiral Percy Noble, who thanked him for 'the best dinner I have eaten in years', and Admiral Bromley, who complimented him on his 'excellent' wines. Sinclair's most influential supporters within Whitehall, besides Vansittart, were the two other most powerful civil servants of the time: Sir Maurice Hankey, cabinet secretary from 1916 to 1938, and Sir Warren Fisher, permanent secretary at the Treasury and head of the civil service from 1919 to 1939. Together, Vansittart, Hankey and Fisher composed the Secret Service Committee which had at least notional responsibility for overseeing the intelligence services. When Sinclair fell ill in March 1939, well before it was clear that his illness would prove fatal, Fisher wrote him an extraordinarily affectionate letter which began 'Hugh dear' and ended 'Bless you, with love, Warren'.[45]

Neville Chamberlain's appointment as prime minister in May 1937 gave Sinclair for the first time a foothold at 10 Downing Street. Chamberlain had been schooled in the importance of intelligence as well as in the art of fly-fishing by his confidant Joseph Ball, ex-head of the MI5 Investigation Branch, who ran agents for Conservative Central Office within Labour Party headquarters much as he had formerly run agents for MI5 within Communist Party headquarters. The Czech crisis of May 1938—four months before Munich—won Sinclair the ear of the prime minister. It seems likely that Hitler did not plan an invasion until the autumn of 1938. Sinclair however, reported that the Führer had plans for an immediate invasion. Chamberlain believed the intelligence reports and warned Hitler not to go ahead. When Hitler failed to launch an attack he had probably never planned, the prime minister congratulated both himself and SIS.[46]

Thereafter Sinclair began to emerge as a policy adviser as well as an intelligence chief. At Munich he pressed strongly that the Czechs accept 'the inevitable' and surrender the Sudetenland: they should 'realise unequivocally that they stand alone if they refuse such a solution'. Britain, for her part, should continue with a policy of calculated appeasement. Sinclair also urged Chamberlain to beware of a pact with Russia, insisting that the Red army 'could do nothing of real value'. Significantly, before Admiral Drax left for Moscow in August 1939 in an abortive attempt to reach agreement with the Russians, Sinclair both briefed him on the negotiations and arranged for him to see Chamberlain. 'It's an infernal shame', he told Drax, 'that they should send you to Moscow to try and clean up the mess that has been made there by the politicians'.[47]

The growing influence of SIS on foreign policy with the approach of the Second World War was reflected also in the increasing authority of the head of the political section, Major Malcolm 'Woolly' Woollcombe. Woollcombe had been appointed Foreign Office liaison officer at SIS headquarters in 1921 but probably did not gain the ear of the permanent undersecretary until Vansittart's appointment in 1930. Van found Woollcombe's intelligence 'Summaries on Germany' 'most thorough and valuable'. He wrote to Woollcombe in December 1936: 'Indeed I would say that your work as a whole is invaluable to me in this Office'. In the Birthday Honours List of 1939 Woollcombe and Maurice Jeffes, head of the passport control organisation which provided cover for most SIS station chiefs abroad, received the CMG, thus becoming the first SIS headquarters officers (save for Cumming and Sinclair) to be decorated for their work. The warm congratulations showered on Woollcombe from senior Foreign Office officials went some way beyond the demands of conventional politeness. Cadogan wrote 'to say how convinced I am that no-one ever deserved it more'. Gladwyn Jebb (later Lord Gladwyn), Cadogan's private secretary, added: 'Nobody has helped the Foreign Office more than you have done during these last difficult years . . .'. Sir Nevile Bland, the British minister in the Netherlands, complimented Woollcombe on 'the admirable way in which you built up your liaison work with the Foreign Office from nothing at all'. Evelyn Sinclair, Quex's sister, housekeeper and assistant, interpreted Woollcombe's CMG as a sign 'that the office [SIS] is no longer ignored in official quarters'.[48]

Some of Woollcombe's intelligence summaries attracted the favourable attention of Neville Chamberlain as well as the Foreign Office. In a summary by Woollcombe entitled 'Germany and Colonies' of February 1938, the prime minister underlined a report that 'high personages in the colonial movement' were now in favour of '"one large compact area"—yielding tropical produce, rather than affording facilities for settlement', and wrote in the margin: 'What did I say'.[49] The SIS policy document circulated by Sinclair within Whitehall during the Munich crisis was, almost certainly, drafted by Woollcombe. Sir Warren Fisher called it ' a most excellent document'.[50]

But though both the prime minister and the Foreign Office had come to value SIS and the intelligence it produced, they had yet to learn how to interpret it. Because of the lack of any adequate system of assessment, the main influence of secret intelligence on British foreign policy during the final year of peace was to sow confusion. A stream of intelligence flowed into Whitehall varying from excellent to dreadful—and Whitehall often found it impossible to tell the difference. The Joint Intelligence Committee, founded in 1936, but still virtually boycotted by the Foreign Office, had barely begun to coordinate intelligence assessment. As Captain (later Admiral) J. H. Godfrey discovered on becoming Director of Naval Intelligence in January 1939, 'There were so many authentic rumours about Germany's intentions that, whatever happened, *someone* could say "I told you so"'. Whitehall, as Godfrey later acknowledged, 'swallowed whole' a series of German plants. In February 1939 false intelligence reports of German preparations for a surprise attack on Holland persuaded the cabinet to recognise a reality it had struggled to evade ever since the First World War: that British security had to be defended on the continent as well as on the high seas, and that continental defence required firm commitments to continental allies. It was ironic that this major turning point in British policy—the acceptance of a continental commitment—was prompted not by the real threat to Czechoslovakia but by an illusory threat to Holland. By Easter 1939 Whitehall was demoralised by the hopeless confusion of its intelligence assessment. The Admiralty took seriously false reports of an impending surprise attack on the Home Fleet and a non-existent U-boat menace in the South Atlantic. The Foreign Office, meanwhile, dismissed accurate intelligence on Italian plans to invade Albania. Cadogan confessed miserably that even when he correctly identified which intelligence reporters were accurate, 'It just happened that these were correct; we had no means of evaluating their reliability at the time of their receipt'.[51]

Whitehall's continuing inability to distinguish good intelligence from intelligence plants was demonstrated in spectacular fashion by the Venlo incident in the early months of the war. Major Richard Stevens, the SIS station chief in the Netherlands, and another SIS officer, Captain Sigismund Payne Best, were contacted by Germans claiming to be senior army officers engaged in a plot to remove Hitler from power. The alleged plotters were in reality officers of the *Sicherheitsdienst* but they successfully deceived Whitehall as well as Stevens and Best. On 9 November, after several weeks negotiations about peace terms, Stevens and Best were lured to the Dutch border town of Venlo, kidnapped and taken to Germany where they were given starring roles in a Gestapo publicity stunt involving an alleged attempt on the Führer's life.[52]

Ever since the Second World War there has been a tendency to blame the Venlo fiasco simply on the incompetence of SIS and on the bungling of Stevens and Best in particular. But Venlo would never have been possible without serious misjudgements by both the Foreign Office and Downing Street. At the time the Foreign Office had the greatest confidence in Stevens. Sir Neville Bland, the British minister in the Netherlands, wrote to congratulate Sinclair on the choice of Stevens. 'Stevens', he wrote, 'is being quite admirable: you couldn't have done better when you chose him'.[53] Hankey, now minister without portfolio but with special responsibility for the intelligence services in Chamberlain's war cabinet, was equally enthusiastic. He described Sinclair's secret report on Stevens' and Best's negotiations with the bogus German conspirators as 'one of the most cheering documents I have read'—and added confidently: 'Here is someone who is getting results'.[54] Even after Stevens and Best had been kidnapped at Venlo, both the Foreign Office and Whitehall as a whole failed to realise that they had been taken in. Ten days after the kidnap Cadogan was still drafting notes on peace terms to pass to the alleged German conspirators. Finally, on 22 November the SD tired of continuing the charade and radioed a mocking message using the conspirators' callsign to tell SIS it had been duped.[55]

The humiliation of Venlo was swiftly followed, however, by a remarkable intelligence renaissance. By the time Stevens and Best were captured by the Germans a major new intelligence recruitment was under way, the nucleus of the ablest team of cryptanalysts yet assembled anywhere in the world was in place at Bletchley Park, and the foundation was being laid for the Double Cross System which was to lead the Germans into intelligence traps vastly more important than Venlo. Thanks to a vastly improved system of assessment, the best raw intelligence in British history was used to shorten the Second World War. There seems, at first sight, little connection between the problems of prewar intelligence assessment and the spectacular wartime successes. The prewar failures, however, provided part of the inspiration for the wartime intelligence renaissance. As Cadogan ruefully acknowledged, the intelligence confusion of 1939 revealed 'a situation that must be remedied'.[56]

Notes

1. PRO index no. 27766 to the Cabinet Conclusions, Nov. 1919–Dec. 1921.
2. A. G. Denniston, 'The Government Code and Cypher School Between the Wars', *Intelligence and National Security*, I (1986), no. 1, pp. 55.
3. House of Commons: Education, Science and Arts Committee, Session 1982–3, *Public Records: Minutes of Evidence*.
4. Ibid., pp. 76–7.
5. *Intelligence and National Security*, I (1986), no. 1.
6. 'Gordon Welchman, Sir Peter Marychurch and "The Birth of Ultra"', ibid., I (1986), no. 2.
7. Christopher Andrew, *Secret Service: The Making of the British Intelligence Community* (London, 1985), pp. 3, 85.
8. See the article in this volume by Peter Morris; and John Ferris, 'Whitehall's Black Chamber: British Cryptology and the Government Code and Cypher School, 1919–1929', *Intelligence and National Security*, II (1987), no. 1, p. 55.
9. Christopher Andrew and Keith Neilson, 'Tsarist Codebreakers and British Codes', *Intelligence and National Security*, I (1986), no. 1.
10. Andrew, *Secret Service*, ch. 2. F. H. Hinsley *et al.*, *British Intelligence in the Second World War*, I (London, 1979), pp. 16–17.

11. 'Reduction of Estimates for Secret Services', 19 March 1920, House of Lords Record Office, Lloyd George MSS F/9/2/16.

12. Andrew, *Secret Service*, ch. 2.

13. Ibid., pp. 52–7.

14. Randolph S. Churchill, *Winston S. Churchill* (London, 1966–), vol. II, companion vol. II, pp. 1120–1, 1342–3. Martin Gilbert, *Winston S. Churchill*, vol. III, companion vol. II, p. 1428. Curiously, there is no mention of Kell in the text of the Churchill biography.

15. Piers Brendon, *Winston Churchill*, paperback edition (London, 1985), pp. 57–8. Christopher Andrew, 'Churchill and Intelligence', forthcoming in *Intelligence and National Security*, III (1988), no. 2.

16. Andrew, *Secret Service*, pp. 106–7, 307.

17. Eunan O'Halpin, 'British Intelligence in Ireland, 1915–21', in Christopher Andrew and David Dilks (eds.), *The Missing Dimension: Governments and Intelligence Communities in the Twentieth Century* (London, 1984).

18. Andrew, *Secret Service*, pp. 108–11.

19. James to Sinclair, 30 April [1921], National Maritime Museum, Admiral Sir Hugh Sinclair MSS 81/091. These papers, like the Woollcombe MSS and some of the other documents cited below, were unavailable to me during the writing of *Secret Service*.

20. Memorandum by R. L. Nicholson (DSD), 4 March 1919; memorandum by Sinclair, 30 April 1919; Admiral secret circular, 24 Oct. 1919; unsigned minute, 2 Sept. 1921; E. H. Robinson (Foreign Office) to C. E. Horsey (Admiralty), 18 March 1922, PRO ADM 1/8577/349.

21. Ferris, 'Whitehall's Black Chamber', appendix 2. The relative consistency in the number of 'flimsies' circulated by GC&CS, however, conceals larger fluctuations in the amount of traffic which it 'handled'. Ferris's figures, for example, suggest no significant change in the number of 'flimsies' during the period 1929 to 1936. But a memorandum by Denniston reveals a jump in 'traffic handled', due to the signals generated by the Italio-Ethiopian War and Spanish Civil War, from 10,618 cables in the last quarter of 1934 to 13,990 in the last quarter of 1936. GC&CS, it appears, selected for 'publication' a relatively constant number of 'flimsies' from a fluctuating number of intercepts. Minute by Denniston, 6 Jan. 1937, PRO FO 366/978 X7105.

22. Andrew, *Secret Service*, chs. 9, 10.

23. Churchill to Austen Chamberlain, 21, 22 Nov. 1924, Birmingham University Library, Chamberlain MSS AC 51/58, AC 51/61.

24. CP 3105, 31 July 1921, India Office Library Curzon MSS Eur. F112/302.

25. Rumbold to Oliphant, 18 July 1923, Bodleian Library, Oxford, Rumbold MSS Dep. 30: cited in the article below by Jeffery and Sharp.

26. Andrew, *Secret Service*, pp. 296–7.

27. Comte de Saint-Aulaire, *Confession d'un vieux diplomate* (Paris, 1953), pp. 628–9.

28. Andrew, *Secret Service*, pp. 296–7. The excellent article in this collection by Keith Jeffery and Alan Sharp possibly errs on the side of charity when assessing Curzon's weaknesses in the handling of intercepts. Other foreign secretaries did not collapse in tears when meeting an opposite number whose perfidy had been revealed by intercepts; they did not publicly taunt a foreign power with the breaking of their codes; nor did they refuse for months on end to see the ambassador of a friendly power whose intercepted telegrams had caused personal offence. Curzon did.

29. Andrew, *Secret Service*, pp. 292–3, 331–3.

30. *Parliamentary Debates (Commons)*, 5th series, CCVI, 24 May 1927, col. 1848.

31. Information from the Cambridge historian, Mr Christopher Morris, who worked at Bletchley Park during the Second World War.

32. Andrew, *Secret Service*, p. 332.
33. Ibid., chs. 9, 10.
34. Ibid.
35. Information from Woollcombe's son, Mr Robert Woollcombe. See his letter to *The Times* of 18 Oct. 1977.
36. J. D. Gregory to Sinclair, 21 March 1928, Sinclair MSS 81/091.
37. Andrew, *Secret Service*, p. 345.
38. Lord Vansittart, *The Mist Procession* (London, 1958), pp. 397–8.
39. Andrew, *Secret Service*, pp. 362–71.
40. Memo by Vansittart, 28 May 1935; Sir John Simon to Moscow embassy, 30 May 1935, PRO FO 371/19467 N2761.
41. Special Branch report, 29 March 1935, PRO FO 371/19467 N1781.
42. 'Order of priority of foreign countries from SIS point of view', n.d. (1935 or 1936), PRO WO 106/5392. On intelligence assessment of the Japanese threat see Christopher Andrew, 'The Growth of Intelligence Collaboration among the English-speaking Peoples', *The Review of International Studies* (forthcoming).
43. Andrew, *Secret Services*, pp. 352–4, 376–7.
44. Ibid., pp. 343, 382–6.
45. Noble to Sinclair, 19 July 1935; Bromley to Sinclair, 19 July 1935; Fisher to Sinclair, 20 March 1939; Hankey to Sinclair, 31 Oct. 1939, Sinclair MSS 81/091.
46. Andrew, *Secret Service*, pp. 339–40, 392–4.
47. Ibid., pp. 398–9, 422.
48. Vansittart to Woollcombe, 14 Dec. 1936; Cadogan to Woollcombe, 13 June 1939; Jebb to Woollcombe, 12 June 1939; Bland to Woollcombe, 10 June 1939; Evelyn Sinclair to Woollcombe, 8 June 1939, Woollcombe MSS. I am very grateful to Mr Robert Woollcombe for permission to quote from these papers which are in his possession.
49. Woollcombe, 'Germany and Colonies', Most Secret, 3 Feb. 1939, copy marked 'No.1. Prime Minister', with marginal comment by Chamberlain, Woollcombe MSS.
50. Woollcombe, 'What Should We Do?', 18 Sept. 1938; Fisher to Sinclair (copy), 20 Sept. 1939, Woollcombe MSS.
51. Andrew, *Secret Service*, pp. 408–20.
52. Ibid., pp. 433–8.
53. Bland to Sinclair, 27 Oct. 1939, Sinclair MSS 81/091.
54. Hankey to Sinclair, 31 Oct. 1939, ibid.
55. Andrew, *Secret Service*, pp. 438–9.
56. Ibid., p. 411.

Crown copyright material in the Public Record Office and the India Office Library cited in this article appears by permission of the Controller, H.M. Stationery Office.

1914: The Safety of Ciphers and the Outbreak of the First World War

JEAN STENGERS

On 1 December 1914 the French Government published its *Yellow Book* on the origins of the war. It was a momentous act of policy, which was echoed in the press:[1] here was the official French version of the course of events which had led to the European conflict.

One of the key documents of the volume was No 118. It was the telegram sent by Maurice Paléologue, the French ambassador in Petersburg, on 31 July 1914. The text ran as follows:

> As a result of the general mobilisation of Austria and of the measures for mobilisation taken secretly, but continuously, by Germany for the last six days, the order for the general mobilisation of the Russian army has been given, Russia not being able, without most serious danger, to allow herself to be further outdistanced; in fact she is only taking military measures corresponding to those taken by Germany. For imperative reasons of strategy the Russian Government, knowing that Germany was arming, could no longer delay the conversion of her partial mobilisation into a general mobilisation.[2]

We now know that this text was an almost complete fabrication (it has been called the 'King'—or 'Queen'—of political falsifications). Paléologue's authentic telegram on 31 July had been simply:

> Order has been given for the general mobilisation of the Russian army (La mobilisation générale de l'armée russe est ordonnée).[3]

The explanation of this decision which the *Yellow Book* added in the first place ('As a result of the general mobilisation of Austria'—'En raison de la mobilisation générale de l'Autriche') was not a pure figment of the imagination of the authors of the compilation. It corresponded to what the French

29

authorities had explicitly stated as early as 1 August. On 1 August Poincaré explained to the British ambassador in Paris that the 'Emperor of Russia did not order a general mobilisation until after a decree of general mobilisation had been issued in Austria'.[4] The *Yellow Book* simply followed that early version.

As this version was absolutely erroneous—the Austrian general mobilisation did not precede that of Russia—two questions arise. Firstly, where did the error originate. Secondly, was it a deliberate error—let us call it a 'trick'—or was it made in good faith? These two questions must be asked and answered at four levels, corresponding to four different aspects of the problem:

1. The Russians' action and the information they gave about that action.
2. The information provided by Paléologue to his government.
3. The way the French authorities interpreted the Russian decision immediately after it had been taken.
4. The way the authors of the *Yellow Book* justified it.

I THE RUSSIANS

The complicated story of the Russian mobilisation (or rather mobilisations, as there was a partial and a general one) has not been completely disentangled. Here are the six successive stages which must be distinguished to make the story coherent:

1. *24 July:* The Council of ministers presided over by Goremykin, the Chairman of the Council, meets in the afternoon. It was a meeting which was hastily convened after the news of the Austrian ultimatum to Serbia had been announced in the morning. Until quite recently nothing was known about the debate which took place during that meeting. This was probably the most serious gap in our knowledge of the events of July 1914. We now have the testimony of at least one of the ministers, Peter Bark, the Minister of Finance. It shows that after a lively discussion the Council decided to take a firm stand: Serbia had to be supported, even if it meant war.[5] As a result, one of the resolutions of the Council was:

> to charge the War and Naval Minister . . . with the task of entreating the most gracious assent of (His) Imperial Majesty to a proclamation of mobilisation of the four military districts of Kiev, Odessa, Moscow and Kazan, . . . should the subsequent course of events so require.[6]

This meant adopting the principle of a partial mobilisation against Austria.

2. *25 July:* The Tsar gives his personal assent to the decision taken the day before. 'Should it prove necessary to proclaim mobilisation, in view of the fact that operations are to be confined solely to action against Austria, His Majesty has commanded that mobilisation shall take place in the military districts of Kiev, Odessa, Kazan and Moscow'.[7]

Various military measures of the kind necessitated by an eventual war were also taken immediately. But none of these measures, however important, was tantamount to mobilisation. The diary of the Russian Foreign Office describes them as follows:

> It was decided not to order mobilisation as yet, but to undertake all the preparatory measures for accelerating it should it become a necessity.[8]

3. *29 July, in the morning:* after the declaration of war on Serbia, the Tsar signs the *ukase* for the partial mobilisation against Austria. There have been some discussions about this *ukase*. It has sometimes been doubted whether it was actually signed.[9] And, if signed, was it a firm decision which had to be put into effect?[10]

A crystal-clear document—quoted here for the first time—leaves absolutely no doubt about the course of events. It is the diary kept by Marchioness de Laguiche, the wife of the French military attaché at Petersburg, General Marquis de Laguiche.[11] The Marchioness de Laguiche took very precise day-to-day notes of what her husband told her. The entry for 29 July in her diary begins with the first important news of the day:

> Janushkevich (the Chief of the General Staff) called Pierre [i.e. General de Laguiche] to-day to inform him that His Majesty had just signed the order of mobilisation for Kiev, Odessa, Kazan, Moscow. Nothing elsewhere, to avoid giving offence to Berlin. . . . At one minute past midnight the order for mobilisation against Austria will be issued ('sera lancé'). According to Janushkevich one must not equate war and mobilisation. As he is convinced of Emperor William's desire for peace, he believes that as a result of the decisions of this night German pressure will be brought to bear upon Austria and that the latter will calm down.

4. *29 July, around 8.00 p.m.:* A conference takes place between Sazonov, the Minister for War and the Chief of the General Staff. The three men come to the conclusion that 'in view of the small probability of avoiding a war with Germany it was indispensable to prepare for it in every way in good time, and that therefore the risk could not be accepted of delaying a general mobilisation later by effecting a partial mobilisation now'. This conclusion is 'at once reported by telephone to the Tsar', and the Tsar 'authorised the

taking of steps accordingly'—i.e. he gives his assent to the general mobilisation.[12] The French Military Attaché is informed that Russia 'is extending its order for mobilisation' ('étend son ordre de mobilisation').[13]

5. *29 July, around 10.30–11.00 p.m.:* The Tsar changes his mind. He telephones to the Minister for War from Peterhof and revokes the order for general mobilisation. The news is immediately transmitted to the Foreign Office. 'At about 11.00 p.m. the Minister for War informed the Foreign Minister by telephone that he had received orders from the Tsar to stop the general mobilisation'.[14] Again, the French military attaché is warned without delay, and Baron Schilling, the *chef de cabinet* of Sazonov, gives him the explanation for this development which was that the Tsar had been impressed by a telegram he had received from Emperor William II.[15]

The cancellation of the order for general mobilisation meant that the Russians reverted to the partial mobilisation against Austria. Janushkevich told Laguiche that the order now being sent was: mobilisation would be 'limited to the thirteen army corps previously mentioned'.[16]

The first day of mobilisation began at midnight on 29 July.[17] The Smolensk garrison, in the district of Moscow, got the order by telegram on 30 July at 4.50 a.m.[18] During the same day, the news of the partial mobilisation was announced by the Russian newspapers and by the news agencies.[19]

6. *30 July:* Strong pressure is brought to bear upon the Tsar in order to make him accept a general mobilisation. He is told that the German as well as the Austrian military measures do reveal aggressive intentions, and that Russia would be in danger if she allowed her partial mobilisation to disorganise her subsequent—and apparently inevitable—general mobilisation.

The most powerful plea was that of Sazonov, who called on the Tsar at Peterhof in the afternoon. 'I began my report at ten minutes past three and ended at four', Sazonov recounts.[20] After some discussion—which may have taken some time for the Tsar was very hesitant[21]—Nicholas finally assented: 'You are right. There remains for us nothing but to accept the challenge. Transmit my order for mobilisation to the Chief of the General Staff'.[22]

Sazonov left the Tsar's office, and from the ground floor of the Palace, where there was a telephone, transmitted the order to General Janushkevich.[23] The time must have been around 5.00 p.m.[24] The official telegraphic orders of the General Staff to the districts which had not yet been mobilised were sent at about 7.00 p.m.[25]

Early on the morning of 31 July, about 4.00 a.m., the pink notices summoning men to the colours were posted up on the walls of Petersburg.[26] 31 July was announced as the first day of the general mobilisation.

So far, no mention can be found in the Russian documents—nor in the information given by the Russians—of any influence the Austrian general mobilisation might have had upon their decisions. This is quite understandable as the general mobilisation of Austria was only announced on 31 July.

The first—but a little ambiguous—mention of such an influence appears in a telegram sent by the Tsar to the King of England on 2 August. The text was released to the press and it was published by *The Times* on 5 August. The Tsar wrote:

> Austria's declaration of war on Serbia forced me to order a partial mobilisation, though, in view of the threatening situation, my military advisers strongly advised a general mobilisation owing to the quickness with which Germany can mobilise in comparison with Russia. I was eventually compelled to take this course in consequence of complete Austrian mobilisation, of the bombardment of Belgrade, of concentration of Austrian troops in Galicia and of secret military preparations being made by Germany.[27]

This is a bit equivocal, as the Tsar avoids the expression 'general mobilisation' which was however a standard one. He speaks of a 'complete' Austrian mobilisation. This is not fundamentally different from what he wired to the German Emperor on 31 July at 2.55 p.m.: 'It is technically impossible to stop our military preparations which were obligatory owing to Austria's mobilisation'.[28] Austria's war against Serbia evidently meant a large degree of mobilisation of her forces—eight corps, i.e. half the Austro-Hungarian army, the Russian ambassador wired from Vienna on 28 July.[29] 'Complete mobilisation' was in this context a rhetorical amplification, and it verged dangerously on the idea of a 'general mobilisation'. But since the Tsar's telegram was written with an eye on its eventual publication the equivocation was quite conceivably deliberate.[30]

II MAURICE PALÉOLOGUE

Maurice Paléologue, the French ambassador in Petersburg, is one of the most vilified protagonists of the July 1914 drama. As regards France, only Raymond Poincaré is described by some historians in colours as black as those which are used for him.

Indictments against Paléologue are found everywhere, not only in semi-pamphlets like the works of Georges Demartial[31], but in the works of the most temperate historians. He was, it is said, an extremely bad informant, who did not care, or did not want, to inform his government about important things which were taking place in Petersburg and about what he was doing himself; moreover he allegedly exercised a very bad, bellicose influence on the Russian government. The most detailed and severe indictment is probably that of Albertini, which piles up critical observations about the 'large lacunae in Paléologue's diplomatic correspondence, which intentionally kept Paris in the dark about what was going on at St Petersburg', about the 'high-handed way in which Paléologue kept his government in the dark . . . for fear the Quai d'Orsay should intervene with demands for restraint and negotiations for a compromise', about the way the French ministers were 'deceived by Paléologue', etc.[32] But Pierre Renouvin also says more mutedly but with great severity that 'it seems evident that Maurice Paléologue deliberately concealed from his government some information of capital importance'.[33]

We shall not try here to examine Paléologue's case in a systematic way. We shall limit ourselves to a few remarks.

Firstly, concerning Paléologue's feelings and his alleged personal policy, a most important testimony in that respect, which must be taken into serious consideration, is that of Marchioness de Laguiche. She writes in her diary on 31 July:

> Paléologue has an immense admiration for Sazonov, for he will be the most vilified, the most unpopular man in the country if he avoids war, and in spite of that nothing deters him from working in that direction—('Paléologue a pour ce dernier [=Sazonov] une admiration sans bornes, car il sera l'homme le plus vilipendé, le plus impopulaire de son pays s'il évite la guerre, et cependant rien ne le détourne de travailler dans ce sens').

Let us translate: the Russian opinion is bellicose. In spite of that, Sazonov struggles to save peace, and Paléologue admires him immensely for it.

Nobody will dare to assert that this summarizes the whole of Paléologue's attitude (or the whole of Sazonov's)—there are other items of information like that of a Frenchman who calls on Paléologue on the very same day, 31 July, and who writes: 'M. Paléologue paraît tout à fait certain de la guerre et s'en réjouit presque, en songeant que la situation actuelle est la plus favorable que l'on ait jamais pu espérer'[34]—but the first-hand testimony of Madame de Laguiche certainly shows that the man's feelings were much more complex and, probably, flexible, than has been asserted.

As regards his personal policy, one may wonder—but this is much more hypothetical—whether he was not encouraged in his sense of independence by the poor opinion he must have formed of the French Prime Minister and

Minister of Foreign Affairs, Viviani, during his stay in Petersburg. Viviani had openly showed how little interested he was in the discussions with the Russians; his prime interests were the news of the trial of Madame Caillaux, and the correspondence he sent to his mistress by the diplomatic bag.[35] With such a minister, the French ambassador may have felt that the great political game was his.

But our main concern here is about the information he sent to Paris. It cannot be denied that it was very poor. But three points—and they are all very important—must be made in that respect:

1. Paléologue was handicapped by the poor quality of his own information. This was deliberately organised by the Russians. Two extraordinary examples appear in the diary of Madame de Laguiche:

> —in the evening of 29 July, a little after 10.00 p.m., the French military attaché was informed by the Russian military authorities that a general mobilisation had been ordered. 'On prie Pierre d'aviser Paris, mais de n'en parler à Paléologue qu'à minuit, son manque de discrétion étant connu!'. Paléologue was thus punished for his lack of discretion: he should be told of the general mobilisation only after some delay.

> —during the night of 29–30 July, a little after midnight, Laguiche was asked to go to the Pont aux Chantres, the Ministry of Foreign Affairs, where Chambrun, the first secretary of the French embassy, was going to wire to Paris the news of the general mobilisation. There, Schilling, the chef de cabinet of the minister, took him aside and told him of the Tsar's counter-order. But it was a secret: 'A vous seul au monde je le confie, pas un mot au rayon, ni Basily [the Deputy-Director of the Chancery at the Russian Ministry of Foreign Affairs] ni personne ne le sait'. 'Pas un mot au rayon': that meant not one word to the staff of the embassy, including the ambassador himself.

On the whole, Madame de Laguiche draws this conclusion: 'Charmante situation de Pierre vis-à-vis de Paléologue!'

In fact, Paléologue was told of the general mobilisation not at midnight by Laguiche, but around 11.00 p.m. by Basily, who called on him at the embassy.[36] And after that, necessarily, he had to be told of the reasons for the Tsar's change of mind: secrecy proved impossible. But it was a question of only a few minutes: if Basily's visit had been scheduled just a bit later, it would have been cancelled when the counter-order arrived from Peterhof, and the unfortunate Paléologue would have known neither of the order for general mobilisation nor of the counter-order.

To what we know from Madame de Laguiche's diary let us add what we can almost certainly deduce from Paléologue's own messages. On 30 July at 9.15 p.m. Paléologue sent a telegram to Paris in which he quoted the conversation he had just had with Sazonov. The Minister had told him that 'the Russian government had decided to proceed secretly to the first measures of general mobilisation'.[37] At that time, let us remember, a much graver decision had already been taken: it was general mobilisation in the full sense of the word, without any reservation. This had been manifestly concealed from Paléologue , whose 'lack of discretion' seemed dangerous; he received only a half-truth. . . .

2. A second handicap from which Paléologue suffered was that, on one occasion at least, he was overruled by Laguiche. When, after Basily's visit on 29 July, he sent Chambrun to the Pont aux Chantres to wire Paris, the last sentence of his telegram, in his minute, was: 'the Russian Government has decided to "commencer secrètement la mobilisation générale"'[38] (this news he had just received from Basily). After Schilling's secret confidence— which Janushkevich confirmed to him immediately afterwards—Laguiche ordered Chambrun to suppress this last sentence. 'Pierre', writes Madame de Laguiche, 'arrive à leur (=Chambrun and Basily) faire supprimer la dernière phrase du télégramme annonçant la mobilisation générale'.[39] Next morning Paléologue was furious: 'Paléologue appelle Pierre, il est furieux contre Pierre et Chambrun d'avoir supprimé la fin de son télégramme'. He was furious, but it was too late.

3. The gravest handicap for Paléologue however—and here we come to the core of our analysis—was that the embassy cipher, for his wires to Paris, was unsafe.

Several allusions have already been made to that fact.[40] We now have definite proof that this was the case. It comes once again from the diary of Madame de Laguiche. When, on the night of 29–30 July, Chambrun left the French embassy for the Pont aux Chantres, accompanied by Basily, to wire to Paris the news of the general mobilisation, he told Laguiche: 'Nous allons le télégraphier au Ministère, *le chiffre de l'Ambassade n'étant pas sûr*'. The telegram sent from the Pont aux Chantres was delivered to the Russian Embassy in Paris, which sent the decrypt to the Quai d'Orsay.[41] 'Le chiffre de l'Ambassade n'étant pas sûr': this is really the key to a most important story.

It explains Paléologue's partial impotence when it came to informing his government. The most important criticism directed against him—and it has sometimes been a harsh criticism—was that he had failed to inform Paris of two vital Russian decisions: the decision for general mobilisation on 29 July, and the cancellation of this measure.[42] Albertini gives it a central place in his indictment.[43] Paléologue himself never answered that criticism. However, the answer was a very simple one: the French ambassador was paralysed. He could neither send the news by the Embassy cipher—that would have meant running the risk of letting the Germans know—nor use the Russian cipher: the Russians would not have liked to see the French Government informed of their vacillations. So he remained silent. The fact that he later never answered his critics is perhaps best explained by the tacit law that problems of ciphers must not be discussed publicly.[44]

Paléologue's predicament, on 30 July, led him to what he was obliged to do, namely change the embassy cipher. He announced it in a telegram sent at twenty-five past midnight: 'Je me servirai dorénavant des tables de chiffre I.G.I.'[45] For this announcement he certainly took particular precautions—perhaps sending the telegram by a circuitous route—for the wire only reached the Quai d'Orsay at 11.15 p.m., that is, if one takes into account the difference of time between Paris and Petersburg (2 hours), more than 24 hours later.[46]

At any rate, it was most probably this new cipher that Paléologue used for his important telegram of 9.15 p.m.—the conversation with Sazonov—which we mentioned a moment ago.

And so we come to his vital telegram of 31 July: 'La mobilisation générale de l'armée russe est ordonnée'.

The order had been given, but the Russians wanted to keep it secret as long as possible. They had wanted that secrecy on the evening of 29 July (hence Paléologue's minute: 'commencer secrètement la mobilisation générale'). They wished it this time too. As stated in the diary of the Russian Foreign Office, 'to avoid rendering our relations with Germany more acute the Minister for Foreign Affairs deemed it desirable to proceed to the general mobilisation as far as possible secretly and without making any public announcement concerning it'.[47]

It seems as though Paléologue had not complete confidence in the new embassy cipher. He did not use the Russian cipher either. He chose a third solution: sending his telegram by the Scandinavian route, so as to avoid any interception by Germany. This was not extravagant; the day before his Belgian colleague at Petersburg had chosen the same route also for security reasons.[48] But in Paléologue's case, the result was, as we shall see, that his wire took nearly 12 hours to arrive at the Quai d'Orsay. This delay had enormous consequences for the interpretation the French authorities would give to the course of events.

The irony is that, as Albertini rightly observes, Paléologue might as well have sent his telegram en clair.[49] What kind of secrecy was still needed when the notices of mobilisation were on the city walls? And Paléologue, according to his own testimony knew they were there.[50] But once instructions had been given—and they were asking for secrecy—the ambassador's duty was to stick to them.[51]

III AT THE QUAI d'ORSAY, 31 JULY–1 AUGUST, 1914

In the third volume of his *Origins of the War of 1914*, Luigi Albertini devotes a long chapter to 'The legend that the Austrian general mobilization preceded that of Russia'.[52] After assembling and examining all the available documents—and this is a game played by an expert—Albertini comes to the conclusion that one of the origins of the legend is a deliberate lie by the Quai d'Orsay and by Poincaré.

Is it possible that the Paris officials misunderstood the train of events, and believed that the Austrians had mobilised first, and that the Russian mobilisation was but a counter-measure to the Austrian mobilisation? Albertini thinks not. In his view, they must have known what had actually happened.

But they immediately—to quote Albertini's own words—'excogitated a trick'.[53] News of the two general mobilisations had come on 31 July. By 1 August, the trick was ready. When Poincaré met Bertie, the British ambassador in Paris, when Margerie, the 'Directeur de la Politique' at the Quai d'Orsay, met the same Bertie a few hours later, when Viviani wired instructions to his ambassador in London, Paul Cambon, the three of them offered the same version of the events of the previous day: Russia had ordered a general mobilisation of her army *after* Austria had done so.[54] This was deliberately 'falsifying the facts'[55] so as to put the blame on Austria.[56]

Is such an interpretation a convincing one? First of all, the documents do prove, I think, that the Paris officials may quite possibly have been deceived as to the chronology of mobilisations by their own informants. The Quai d'Orsay got the news on 31 July and in the early hours of 1 August, from four successive sources. First came a telegram from Jules Cambon, in Berlin, saying it seemed that the Auswärtiges Amt had been informed that 'Russia had just decided on total mobilisation in reply to Austrian total mobilisation'.[57] Then, later in the day, came two telegrams from the two capitals where mobilisation had taken place, Petersburg and Vienna. Paléologue, from Petersburg, and Dumaine, from Vienna, both briefly announced that the order for general mobilisation had been issued.[58] Paléologue's wire was sent first—about seven hours before Dumaine's—but, owing to the delay in its transmission, it arrived in the Quai d'Orsay later than Dumaine's.[59] This, in these terribly tense hours of hurried diplomatic work, which were not particularly favourable to the cool application of the rules of historical criticism, may have proved a second source of misunderstanding. Finally, in the early hours of 1 August came a new telegram from Paléologue, in which the French ambassador quoted the Tsar as having asserted that the Russian mobilisation 'was solely motivated by the previous mobilisation of the Austro-Hungarian army'.[60] So if we believe in the Quai d'Orsay's and in Poincaré's ingenuousness, we can explain their mistake in a quite plausible way: they were put on the wrong track by the first information received from Cambon, they misinterpreted accordingly the two telegrams of Dumaine and Paléologue and were finally confirmed in their error by Paléologue's wire quoting the words of the Tsar.

But was there any ingenuousness in Paris on 1 August? Albertini, as we said, does not think so. His description is that of mischievous statesmen contriving a 'trick'. I think his interpretation stumbles in that respect against an often elusive but supreme truth in history: the psychological truth.

To accept Albertini's views means that Viviani, Poincaré and Margerie would have been deliberate liars and also, undoubtedly, very stupid liars. They were falsifying simple and important facts, and offering that falsified version to another nation—England—while there was every chance that, with its own information, the British Government would have known the truth and so would immediately have seen through the French falsification. At a crucial moment, when England was still hesitating, they were giving her the strongest reasons to doubt the French as well as the Russian good faith. And these indescribable muddlers were Viviani, Poincaré and Margerie!

Only one conclusion remains open: we must, I think, necessarily believe in the Quai d'Orsay and in Poincaré's perfect integrity.[61] At the root of their mistake was the delay with which Paléologue's wire had reached Paris. Paléologue minuted his telegram at 8.30 a.m.[62] For reasons which are not absolutely clear—he speaks of some trouble and agitation at the Russian telegraphic office, but doubts have been expressed about this explanation[63]—the wire was actually sent only at 10.43 a.m. Then began the long Scandinavian route.[64] The time of arrival at the Quai d'Orsay was 8.30 p.m. This was before decipherment.[65] The supplementary delay required for the decipherment—and this, in spite of the fact that the text was very short, was perhaps not such an easy operation—helps to explain that Viviani, when sending a telegram to Paléologue at 9.00 p.m. had not yet received the ambassador's wire.[66]

Can the Quai d'Orsay have overlooked the fact that Paléologue's wire had suffered from such a long delay? Quite easily, I think, as it was accustomed to receive the telegrams from the main European capitals at generally normal speed. At the end of July 1914, the telegrams from London took from a hundred minutes to three and a half hours (with one case of a delay of nearly five hours), those from Berlin took from ninety-five minutes to three or four hours (with one case of nearly seven hours); the traffic with Vienna was somewhat more irregular, and the delay varied from a little more than two hours in one case to an average of three or four hours, and in three cases to more than seven; the telegrams from Brussels took from some twenty minutes to two or three hours. The telegrams from Petersburg ordinarily also reached Paris at normal speed; until 31 July, they had taken from two and a half hours to a maximum of six hours.[67] Paléologue's wire about the Russian general mobilisation was an exception (along with the telegram about the change of cipher, but this must have been a special case)—so it is not difficult to understand that, in the hurry and agitation of the time[68], the exception went unnoticed.

The question of the cipher was at the root of the matter.

IV   THE YELLOW BOOK

We have little information about the compilation of the *Yellow Book*. It is generally agreed that the main author of the work was Philippe Berthelot, Deputy Director for Political Affairs.[69] Berthelot had been one of the main participants in the Quai d'Orsay in all the diplomatic activities of July 1914.[70] On 1 August he had certainly believed what Viviani, Margerie and Poincaré also believed. In the *Yellow Book* he stuck to that version quite firmly. This meant doing two things: adding to Paléologue's authentic wire the long comments which were a complete fabrication; and doctoring Dumaine's telegram announcing the Austrian mobilisation. The telegram was:

> L'ordre de mobilisation générale vient d'être donné aux armées austro-hongroises. Tous les hommes de dix-neuf à quarante-deux ans sont appelés.[71]

In the *Yellow Book* it became:

> La mobilisaton générale atteignant tous les hommes de 19 à 42 ans a été décrétée par le Gouvernement austro-hongroise *ce matin à la première heure*.[72]

In making these two alterations, was Berthelot still acting in good faith[73] or was he, this time, contriving a trick? This is a problem which I have been examining for over twenty years, and I have not been able to make up my mind.

Berthelot may have stuck to his original views without realizing his mistake. Nothing he had read in the British *Blue Book* could have aroused his doubts (the telegram of Buchanan, the British Ambassador in Petersburg, announcing the Russian general mobilisation, was printed in the *Blue Book* with the date of 31 July, but without any precise mention of time).[74] On the contrary, he may have been confirmed in his views by the telegram of the Tsar to King George V. He may have believed that Dumaine's telegram was sent from Vienna at 5.00 *a.m.*, whereas it had been sent in fact at 5.00 *p.m.* This would mean that he believed what he wrote.

But there are difficulties. The main difficulty is that any clear-minded reading of the series of Dumaine's telegrams shows that his crucial wire cannot have been sent at 5.00 *a.m.* But this is the result of an exercise of historical criticism which was perhaps not part of Berthelot's brief. Officials and historians are two different races.[75]

At any rate, apart from the misconception about the Austrian mobilisation, the fabricated No. 118 of the *Yellow Book* was not at all bad history. The Tsar had actually decided for general mobilisation (there was naturally no allusion to his hesitations and vacillations, and Berthelot probably did not even know of them) because of what his generals and ministers told him about the dangers of German military preparations.

In this rather obscure story, one thing at least is certain: the version of the *Yellow Book* was fully accepted and adopted by its French readers. It became the official French version. More than ten million copies were sold of the booklet *Qui a voulu la guerre?* by Emile Durkheim and Ernest Denis.[76] The authors, two professors at the Sorbonne and moreover two very reputed scholars, piously write:

> L'Autriche n'avait encore mobilisé qu'une partie de ses troupes. Mais le 31 juillet, à la première heure, la mobilisation générale était décrétée: tous les hommes de 19 à 42 ans étaient appelés. La mesure était grave . . . A cette nouvelle, la Russie jugea naturel de prendre les mêmes précautions . . . Le 31 juillet, vers le milieu de la journée, la flotte et l'armée tout entières furent mobilisées.

Durkheim and Denis underline 'ce fait capital que la mobilisation générale autrichienne a été antérieure à la mobilisation générale russe'.[77]

If Berthelot had been guilty of conscious distortion, it would illustrate Demartial's caustic dictum about France:

> Le droit de guerre et de paix appartient au Pouvoir exécutif qui peut, pour tromper la nation sur les causes de la guerre, déposer de faux documents devant les Chambres. . . . Les académiciens sont chargés de faire croire qu'ils sont vrais.[78]

Apart from Berthelot himself—whose case must remain undecided—those who believed what they found in the *Yellow Book* were, needless to say, perfectly innocent. They were just victims. The most illustrious victim was Raymond Poincaré himself. In his lectures about *Les origines de la guerre*, as late as 1921, he still quoted the telegrams of Dumaine from Vienna and of Paléologue from Petersburg, as he had found them in the *Yellow Book*.[79]

The truth was revealed only in 1925, when Pierre Renouvin, who had been allowed to see some original documents, published Paléologue's authentic telegram of 31 July in his *Origines immédiates de la guerre*.[80] It was the beginning of the end for the legend.

But a legend there had been—a formidable misconception about the course of events which had led to the war. And at the bottom of the misconception and of the legend, there was a question of ciphers.

APPENDIX

As we have referred to Marchioness de Laguiche's diary piecemeal, it may be useful to print here the full text of the entries for 29 July and 30 July:

*16/29 juillet 1914**—Januschkevich a appelé Pierre aujourd'hui pour lui dire que Sa Majesté venait de signer l'ordre de mobilisation pour Kiev, Odessa, Kazan, Moscou. Rien autre part pour ne pas froisser Berlin, et le désir d'être correct est tel que Soukhomlinov et Januschkevich avaient proposé d'aller voir Pourtalès et Chelius pour leur prouver qu'on n'en veut pas à l'Allemagne. Sazonov a trouvé cela exagéré, et Januschkevich a simplement fait venir Eggeling, lui affirmant le vif désir de ne pas blesser l'Allemagne, mais ne cachant pas qu'on était mécontent de l'Autriche, et que des mesures préparatoires étaient prises. Eggeling riposta aigrement: 'Evidement! on ne peut guère en faire plus, puisque l'armée russe est en pleine mobilisation!'. 'Non, reprit tranquillement Januschkevich, je vous donne ma parole d'honneur que jusqu'à présent, 3h. 06, aucun ordre de mobilisation, même partielle, n'a été donné, mais évidemment cela n'implique point qu'il ne le sera pas'. Quoique un peu rasséréné, Eggeling lança encore 'qu'à Vilna la réquisition des chevaux avait eu lieu'. 'Fait d'une erreur, geste d'un exalté, riposta Januschkevich. C'est arrivé en France l'an passé, et l'Allemagne n'y a pas vu de casus belli'. Devant Eggeling, il ordonna une enquête et poussa le sang-froid jusqu'à déclarer que la Russie comptait sur l'Empereur Guillaume pour détendre la situation, et que si l'Allemagne prouvait à la Russie le moindre acte dirigé contre elle*, satisfaction lui serait donnée sur l'heure.

En attendant, à minuit une minute l'ordre de mobilisation contre l'Autriche sera lancé. Selon Januschkevich guerre et mobilisation ne sont pas à confondre, et

---

* The first date is the date of the Julian Calendar, which was still in use in Russia; the second date is the date of the Gregorian Calendar.

convaincu des désirs pacifiques de Guillaume, il croit que grâce aux décisions de cette nuit la pression allemande agira sur l'Autriche qui se calmera.

A 10 heures, une automobile de la Guerre vient chercher Pierre; à 11 heures il rentre, nous disant qu'il y a eu un échange de télégrammes entre les deux Empereurs affirmant leurs désirs pacifiques, mais que Pourtalès est survenu un peu après déclarant que si la Russie ne contremandait pas tous ses préparatifs, l'Allemagne s'estimerait en droit d'en tirer les conséquences les plus graves. Du coup la Russie étend son ordre de mobilisation; on prie Pierre d'aviser Paris, mais de n'en parler à Paléologue qu'à minuit, son manque de discrétion étant connu! . . .

17/30 juillet 1914—A deux heures trente du matin, mon pauvre Pierre rentre enfin. Quelle nuit! Comme à minuit il arrive à l'Ambassade, il trouve Basili et Chambrun sortant, disant: 'Vous savez, mobilisation! Nous allons le télégraphier au ministère, le chiffre de l'Ambassade n'étant pas sûr'. Paléologue demande à Pierre s'il était au courant: 'Oui, et j'attendais l'heure où on m'avait permis de vous en parler'. A ce moment arrive un envoyé de Januschkevich priant Pierre de ne rien dire et de venir le trouver. Pierre y court, passant d'abord au Pont aux Chantres pour arrêter Basili et Chambrun. Là, Schilling le prend à part et lui dit: 'A vous seul au monde je le confie, pas *un* mot au rayon, ni Basili ni personne ne le sait. L'Empereur Guillaume a encore télégraphié à notre Empereur, le suppliant d'arrêter ses préparatifs, lui jurant que s'il ne continue pas, il arrivera à calmer les Autrichiens; on va donc retarder l'ordre de mobilisation'.

Pierre file à l'Etat-Major, où Januschkevich lui tient identiquement le même langage et disant que d'après cela on se bornait aux 13 corps d'armée déjà cités. Pierre trouve Monkevitz se demandant ce qui a pu se passer et répétant: 'Oh! si l'on pouvait couper ce fil de Peterhof!'.

Pierre repart pour le Pont aux Chantres et trouve Basili et Chambrun enragés pour envoyer leur télégramme à sensation, ne comprenant rien au contre-ordre; enfin Pierre arrive à leur faire supprimer la dernière phrase du télégramme annonçant la mobilisation générale. Pendant ce temps-là, Sazonow et Pourtalès discutaient, Sazonow disant qu'on en avait assez des différents sons de cloche, qu'il fallait savoir à quoi s'en tenir. A 2 heures 1/2, le conciliabule continuant, Pierre est rentré se coucher.

L'impression de Schilling est qu'on a reculé pour mieux sauter et que le tabac n'est qu'un peu retardé. Charmante situation de Pierre vis-à-vis de Paléologue! A 9 heures l'Ambassade d'Allemagne téléphone à Maria [the German maid of the Laguiches] d'être prête à filer aujourd'hui ou demain au plus tard. La maison est sens dessus dessous, les fausses nouvelles circulent. Paléologue appelle Pierre, il est furieux contre Pierre et Chambrun d'avoir supprimé la fin de son télégramme. On ne pouvait cependant signaler une mobilisation qui n'existe pas encore!

L'Autriche a fait savoir que si la Russie mobilise, de son côté elle ripostera par une déclaration de guerre.

Notes

1. *Le Temps*, 1 December 1914; *The Times*, 1, 2 and 3 December 1914.
2. *Ministère des Affaires étrangères. Documents diplomatiques. 1914. La Guerre européenne* (Paris, 1914) better known as the *Yellow Book*, p. 129.
3. *Documents diplomatiques français, 1871–1914*, 3rd series, XI (Paris, 1936) (henceforth *DDF*), p. 356, no. 432.
4. Bertie to Grey, 1 August 1914, in *British Documents on the Origins of the War, 1898–1914*, XI (London, 1926) (henceforth *BD*), p. 243, no. 403.
5. Peter Bark, MS *Memoirs*; New York, Columbia University Libraries, Rare Book and Manuscript Library, Kakhmeteff Archive, Bark Papers, Box 1. Used for the first time by D. C. B. Lieven, *Russia and the Origins of the First World War* (London, 1983), pp. 141–4. See my comments in my forthcoming article 'Le rôle de l'opinion publique dans la genèse d'une guerre: 1870 et 1914', in *Europa vor dem Krieg von 1870. Mächtekonstellation, Konfliktfelder, Kriegsausbruch*, Kolloquium des Historischen Kollegs München 1985 (Munich, 1987).
6. *Die Internationalen Beziehungen im Zeitalter des Imperialismus. Dokumente aus den Archiven der Zarischen und der Provisorischen Regierung*, ed. by Otto Hoetzsch, 1st series, V (Berlin, 1934), pp. 25–6, no. 19; Immanuel Geiss, *Julikrise und Kriegsausbruch 1914*, vol. 1 (Hanover, 1963), pp. 354–5, and *July 1914. The Outbreak of the First World War. Selected Documents* (London, 1967), pp. 186–7. Cf. also *How the War Began in 1914. Being the Diary of the Russian Foreign Office from the 3rd to the 20th (Old Style) of July 1914*, ed. by W. Cyprian Bridge (London, 1925) (henceforth *How the War Began*), p. 30.
7. *Die Internationalen Beziehungen*, op. cit., p. 67, no. 79; not reproduced in Geiss's collection; *How the War Began*, p. 34. See also Luigi Albertini, *The Origins of the War of 1914*, transl. by I. M. Massey (henceforth Albertini), II (London, 1953), pp. 304–5. Paléologue is informed and sends the news to his government: 'Au Conseil des Ministres qui a été tenu ce matin à Krasnoïé Sélo sous la présidence de l'Empereur, le Gouvernement russe a décidé *en principe* de mobiliser les treize corps d'armée qui sont éventuellement destinés à opérer contre l'Autriche. Cette mobilisation ne sera rendue effective et publique que si le Gouvernement austro-hongrois prétend contraindre la Serbie par la force des armes' (telegram of 25 July, at 6.22 p.m., in *DDF*, p. 52, no. 50).
8. *How the War Began*, p. 34.
9. L. C. F. Turner, 'The Russian Mobilization in 1914', *Journal of Contemporary History*, III (1968), p. 85, n. 54; revised version of the article in Paul M. Kennedy (ed.), *The War Plans of the Great Powers, 1880–1914* (London, 1979), p. 268, n. 38. Doubts are due mainly to the fact that there is no mention of the *ukaze* in the diary of the Russian Foreign Office (*How the War Began*).
10. Negative answer in Albertini, II, p. 555.
11. Copy communicated to the author by Princess de Merode-Westerloo, to whom we wish to express our respectful thanks. Princess de Merode-Westerloo is the daughter of Marchioness de Laguiche. Extracts from the diary have already been published (with a few minor errors, which we correct here) in J. Stengers, 'July 1914: Some Reflections', *Annuaire de l'Institut de Philologie et d'Histoire Orientales et Slaves*, XVII (1963–5), pp. 146–8.
12. *How the War Began*, p. 50; Albertini, II, pp. 555–6.
13. Diary of Marchioness de Laguiche; see Appendix.
14. *How the War Began*, p. 50.
15. Diary of Marchioness de Laguiche; see Appendix.
16. Ibid. New developments, the French embassy wires to Paris, have 'décidé le Gouvernement russe, cette nuit même, à ordonner la mobilisation des treize corps destinés à opérer contre l'Autriche' (*DDF*, p. 230, no. 283; telegram dated 29 July and bearing the name of

Paléologue, but which was actually sent on 30 July a little after midnight and under the supervision of Laguiche: see below).

17. R. Hoeniger, *Russlands Vorbereitung zum Weltkrieg. Auf Grund unveröffentlicher russischer Urkunden* (Berlin, 1919), pp. 108–9.

18. Ibid.

19. 'Saint-Pétersbourg, jeudi 30 juillet. – Les journaux enregistrent le décret de mobilisation comme une mesure prévue et fatale' (telegram from the Havas-Reuter Bureau in Brussels, published by several Belgian newspapers: see for instance *L'Indépendance Belge* and *La Gazette*, 31 July 1914). The German Ambassador in Petersburg, Pourtalès, announces the mobilisation of the fourth military district in a telegram sent at 11.00 a.m. (I. Geiss, *Julikrise und Kriegsausbruch*, op. cit., II, p. 360). See also the despatch sent on 30 July by the Belgian chargé d'affaires in Petersburg, de l'Escaille: 'Ce matin à 4 heures, [la] mobilisation était publiée' (cf. about this despatch, below note 48).

20. Quoted by Nicolas de Basily, *Memoirs* (Stanford, 1973), p. 100.

21. Cf. *How the War Began*, p. 65.

22. Nicolas de Basily, p. 100.

23. *How the War Began*, p. 66; Maurice Paléologue, *La Russie des Tsars pendant la Grande Guerre*, I (Paris, 1921), p. 39.

24. Cf. Sazonov's foreword to *How the War Began*, p. 9.

25. R. Hoeniger, op. cit., p. 112. Perhaps even a bit earlier: cf. Pierre Renouvin, *Les origines immédiates de la guerre*, 2nd edn (Paris, 1927), p. 780, and *Die Internationalen Beziehungen*, p. 198, n. 1.

26. The time—an approximate one, naturally—is that indicated by the British military attaché (*BD*, p. 246, no. 410) and by the correspondent of the *Kölnische Zeitung*: cf. Richard Ullrich, 'Herrn Paléologues Meldung der russischen allgemeinen Mobilmachung', *Berliner Monatshefte*, August 1933, p. 781. According to *The Times* correspondent, these 'curt notices on pink paper' were posted up at midnight (*The Times*, 1 August 1914, p. 7).

27. *BD*, p. 276, no. 490; *The Times*, 5 August 1914, p. 5.

28. I. Geiss, *July 1914*, op. cit., p. 323; Albertini, III, p. 56.

29. Albertini, II, p. 545, and III, p. 127.

30. There is however another and more simple explanation: it is the general lack of precision of the Tsar in the wording of his telegrams. The best example is that of his telegram of 30 July to Emperor William II, which was such a masterpiece of clumsiness that it provoked an uproar in Berlin (cf. Hans Hallmann, *Um die russische Mobilmachung. Diplomatische Studien zum Ausbruch des Weltkrieges* (Stuttgart, 1939), pp. 48–9 and 65–6; Albertini, II, p. 560, and III, pp. 2–6).

31. 'Voilà comment l'ambassadeur de France renseignait son gouvernement. Il lui télégraphiait des faussetés, et ne lui disait rien des faits les plus graves, les plus dramatiques' (G. Demartial, *L'Evangile du Quai d'Orsay* (Paris, 1926), p. 46).

32. Albertini, II, pp. 327, 568, 585, 586, 587, 588, 613, 616–7, 621, 625, 626.

33. 'Les origines de la guerre de 1914. Réponse de M. Pierre Renouvin à M. Albert Fabre-Luce', *Le Monde*, 19 August 1964. See also H. Hallmann, op. cit., pp. 80 ff. 92, 101, 128 and 148–50; G. Krumeich, *Aufrüstung und Innenpolitik in Frankreich vor dem ersten Weltkrieg* (Wiesbaden, 1980), p. 269 ('die Desinformationen Paléologues'), and *Armaments and Politics in France on the Eve of the First World War* (Leamington Spa, 1984), p. 227 ('Paléologue's deliberate misinformation'); John F. V. Keiger, *France and the Origins of the First World War* (London, 1983), p. 159.

34. 'L'Esprit public en Russie. Journal d'un mobilisé', *Le Correspondant*, 10 September 1914, p. 756.

35. Cf. G. Krumeich, *Aufrüstung und Innenpolitik*, op. cit., p. 258, n. 152 (extract from Poincaré's diary), and *Armaments and Politics*, op. cit., p. 291, n. 153 (idem); Comte de

Saint-Aulaire, 'De Viviani à la Jeanne d'Arc de Bernard Shaw', *Oeuvres libres*, April 1953, p. 114; Gabriel Hanotaux, *Carnets, 1907–1925* ed. by G. Dethan (Paris, 1982), pp. 430–1 (reminiscences of Paléologue).

36. M. Paléologue, *La Russie des Tsars*, I, p. 35; *DDF*, p. 592 (note of Paléologue).

37. 'Le Gouvernement russe a résolu de procéder secrètement aux premières mesures de mobilisation générale' (*DDF*, p. 297, no. 359).

38. *DDF*, p. 230, n. 5.

39. There was no initiative by Chambrun himself, as Paléologue has asserted (*DDF*, p. 230 n. 5).

40. Cf. R. Recouly, *Les heures tragiques d'avant-guerre* (Paris, 1922), pp. 160–1 (Recouly was informed by Basily); Y. Danilov, *La Russie dans la guerre mondiale, 1914–1917*, French transl. (Paris, 1927), p. 39 (same source); Nicolas de Basily, *Memoirs*, p. 96; Albertini, II, pp. 586–7.

41. *DDF*, p. 230, no. 283 and p. 258, no. 302.

42. See for instance Jules Isaac, *Un débat historique. Le problème des origines de la guerre* (Paris, 1933), p. 199.

43. II, p. 587.

44. This may explain also why telegrams about the problems of ciphers were not published in the *DDF* (see the list of telegrams, pp. 616–20); this may have been a deliberate omission.

45. Unpublished telegram in the quai d'Orsay Archives; kindly communicated by the Head of the Archives, M. Georges Dethan, to whom I express my warm thanks.

46. Ibid. In the first paragraph of this telegram, Paléologue wrote: 'Je vous adresse par l'entremise de l'Ambassade de Russie et sous le couvert du chiffre russe un télégramme secret No. 304' (No. 304 was the telegram sent from the Pont aux Chantres). The number of the telegram in the series of Paléologue's wires can thus be ascertained: it is No. 305 as mentioned in the list of *DDF*, p. 619.

47. *How the War Began*, p. 69.

48. 'Comme j'ai eu l'honneur de vous le télégraphier aujourd'hui (Tél. 10), tout espoir de solution pacifique paraît écarté . . . Je me suis servi pour mon télégramme de la voie via Stockholm par le Nordisk Kabel comme plus sûre que l'autre' (despatch of Baron de l'Escaille, Belgian chargé d'affaires at Petersburg, of 30 July 1914, to the Belgian Minister of Foreign Affairs; de l'Escaille had committed this despatch to the care of a messenger who posted it in Berlin to a private address in Brussels; but these elaborate precautions were useless for the mail was intercepted by the German Post Office; the despatch was published in the German press in September 1914—see the text in F. Roches, *Manuel des origines de la guerre* (Paris, 1919), pp. 364–8, and in the *Amtliche Dokumente zur Geschichte der europäischen Politik, 1885–1914*, 1st supplementary vol., *Belgische Aktenstücke, 1905–1914*, new edn (Berlin, 1925), pp. 328–33; on the story of the interception, Archives of the Ministry of Foreign Affairs, Brussels, Classement B, No. 34, Correspondance politique Russie, 1914). The decrypt of the telegram of 30 July referred to in this despatch—the telegram No. 10—figures in the same file of the Foreign Ministry Archives; there is no indication on it of either the time of departure or the time of arrival, but a stamp seems to show that it reached the Ministry only on 31 July.

49. Albertini, II, p. 623.

50. Interview by Madol in 1933: H. R. Madol, 'Qui a voulu la guerre? 2. M. Maurice Paléologue', in *Vu*, 15 March 1933, and A. von Wegerer, 'Qui a voulu la guerre?', *Berliner Monatshefte*, April 1933, p. 378; see also *DDF*, p. 594 (note of Paléologue), and M. Paléologue, *La Russie des Tsars*, I, p. 40.

51. A despatch of the Belgian minister in Petersburg, Count de Buisseret, has here some relevance. Buisseret writes on 31 July: 'En arrivant ce matin à Saint-Pétersbourg, je suis allé voir l'Ambassadeur de France. M. Paléologue m'a dit ce qui suit: *La mobilisation est*

générale. En ce qui concerne la France, elle ne m'a pas encore été notifiée, mais on ne peut en douter. M. Sazonow négocie encore . . .' (Brussels, Foreign Ministry Archives, file quoted supra; published in the second Belgian Grey Book: *Royaume de Belgique. Correspondance diplomatique relative à la guerre de 1914–1915*, II (Paris, 1915), p. 17, no. 17). 'Elle ne m'a pas encore eté notifiée': this may be the key to Paléologue's attitude.

52. III, pp. 112–65.

53. p. 119.

54. Cf. *BD*, p. 243, no. 403, and p. 254, no. 428; *DDF*, p. 419, no. 523.

55. Albertini, III, p. 140.

56. Albertini's interpretation has met with the approval of A. J. P. Taylor. Taylor writes in his review that 'the French certainly cheated . . . [when] they invented the legend that Austria's mobilization preceded Russia's and provoked it' (*English Historical Review*, LXXIII, 1958, pp. 322–3).

57. *DDF*, p. 336, no. 402. How such a version could have come to the ears of the French Ambassador, remains a mystery. Wegerer's tentative explanation—that Cambon must have got the news from his Russian colleague in Berlin—seems groundless (see A. von Wegerer, *Der Ausbruch des Weltkrieges 1914*, t. II (Hamburg, 1939), p. 228, and the objections of Bernadotte E. Schmitt, 'July 1914 once more', *Journal of Modern History*, June 1941, p. 232).

58. *DDF*, p. 356, no. 432, and p. 348, no. 419.

59. The telegram from Petersburg was sent at 10.43 a.m., East European time, that is, at 8.43 a.m., Paris time, the telegram from Vienna at 5.00 p.m., Central European time, or 4.00 p.m., Paris time.

60. *DDF*, pp. 370–1, no. 454.

61. Poincaré himself, it must be noted, strongly asserted later that he and the French Government had made their mistake in absolute good faith (R. Poincaré, *Au service de la France*, IV, *L'Union sacrée, 1914* (Paris, 1927), pp. 445–6; R. Gérin and R. Poincaré, *Les responsabilités de la guerre. Quatorze questions. Quatorze réponses* (Paris, 1930), pp. 149 and 153).

62. *DDF*, p. 357 n. (extract from Paléologue's diary).

63. Ibid.; see also Paléologue's interview in 1933 by Madol (H. R. Madol, "Qui a voulu la guerre?', op. cit., and A. von Wegerer, "Qui a voulu la guerre?', op. cit., p. 378). Objections by R. Ullrich, 'Herrn Paléologues Meldung', op. cit., p. 783. The question is discussed by Albertini, II, pp. 622–3.

64. This meant using 'la voie des réseaux scandinaves et des câbles anglais, intinéraire d'un mécanisme très compliqué' (interview by Madol, loc. cit.); see also *DDF*, p. 357 n.

65. Cf. *DDF*, p. ix; P. Renouvin, *Les origines immédiates de la guerre*, p. 182, n. 1; R. Poincaré, *Au service de la France*, IV, p. 456.

66. *DDF*, p. 360, no. 438. Cf. R. Poincaré, loc. cit.

67. All this is based on the data of the *DDF*.

68. An important element must be added here: the agitation was particularly great in the evening of 31 July, when the news of the assassination of Jean Jaurès was announced and there were such serious fears of popular reactions that the ominous words of 'civil war' were heard at the Council of Ministers (Abel Ferry, *Carnets secrets, 1914–1918* (Paris, 1957), p. 26; J. J. Becker, *1914: Comment les Français sont entrés dans la guerre* (Paris, 1977), pp. 238–9). This was the worst time indeed for a critical assessment of diplomatic documents.

69. Jules Isaac, 'Observations complémentaires sur les Documents français', *Revue d'Histoire de la Guerre Mondiale*, XV (1937), p. 24. On Berthelot, cf. A. Bréal, *Philippe Berthelot* (Paris, 1937); G. Suarez, *Briand. Sa vie. Son œuvre*, III (Paris, 1939), pp. 174–8 and passim; R. D. Challener, *The French Foreign Office: The Era of Philippe Berthelot*, in Gordon A. Craig and Felix Gilbert (ed.), *The Diplomats, 1919–1939* (Princeton, 1953). Abel Ferry described him as an 'homme intelligent, âpre, au masque florentin, à l'âme

florentine', as a 'génie paradoxal et faux, orgueilleux de soi-même et méprisant aux autres' (*Carnets secrets*, p. 153 and p. 184).

70. See *DDF*, p. 628, Index sub v° Berthelot; cf. also R. D. Challener, loc. cit.

71. *DDF*, p. 348, no. 419.

72. *Ministère des Affaires étrangères. Documents diplomatiques. 1914*, p. 127, no. 115.

73. This seems to be the opinion of Pierre Renouvin ('La politique française en juillet 1914 d'après les Documents diplomatiques français', *Revue d'Histoire de la Guerre Mondiale*, XV (1937), p. 13, n.3).

74. Even now, it must be noted, in spite of its publication in the *BD* (p. 218, no. 347), we do not know for certain at what time Buchanan's telegram was sent. There is still a small mystery there. The time of its receipt at the Foreign Office is certain: 5.20 p.m. on 31 July (*BD*, p. 218, note of the editors; the text of the telegram was initialled on 31 July by Sir Eyre Crowe and G. R. Clerk: see F.O. 371/2159, No. 35076). The time of despatch from Petersburg was 6.40. Was it 6.40 *p.m.* on *30 July*, as the editors of the *BD* believe (loc. cit.)? This seems impossible to reconcile with the contents of another telegram of 30 July, sent at 11.25 p.m. (*BD*, p. 210, no. 328). Is it then, as Albertini thinks, 6.40 *p.m.* on *31 July* (Albertini, III, p. 137)? This is also most improbable, not only because the telegram would have taken only forty minutes in transmission, but because, above all, Buchanan was not such a bad ambassador as to send late in the afternoon a piece of information of vital importance which his French and German colleagues had already sent to Paris and Berlin in the morning (Paléologue's wire, as we have seen, was sent at 10.43 a.m.; Pourtalès's wire left at 10.20 a.m., and the telegram of Chelius, the German military plenipotentiary at the Russian Court, followed immediately at 10.30 a.m.: cf. I. Geiss, *Julikrise und Kriegsausbruch*, II, p. 455, and 'Ergänzungen zu den Deutschen Dokumenten zum Kriegsausbruch', *Berliner Monatshefte*, February 1937, p. 162). So we are left with only one option: 6.40 *a.m.* on *31 July*. This would mean that Buchanan's wire took nearly thirteen hours to reach London. As Jules Isaac rightly says, there is 'une sorte de mystérieuse fatalité qui pèse sur tous les documents français et anglais concernant la mobilisation générale russe' (*Un débat historique*, p. 209, n.2).

75. Even if Berthelot saw through his initial mistake, he may have felt compelled to stick to his guns for the simple reason that the initial erroneous version had already been publicised in the British *Blue Book*, and publicised, so to speak, with a French signature. The *Blue Book* had made known the conversations of Sir Francis Bertie with Margerie and Poincaré on 1 August, where both Margerie and Poincaré had explained that the Russian mobilisation had followed the Austrian mobilisation (*Blue Book*, No. 126 and No. 134). Berthelot felt perhaps that he was no longer free to tell the truth.

76. G. Demartial, *L'Evangile du Quai d'Orsay*, op. cit., p. 104.

77. E. Durkheim and E. Denis, *Qui a voulu la guerre? Les origines de la guerre d'après les documents diplomatiques* (Paris, 1915), pp. 41–2; also pp. 64–5. There are more lucid treatments of the problem by J. W. Headlam, *The History of Twelve Days, July 24th to August 4th, 1914* (London, 1915), pp. 218–20 (who concludes that 'the mobilisation of Austria and Russia must have been almost simultaneous'), and by Joseph Reinach, *Histoire du douze jours (23 juillet–3 août 1914). Origines diplomatiques de la guerre de 1914–1917* (Paris, 1917), pp. 424–6, but their critical remarks were not strong enough to tarnish the official version.

78. G. Demartial, *La haine de la vérité* (Paris, 1939), p. 57. On Georges Demartial's interesting personality, cf. Félicien Challaye, *Georges Demartial, sa vie, son œuvre* (Paris, 1950); G. Thuillier, 'Un fonctionnaire syndicaliste et pacifiste: Georges Demartial (1861–1945)', *Revue Administrative*, 1976, pp. 355–64; H. Josephson (ed.), *Biographical Dictionary of Modern Peace Leaders* (Westport, 1985), pp. 203–5.

79. R. Poincaré, *Les origines de la guerre* (Paris, 1921), p. 261; cf. Albertini, III, pp. 145–6.

80. Paris, 1925, p. 146; 2nd edn, (Paris, 1927), p. 181.

The Surveillance of Indian 'Seditionists' in North America, 1905–1915

RICHARD POPPLEWELL

Indian 'agitators' abroad before the First World War generally feared the efficiency of the overseas intelligence system of the British Empire. At home they were familiar with networks of police informers, while in the United States their fears were strengthened by the past experience of their Irish-American sympathisers. After the Civil War the latter built up a military organisation with which they hoped to conquer Canada. Yet their most secret plans fell into British hands thanks to the famous informer 'Henri le Caron'.[1] Despite such a reputation, however, British intelligence arrangements in North America were not extensive. Neither the War Office nor the Admiralty ran networks of agents in North America before the Great War, being represented solely by the military and naval attachés at Washington. The activities of the Secret Service Bureau, which was founded only in 1909, were directed almost entirely against Germany.[2]

The Department of Criminal Intelligence of the Government of India had the specialised task of gathering information about the Indian enemies of the Empire. It was established in 1904 with the basic duty to collect and collate information received from the new Criminal Investigation Departments of the separate Indian local governments, and to watch the Indian press at home and abroad. But in no sense did the DCI constitute an Imperial secret police force. It had a small personnel; there were originally intended to be only 26 men on its staff. The Department was headed by the Director of Criminal Intelligence, who at first had only one assistant of officer rank. The other members of the Department belonged to either the clerical staff or to the 'menial establishment'.[3] Additions were made in 1906 and in 1908, but the DCI's formal establishment remained very restricted, though its strength could be increased by the secondment of detectives from the local Criminal Investigation Departments to work under it on special enquiries.[4] In 1904 the Secret Service fund of the DCI amounted to only Rs. 12,000. By 1912 this allotment had increased to Rs 50,000 and in 1913 went up to Rs. 100,000;[5] this was not a large sum, particularly when the concerns of the DCI extended outside India.

The reasons why the Department of Criminal Intelligence had only a small staff and restricted budget were neither the parsimony nor the poverty of the Government of India, but the maintenance of a strict demarcation line separating it from the police force. The DCI was discouraged from becoming an investigating department, originally being intended to restrict itself exclusively to the processing of information received from local CIDs. Such an artificial division could not be maintained for long, but the general principle held good that the DCI should not, as far as possible, interfere in the jurisdictions of the local investigation agencies for fear of conflict,[6] and because the Government of India and Parliament were deeply concerned that the Empire should not possess an imperial secret police like the Russian Empire.[7] Moreover, in dealing with Indian agitation abroad the problems of distance strongly encouraged the Department to operate through existing local intelligence agencies whenever possible. By 1910, however, the virtual refusal of Scotland Yard to operate outside London necessitated the direct establishment of a small-scale Indian secret service operation on the Continent.[8]

The DCI performed an important imperial function just by collecting and assessing information about both unrest in India and the activities of Indian agitators abroad, which came from various, often irregular, sources. While the system of Indian intelligence abroad was of a very *ad hoc* nature it did have a centre. Moreover, the Director of Criminal Intelligence was a highly paid and experienced officer, intended by the Police Commission of 1903, which established the new Department, to hold a position of authority within the Government. His status encouraged the effective supply of intelligence to the Indian Government.[9] The first to occupy the post was Sir Harold Stuart, who went on to become Indian Home Secretary in 1907, being replaced as Director by Mr Charles Stevenson-Moore; the latter was in turn succeeded by Sir Charles Cleveland in February 1910. Cleveland remained Director of Criminal Intelligence almost continuously until 1919.

The first serious outbreak of Indian unrest within India itself occurred in 1907.[10] Soon afterwards centres of Indian agitation appeared abroad. The

British had not expected this offshoot of the world-wide Indian diaspora of the later nineteenth century. The first centres of serious concern to India were London and Paris. Most serious of all by 1913 was evidence which suggested a large-scale Indian conspiracy in the United States. At times these revolutionary centres abroad were considered by the DCI to be a greater threat than those within India.

The first Indians in America to concern the DCI were not revolutionaries but priests of the Hindu-fundamentalist Vedanta Society, formed in the 1890s by Swami Vivekananda (1863–1902). The Vedanta Temple at New York in particular was suspected of encouraging 'seditious' Indian students. Until 1905 the information which the Indian authorities received about the United States came entirely from the American press.[11] This situation seemed inadequate to the newly-formed DCI, which felt that the United States was the country most attractive to Indian exiles, for besides a tradition of political toleration, it offered to the Indian student unrivalled opportunities of education.[12]

New York, the first centre of Indian unrest in the United States, was also the stronghold of Irish nationalism. The Republican Clan-na-Gael and their newspaper the *Gaelic American* welcomed the first Indian agitators to arrive in New York in 1905 with open arms. The Irish-American leader George Freeman had hopes of a revolt in India backed by the Clan-na-Gael.[13] Though the British were anxious lest the Irish provide Indians with firearms or with experience of bomb-making they did not overreact to this potential menace.

Since the 1860s British, Irish and American agents had worked in the employ of the British Home Office within Irish-American circles. In 1905 the Home Department of the Government of India contacted the Home Office through the India Office and arranged that its New York agency should provide India with intelligence. This was agreed upon and the India Office started to receive direct information from America. By March 1908 at the latest, the New York agency was in receipt of a subsidy from Indian revenues. In 1910 the maintenance of the agency cost India £300 a year.[14] In return a weekly report on Indian affairs was sent to the India Office.

The Home Office agency was not extensive. Its activities were restricted almost entirely to New York, and it provided next to no information on Indians elsewhere in the United States. In 1905 the agency had only one full-time agent, F. Cunliffe Owen, who was not reinforced by another permanent agent until the middle of 1911.[15] Cunliffe Owen obtained information on Indians 'partly through personal investigation of [his] own, and partly through specially selected newspaper reporters'.[16] He claimed to have supplemented the Indian subsidy out of his own pocket in his eagerness to lead Americans from

> the fallacious belief that the Land of Hind would be happier and more ably governed by irresponsible, ill-educated and dishonest Baboos than under the honest and experienced administration of the Viceroy and his splendid corps of English civil servants.

Cunliffe Owen himself, or one of his hired reporters, posed as a member of the Clan-na-Gael, becoming intimate with George Freeman and with Myron Phelps, an American lawyer who at the end of 1907 formed his own society for Indian students, the Society for the Advancement of India. By May 1909 he was one of only five or six whites attending the meetings of New York's main Indian club.[17]

In a general review of the Home Office agent's performance in 1911 the Government of India listed the kind of tasks he had performed.[18] Cunliffe Owen had read the American newspapers on India's behalf. He had traced some notable 'seditionists' for the DCI, and gathered some quite detailed information about some of them. More importantly, he had warned India that some of the nationalists in America had international connections. Two American sympathisers were in contact with the coterie of Indian revolutionaries in Paris who were subsidising Freeman. At times this intelligence gave cause for real concern. The Home Office agent first brought to notice that arms were being exported to India for revolutionary purposes.[19] At the end of 1908 he mentioned a rumour that the SS *Moraitis*, carrying thousands of Mauser pistols, had sailed from New York for the Persian Gulf. This news stimulated considerable Foreign Office activity, which came to a farcical conclusion when the Consul at Smyrna discovered that the ship was carrying only bicarbonate of soda.[20] Also in 1908 the agent provided detailed information about 'seditious' utterances made by one of the most important Indian Princes, the Gaekwar of Baroda, on his visit to New York. Cunliffe Owen later recalled that

> So intimate was the connection between the Gaekwar's students here in America and the perpetrators of the anti-British outrages in India, that I and others here aware of the fact, were convinced that the Gaekwar would be deposed on the strength of the evidence obtained.[21]

However, despite the occasional scare, the Home Department and the DCI felt that the Cunliffe Owen's agent's reports furnished little of interest. Largely this was because of a slump in the activity of the Indian and Irish nationalists in 1909. Both the two main Indian nationalist societies in New

York failed within a short time of their foundation. They attracted little support from the Indians in New York, and almost none from American whites. Cunliffe Owen, however, attributed the revolutionaries' lack of success to his own ability in invoking against them 'quiet influences of one kind and another, especially on the part of powerful people'.

In April 1910 a meeting of the Indo-American Society was held in order to wind up the club. The Clan-na-Gael leadership believed that the movements of the Indian agitators had been reported to the British authorities by one of the English or American members of the society, and that the Indians would be safer if they formed an exclusively Oriental society.[22] When the Indians followed this advice the Home Office agent found it very difficult to provide information about them. He complained that

> it seems impossible to get the right sort of Agents to tackle [the surveillance of Indians] and invariably it comes back to the basis of the need of a native to handle the business properly, as no sooner does the ordinary Agent begin to get familiar with the interested parties than they become suspicious and close up like an oyster.

In forwarding this letter to the India Office the Home Office added that the employment of at least one native Indian agent in New York was 'very essential', as English and Irish agents were 'practically useless' in Indian circles.[23] Exactly the same problems were experienced by the Special Branch of the Metropolitan Police in this period, even though India depended upon them for the bulk of its information about the activities of Indian agitators in London.[24]

The use of spies picked by the Director of Criminal Intelligence and sent out from India was first suggested in 1907 by Sir William Lee-Warner, the senior member of the Council of India in London. In a private letter to Sir Harold Stuart, the Indian Home Secretary, he suggested that an agent should be sent to London under the disguise of a student, work his way into the confidence of the Indian agitators in London, and then go to America. Sir Harold Stuart replied that it would be difficult to secure a suitable man, and that even if one were found he might well fall under suspicion and be exposed to great risks. Perhaps most importantly, the Liberal Secretary of State for India, Lord Morley, would not wish to spend money on such a 'dirty business'.[25] After discussion the Home Department came to view the idea more favourably, but did not act upon it immediately.[26]

On occasion the DCI or the local CIDs persuaded natives leaving for America to send back reports on the state of Indian feeling there. Alternatively they encouraged natives of India at home to persuade their relatives abroad to supply information. Though these practices were a far from reliable way of gathering intelligence, they were used by the DCI in at least one case to make up for the Home Office Agency's inability to operate outside New York. An informer named Mahomed Husain provided details from Chicago. His reports were soon found useless and discontinued. Later Mahomed Husain went mad and in July 1911 started shooting indiscriminately with a magazine-rifle at passers-by outside the Chicago Opera House. He claimed on arrest that he had been prompted to do this by the 'tyranny of the British Government'. He was so obviously insane that the Government of India escaped compromise.[27]

A more regular means of supplementing the Home Office agency's information was to employ Pinkerton's detective agency. This was an idea particularly favoured by the Viceroy and former Governor-General of Canada, Lord Minto, and to which the Foreign Office had recourse on occasion.[28] However, Sir Harold Stuart wrote in January 1909 that it would probably prove less expensive and more effective if the DCI were to send its own agent to America.[29]

When the Department of Criminal Intelligence despatched their own native Indian agent on a short mission to the United States and Canada in 1910 it was pleased with his performance. It noted that the reports submitted by the Home Office agent compared very unfavourably with those of 'his coloured rival'. The latter reported that a large number of Indians in North America were 'full of anti-British and revolutionary ideas', but that they had not formed themselves into effective organisations; rather they were 'dotted about in many places in Canada and America'. This intelligence persuaded the Government of India that there was no foreseeable need to employ a permanent agent. The Director of Criminal Intelligence, Sir Charles Cleveland concluded in July 1911,

> It would mean our employing several Indian agents if we wanted to keep in close touch with all that is going on among Indians over there but for the present it is sufficient to know the general trend of things as, I think, we do know it. When we have reason to suspect anything immediately dangerous we can adopt measures of our own.[30]

Far from finding the situation in America dangerous in 1911 the DCI and the Home Department even considered stopping the subsidy to the Home Office agent. H. H. Risley, Under-Secretary at the India Office, summed up the issues thus:

> The decision appears to turn on the question whether there is a prima facie reason to suppose that anything really dangerous is going on in America. The weekly

reports do not seem to disclose much reason for the supposition. Isolated items are interesting, but not of great value in themselves. On the other hand, evidence of a real organisation would be very valuable. But have the Government of India reason to think that one exists? If they have not, it is not much use paying Agents to try to find one.[31]

The Director of Criminal Intelligence replied that he was reluctant to cut himself off from his sole direct source of information in North America, for despite the absence of a revolutionary organisation among the Indians there was still reason to fear 'desperate enterprises in India on the part of individuals'. The Indian Government still maintained the Home Office agency on the outbreak of World War One.[32]

The weekly reports of the Director of Criminal Intelligence give a good indication of how American intelligence was interpreted in India from week to week. From 1907 to 1911 the DCI seems to have been uncertain whether the Indians in New York were mainly concerned with politics, with money, or with chasing white women.[33] By the end of 1908 the last two factors were usually felt to predominate. The weekly reports cite many cases where Indians were allegedly only posing as freedom fighters in order the better to acquire donations from the American public.[34] The Indian authorities saw the vast majority of Indian agitators abroad as moral degenerates of one kind or another.[35] They held the allegedly unsavoury personal habits of Indian agitators to be an extension of what they considered the immorality of their political opinions, namely their opposition to the Empire. This contempt combined with the basic uneventfulness of Indian and Irish affairs on the East Coast discouraged the Indian authorities from over-reacting to the far more dangerous situation among the Indian settlers on the West Coast which had developed by 1913.

Before World War One both the affairs of Indians on the Pacific Coast and their surveillance by the Imperial Authorities were conducted in near independence from the East Coast. Until the outbreak of war the only links between the intelligence agents in the two areas were the India Office in London, and the Department of Criminal Intelligence itself, thousands of miles away. By 1913 India was already the beneficiary of various ill assorted methods of surveillance on the East Coast: the Home Office Agency, informers controlled form India, a DCI spy sent on a 'round trip' to America, and Pinkerton's. Events on the West Coast were not to break this *ad hoc* pattern.

Sikhs from the Punjab and Hong Kong began to enter British Columbia in large numbers from 1905 onwards and were confronted by the large-scale white hostility to Asians already experienced by British Columbia's Chinese and Japanese communities.[36] The situation in Canada soon became disturbing from an Indian as well as a Canadian point of view. The vast majority of Indian immigrants to Canada were Sikhs, representatives of what the Government of India esteemed as one of India's 'martial races'. In September 1907, while the Punjab was going through the most active period of unrest which it experienced before the First World War, a serious race riot broke out in the Asian quarter of Vancouver. This led to a Government investigation under Mackenzie King from May to June 1908,[37] and to a secret mission by T. R. E. McInnes, the personal agent of the Minister of the Interior who enquired into the whole question of Asiatic immigration into British Columbia.[38]

McInnes singled out several agitators among the Sikhs, the most important of whom was the young Bengali, Tarak Nath Das. Like the Indian authorities McInnes despised the 'seditionists' as extortionists and confidence tricksters, and denied their claim that there would be serious danger to the Empire if Indians were shut out of Canada. He noted that Das, who had recently set up a paper, *The Free Hindusthan*, had nothing in common with the Sikhs. Not one in a hundred Punjabis could read the English language in which the paper was written. He believed that the agitators were pressing for the lifting of the immigration laws simply so that they might have more of their compatriots to fleece in Canada.[39]

In July 1908 the Vancouver police were instructed by Ottawa to make enquiries about Indians who were collecting money to be sent to revolutionaries in India.[40] At this time Canadian military intelligence also showed a fleeting interest in Indian affairs. Lieutenant W. MacLeod, Sub-Divisional Officer, Vancouver, forwarded the mailing list of the *Free Hindusthan* to his superior, Major Rowland Brittain, district intelligence officer.[41] The Canadians informed the British military attaché at Washington that Taraknath Das was receiving military training at a college in Vermont. The attaché transmitted this information to the War Office, and to the United States General Staff at Washington. The Americans instituted enquiries through a training officer at the college, who reported that Das had no military ability and was not to be feared in any way.[42]

More positive action against the Indian agitators in British Columbia came not from the Intelligence service but from an officer of the Vancouver Immigration Department, William Hopkinson. Though in the Canadian service, Hopkinson was an Englishman who had lived most of his life in India, and was acutely aware of the potential danger to India of events in Canada. His father had been one of the military escort of Sir Louis Cavagnieri massacred at Kabul in 1879, leaving him and his mother stranded at Lahore.[43] In effect Hopkinson was born into the service of the Empire, speaking Punjabi and other Indian languages fluently. He had served in the Indian Police since the age of sixteen, first in the Punjab, and then at Calcutta from 1901 to 1907. There he attained the rank of sub-inspector. At the end of 1907 he went to Canada on two years' leave, unconnected with the Indian Police, and was employed by the Vancouver Immigration Department as interpreter soon after his arrival.[44] Hopkinson was annoyed to discover that Taraknath Das had set up his press near Vancouver. He reported this to a local correspondent of *The Times*, W. L. Creppin, who published an article describing Das's alleged activities. As a result the press moved across the border to Seattle.[45]

The initiative in the surveillance of Indian agitators on the Pacific Coast at this time came entirely from the Canadian side and not from India, let alone from the War Office. The Department of the Interior placed a full-time agent in Vancouver after the failure of a scheme to remove the unwelcome Indians of British Columbia to Honduras. At the beginning of November a Canadian delegation headed by Mr Harkin, the chief clerk of the Ministry of the Interior went to British Honduras, accompanied by Teja Singh and a small Indian delegation. The Canadians blamed the failure of the resettlement plan on Teja Singh's claims that the Sikhs were earmarked for slave-labour and that Hopkinson had tried to bribe the Indian delegates to give a favourable report. As a result the Prime Minister, Sir Wilfrid Laurier, placed Teja Singh under the surveillance of the Vancouver Police.[46]

The Governor-General, Earl Grey, agreed with Laurier that in the current state of unrest in India it was important to keep a close watch on all events which might be seized upon by agitators in India. He ordered the Department of the Interior to keep him regularly informed on Indian affairs in British-Columbia.[47] In December 1908 Grey requested that Laurier send the MP and future Prime Minister, Mackenzie King, to India to brief that Government on the situation in British Columbia. Mackenzie King had already concluded that in any future enquiry into Indian affairs, Hopkinson of the Immigration Department would be 'in a position to render special services'.[48] Hopkinson also impressed the Governor of Honduras, Colonel Swayne, who came to Ottawa at the end of 1908. He wrote on 7 January 1909:

I think it is important that the doings of the Brahmin section be closely watched. There is presumptive evidence that they have a close connection with the agitators in Bengal. I do not think a better man than Mr Hopkinson of the Calcutta police could be found for this work. He has already managed to get a knowledge of their affairs, and Mr R. S. Chamberlain, Chief of the Police of Vancouver, with whom I unofficially spoke on the matter would have no objection to his doing this.[49]

As a result of this recommendation Hopkinson was employed by the Department of the Interior as 'Dominion Police Officer on special duty at Vancouver' for the special purpose of the enquiry into the Indian agitation there. At Canada's request he was placed in communication with the Calcutta Police. In the course of 1909 he resigned from the Indian Police, and in February was formally engaged by the Department of the Interior on a salary of $100 per month. For the next two years he was officially a member of the Immigration Department at Vancouver. He did not receive a commission in the Dominion Police until January 1911.[50]

From 1909 to 1914 Hopkinson to all intents and purposes constituted India's intelligence system on the Pacific Coast. His role was in many ways anomalous. He ceased to be an Indian officer when he took up his duties in India's cause. The Department of Criminal Intelligence was not even informed of his appointment as special agent of the Ministry of the Interior. On 19 April 1909, Stevenson-Moore for the second time argued against using his services. But he was informed in July by Ottawa's Commissioner of Police, that Hopkinson had been employed by the Department of the Interior since the beginning of the year.[51] His reports were sent by the Governor-General's Office to the Colonial Office in London, not direct to the India Office. Hopkinson's mission, though secret, was not entirely concealed from the Indian agitators. Hopkinson and Taraknath Das were already personally acquainted in 1908, when Hopkinson had forced Das to resign a post as Indian interpreter with the U.S. Immigration service by giving the Americans details of his 'seditious' activities. In return Das denounced him as a secret agent in a Canadian newspaper even before he had become one.[52]

Hopkinson was not even provided with facilities for typing his reports in secrecy. His wife acted as his unpaid secretary.[53] However, the employment of a Canadian agent in India's interests suited the DCI's policy of avoiding direct involvement in investigation as far as possible. The discovery of extensive British or Indian Secret Service activity within the United States would have had serious diplomatic consequences. The British Ambassador, Sir Cecil Spring-Rice, wrote in May 1914 that even representations against an Indian agitator would at once galvanise anti-British sentiment and the Irish press.[54]

Early in 1909 Hopkinson and Harkin of the Canadian Ministry of the Interior proposed an extension of the surveillance of Indians into the United States. The Sikh leader Teja Singh had business dealings in California, while Taraknath Das printed the *Free Hindusthan* at Seattle. Another prominent agitator, Guru Dutt Kumar, often visited Das there from Vancouver.

Harkin and Hopkinson proposed that mail to these agitators from places with a large Hindu population should be intercepted and that agents should be sent to obtain information about the agitators' activities in the United States. Inside Canada they recommended that enquiries be made among banks and express companies about the financial transactions of Vancouver Indians.[55] These proposals were rejected by Sir Richmond Ritchie, the senior Under-Secretary at the India Office, who argued that there might be serious consequences if the Canadian Police increased the supervision of suspects, without the despatch by the India Office of an experienced officer to co-ordinate the surveillance. Ritchie felt the best way to obtain intelligence of Indian affairs inside the United States was by examining correspondence to and from America inside India.[56] Systematic postal censorship of the Indians' mail in Canada was not instituted until 1914.[57]

Hopkinson's one-man intelligence agency worked to the satisfaction of the Canadian Ministry of the Interior, the India Office and the Government of India. Because he had a 'good knowledge of Indians'[58] and spoke Indian languages, Hopkinson found it easy to make contacts within Indian circles, unlike the Special Branch of the Metropolitan Police and the Home Office Agency at New York. He had already made friends among the Sikhs before his appointment as special agent.[59] India was thus spared additional irritating requests for assistance from Canada for the loan of her secret agents. From 1908 to 1914 Hopkinson built up an effective system of informers which was a significant faction within the Sikh community by 1914. There is some evidence that Hopkinson personally infiltrated Indian circles. His main accomplice, Bela Singh, declared before a Canadian court in 1914 that 'he used to dress in a turban with a false beard and moustache and old clothes and go to the temple'.[60]

Hopkinson performed the dual role of imperial intelligence agent and agent of the Ministry of the Interior, besides working as immigration inspector. He reported regularly to the Deputy Minister of the Interior, W. W. Cory upon 'sedition' among the Indians, their economic well-being, and all attempts to break the Canadian immigration laws. His reports show clearly that as a Canadian citizen he personally approved of his new country's strict immigration policy, which the Government of India wished to see relaxed.

Though he received no directives from the DCI, Hopkinson seems regularly to have contacted the Indian Police. He reported that Taraknath Das's colleague, G. D. Kumar, held a meeting at which he denounced him as being responsible for all the house-searches which the police had made at the homes of the audience's relatives in India. Then the Indians offered one

Harnam Singh $1,000 to bring some charge against Hopkinson and a colleague so that they would both be thrown out of the immigration service.[61] Hopkinson was hated by the 'disloyal' Sikhs all the more because they realised that he upheld the immigration laws. His informers reported that at a meeting in Vancouver in June 1910 he was held personally responsible for Sikh immigration problems and for keeping Sikh women out of Canada.[62]

Besides reporting the acquisition of arms by Indians, Hopkinson paid close attention to their contacts with Western left-wing movements. In March 1912 he received information that Husein Rahim, a prominent Vancouver agitator, had boasted that he would vote in the Canadian elections on the 28th of that month, although Indians in Canada were disenfranchised. On that day Hopkinson found Rahim acting as scrutineer at the polling station where he himself was to cast his vote. He had Rahim arrested, and accompanied the police in searching his house. There he found a large amount of anarchist, Industrial Workers of the World and Socialist literature. Hopkinson regarded this as a 'very serious matter' because until then the Indians had never identified themselves with a political party. He concluded that the real danger was the effect which such 'Socialistic and Revolutionary teachings' would have 'on the people in India on the return of these men primed with Western methods of agitation and Political and Social equality.'[63]

Despite his obvious efficiency in securing informers inside Canada, Hopkinson felt frustrated at the end of 1911 by his inability to find Indians trustworthy enough to operate within the United States. His main immediate concern was to prevent Taraknath Das's naturalisation as a US citizen lest he take advantage of this status to return to India and cause trouble at the forthcoming Coronation of George V.[64] In the Autumn of 1911 Hopkinson made a nineteen day tour of the US Pacific coast. At San Francisco he met Inspector Ainsworth of the US immigration service to discuss Das's activities. Ainsworth professed his astonishment that the British Government had never taken notice of the activities of the Indian students at Berkeley University. Hopkinson was particularly disturbed when he discovered that knowledge of explosives was widespread among the Indians on the Pacific coast, and that some of them were connected with notorious revolutionary societies in Bengal.[65]

The substance of the report submitted by Hopkinson found its way back to the recently-appointed British Consul-General in San Francisco, Alexander Carnegie Ross. He countered Hopkinson's implied criticism of his Office by saying that its staff was too small to make a detailed investigation among Indians, and that

> As Mr Hopkinson points out his enquiries were of a superficial character . . . It seems unfortunate that when he called at the Consulate he was unable to produce any document showing that he was a Government Official of any sort . . . .[66]

But Hopkinson's mission to America of 1911 had positive results. At Seattle, an American immigration inspector, Hunter, agreed to state on oath what he knew of Taraknath Das. Das was not granted naturalisation until 1914. More importantly Hopkinson started a network of informers within the United States; from this time onwards the Indian 'agitators' on the Pacific Coast were never to be free of British informers. The latter came from widely different backgrounds. Upon his first arrival in San Francisco, Hopkinson called on the priest of the local temple, Swami Trigunatita, whom Das had once threatened and whose protégé he had personally beaten up. Hopkinson offered him protection, and thus secured the support of a very well-placed member of the Indian community.[67] Hopkinson read that Taraknath Das had once been hissed off the stage when he had presented a San Francisco women's group not with a discourse on Indian philosophies, but with a fiery denunciation of the British Raj.[68] He then contacted Mrs Jean Sinclair, one of the leaders of the women's group, who offered to give him information on Das's white female supporters, over whom, Hopkinson believed, Das had an almost hypnotic hold.

Hopkinson did not return to San Francisco until January 1913. The British Consul-General, Carnegie Ross, introduced him to two Indian students of Berkeley University, Surendranath Guha and Edward Pandian, who volunteered reports that at the end of December 1912 one Har Dayal held a dinner at the University to celebrate the attempted assassination and wounding of the Viceroy, Lord Hardinge, on the latter's State Entry into Delhi.[69] This event prompted the British authorities in Delhi and in London to view Indian agitation in America in a much more serious light.

In 1913 Indian 'agitators' on the Pacific Coast became more united and better organised than before, thanks in large part to the charismatic leadership of Har Dayal. He was the first Indian leader in North America to see that the ill-educated Sikhs of the United States and Canada could provide mass support and funds which the nationalist movement in exile needed. His cause was given vital assistance by the unremitting severity of the Canadian immigration laws which damned the Empire in the minds of the Sikhs. The first major step to uniting Hindu intellectuals and Sikh farmers was taken when the Hindu Association of the Pacific Coast was formed in May 1913. By the Autumn, Har Dayal had set up a revolutionary paper at San Francisco together with his own revolutionary party, taking its name from that of the paper, *Ghadr*, or revolt.[70] By the outbreak of the First World War *Ghadr* was being despatched throughout the British Empire, printed in numerous Indian languages.

The increasing virulence of the Indian agitation on the Pacific Coast was accompanied by a strengthening of Hopkinson's ability to provide intelligence. In 1913 he was given greater assistance by the Foreign Office and by the Indian authorities, while by his own efforts he extended the contacts with informers and with US immigration officials begun in 1911. On 12 February 1913 Ross, the Consul-General at San Francisco, was officially ordered by the Foreign Secretary, Sir Edward Grey, to co-operate with Hopkinson.[71] Ross by now was content to be guided by Hopkinson's expert knowledge of Indians and India, and put loyal Indians who volunteered information in contact with him.

In January 1913 Hopkinson attended two meetings at which Har Dayal lectured on Anarchist subjects. He was accompanied by Mr A. Tilton Steele, an accountant who, like Hopkinson, had been brought up in India, and had clashed with Har Dayal in the columns of the San Francisco *Bulletin*.[72] Hopkinson persuaded him to act as his unpaid deputy during his absence from San Francisco. In July 1913 Steele attended a course of lectures delivered by the American 'high priestess' of anarchism, Emma Goldman, in the hope of hearing Har Dayal deliver a speech which would give evidence needed to present him as a political undesirable to the US authorities.[73] Hopkinson's relationship with immigration officials at San Francisco and at Seattle became very close in 1913. They were much more favourably disposed to Britain's desire to control Indian agitators in the United States than were the authorities at Washington. Hopkinson's personal contacts with these officers enabled the British to secure American assistance without approaching the State Department. Hopkinson was so trusted by the American Immigration Officials that in 1913 they employed him as the official US 'Hindu' interpreter at Vancouver, and allowed him to send his informers on missions across the border.[74] The San Francisco officials also assisted Hopkinson's efforts to remove Har Dayal from the United States. Mr Edsall, assistant commissioner at the Seattle immigration station, promised him that if he was given documents implicating Har Dayal with anarchism, then the Immigration Department would investigate his case with a view to deportation.[75] Hopkinson was even allowed to hire a clerk inside the San Francisco Post Office, so that he could intercept Har Dayal's mail.[76] When Har Dayal gave a lecture at Seattle in January, US immigration officers attended at Hopkinson's request.

Hopkinson eventually secured the agreement of the Washington Administration to Har Dayal's deportation because it regarded him as far more obnoxious than other Indian nationalists. Har Dayal was one of the few Indian agitators abroad for whom the term 'anarchist' was not merely a term of British opprobrium, but an objective statement based on his own speeches in support of the Industrial Workers of the World. Moreover, his supporters occasionally threatened US officers with violence if he was deported.[77] In January 1913 the Department of Justice even granted a request from the Foreign Office that Clayton Herrington, its 'Special Agent' at San Francisco, should assist Hopkinson. As a result Hopkinson was given a list of the Hindu students attending Berkeley and an account of the events leading up to Har Dayal's expulsion from his teaching post at Berkeley for overzealous advocacy of free love.[78]

By April 1913 Hopkinson claimed that he had only to give the word and the US Immigration authorities would effect Har Dayal's deportation. Even though Har Dayal was a special case in American eyes, it is unlikely that the State Department would have responded so favourably to British wishes were it not for Hopkinson's skill in winning the support of local American officers and in assiduously building up the case against Har Dayal. Vital to the success of the case was Hopkinson's official status in Canada. Because he was not an agent of the Indian Government the Indian agitators or their sympathisers within the American administration would not readily be able to represent him as the henchman of a 'repressive colonial regime'. The campaign against Har Dayal, like that against Taraknath Das two years before, was devised and instituted by Hopkinson in complete independence from the Indian Government.

However, unknown to the Americans, Hopkinson was finally given discreet support by the Indian Government in 1913. The question of the deportation of Har Dayal was too important an issue for a junior officer like Hopkinson to bring to a conclusion on his own. This precipitated discussion about employing Hopkinson as an agent by the Indian authorities. In April Hopkinson travelled to London in order 'to get his position in Vancouver placed on a satisfactory basis'. At the India Office he was briefed on the world-wide situation of Indian 'agitation' by Major John Arnold Wallinger, a deputy-superintendent of the Bombay Police, who was in charge of Indian secret service operations in Europe. Wallinger was 'favourably impressed with Hopkinson', while the Director of Criminal Intelligence found his reports of 'increasing value'. As a result in April the Home Department granted Hopkinson an allowance of £60 a year as a 'retainer' and another £60 a year to spend on acquiring information.[79] The money was paid out of the Department of Criminal Intelligence's Secret Service fund. In return the DCI started to receive a large number of reports from Hopkinson, while through Wallinger, the Director of Criminal Intelligence was able to recommend action to Hopkinson and provide him with advice.[80]

This improvement of the links between India and intelligence gathering in North America came precisely three years after the Government of India had extended their direct sources of Indian intelligence in Great Britain and in Europe. In 1910 Wallinger had been sent to London to supervise the surveillance of Indian 'anarchists' on the Continent and in America. He set up a small-scale secret service operation with about half a dozen, probably part-time, agents in the major cities of Europe. Such control as he had over American intelligence before 1913 was probably confined to receipt of information from, and the despatch of directives to the Home Office agency in New York.[81] Once put in direct touch with Hopkinson in 1913, he was the first to receive reports from Canada, and transmitted them himself to the DCI. The Government of India was not yet consciously moving towards the creation of a truly imperial intelligence system under which the Department of Criminal Intelligence controlled a heterogeneous but world-wide network of agents. It is true that Wallinger's system of intelligence on the Continent was not much smaller in scale than that of the Secret Service Bureau, while the quality of Indian intelligence from North America was certainly better than that at the disposal of the British Secret Service. However, the Government of India had not planned to take on such an imperial role, and in 1913 did not intend to continue it. The intelligence from its agents abroad solely concerned Indians and their plots.

Moreover, both Wallinger and Hopkinson were employed by the Government of India on a short-term basis; as in the case of the Home Office agency at New York, the continuation of their work and the maintenance of their subsidy was subject to review every year by the Home Department.[82] The Government of India were so uneasy about employing agents in the United States that they even proposed to spy on Hopkinson's work. In May 1913 the Director of Criminal Intelligence suggested getting in touch with someone who was going to America to check up on him.

The *ad hoc* nature of the Indian intelligence system was epitomised by the relations between Wallinger and Hopkinson. Despite his superior rank,

Wallinger acted not as Hopkinson's chief but as his advisor. The two men still served different administrations and saw Indian affairs from slightly different viewpoints. In June Hopkinson forwarded a secret circular of the Department of Criminal Intelligence to the Canadian government. Wallinger complained that he had no right to do so as the document was secret and the property of the Government of India. Hopkinson replied to Wallinger that he had circulated the Department of Criminal Intelligence's formula with a view to keeping the Canadian government in touch with all information received, from whatever source.[83] The arrangement generally worked smoothly. Wallinger described Hopkinson's work as 'of a most meritorious and useful character.'[84]

Wallinger instructed Hopkinson to ask the US authorities to deport Har Dayal. Previously Hopkinson had been unsure whether the information he had collected should be used, because under US law an 'undesirable alien' was deported to the country whence he arrived. In Har Dayal's case this meant Martinique. Wallinger, who was better equipped to look at Indian 'agitation' from a global viewpoint, decided that Har Dayal would be much less dangerous if under the eyes of the French Police, with whom he was on excellent terms.[85]

In February 1914 the American immigration authorities arrested Har Dayal. He immediately broke bail and, to the annoyance of the British, fled to Switzerland. Though this loss did not at first weaken the Ghadr party in North America, the lack of a strong leader was later to prove disastrous to their cause. The continued vigour of the Ghadr party was all the more worrying as the political situation in Europe was worsening. *Ghadr* did not disguise its opinion that England's embroilment in a European war would be the opportunity for revolution in India. Wallinger was anxious to persuade the Americans to give more assistance by revising the manifests completed by Indians for the US immigration authorities, thus making it easier for the British to trace them. This was not asking much of the Americans, but it involved Hopkinson in a sensitive political task when in January 1914 he discussed the matter with Mr Caminetti, the US Commiss-ioner General of Immigration, who was not well-disposed to allow Britain to control Indians in the United States.[86] The manifests, nevertheless, were revised on the basis of a specimen drawn up by Wallinger which Hopkinson presented to Caminetti.[87]

Hopkinson felt that the best way of dealing with the Indians was to rely on the ability of consulates in the United States to watch their movements. He exaggerated the ability of the Foreign Office to perform continual surveillance, wrongly believing that all the Consulates in centres of Indian population had secret agents attached to them.[88] As late as 1914 Carnegie Ross complained that

> no provision has been made by the Government in connection with this Consulate-General for making enquiries regarding seditious Indians.[89]

He noted that the only secret service assistance which he received in dealing with Indian agitators abroad came from Hopkinson.

The Secretary of State for India, Lord Crewe, wrote in April 1914 to the Viceroy, Lord Hardinge, arguing that a better intelligence organisation was needed for the Pacific coast.[90] The Governor-General of Canada, the Duke of Connaught, wrote to the Colonial Secretary, Harcourt, in May that though Hopkinson was 'an energetic and excellent official':

> It is, however, highly undesirable that this work should be dependent on the existence of a single individual. In the first place, Mr Hopkinson has to cover the entire country from San Francisco to New York and from the Canadian to the Mexican frontier. In the second place, the entire system—if system it can be called—is dependent on one man. If anything happened to Mr Hopkinson, the work would automatically collapse.

Canada was not willing to pay for any improvements in the system. The Governor-General argued that Hopkinson ought to be transferred back to the Indian Police. He felt that Hopkinson's work was of Imperial rather than Canadian interest; yet despite the subsidies paid to him by India, the major part of his salary and his costly trips to the United States were met from Canadian funds. The Duke of Connaught believed there was a danger that this expenditure might become known to Members of the Canadian Parliament, and cause complaints which would severely compromise Hopkinson's work.[91]

Wallinger persuaded the India Office not to take the Governor General's advice:

> the permanent transfer of Mr Hopkinson to the Indian Government would entirely destroy Mr Hopkinson's usefulness. He is now, by very reason of his multifarious offices . . . in a position to do some delicate work for us without having suspicion drawn upon himself. Once he is removed from these offices he would be a marked man. Moreover, his permanent appointment to an Indian Service entails the entry of his name in some official list, together with the announcement that he is on deputation. Mr Hopkinson's appearance on any Indian record whatsoever would practically mark him down as being on secret duty under the Government of India in Canada.[92]

In August 1914 the Canadian Deputy Minister of the Interior, W. W. Cory, met Wallinger and Malcolm Seton, the Secretary of the Judicial and

Public Department, in London. He convinced the India Office that some expansion of the Pacific Coast intelligence system was necessary because of the strength of the Ghadr party. He did not feel that Hopkinson was suitable to be put in sole charge of an agency in America and Canada, though he recommended him as a 'very suitable worker under superior guidance'.[93] For five years Hopkinson had, of course, been such a one-man agency. However, he was a junior officer of only 35 years of age. Moreover, he probably lacked the sort of 'clubability' which seems to have been considered an essential part of the make-up of senior secret service officers.[94]

Wallinger was certainly mistaken when he said that Hopkinson's 'multifarious duties' kept him out of the lime-light. The conflict between his duties as intelligence agent and immigration officer was in the end fatal. On 23 May 1914 a Sikh entrepreneur from Singapore, Gurdit Singh, challenged the Canadian immigration laws, arriving at Vancouver with 376 Sikhs from Asian ports on board the *Komagatu Maru*. They were refused permission to land, and did not leave until 23 July. As interpreter at the Immigration Office Hopkinson naturally handled the negotiations with Gurdit Singh, for which he was greatly commended by the Home Department of the government of India. He gained intelligence of what was going on inside the ship from an Indian army doctor named Ragunath Singh.[95] Hopkinson acted as a very important restraining influence upon the more bellicose Canadians, prominent among whom was his superior within the Immigration Department, Malcolm Reid. Hopkinson stopped Reid's plan to get rid of the Indians on the *Komagata Maru* simply by starving them.[96] Finally the Canadians decided to seize possession of the ship before dawn on 19 July. Hopkinson tried courageously but unsuccessfully to parley with the Sikhs fifteen minutes before the assault. The attempt to board the ship failed ignominiously before a barrage of missiles from the Sikhs, but the whole affair inevitably brought Hopkinson into public prominence. A journalist claimed that the Sikhs were particularly aiming for him when they hurled missiles at the boarding party. Hopkinson, it was said, only avoided serious injury when someone pulled off his immigration officer's cap.[97]

The two-month wait of the *Komagata Maru* in Vancouver whipped the Vancouver Sikh community into a frenzy and gave a great fillip to the Ghadr party. The Vancouver Chief of Police believed that drastic action ought to be taken against the 'seditious party' lest they take revenge on officers of the Immigration Department.[98] The two conspicuous officers whom he had chiefly in mind were doubtless Hopkinson and Reid. In July 1914 Hopkinson learnt that some Indians had tried 'to buy a bomb' in Vancouver.[99] The Canadian Immigration authorities caught one Mewa Singh returning from the United States in possession of two revolvers. The first victims of Sikh vengeance were the Sikhs loyal to Hopkinson led by Bela Singh. One Harnam Singh of Patiala was found with his throat slit.[100] On 3 September another of the faction, Arjan Singh, was shot by Ram Singh, a member of the Sikh Temple Committee, which was the centre of 'sedition' among Vancouver Sikhs. The 'seditionists' trapped Bela Singh himself as he was praying for one of his dead friends inside the Vancouver Gurudwara. Bhag Singh, the priest, advanced towards him with an unsheathed holy sword, but Bela Singh drew a revolver, shot the priest and another Sikh dead, wounded seven others, and made his escape.[101]

The Vancouver press expected the trial of Bela Singh, 'the Hindu Adonis', to be a sensational one. But the cover story they got was other than they had expected. On 21 October 1914 Hopkinson was waiting outside the Court room at Victoria to testify in favour of Bela Singh when Mewa Singh shot him at point blank range in the chest. He fell to his knees, catching his assailant round the thighs. Mewa Singh then struck him on the head with a revolver, Hopkinson released his hold, and Mewa Singh shot him five times more with a second pistol. He died five minutes later.[102]

Events in the United States also reached a climax at about the same time. The Ghadr leadership put into effect plans to send bands of revolutionaries to cause mutiny and revolt in the Punjab. The consulate at San Francisco and the Canadian immigration authorities had no trouble in passing on notice of the large number of Indians leaving to the Indian authorities. The Director of Criminal Intelligence credited the success in detecting the Ghadr exodus to the small intelligence system built around Hopkinson.

> As the results of the existing agency in Canada and the United States of America, and of the co-operation of other representatives in Japan and Singapore, we knew a lot of Indians were returning to India with some firearms, We also knew that at one time a proportion of the returning had been seriously tainted with the 'Ghadr' propaganda. . . . practically we had all possible information about these people. The most extended intelligence agency abroad could not have told us more than we had been told, as no agency could have correctly foretold their state of mind on arrival in India.[103]

The Indian authorities were not sure what the effect of the death of Hopkinson would be. Wallinger wrote to Cleveland on 30 October 1914,

> The blow delivered by the terrorists may be said to be both morally and materially a very serious one. For the present we shall be left without any information from America whatever, which I think is a most deplorable thing.[104]

The Secretary of State for India wrote, 'I do not know of anyone who could fill the place of Hopkinson'.[105] But the British authorities soon concluded that they did not need anyone to replace Hopkinson in all his many functions. The whole situation in America changed upon the outbreak of the Great War. Within months of its beginning many of the most active leaders from North America were either in Germany—in particular Har Dayal and Taraknath Das—or else were involved in the plot in India, or were in British custody.

Cleveland wrote to the Home Department,

> At the present stage the practical question is not the intelligence abroad, but how to deal with seditious activities in India. If we can deal wih the 'Ghadr' people already in India and with those who come to India during the next few months we shall have won our big fight. Intelligence from abroad may be useful to us during the next few months but it will not by any means be the most important factor, We have enough to go on and enough to tackle for the decision of the fight. The doings of the returned and returning 'Ghadr' people in India itself are now our primary objects of watch and action.[106]

The Home Department concluded that it was now the whole Pacific and the Far East, rather than just the West Coast of North America which needed to be watched.[107]

India initially considered sending an Indian officer to replace Hopkinson in Canada. However, there was some objection to this.[108] Cory assured Wallinger that Malcolm Reid was in general familiar with Hopkinson's work and was assisted by Hopkinson's own assistant in the Immigration Department, Mr Gwyther, though they were not in a position to do all the work of Hopkinson.[109] Reid's understanding of the wider implications of Indian affairs in North America was incomplete. He believed, for example, that the Ghadr exodus had taken place because the Amir of Afghanistan was recruiting an army to invade India.[110] In March 1915 a officer named A. L. Jolliffe took Hopkinson's place as 'Dominion Immigration Officer'. His background is unknown. He received information from the consulates in the Pacific regarding the revolutionaries and made enquiries on their behalf. Hopkinson's faction of informers also lived on. After 1915 the Canadian Sikhs were effectively neutralised as a force of any concern to the Empire because of their own internal squabbles, and also because of their suspicion of the Ghadr leadership in San Francisco. There were 2,100 Hindus in British Columbia at this time, about 200 of whom were reputed to be 'seditious'. The Ministry of the Interior even at one point considered deporting Bela Singh.[111]

Unlike Hopkinson, Jolliffe did not operate within the United States.[112] The British Secret Service, on the other hand, was non-existent in the

United States at the outbreak of war. In August 1914 the naval attaché at Washington, Captain Guy Gaunt, recommended himself to the Admiralty as secret agent.[113] There is some parallel here with Hopkinson volunteering himself as agent on behalf of India five years before. Gaunt was reinforced only in 1916 with the arrival of Major Norman Thwaites, and an agent from MI1c (later to become the Secret Intelligence Service, SIS), Sir William Wiseman.[114] Thwaites later complained of the exiguousness of the Intelligence establishment in New York.[115]

The small scale of British Secret Service activity in America would not have allowed the continuous surveillance of Indians. However, now that the Ghadr party had shot its bolt by acting against the Punjab and so deprived itself of most of its leadership in America, intelligence on the activities of Indian agitators in America became of very much less importance than the need to watch German and Irish plotting. The Ghadr party was relatively so unimportant that at the end of 1915, when India was setting up an intelligence agency for the whole Pacific and Far East under David Petrie, an intelligence conference in London, at which Wallinger was present, decided that it was not worth placing an Indian agent at San Francisco for fear of prejudicing the operations of MI1c and Naval Intelligence.[116] It was easy for India to thwart Ghadr plots on the spot in India and the Far East. The effective operation of Petrie's intelligence system, which drew together the efforts of Indian Police officers, informers and consular officials, allowed India to do without its own agents in the United States.[117]

The familiar problem of avoiding the displeasure of American public opinion became more important than ever after the outbreak of war. The British Empire necessarily took a very different attitude to secret service work than did the Germans. While the British generally were anxious to keep a low profile, German agents behaved aggressively, at times arranging the sabotage of British shipping. Britain had convoys and colonies open to attack; the Germans had not. The roles of British Naval Intelligence and MI1c were defensive: to learn about German plans and to use this knowledge to destroy Germany's moral standing in the eyes of the American Administration. In the propaganda war Germany's trump card was the support of many Irish-Americans who represented Great Britain as an 'exploitive colonial power' in Ireland. The Ghadr party tried to do the same, though, unlike the Irish, they were not a force in American politics. Nevertheless, it was crucial during the years of the War, even after America's entry, that the Indian government should not have a visible secret service presence in the United States for fear of affording credibility to German-backed propaganda. There was no British or Indian secret service activity directed towards the prosecution of the Ghadr party in America until after the United States entered the War.

The absence of the Indian secret service from America by no means cut India off from direct sources of information there. Soon after the outbreak of war the British consulates throughout the United States were given orders to watch Indian affairs, as was Thwaites in New York.[118] The American Department of the Foreign Office under Sperling became the centre of an inter-departmental committee dealing with the Ghadr conspiracy throughout the Far East. However, this involvement depended heavily on the aptitude of the Consulates at key points performing effective intelligence work; this was something which they had not been trained to do before the War. Indian intelligence benefited during the War from the natural ability for intelligence work of Carnegie Ross at San Francisco. Ross proved a capable controller of informers, many of whom had been employed by Hopkinson. Nevertheless, throughout the War, the consulate at San Francisco was not provided with an expert on Indian affairs. Ross professed himself unable to gauge the true value of the intelligence produced by his informers.[119]

By far the most important of these men was the Parsi V. D. Bagai. He had been encouraged by the C.I.D. of the North–West Frontier Province to give information on 'sedition' before he left for America, and offered his services to Ross. He had intimate knowledge of the plans of the Ghadr party, being a friend of Ram Chandra, the secretary of the party and editor of the *Ghadr* newspaper,[120] who entrusted Bagai with details of his finances. Bagai's reports revealed clearly the weakness of the party. Both the Germans and many of the Sikhs distrusted Ram Chandra as an embezzler. By mid-1916 there was an open split when Bhagwan Singh made a bid to take over the Ghadr party.

In May 1916 a senior secret service agent with a brief to watch Indians in North America arrived in Vancouver.[121] He was Robert Nathan, an Indian Police Officer who had been seconded to MI5. He remained directly under the head of MI5, Vernon Kell, and was not controlled by the Indian DCI.[122] In America he was probably subordinate to the MI1c station chief, Sir William Wiseman. Nathan took over control of Ross's informers,[123] and thus had at his disposal the experience and contacts accumulated at the San Francisco consulate since Hopkinson's first visit there in 1911. Unlike Hopkinson, Nathan kept a very low profile in the United States even after America's entry into the War.[124] Only after this was it possible for the British to secure the support of the American Government for the prosecution of the Ghadr party. Nathan had the task of helping the Americans to draw up the case against the Ghadr party, which was hopelessly compromised. The British Authorities attached great importance to the prosecution of Ghadr, as is indicated by the standing of the MI5 officer, Alexander Marr, whom they despatched to assist Nathan in 1917. Before the War he had been secretary of the Political Department of the Government of Bengal.

The prosecution of the Indian conspirators resulted in the longest legal case in American history, the San Francisco Conspiracy Trial. All the leaders of the Ghadr party were sentenced to imprisonment on 30 April 1918. The light sentences imposed show how insignificant a matter Indian plotting against the British Empire was to the American authorities. The often reluctant co-operation of Canadian, British and Indian agencies in the surveillance of the Indian diaspora in North America over the previous decade marked none the less an important stage in the development of intelligence collaboration within the British Empire.

Notes

1. For Fenian activities in America in the nineteenth century see J. A. Cole, *Prince of Spies: Henri Le Caron* (London, 1984), and K. R. M. Short, *The Dynamite War* (Dublin, 1979).
2. C. M. Andrew, *Secret Service. The Making of the British Intelligence Community* (London, 1985), Chapter 2.
3. Judicial and Public department (J&P) 826/04 in India Office Library and Records, L/PJ/6/670: The Establishment of a Central Criminal Investigation Department in India. Statement of Proposition for Revision of Establishment.
4. In 1906 the DCI was reinforced by the addition of a 'Sub-Executive Establishment' of 4 Inspectors for investigations within India, and by the appointment of an Assistant Director. J&P. 2222/06 in L/PJ/6/770: Criminal Intelligence Department: Proposed Additions to Staff. In 1908 James Campbell Ker was appointed personal Assistant to the Director. J&P. 826/08 in L/PJ/6/854.
5. H.D.(B): November 1913, nos. 62–3. Note by R. Hughes-Buller, Director of Criminal Intelligence, 13 September 1913.
6. *Note on the Proposed establishment of a Criminal Investigation Department* by Sir Andrew Fraser, 25 April 1903. In J&P. 826/04 with L/PJ/6/670.
7. See Demi-official from Sir J. H. LaTouche to Sir Andrew Fraser, 7 March 1903, in L/PJ/6/670. op. cit., *Hansard*, 1909, vol. II. 'Director of Criminal Intelligence'.
8. Note by C. J. Stevenson-Moore, dated 21 September 1909 in Home Department, (Political) Proceedings: A Series [H.D.(A)]: January 1911, nos. 52–64. Deputation of Mr Wallinger to England. For Indian Intelligence operations in Great Britain and on the Continent see my forthcoming article in *Intelligence and National Security*.
9. The DCI furnished the Home Department and the local Governments with intelligence summaries on Indian unrest at home and abroad every week in the shape of the *Weekly Reports of the Director of Criminal Intelligence*.
10. In his preface to J. C. Ker's *Political trouble in India, 1907–1917*, Sir Charles Cleveland wrote that "Previous to 1907 criminality in Indian politics was not a general feature though there were some manifestations and some underground preparations for it." Ker believed

SURVEILLANCE OF INDIAN SEDITIONISTS IN NORTH AMERICA

that with their 'customary veneration for anniversaries the Hindu revolutionary leaders. . . . naturally attached special importance to the fiftieth anniversary' of the Mutiny, 'which marks roughly the beginning of the modern phase of revolutionary activity in India.'

11. Home Department, (Political) Proceedings: Deposit [H.D(D)]: August 1911, no. 17. Employment of agents in America. Note signed 'B.E.S.', 28 June 1911.
12. J. C. Ker, op. cit., pp. 215–19.
13. For the importance of George Freeman in Irish-Indian affairs see Weekly Reports of the Director, Criminal Intelligence (Weekly Reports), Report for the Week Ending 9 March 1915 in Home Department, (Political) Proceedings: B Series [H.D(B)]: April 1915, nos. 412–15.
14. H.D.(D): August 1911, no. 17. Employment of Agents in America.
15. Ibid. Note by A. B. Barnard, Deputy-Director of Criminal Intelligence, 28 November 1911.
16. F0115 1908 (113). P&S. (Political and Secret Department) 3000/08 in L/PS/3/438.
17. Weekly Report for 17 April 1909, in H.D.(B): June 1909, nos. 108–14. The association was by this date called the *Indo-American Club*.
18. Employment of Agents in America, op. cit.,
19. Weekly Report for 5 September 1908, nos. 1–8.
20. Political and Secret Department, nos. 3000, 3101, 3133 and 3150 in L/PS/3/438.
21. F0115 1908, op. cit.,
22. Weekly Report for 23 April 1910, in H.D.(B), June 1910, nos. 17–25
23. Employment of agents in America, op. cit., Quoted by H. H. Risley in letter to DCI of March 1911.
24. See, for example, Morley Papers, MSS.EUR.D.573/4. Letter to Minto, 4 June 1908.
25. Stuart, unlike Lee-Warner, refused to act behind Morley's back.
26. H.D.(D): June 1909, No. 30: Papers connected with the employment of Pinkerton's detective agency.
27. Weekly Report for 12 September 1911, in H.D.(B), October 1911, nos. 46–9.
28. For example, in 1911 the Foreign Office made enquiries through Pinkerton's when the Home Office informed them that an anarchist in Bessemer, Michegan, intended to sail to England and assassinate George V. F0371 1270, file 787.
29. Note by E. N. de Rhe, in *Employment of Agents in America*, op. cit.,
30. Note by C. R. Cleveland, 8 July 1911, in *Employments of Agents in America*, op. cit.,
31. Employment of Agents in America, op. cit., Letter from H. H. Risley to DCI dated March 1911.
32. H.D.(B): February 1913, nos. 53–5. Home Office Secret Agent.
    H.D.(D): December 1913, No. 8. Home Office Secret Agent.
33. For example the DCI made sure that the Government of India and the local Governments learned the full details of a scandal concerning the old suspect, Swami Abhedananda; 'Swami Abhedananda has at last been exposed in New York by a Mrs Beauley of Manhatten, and a considerable number of his feminine admirers have left the Vedanta Society in consequence. Mrs Beuley's grievance is that the Swami has been captivated by 'a certain young woman'—a 'Chinese blonde'—too fat for her height, ignorant, and not even prepossessing in appearance,' and she regrets, in a strange language used by the followers of the cult, that "the discordant woman got a hold on the Swami's psychic soul".' Weekly Report for 27 June 1911, in H.D.(B): July 1911, nos. 1–4.
34. For example, in the Weekly Report for 27 June 1911, op. cit., the DCI claimed that by telling tales of British oppression in India 'it is said to be very easy to reap a rich harvest . . . from credulous Americans of the class that provides recruits for the Vedanta Society.'

35. In the DCI's compilation of History Sheets, *Indian Agitators Abroad. Containing short accounts of the more important Indian Political Agitators who have visited Europe and America in recent years, and their sympathisers* (Simla, 1911), V/27/262/1, few offenders are accused of purely political offences.

36. For a general discussion of Indian immigration into British Columbia see T. G. Fraser, 'Canada and the Sikh problem', 1907 to 1922, *Journal of Contemporary History* (1977).

37. C042 914, Grey to Elgin.

38. Ibid. McInnes's existence was so secret that the Governor-General did not know of it until the trouble with the American Exclusion Leagues.

39. C042 919.

40. H.D.(D): November 1908, No. 6. Note by the DCI on the anti-British movement among natives of India in America.

41. J&P. 1309/09 (4452/08) with L/PJ/6/930. For other references to Canadian Military Intelligence see C042 929 (2904,3723,10826)

42. H.D.(A): February 1911, nos. 98–101: Information regarding Tarak Nath Das who is receiving military training at the Norwich University, Vermont.

43. Extract from the *Daily Province* contained in H.D.(A): January 1915, nos. 3–6.

44. Note by Cleveland, 7 December 1914, in H.D.(A): January 1915, nos. 3–6.

45. C042 920. Memorandum by Mackenzie King (Undated). J&P.320/09 with L/PJ/6/930. Report on sedition and immigration in Canada by Col. Swayne.

46. J&P.320/09 with L/PJ/6/930. Colonial Office to Governor General, September 1908. Ibid, Report by Col. Swayne. Ibid. Governor General to Colonial Office, 11 December 1908.
J&P. 1309/09 (4591/08) Governor General to Colonial Office.

47. J&P.320/09 with L/PJ/6/930 Governor General to Sir Wilfred Laurier, 3 December 1908.

48. C042 920 (29488) Mackenzie King to the Canadian Minister of Labour, Radolphe Lemieux.

49. J&P. 320/09 with 1309/09. Memorandum of matters affecting the East Indian community in British Columbia by Colonel E. J. E. Swayne.

50. J&P 568/11 in L/PJ/6/1064, Hopkinson to Cory, 11 January 1911.

51. H.D.(A): January 1915, nos. 3–6.

52. Quoted by Mackenzie King in C042 920.

53. Wallinger to Cleveland, 28 August 1914, in H.D.(A): December 1914, nos. 96–8.

54. Sir Cecil Spring-Rice to Sir Edward Grey, in H.D.(A): December 1914, nos. 96–8.

55. Memorandum by Harkin in J&P.1309/09 (1882) with L/PJ/6/930.

56. Minute Paper drawn up by Ritchie in J&P.1309/09 (1882).

57. H.D.(A): December 1914, nos. 96–8. Question of putting *Ghadr* on the list of publications prohibited from transmission by post to India.

58. H.D.(B): June 1913, nos. 5–17. Note by W. S. Marris.

59. Undated Memorandum of Mackenzie King in C042 920.

60. J&P.568/11 (56) with L/PJ/6/1064. Hopkinson was not a master of disguise. When the Sikh temple at Victoria was dedicated he told Cory he doubted whether any whites would be allowed to attend the ceremony, but that since he had sent his Indian agents to attend he would know what happened all the same. J&P.568/11 (4161).

61. J&P.568/11 (2818)

62. J&P.568/11 (1133)
J&P.275/12 in L/PJ/6/1137 (1794, 2012, 2551).

63. J&P.275/12 (3001/11) with L/PJ/6/1137.

64. J&P.275/12 (3001/11)
J&P.275/12 (4803/11)

65. J&P.275/12 (1257)
66. J&P.275/12 (4355/11)
67. J&P.275/12 (4530/11)
68. J&P.275/12 (4803)
69. C042 978 (7054)
70. See E. C. Brown, *Har Dayal: Hindu Revolutionary and Rationalist* (University of Arizona Press, 1975)
71. F0115 1731
72. H.D.(B): June 1913, nos. 5–17. Letter from Hopkinson to Cory, 31 January 1913.
73. Ibid. Letter from Hopkinson to Cory, 17 February 1913.
74. C042 980 (29650)
75. C042 970 (25503)
76. H.D.(B), June 1913, nos. 5–17. Letter from Hopkinson to Cory, 17 February 1913.
77. J&P. 871/14 in L/PJ/6/1302.
    CO42 978 (8778).
78. CO42 970 (25503).
79. H.D.(B): November 1913, nos. 62–3.
80. H.D.(A): December 1914, nos. 96–8.
81. Note by C. J. Stevenson-Moore, dated 21 September 1909 in Home Department (Political) Proceedings: A Series [H.D.(A): January 1911, nos. 52–64. Deputation of Mr Wallinger to England.
82. From 1912 until the eve of the Great War the Indian authorities did not take seriously the threat from the Indian revolutionaries in Paris whom it was Wallinger's basic original task to watch. The continuation of his mission was due to the Home Department's desire to err on the side of caution, and to Wallinger's own ability. See H.D.(A): November 1911, no. 87.
83. CO42 981 (41409).
84. H.D.(A): June 1915, nos. 3–6. Wallinger to Cleveland, 30 October 1914.
85. H.D.(B): June 1913, nos. 5–17. Wallinger's letter of 4 April 1913.
86. CO42 979 (19818).
87. H.D.(A): December 1914, nos. 96–8.
88. CO42 979 (19818).
89. CO42 980 (259559).
90. Hardinge Papers, vol. 97, no. 249a from Secretary of State.
91. H.D.(A): December 1915, nos. 96–8. Governor General to Harcourt, 20 May 1914.
92. Ibid. Undated memorandum by J. A. Wallinger.
93. Ibid. Wallinger to Cleveland, 28 August 1914.
94. See in various places, C. M. Andrew, op. cit.
95. CO42 980.
96. CO42 980 (29650).
97. CO42 980 (29647).
98. Weekly Report for 27 October 1914, in H.D.(B): Demceber 1914, nos. 218–22.
99. CO42 980 (29650).
100. For the events leading up to the Sikh Temple shooting case see Weekly Report for 27 October, op. cit.
101. J&P. 5372/14 (5166) with L/PJ/6/1341. See also Weekly Report for 27 October, op. cit. The Director of Criminal Intelligence, like some members of the India Office, wondered whether Bela Singh needed to shoot nine men with two revolvers in pure self-defence. However, on the basis of this story Bela Singh was acquitted of the charge of murder by a Canadian Court.

102. J&P. 5372/14 (4987).
103. H.D.(A): December 1914, nos. 96–8.
104. H.D.(A): January 1915, nos. 3–6.
105. Hardinge papers, vol. 97, no. 249a from Secretary of State.
106. H.D.(A): December 1914, nos. 96–8.
107. Ibid. Note by C. R. Cleveland, 8 December 1914.
108. Ibid. Note by R H. Craddock, 10 December 1914.
109. Ibid. In the past Reid and Gwyther had effected the surveillance of Indians during Hopkinson's trips to the USA.
110. Ibid. Note by H. Wheeler, 7 December 1914.
     J&P, 5372/14 (4987).
111. See generally the reports of Consul-General Ross in FO371 and FO115. A concise account of the Ghadr Party's troubles is contained in J. C. Ker, op. cit., pp. 252–61.
112. There are very few documents relating to him. However, Ross always wrote to him at Vancouver, while Ross complained before 1916 of having *no one* to help him assess the value of his Indian intelligence.
113. Guy Gaunt, *The Yield of Years*, p. 135.
114. See Andrew, op. cit., pp. 208–9, and W. B. Fowler, *British-American Relations, 1917–1918. The Role of Sir William Wiseman* (Princeton, 1969).
115. Norman Thwaites, *Velvet and Vinegar*, p. 150.
116. H.D.(A): June 1916, nos. 285–95. Deputation of Mr D. Petrie as Intelligence officer for the Far East in connection with Indian sedition.
117. So effective were Petrie's operations, assisted by the difficulty of terrain in Siam, which restricted all movement to India to a very few roads, that Basil Thomson, the head of the Special Branch of the Metropolitan Police, recorded in his diary for May 1916: 'the precautions were so elaborate that no Indian could hope to go through India by way of the Pacific. They must all go through Europe and consequently to my room in Scotland Yard.'
118. FO115 1780. Thwaites, op. cit., p. 145. He was first ordered to watch Indians in 1916.
119. FO115 2067 (no. 123). Letter from Ross to Viceroy, 12 May 1916.
120. Ibid. FO115 2067 (No. 23). Letter from Ross to Viceroy, 24 January 1916.
121. FO115 2067 (no. 128). Letter from Ross to Viceroy, 16 May 1916.
122. That he was not in Naval Intelligence or MI1c, the two existing British Intelligence organisations in America was not important. There was much overlapping of the different British intelligence organisations in the United States during World War One.
123. FO115 2067 (no. 140). Letter from Ross to Spring Rice, 15 June 1916.
124. Weekly Reports of DCI Report for Week Ending 27 July 1918. H.D.(B): July 1918, nos. 413–16.

Intelligence and its Interpretation: Mesopotamia 1914–1916

PETER MORRIS

The outbreak of war with Turkey in November 1914 confronted the Entente Powers with major new problems. For none was this more true than for Great Britain. It greatly widened the geographic scope of the British war effort, complicated the strategic patten and served to enhance nationalist feeling throughout a wide area of the Near and Middle East. For the Government of India the consequences were particularly serious. The expeditionary force sent to Mesopotamia, known as Force D, was to grow into a major military undertaking, straining the human and material resources of India as it strove to meet its steadily growing requirements as well as to support a large military commitment on the Western Front and in Egypt and East Africa. The humiliating surrender at Kut in April 1916 had significant repercussions on the self-confidence of the Government of India and badly damaged that of its armed forces; the parliamentary Commission of Inquiry set up in August 1916 censured many leading officials from the Viceroy downward. Whilst defective intelligence gathering and assessment was not solely to blame, there can be little doubt that it had a part to play in both the outbreak of war with the Ottomann Empire and in the military debacle at Kut.

Long before 1914 the Ottomann Empire of which Arabia and Mesopotamia were part had attracted the attention of intelligence gatherers both official and unofficial. The principal group active in the Gulf area and in Mesopotamia were the personnel of the Government of India's Political Service, a carefully chosen group of officers largely drawn from the Indian Army and trained for use as advisers to native rulers within India and as the equivalent of a diplomatic service in representing that Government to foreign rulers within its area of interest. By the beginning of the twentieth century the major centre of activity in the Gulf was the Persian port of Bushire, where the official combining the offices of British resident, consul general for the Gulf and Southern Persia and agent of the Viceroy had his headquarters. Responsible to him were subordinate officers functioning as consuls and vice consuls in Arabia and southern Persia and native agents and newswriters who provided a steady flow of information which was passed on to the Foreign Department of the Government of India at Simla. Despite their military background the intelligence accumulated and forwarded was lagely political and economic. It was to this service that officers such as W. H. I. Shakespear, C. C. R. Murphy, A. T. Wilson, N. N. E. Bray and G. E. Leachman belonged. By 1914 they had developed a collective view of the peoples of the area. They were pro-Arab, patronising or contemptuous of Persians, and anti-Turkish. They believed the end of the Ottomann Empire was in sight and welcomed its demise. They were eager advocates of close contacts with local arab chieftains and keen supporters of those wishing to throw off Ottomann suzerainty. In their enthusiasm they often stretched their instructions to the limits: or flagrantly disregarded them.[1] Added to this was the further conviction that British paramountcy in the Gulf was under increasing threat from Germany. The appearance of a regular German steamship service by the Hamburg-Amerika line, the dispute over the oxide deposits on Abu Musa island, the activities of the Wonckhaus trading house and the appointment of a German consul to Bushire were all interpreted as indications of the inroads being made by German political and economic influence. Taken together, these attitudes were probably closer to those of British official opinion in London than they were to opinion in Simla.

Whilst the development of the British intelligence services before 1914 has been analysed in the first chapters of Christopher Andrew's *Secret Service*,[2] no such account exists for India. There, military intelligence was the affair of the Military Department of the Government of India just as political intelligence fell to the Foreign Department. The impetus to develop a military intelligence organisation in the Office of the commander-in-chief came from fears of Russian expansion and of what was seen as a growing threat to the northern frontiers of India. From the start therefore the thrust of the intelligence gathering and collating effort was directed toward central Asia and Persia and the traditions and assumptions of the Indian service were Russian-oriented. The first appointments for intelligence work were authorised in October, 1874 when it was agreed that each summer two officers would be temporarily deputed to gather and collate information. This was a watered down version of the suggestion that a full intelligence branch be established in India paralleling that already set up in the War Office in London. Deferred on grounds of cost, the proposal re-surfaced in 1877 and was finally authorised in January 1879, and the Intelligence Branch of the Quartermaster-General's Department began to function under Lieutenant-Colonel G. E. L. Sanford in March 1880. From the outset attempts to link together the work of the Indian and London Branches ran into difficulties. The attempt to attract personnel from London met with the refusal of the preferred officers and the Indian authorities had eventually to settle for Captain M. S. Bell who was far from being their first choice. Six surveyors of the Royal Engineers recruited for the topographical work of the new Department proved entirely unsuitable and had to be shipped home to Britain in 1881.[3] The staff of five officers, only three of whom were permanent, together with thirteen draftsmen and an office staff of fifteen struggled to amass and render usable information derived largely from others. Paying the travelling expenses of its own officers on intelligence gathering journeys, it relied mainly on information derived from army officers travelling whilst on leave, to whose expenses it contributed should they provide useful reports, on that sent in unsolicited by officers with a self-proclaimed bent for the work, such as Lieutenant A. T. Wilson,[4] on sponsored translations of works from foreign languages and on maps, books and periodicals which it purchased.[5] The system was not however satisfactory, and the Government of India took the opportunity of the appointment of Lieutenant-General Henry Brackenbury as military member of the Viceroy's Council to review its operation. Brackenbury was a former head of the Intelligence Department of the War Office and a committee under his chairmanship in April 1892 urged a reorganisation along the lines of the Intelligence Branch in London. It came into force in August 1892. Under it the staff was increased by one third and the expenses by two thirds, and the enlarged Department was divided into four sections each responsible for a specified geographical area. The Western Section, known as W, corresponding roughly to sections D and E of the London Department, covered Russia in Asia, Persia, Turkey in Asia, the province of Baghdad and secured information about the wider Russian Empire from the War Office.[6] Though amalgamated with the Mobilisation Branch in 1903 when its staff was further increased,[7] this basic structure was retained until 1914.

The working of the Branch continued to give cause for concern. Lord Kitchener, whilst commander-in-chief, concluded that the collection of peacetime intelligence was very defective and complained that no measures existed to amplify it in wartime. He was concerned that information was derived from only two main sources: officers of the Intelligence Branch on infrequent tours to collect military intelligence, and from the Foreign Department which relayed that provided by the Political Service. The former depended wholly on funds being available whilst the latter was largely political. Those who provided information to the officers of the Political Service were civilians without military training and concerned with economic and political matters. Kitchener, planning for war with Russia, decided it was essential for the Intelligence Branch to recruit its own agents who could be trained and sent into central Asia in disguise to collect the necessary information. Called by him an Intelligence Corps, it was linked directly to the Intelligence Branch by a specially appointed staff captain who was responsible for a body of thirty carefully selected and trained sepoys. The system was in operation by 1906 though it was oriented to central Asia, Afghanistan and northern and eastern Persia and not to the Gulf.[8] In a parallel effort to increase efficiency and avoid reduplication of effort, the spheres of responsibility of London and Simla intelligence organisations were demarcated in January 1905. Simla was thenceforth responsible for Aden and the Protectorate, Arabia east of a line from the Straits of Bab al-Mandab to Basrah, and for Persia and the Gulf, as well as other areas. London assumed responsibility for the rest of Arabia and the Ottomann Empire, and the Russian Empire. Central Asia was to be shared.[9] This demarcation was to be important for the Mesopotamian campaign, for divided intelligence responsibilities led to the relative neglect of the area through which the line of demarcation ran. Not only was Simla preoccupied with the Russian threat: the thrust of intelligence-gathering operations based on London was not directed to Mesopotamia. As the exhaustive account in Winstone's *Illicit Adventure* shows, very few of the official and unofficial intelligencers active in the Ottomann Empire were involved in Mesopotamia. They concentrated on Palestine and the Lebanon and made their headquarters at Damascus and Cairo. Travelling in and collecting information about Mesopotamia was the monopoly of Shakespear, who was primarily interested in the arab tribes of the peninsula; of Leachman, who was at least as interested in these same tribes as he was in Mesopotamia; and of Gertrude Bell. Even allowing for their formidable talents it was a thin coverage.

Further developments before 1914 illustrated the slowly growing professionalism. The first was in the area of cipher-breaking. Here too the Government of India was preoccupied with Russia. When in May 1904 permission was first sought to intercept coded telegrams using the Indian telegraph system and to use the accumulated information thus acquired to break the codes, the object was telegrams passing to and from Russian representatives. Despite the moral scruples of the Viceroy, Lord Ampthill,

Lord Kitchener and the War Office were enthusiastic supporters of the proposal which was agreed on the grounds that there were strong reasons for thinking Russian representatives to be in touch with anti-British native elements whom they supported with money and advice. The potential of the operation quickly became apparent. Thanks to the role played by India in the world-wide telegraph system, much ciphered traffic from various foreign Powers flowed over its lines offering the possibility of gathering and utilising a considerable body of information. By 1907 permission had been given for the systematic collection of all coded telegrams using the Indian telegraph lines, the decision being justified by the argument that 'we are in this respect only following the practice of all the Great Powers, who . . . make a practice of tapping all telegraph lines passing through their territory'. The information thus accumulated had however to be used. The first telegraphic interceptions had been sent from India to the War Office, which had been unable to crack the codes. Consequently on 1 July 1906 the Government of India had set up its own, highly secret, code breaking operation. Major G. R. M. Church, a statistician of the Telegraph Department and a key censor based at Aden during the Boer War, and Captain G. S. Palmer, a first rate Russian linguist, were set the task of establishing a data base on the Russian language and of statistically analysing the codes. By September 1907 they had broken the cipher used by General Linievich, the Russian commander-in-chief in Manchuria, and that used in Iran by the Russian consul-general at Mashhad and had turned their attention to other Russian ciphers. Officially sanctioned for a further year, their work was extended for five years in 1908 before being made permanent in 1913. To what extent they had succeeded in breaking other Russian codes remains at present unclear. It seems probable however that their major efforts had been directed at those used locally, of direct interest to the Government of India rather than at those with wider, international application. In any case the operation remained small, and by 1914 the great increase in wireless traffic was spawning so many ciphers that it was estimated in time of war at least thirty officers would be needed to censor telegrams and wireless traffic. It was envisaged that the new section would form the nucleus of a cipher school.[10]

The second new development was wireless. The Government of India had shown early interest in experiments and trials with portable wireless equipment carried out by the Royal Engineers in Britain at the turn of the century, but it was not until late 1907 that it seriously began to consider establishing wireless stations. Between then and 1914 major interest focussed on the nautical aspects, with the pace being set by the naval authorities anxious to improve communications with vessels at sea. It was the Royal Navy too which was interested in wireless installations in the Gulf as an aid to intercepting gun-runners. It was thus not surprsing that in August 1914 those stations already established were at Calcutta, Karachi and Bombay, with a further one under construction at Madras. Each had a normal range of six hundred miles over land.[11] As for the Gulf, despite considerable enquiry and the devising of several proposals, there were as yet no permanent installations. The one at Jask, with a range also of six hundred miles, had begun operation at the end of 1909 as an adjunct of the telegraph office, but as it was intended to move it higher up the Gulf to a location still to be decided, it lacked permanent accommodation of its own. There had been frequent talk of additional temporary stations with a range of between 200 and 300 miles each at Bahrain, Dubai, Kuwait, Bandar Abbas, Lingah and Bushire in an effort to speed intelligence of gun-runners,[12] but the only other station operating in 1914 apart from Jask was at Bushire where naval personnel had set up a small wireless station at the telegraph office to ease communication with the resident.[13]

By 1914, therefore, the Government of India disposed of the nucleus of an effective intelligence system. It was, however, largely concerned with Russia, seen as the principal source of danger, and not with the Ottomann Empire. The gathering and assessment of intelligence from the latter was divided between London and Simla and the line of demarcation ran, crucially, through Mesopotamia. There were major doubts, expressed as late as 1904, whether the machinery existed for the rapid augmentation of intelligence gathering during wartime and the very small number of experts at work in the Intelligence Branch, in the wireless service and in cryptographic work suggested it would be difficult rapidly to expand. Underlying everything was the question of interpretation of intelligence, and there were many in London and at Simla on the eve of war in 1914 who had already made up their minds.

When British officials looked back after the war there was considerable agreement amongst them that the involvement of Turkey was inevitable, the outcome of consistent German intrigue since at least 1875. Active Turkish belligerence had been posponed so as to permit the fullest possible military preparation and especially the flow of German personnel and material to bolster the weak Turkish armed forces. In the meantime the Ottomann Empire had undertaken a series of unfriendly acts which proved her commitment to the Central Powers. Two examples of such writings illustrate the point. N. N. E. Bray commented in a 1936 biography of his fellow political officer Lieutenant-Colonel Leachman:

It was plain to many that the next European war, which was obviously impending, and had only been averted in 1911 by the narrowest of margins, would certainly vitally affect our interests in Arabia or Persia, if not in both these regions. Turkey was the friend of Germany and German ambitions envisaged the extension of her influence to the Persian Gulf. The deductions were obvious. . . .[14]

The official history of *The War in the Air* commented:

Before Turkey entered the war in October 1914 she gave evidence of hostility to Great Britain, and among other acts she strengthened her forces in Lower Mesopotamia.[15]

By the end of October 1914, before war began, the Foreign Office was busily preparing its draft bluebook on the outbreak of hostilities with the Ottomann Empire. Turkish enormities were listed: the permission afforded the *Goeben* and *Breslau* to pass into the Straits and the subsequent fate of the two vessels and their German crews; the anti-Entente attitudes of local Turkish officials; mobilisation and troop movements of a threatening nature against both Egypt and Russia's Caucasian frontier; commandeering of the property and goods of Entente subjects; the detention of British merchant vessels in the Dardanelles; the removal of Admiral Limpus and other members of the British naval mission from executive control of the Turkish navy; the flow of German men and war equipment; unilateral Turkish renunciation of the capitulations and commercial treaties and attempts to raise import duties; the closure of foreign post offices in the Empire; protests that British ships were using the Shatt al-Arab route to and from Moham- merah. A formidable list, each and every item had been carefully noted and added to the recital of grievances. British official opinion had long made up its mind. As G. R. Clerk had pointed out at the end of August:

Turkey's 'neutrality' is demonstrably non-existent and it is a question whether the only way to save the situation might not be to rush through the Dardanelles, desperate though such a situation may seem.[16]

This assessment, however, was not the result of calm and dispassionate examination, and noticeably absent was any attempt at a parallel statement of Turkish grievances or an examination of the interaction of the two sets of complaints, whilst the air of apparent cool appraisal and analysis hid a very different reality.

From the outbreak of war official opinion was convinced it was only a matter of time before Turkey would join the Central Powers. If the then military secretary in the India Office was to be believed,

> Both Lord Crewe and I from the very outbreak of the war were fully convinced that Turkey sooner or later would be involved, in which case the great danger of a Pan-Islamic combination against us in India would become both imminent and vital.[17]

Others shared this view. As August passed every piece of information from the Ottomann Empire was scrutinised and utilised to confirm and harden the opinion already formed. Official minutes reveal the process. Sir Eyre Crowe wrote on 16 August:

> The Turks are, and have been, playing with us. I do not believe that any declaration on our part [guaranteeing Turkey's territorial integrity] will have any effect.

A week later his attitude had stiffened further:

> our representations on the subject of British grievances are treated by the Turkish Govt. with undisguised contempt. . . . I do not think we should go on making complaints so long as we are not ready to insist on their being attended to.[18]

And by the end of the month he was writing:

> I have no confidence in the prospect of Turkey remaining neutral, and therefore think we should do wrong to avoid strictly precautionary measures.[19]

Such 'precautionary' measures could however seem very menacing indeed, as would soon become clear. Turkish unfriendliness and suspicions of British intentions had some basis in reality. On 1 August, even before the British declaration of war against Germany, the *Rashidiah* and the *Sultan Osman 1*, two warships being built in Britain for the Ottomann navy, were seized by the Admiralty on the eve of their being delivered. Something of the spirit behind this move may be gauged from Churchill's minute of 8 August. Condemning Turkish claims for compensation for breach of contract as well as the return of the purchase monies, which had been paid in full, he wrote

> The Turks should have back whatever they have paid—no more. And there is no hurry about this. They may join the Germans, in which case we shall save our money. Negotiate and temporise.[20]

Not for the last time was the Admiralty to urge steps with a pronouncedly anti-Turkish bias. It was to authorise hostilities against Turkey on 31 October, five days before war was declared.

This anti-Turkish bias was not confined to London but was shared by officials serving in the Ottomann Empire and Gulf and gave a marked slant to their resumés on the local situation. The consular reports of the animosity of local Turkish officials toward the Entente which began to flow in August 1914 reflect many of the assumptions colouring the interpretation of local developments. Two examples drawn from the Gulf area may serve to illustrate this. The Resident at Bushire reported on 16 August that British employees of APOC at Abadan were nervous 'in view of the expected rupture with Turkey' and urged that an additional warship be dispatched to reassure them. Two days later he was telegraphing

> Bullard, consul at Basrah, writes to me privately August 15th:- 'Emissaries may go from here trying to stir up troubles in India.' Turks, in fact all Moslems, very anti-English.[21]

Greater attention was given to such impressionistic reporting, which agreed with perceived opinion in London, than it was to less highly-coloured appreciations. When the military attaché at Constantinople reported on 23 August that Turkish troop movements were relatively unimportant and that there were no signs of movements via Aleppo and Damascus in the direction of Egypt nor of unusual activity in the Caucasus in the vicinity of the frontier with Russia, his report was filed without comment.

Closer examination of the position in Mesopotamia sheds some light on the deficiencies of the often alarmist reports coming from there in August 1914. As has already been noted, after the war troop movements there were one example of alleged anti-British activity. Reports of such movements began to flow from the latter part of August. On the 27th the consul-general at Baghdad reported troop movements to Basrah; on the 28th he detailed efforts to charter vessels belonging to the Lynch Company to move soldiers. Early in September guns and German personnel were said to be arriving, and claims made that a German ship, the *Ekbatana*, was in position to block the river. October brought reports of the intended movement of soldiers and gendarmes to al-Hasa, of further troop reinforcements at Fao on the mouth of the Shatt, of the impending arrival of naval mines, and on 19 October a claim that a Turkish crew under German officers with a quantity of ammunition was on its way to Basrah where it would take over the German commerce raider, the *Emden*.[22] Once more it seems a formidable list. However it requires some modification.

Once the war was over it became possible to compare this picture with the realities of Turkish military preparation. Based on documents in the fomer Ottomann Ministry of War, C. C. R. Murphy's *Soldiers of the Prophet*, published in 1921, revealed that the forces in the area consisted of local Arabs whose numbers had been hastily augmented by impressing untrained men and who were regarded by their superiors as of little or no military value. In addition there was a single battalion of regular Turkish infantry. No attempts were made to move reinforcements to Mesopotamia until after the British occupation of Basrah in November 1914.[23]

Further doubts must exist as to the realities of the danger of panislamic propaganda in British India. The spectre of panislamic agitation first raised in the 1890s was the subject of a considerable literature after 1900, and for British Indian officials this was the principal source of alarm in the summer of 1914 as their sensitivity on the issue surfaced repeatedly. For Barrow the danger was sufficient to lead him on 10 August to oppose the transfer of British officers from the Indian to the British Army,[24] and was echoed in the response of Sir Arthur Hirtzel, political secretary in the India Office, to the first suggestions of support for Arab aspirations for independence:

> That is a card which it *might* be useful to play, though I am not sure that in the long run the Arabs will not be more dangerous propagandists of Panislam than the Turks.[25]

By the end of August 1914 the assumption that war was inevitable led logically to acceptance of the need to plan a suitable British response. Once more the Admiralty took the lead though interestingly there is no mention of this Admiralty initiative in Sir J. S. Corbett's official *History of the Great War—Naval Operations*.[26] It suggested on 25 August that forces be prepared for an attack on Mesopotamia, important for its location, fertility and proximity to the APOC oilfields of vital interest to the Admiralty. It would also be an encouragement for friendly Arabs whose anti-Turkish feelings should be sustained. Over the next week the case was pressed both officially and unofficially, especially by Admiral Slade in meetings with Barrow between 28 August and 1 September. On the next day Barrow commented in his *Diary*:

> The Turkish menace increasing, I put in a strong minute for the immediate occupation by 'B' Force of Abadan and Muhammerah to protect the oil fields but Lord C[rewe] obdurate.

Though coolly received in India as well as in the India Office the idea did not go away. Tension grew as reports of Turkish preparations and of the flow of German military aid via Bulgaria and Romania continued. Though once more these were unsubstantiated despite attempts to verify them at Bucharest and Sofia, they were given credence. Nicolson wrote, 'If Turkey does go with our enemies I do not think that I could delay encouraging the Arabs to rise.': a view informing the official Foreign Office note of the following day:

> Sir E. Grey is further of opinion that directly Turkey joins Germany, HMG should at once give every support and encouragement to the Arabs to possess themselves of Arabia and the holy places . . . and he would suggest that all preparation for giving effect to this policy at short notice should be put in hand forthwith.[27]

Finally on 24 September Barrow managed to secure Crewe's agreement to start considering the steps urged initially by the Admiralty and now widely accepted

> Sept. 24—The Turkish problem grows more menacing as they are now trying to win over the Arabs to a Jehad against us. Crewe discussed situation and suggested I should talk it over with Shakespear—the Arab explorer.

The only evidence for the first claim was rather nebulous reports from agents in Baghdad and Basrah, summarised by the Resident at Bushire, that letters had been sent to Ibn Saud and other Arab leaders in July 1914 and that the Vali of Baghdad had been told to prepare to fight alongside Germany. It was also rumoured Ibn Saud had been asked to provide men for the Turkish forces. The mention of Shakespear was also significant. Well-known, and distrusted for his single-minded advocacy of the cause of Ibn Saud, his involvement could only lead to more pressure for a British commitment to the Arabs. He met Barrow on 25 September, and the latter wrote in his Diary that he was 'so impressed that I went over to see Hankey at the Defence Committee Office and unrolled to him a plan to despatch a Brigade . . . secretly to the Shatt el Arab. This would commit us to supporting the Arabs and be the desired signal'. He then drew up his memorandum of 26 September, erroneously seen later as the origin of the Mesopotamian Expeditionary Force. Submitted to and approved by the Cabinet on 28 September, Barrow noted impatiently '"Asquith like" it was decided to "wait and see" what the Turks would do for two days!' Others shared his concern: 'Sept. 29 . . . Saw Crowe at F.O. He is still convinced Turkey means war and begged me to press S of S regarding Shatt el Arab.'[28]

Thus at the end of September, a month before war broke out, two immensely important decisions had been made: to assist the internal disruption of Turkey by encouraging the rebellion of disaffected Arab chiefs, and secretly to prepare and dispatch a military force to the Gulf. During the ensuing month they were put into operation. Determined efforts were made to contact what was termed the Arab movement. Shakespear was sent out early in October to visit Ibn Saud; communications were opened with Sayyid Tallib through the consul at Muhammerah (despite the Sayyid's dubious reputation); the Sheykh of Muhammerah was reassured and his neighbour at Koweit asked to use his influence with Ibn Saud. Meanwhile at Cairo representatives of the Pan Arab movement were contacted. As for the military preparations at Bombay, they too formed an integral part of the plan. According to Crowe's minute of 26 September, Shakespear had urged troops be sent to the Gulf to ensure Arab support for Britain. Barrow and Slade told Crowe then that protection of the oil pipeline was only the ostensible reason for the dispatch of the expeditionary force.[29]

If the force was to reach Abadan and Muhammerah it would be necessary to pass through Turkish territorial waters. Unwilling to make the first move, the British objective was to manoeuvre the Turks into actions which would put them in the wrong with muslim opinion in India and elsewhere, the consistent refrain in virtually all documents dating from September and October 1914. Force 'D' was therefore halted at Bahrain, where it arrived on 23 October. As if to emphasise that was not its final destination, it was ordered to remain on board ship. Although the need for secrecy was continually emphasised its eventual destination seems to have been quite widely known as many of those involved in its preparation later recalled. The nature of the craft employed and of the stores and equipment embarked made it obvious.[30]

For the Turks, therefore, it must have seemed as if the British were the ones preparing for war and merely awaiting the right moment to strike. Increasing British contact with dissident Arab tribal and urban leaders in Arabia and Mesopotamia, the obvious military preparations, the dispatch of British Indian agents to Basrah and Baghdad, the unhelpful attitude of British commercial companies such as Lynch Brothers' Tigris and Euphrates Steam Navigation Company and the comings and goings of British officers whose anti-Turkish attitudes were well-known must have suggested impending hostilities. Moreover, British protests against the *Goeben* and *Breslau* must have rung hollow when British warships were violating Turkish neutrality in the Shatt and Turkish complaints at the presence of HM ships *Odin*, *Lawrence* and *Espiegle* were brushed aside, despite private British recognition of the justice of the Turkish case.[31] It is against this background that Turkish military preparations in Mesopotamia ought to be seen. Turkish demands that British warships should not use their wireless transmitters whilst in the Shatt and that the equipment be sealed, reports in October of Turkish preparations to block the Shatt by sinking the *Ekbatana* and laying naval mines, the movement of gendarmes to el Hasa to assert Turkish authority, the placing of guns opposite the mouth of the Karun river to oppose British warships and increasing surveillance over British subjects were all developments of the later part of September and October. It was as likely that they were precautionary measures against a perceived British threat, no doubt exaggerated and emphasised by the Germans, as they were measures for offensive military action. Their effect was to confirm British prejudices and assumptions which predated them. Perhaps most telling of all was the relative strength of the forces at the head of the Gulf when war broke out. In November 1914 though numerically roughly equal, the British was much the superior fighting force which three weeks after landing at Fao had occupied Basrah and comprehensively defeated the Turkish relieving forces.

The assumptions governing the interpretation of information from Turkey in the summer and early autumn 1914 seem to have had their origin in the deep-seated conviction that the various pressures and threats had a common and malevolent origin, Imperial Germany. It was the German hand which guided Britain's main enemies, whether Ottomann Turkey in 1914 or Bolshevik Russia in 1918 and 1919 or Amanullah's Afghanistan or Iranian Nationalists in 1919 and 1920. Whilst understandable, the inability to differentiate old Power rivalry from new nationalist movements was to prove a serious handicap to policy-making. The Turkish case was particularly interesting, for it showed all the hallmarks of what was to come later. The touchy pride of nationalists often led to bewildering demands, apparently trivial but nonetheless significant. The Ottomann Empire had, during its years of weakness, been compelled to submit to humiliatingly unequal treaties which governed the terms of its foreign trade, protected foreign subjects in its law courts, promoted a rival post system, permitted European Powers to interfere in the relations between the Porte and its subjects, and provided economic concessions to foreigners especially in the provision of transport facilities. It was not surprising that the Turkish nationalists or Young Turks who controlled the government of the Empire should take advantage of the War to reassert themselves. They did so in an inchoate and stumbling manner without providing a clear and reasoned explanation of their activities. Those activities however were potentially as much a threat to Germany as to the Entente Powers and if it was the former which was able to take advantage of them in the immediate context of 1914, that owed something to a misinterpretation of intelligence which arose from deeply ingrained attitudes such as those of Clerk:

> I think war with Turkey is undesirable because it means an additional complication, when the hands of the Allies are full enough elsewhere, and because of the Moslem question, but should such a war come, it can only have one result, and HMG and Europe generally will be freed from many burdens.[32]

For him and others such as Wilson and Gertrude Bell the incompetence of Turkish administration and brutality of her periodic assertions of authority alike led to the conviction that the elimination of Turkey from Mesopotamia would be a humanitarian blessing.[33]

Britain declared war on Turkey on 5 November 1914 and on the following day the first party of troops from the expeditionary force landed at Fao. On 22 November the advance guard entered Basrah, formally occupied the next day. Whatever its rationale, in purely military terms the force had been a great success and its victories were widely acclaimed in a Britain starved of military achievement. They also immediately posed problems of objectives. What had been seen as a cardinal objective—the encouragement and sustenance of Arab rebellion—faded from sight as military considerations and questions of political prestige became paramount. Between November 1914 and November 1915 there is little in the military or political records of Ibn Saud or Arab rebellion. If mentioned at all, Arabs are more likely to appear as unreliable and treacherous elements in the military equation, subservient to whomsoever was victorious and a scourge to the defeated.

In these new circumstances Baghdad became an object of military and political ambition, for reasons which a glance at the map of Mesopotamia reveals. A major regional and commercial as well as administrative centre, its fabled past ensured that the public as well as soldiers and politicians had heard of it, which was more than could be said of any other place in Mesopotamia.

Despite later suggestions that Baghdad emerged as a campaign objective only after the occupation of Kut in June 1915,[34] the first mention of Baghdad as an objective came on the morrow of the occupation of Basrah. Sir Percy Cox, former resident in the Gulf, recently foreign secretary to the Government of India and now chief political officer and effectively political adviser to the commander of the expeditionary force raised the matter in telegrams on 23 and 25 November. On the 23rd he asked the Viceroy for a statement of British intention. Noting that the Turks had been heavily defeated, he reported Arab opinion to be favourable and that all reports suggested Baghdad Arabs would welcome British forces. A quick move on Baghdad would, he thought, be easy and anyway it would be hard to avoid taking Baghdad now the campaign was launched. It was the obvious objective. He repeated these views direct to London on 25 November. Oliphant, Clerk, Nicolson and Grey unanimously agreed Baghdad was a valuable prize: for Nicolson 'a great coup', for Clerk a worthy objective and he 'should welcome a decision to go for Baghdad'.[35] Soldiers were much more restrained than civilians. Barrow urged caution. Whilst an advance to Qorna, north of Basra, was militarily desirable, any further move to Baghdad would be hopelessly ambitious. Kitchener, anxious as ever about France, agreed: more troops were needed for an advance on Baghdad and there were none available.[36] The commander of the expeditionary force, General Barrett, was so instructed on 27 November. But once raised, the issue did not go away. At its crux lay the appreciation of the local military position. If that were thought favourable, pressures would build for a forward movement against Baghdad. In the meantime the original major objectives of the expedition remained those Barrow identified: the security of the oilfields and the encouragement of Arab reliance on Britain. A steady step-by-step approach would advance these and have the additional advantage of avoiding specifying future objectives. Yet the attraction of Baghdad was unavoidable. Its capture would be welcome and should circumstances appear propitious there could be little doubt that local commanders would seize them. Indeed they were positively encouraged to think of it. Barrett's successor, Nixon, on appointment was ordered 'after acquainting yourself on the spot with the present situation you will . . . submit a plan for a subsequent advance on Baghdad'.[37] The dilemma was summed up neatly in Grey's minute of 29 November which identified the issue dominant over the next year:

> It should all depend upon whether, if we take Baghdad, we can hold it: and that depends on whether the Turks could bring any considerable force against it to retake it.[38]

A decision depended on the quality and interpretation of information about Turkish troop movements. Once more the question arises whether hopes and aspirations did influence interpretation.

Information relating to Turkish military activities came from a variety of sources, broadly definable as international and local. Human sources remained paramount and there is nothing in the records in London to show the successful interception and use of enemy wireless transmissions. In part this may reflect the expeditionary force's lack of equipment and personnel, discussed below, which shewed lack of appreciation of the potential value of this source of intelligence. It probably also reflects the lack of the necessary raw material. There seems little reason to doubt that Ottomann military traffic used landlines nor that the technological weaknesses of the Empire precluded extensive provision of wireless equipment. In their absence information came from the military attachés in Sofia and Bucharest and from the Legation in Bern. News from the Greek Government was generally discounted as unreliable. More important was Petrograd, relaying information provided by the Russian Government and especially military headquarters in the Caucasus where Colonel Marsh was. Formerly British military attaché at Mashhad where he had been in charge of intelligence gathering in Russian central Asia and Afghanistan, he now acted as liaison officer and was the conduit for the sharing of intelligence. The Caucasus provided some of the earliest and most useful information, though the poor range of wireless transmitters and the mountainous terrain required that news from the Caucasus be transmitted via Petrograd or Bucharest and London. Useful information also came from consuls and from the staff of the Imperial Bank in neutral Iran until Turkish armies and German-inspired native tribesmen occupied Kermanshah, Hamadan and other towns in western and southern Iran. Tehran remained the centre of rumour and gossip it always had been.

Other useful but inevitably adventitious sources of intelligence were recent arrivals from Turkish territory. The value of their contributions depended on their powers of observation, access to sources of information whilst in Turkey and general intellectual power and educational level. Thus information from Christian refugees who fled the Ottomann Empire seems generally to have been of little value whilst the observations of some British residents eventually allowed to leave was of real use, such as that provided in early March 1915 by Sloane of APOC and by Tod of Lynch Brothers.[39] A few participated actively. The APOC engineer Baillie commanded an armed launch during the initial landing at Fao whilst Cowley, one of Lynch Brothers' captains, assumed command of one of the Expedition's naval vessels. In addition, it was later claimed agents were sent on the eve of war, perhaps drawn from Kitchener's Intelligence Corps. Murphy speaks of sending a pathan former cavalryman fluent in farsi to Basrah in September 1914, whilst Winstone claims Major Blacker, later famous for his escapades in Bolshevik central Asia, was also deputed to Basrah for undercover operations.[40] Interestingly, no-one seems to have been sent to Baghdad. These sources supplemented the information already available in Simla, where the General Staff's *Field Notes on Lower Mesopotamia* were collated and published for the use of the expeditionary force in October 1914. Despite the strictures of at least some recipients such as Wilson who commented:

Though ample sources of information were open to them, the Intelligence Departments of the British and Indian Armies had virtually no hand-books of value and had neglected to make use of those that already existed.[41]

The surviving copy in the India Office records suggests that the force commanders and officers were in possession of reasonably accurate information at the outset of the campaign. Once it landed there were local contacts to be cultivated, sometimes offering information voluntarily and the more suspect for that, or recruited and organised by officers such as Leachman or Saunders.[42]

The outbreak of hostilities led to the hurried provision of additional wireless installations, with facilities at Abadan and Bahrain. It was not until autumn 1915 however that the expeditionary force acquired its own facility, though once installed it was rapidly upgraded until by Easter 1916 there was at Basrah 'a permanent and powerful station from which news could be received from Malta or even from the Eiffel Tower'.[43] At the time when the decision to advance to Baghdad was being made, however, there was no direct wireless link and communications with India and London depended on the telegraph system and were slow and liable to disruption. As for aerial reconnaissance that too was in its infancy and Mesopotamia had a very low priority. The first machines did not arrive until May 1915 when a scratch formation was created from territorial units in India and Australian pilots and mechanics. Its aircraft were superannuated machines from training units. During 1915 it gradually grew into a heterogeneous collection of aircraft, usually of obsolete design and dubious reliability or hastily adapted on proving unsuitable for their original function. Even so, air observation immediately proved an enormous advantage, first shown in the advance north from Qorna in June 1915, and the force commanders came to rely upon it. Reliance however had its own dangers. It was the judgement of the pilot as to the significance of events on the ground which determined whether or not they were recorded and reported. Much therefore depended on the experience and skill of the man in the air, yet slow aircraft of limited manoeuvrability were vulnerable to ground fire and the rotary engines and wood and fabric airframes were badly affected by dust, sand and the extremes of heat and humidity. Enemy action and natural conditions combined to shorten the active careers of pilots. Given that other areas had priority their replacement was irregular and seasoned pilots were not sent to Mesopotamia. There were major dangers in depending too heavily on aerial reconnaissance for accurate intelligence. At the vital moment it might well fail as the official history subsequently showed.[44]

It took time for the gathering and interpretation of intelligence on the spot in Mesopotamia to be systematised and refined. It is indeed questionable whether adequate attention was paid at the outset to the military as opposed to the political side of intelligence work or whether adequate personnel were available. Certainly the force as originally constituted under Barrett and subsequently reorganised under Nixon had no designated intelligence officer or cipher officer on its staff. Only in March 1916, with the further expansion under the newly installed Lieutenant-General Sir Percy Lake, was a staff captain for intelligence work added in the form of Captain R. C. Thompson, late of the Inns of Court O.T.C., and an establishment of four cipher officers created. Of the latter only three were actually appointed, two reserve second lieutenants and an army schoolmaster. The weakness of intelligence work was illustrated by the secret *Who's Who in Mesopotamia* compiled in 1916 from the expeditionary force's intelligence files. The overwhelming majority of the entries were recorded after the summer of 1915 and most dated from the winter of 1915–16.[45]

In the circumstances it is not surprising that late in 1914 the force commanders were in a state of uncertainty. They assumed after the occupation of Basrah that Turkish forces would soon be reinforced in an attempt to recapture it. Lacking sources of information of their own and mindful that the area whence such forces would come fell into the sphere of responsibility of the War Office, the General Staff at Simla urgently asked London for information as to Turkish strength in the area. This led to the dispatch on 13 December of the first in a series of appreciations of Turkish strength, drawn from a wide range of international sources. A constant feature was warnings of Turkish reinforcements: on 29 December 10,000 troops en route from Constantinople and the whole 12th corps from Aleppo; in January 1915 the 12th army based on Mosul was moving south; early February brought claims that 35,000 men with artillery were moving to Baghdad; escaped British civilians reported on 10 February that between six and ten thousand soldiers had come to Baghdad. By the end of that month there was a direct conflict of opinion. Kitchener officially warned the Indian commander-in-chief in Simla that the Turkish forces would soon number two or three divisions whilst Cox from Mesopotamia claimed reliable news from Baghdad showed that no reinforcements had yet arrived though some might be on the way. At the end of February Beauchamp-Duff in India was pleading that the conflicting intelligence reaching India from London, Egypt and Mesopotamia made it difficult to appreciate Turkish strength. Fearing a sudden attack by superior forces massed in Mesopotamia he asked for help in formulating strategy. In reply he was told that the strength of Turkish forces had in fact changed little. Overall the picture emerging from the exchanges is one of confusion and constant major changes in assessments of Turkish strength. Some indication of the disparity is provided by the contrast between the War Office estimate of 65,000 made on 15 March and the Simla estimate of 18 March of 20–21,000. In fact the latter was reasonably accurate. When Turkish forces attacked at Shaiba on 12 April they had 10,000 regular Turkish infantry and 1,000 cavalry plus 2,000 Kurds and 10,000 Arab irregulars.[46]

In the light of this it is perhaps not entirely surprising that Nixon seems to have been less anxious to secure information from London than his predecessor had been. There is no evidence on file of appreciations of Turkish strength between April and July 1915. By then the advent of aerial reconnaissance gave local commanders wider opportunities to assess enemy strength. Certainly there was a new self-confidence in the response of Nixon to warnings from London of impending Turkish reinforcements, renewed in August 1915. When Marsh's information that 25,000 troops had gathered in Mosul en route to lower Mesopotamia was relayed to Basrah it was flatly discounted in September.[47] In the renewed advance north to Kut al-Amara following the repulse of the Turkish attack at Shaiba the local intelligence operation seems to have worked well. Nixon reported that extensive use had been made of aircraft which had made possible the tactic employed in the battle and the effective pursuit of the beaten enemy:

> The accurate information obtained during air reconnaisance was of the utmost value in planning the defeat of the enemy and the remarkable skill and powers of observation displayed by Flight-Commander Major H. L. Reilly, R.F.C., contributed in no small degree to the success of the operations.[48]

This successful forward movement up the Tigris and the parallel move up the Euphrates to secure its western flank had taken the expeditionary force from Qorna on 31 May as far as Aziziyah, reached on 3 October, a distance of over 250 miles along a tortuous river. In the planning and execution Nixon had had access to no external information of value and it would not be surprising if he had come to the conclusion that the intelligence available to him locally was sufficient and reliable. With his advance force only about 60 miles south of Baghdad it was time to decide whether or not to move on to that romantic objective.

Barrow at once realised the implications. He minuted on 4 October 'The victory at Kut-al-Amara is of so complete a nature that the idea of pushing

on to Baghdad will certainly be revived', noted the 'glamour' of Baghdad
and the powerful lobby favouring continued advance before concluding

> the ease with which the operation can be carried out will be impressed upon us
> with such cogency and insistence that the proposal will be difficult to resist.

Nonetheless resist it he did. The expeditionary force was already dangerously
extended, local Arab sentiment was uncertain, Turkish reinforcement
probable and defeat or forced retirement would have disastrous effects on
British prestige.[49] Similar caution came from the War Office, whose General
Staff appreciation of 12 October concluded that any advance on Baghdad
would require at least two more divisions and that no move should be made
until they were en route to Mesopotamia. Any move against Baghdad would
be hazardous, and the Staff feared lest Turkish reinforcements exceed what
was anticipated.[50]

Barrow and the War Office were right. Telegrams from Nixon and from
the Viceroy in Simla urged the desirability of moving on Baghdad. Nixon
wired on 30 October that he considered his force 'strong enough to open the
road to Baghdad' whilst the Viceroy urged on 6 October that reinforcements
be sent Nixon from Europe as

> the capture of Baghdad would have such an effect in the Near East and offers such
> important political and strategical advantages as to justify movement . . .

Nixon's own appreciation of the position was provided in additional
telegrams on 8 and 10 October. He estimated Turkish forces at 8,500
infantry, 600 cavalry and 28 guns and was confident he could occupy
Baghdad after a battle at Ctesiphon with the Turkish forces now rallying
there. He would however need another division to hold it once captured,
echoing Grey's preoccupation of the previous November. On 4 October the
Prime Minister referred the whole question to a special sub-committee of the
Committee of Imperial Defence which reported on 16 October. It concluded
that an advance on Baghdad was desirable, that Baghdad was an important
Turkish *place d'armes* and that a prestige-building success was needed at that
stage of the war and that Baghdad was the only possible point at which a
'decisive blow' might be struck. It was prepared to defer to Nixon, as the
man on the spot, and to accept his view that his force was strong enough to
take the city. However it emphasised that occupation must be permanent
and that Nixon would need reinforcements to hold it. No move foward ought
therefore to be made unless reinforcements were forthcoming. On this basis
the Secretary of State telegraphed Nixon that two divisions would be sent as

soon as possible from France and authorised him to proceed to Baghdad provided he thought his existing force adequate.[51]

The decision to advance was therefore dependent on the available intelligence and Nixon's interpretation of it. The ensuing forward movement led to the battle at Ctesiphon on 22-23 November followed by retreat to Kut, where Townshend's force was beseiged until its surrender on 29 April 1916. There was no reason to suppose that Nixon's preparations were in any way different from before. It is clear however that he knew of the strong desire in London and Simla for the occupation of Baghdad, knew that it had been in the minds of his superiors at the time of his appointment and knew that the British authorities were so convinced of the desirability of it as to divert divisions from the Western Front. It would moreover be surprising if at the personal level he did not appreciate the advantages which would accrue to the conqueror of Baghdad.

During October 1915 Nixon reported that some 7,500 Turkish troops were between Aziziyah and Baghdad, only 3,000 of them in front line positions, and that the garrison in Baghdad was negligible. Information from Egypt showed no signs of significant troop movements in the direction of Mesopotamia. It must therefore have been irritating for him to receive in November intelligence of substantial Turkish reinforcements en route to the area. The key information was enclosed in War Office telegrams on 16 and 17 November. The former told Nixon 'Reliable and authentic information has been received that a Turkish expedition is on its way to Baghdad', whilst the latter provided details. The German von der Goltz had left to take command at Baghdad and a force 30,000 strong under Khalil Bey was marching from Erzurum to Iraq. A further telegram of 22 November, the day the battle at Ctesiphon began, assured Nixon of its reliability:

> The sources of our information are Secret Service in the Near East. We had made various enquiries and received corroborative evidence before sending you the information.

Anyway additional confirmation had come from Marsh in the Caucasus, who telegraphed Simla on 17 November that Khalil Bey's force had left for Baghdad from Bitlis, south of Lake Van, about 16 October. This was the first time that intelligence about Turkish troop movements had been sent to Mesopotamia in such clearcut and authoritative form.[52]

Yet Nixon decided not to heed it. No doubt part of the reason was the unhappy experiences at the beginning of the year which cannot have encouraged trust in intelligence sent from London. That no doubt explains his query about the reliability of the sources to which the telegram of

22 November was a response. Moreover he had also been told on 21 October that the War Office thought that there were 9,000 Turkish regulars between his force and Baghdad and that these could not be reinforced for about two months, though possibly as many as 60,000 (that number again) might be sent in the new year. In the light of that it might have seemed to Nixon that the rapid oscillation of estimates of Turkish forces had started again. Yet after allowing for this it remained true that the news did not come as a complete shock to him. He replied on 20 November:

> I have received similar news about a large force under Von der Goltz from my own agents here for over a fortnight, but for various reasons I do not accept their report as conclusive at present.

It is hard not to conclude that Nixon was extremely reluctant to give up the advance on Baghdad and that it would take incontrovertible proof to make him do so. One source of information locally available and which he and his commanders trusted was aerial reconnaissance.

To identify Turkish reinforcements moving southward from Baghdad long-range reconnaissance would be necessary, but owing to accidents whilst making sorties and to shortages of machines and personnel Nixon ordered them to be discontinued on 13 November. Local aerial reconnaissances were made on Townshend's orders on the eve of the battle of Ctesiphon. During them Major Reilly, the most experienced of the four pilots involved, was forced down and the significance of Turkish movements was lost on the others who failed to observe the arrival of substantial enemy reinforcements. The outcome was that when Townshend advanced he expected to find approximately half the 20,000 men and 38 guns actually in position. Neither was he aware of the impending arrival of additional forces under Khalil Bey which came up on 23 November.

In a little more than fifteen months the picture at the head of the Gulf had changed dramatically. A military expedition had been conceived and launched from India, adding to obligations in East Africa, Egypt and France and straining the Government of India's available resources. It had begun the process which led to the destruction of the Ottomann Empire and to British involvement in the tar-baby of Mesopotamia. Though only involving a relatively small number of men, the capitulation at Kut was arguably the worst humiliation suffered by British arms during the War. Contemporaries certainly took that view as the Mesopotamian Enquiry showed and the scramble by officials to divest themselves of responsibility for suggesting and conducting the campaign confirmed. After seventy years the record is still unedifying reading.

There was certainly nothing inevitable about it. Grey wrote later that he did not think the treaty with Germany, kept secret even from a majority of the Turkish Cabinet, made much difference. What made her a belligerent was the success of the pro-German group in the ruling Committee of Union and Progress in convincing their fellows that Germany was likely to be victorious and that by joining the Central Powers Turkey would be more likely to re-establish her independence and further the process of national regeneration. The war gave an opportunity to annul the unequal treaties forced on Turkey. Guarantees of the Empire's territorial integrity were not enough and Grey missed the point when he subsequently wrote

> everything conceivable was done to make it easy and even profitable for Turkey to remain neutral. A promise, in which France and Russia joined, was made to her to see that in any terms of peace at the end of the war her independence and integrity should be preserved.[53]

If that was the best the Entente was prepared to offer it was not surprising that Turkey should go it alone, renouncing capitulations and cramping commercial treaties. The allied reaction to that and British preparations in the Gulf area and intrigues with Arab chiefs can only have served to help those urging Turkish belligerency alongside the Central Powers. The key month therefore was August 1914 when British analyses of information coming from Turkey were crucially influenced by pre-formed attitudes. In its turn much of the intelligence came from men on the spot whose assumptions shaped their reporting in much the same way as happened earlier in the century.[54] It was not a conspiracy but it does suggest that the concept of policy formation based on the cool analysis of political intelligence requires some modification. Information-gathering and policy-formation alike reflect a priori assumptions and aspirations and inter-react in a symbiotic relationship.

As for military intelligence the experiences of the Mesopotamian campaign also suggest caution in assessing its importance. Commanders have always sought information about the activities of their opponents to enable them to plan but during the First World War the possible sources of information increased dramatically. The machinery for collating, analysing and applying it does not seem to have expanded commensurately. It was all very well to leave decisions to the general on the spot, as was done in 1915, but it was essential that he be provided with an organisation adequate for the task and guidance as to the reliability of information coming from outside his immediate jurisdiction. This was not available in 1915. There is nothing in the surviving documents to suggest that local commanders were provided with guidance about the reliability of the sources on which intelligence appreciations were based: hence Nixon's query as to the origins of information of Turkish reinforcements sent him in late November 1915. In the absence of this local commanders could only assess the value of current intelligence by reviewing that of information previously supplied. Perhaps it is inevitable that the need for secrecy and security precludes local commanders from receiving full details of sources yet its absence may lead them to discount its value. There were also difficulties with the utilisation of the most modern technological aids. These provided a new dimension of intelligence gathering yet they were also addictive. Technological weaknesses or the inexperience of human operators might seriously impair their operational value without that being apparent whilst their collapse at a crucial moment could seriously endanger forces whose commanders had become dependent on a technological quick fix. Finally, like civilians, soldiers had assumptions and objectives they were reluctant to abandon. Not surprisingly inconvenient intelligence might be discounted 'for various reasons' left unstated. The consequence could be disaster.

Notes

1. H. V. F. Winstone, *Captain Shakespear, a portrait* (London, 1976); *Leachman: O.C. Desert* (London, 1982); and especially his *Illicit Adventure, The Story of Political and Military Intelligence in the Middle East from 1898 to 1926* (London, 1982).
2. C. Andrew, *Secret Service: The Making of the British Intelligence Community* (London, 1985).
3. India Office Library and Records L/MIL/7/7793. For permission to use this and other Crown copyright material in the India Office Library and in the Public Record Office I am indebted to the Controller, H.M. Stationery Office. Subsequent references will be given as IOLR and the appropriate file number.
4. Sir A. T. Wilson, *S.W. Persia, a Political Officer's Notebook* (Cambridge, 1941).
5. IOLR L/MIL/7/7799.
6. IOLR L/MIL/7/7800.
7. IOLR L/MIL/7/7810.
8. IOLR L/MIL/7/7811.
9. IOLR L/MIL/7/7812.
10. IOLR L/MIL/7/7813.
11. IOLR L/MIL/7/10223.
12. IOLR L/P&S/10/118.
13. IOLR L/P&S/10/298.
14. N. N. E. Bray, *A Paladin of Arabia* (London, 1936), p. 225.
15. Committee of Imperial Defence, Historical Section, *History of the Great War based on Official Documents: The War in the Air*, by W. Raleigh and H. A. Jones, 8 vols (Oxford, 1922–37), vol. V, p. 251.
16. Foreign Office Records, Public Record Office, FO 371/2139. Subsequent references will be given as PRO and the appropriate file number.

17. Private Apologia of Sir E. Barrow, IOLR Eur. Mss. E. 420/17.
18. PRO FO 371/2138.
19. PRO FO 371/2136.
20. PRO FO 371/2137.
21. PRO FO 371/2136.
22. IOLR L/MIL/5/748 and 768.
23. C. C. R. Murphy, *Soldiers of the Prophet* (London, 1921). The same picture emerges from the résumé of a Turkish general staff analysis in Committee of Imperial Defence, Historical Section, *History of the Great War Based on Official Documents: The Campaign in Mesopotamia, 1914–1918*, by Brig. Gen. F. J. Moberly, 4 vols (London, 1923–7), I, appendix VI.
24. Sir E. Barrow, Great War Diary August-September 1914, IOLR Eur. Mss. E. 420/36.
25. Sir A. Hirtzel to G. R. Clerk, 31 August 1914, PRO FO 371/2139.
26. Sir J. S. Corbett and H. Newbolt, *Naval operations. History of the Great War Based on Official Documents*, 5 vols (London, 1920–31), I, pp. 375–6
27. Both Nicolson's minute, dated 31 August 1914, and the Foreign Office note are in PRO FO 317/2139.
28. Winstone, *Captain Shakespear*. Barrow, Great War Diary, IOLR Eur. Mss. E. 420/36.
29. PRO FO 371/2139, FO 371/2140
30. A. T. Wilson, *Loyalties-Mesopotamia 1914–1917* (Oxford, 1930), p. 8.
31. PRO FO 317/2142
32. Minute by G. R. Clerk, 12 October 1914, PRO FO 371/2142
33. For detailed accounts of the Mesopotamian campaign see: Moberly, op. cit., Wilson, *Loyalties*, A. J. Barker, *The Neglected War: Mesopotamia 1914–1918* (London, 1967).
34. Corbett, *Naval Operations*, 1, p. 181.
35. PRO FO 371/1243 and 1244.
36. PRO FO 371/2144.
37. IOLR L/MIL/5/750.
38. PRO FO 371/1243.
39. PRO FO 371/2141 and IOLR L/MIL/5/750.
40. Murphy, *Soldiers*, p. 48; Winstone, *Illicit Adventure*, p. 208.
41. Wilson, *Loyalties*, p. 40.
42. The *Field Notes* are in IOLR L/MIL/17/15/48. Leachman's methods are described in Gray, *Paladin*, pp. 265 ff., and in Winstone, *Leachman*, p. 150. For Saunders, see L. D. Dunsterville, *The Adventures of Dunsterforce* (London, 1932).
43. Black Tab [pseud], *On the Road to Kut* (London, 1917), p. 245.
44. Jones, *War in the Air*, V, pp. 250 ff.
45. IOLR L/MIL/17/15/79 i–iii and L/MIL/17/15/51.
46. IOLR L/MIL/5/749 and 750.
47. Ibid.
48. IOLR L/MIL/17/15/101. This is confirmed by Maj. Gen. Sir C. V. F. Townshend, *My Campaign in Mesopotamia* (London, 1920), pp. 108 ff.
49. IOLR L/MIL/5/752.
50. IOLR L/MIL/5/753.
51. Ibid.
52. Ibid.
53. Sir E. Grey, *Twenty Five Years, 1892–1916*. 2 vols (London, 1925), II, p. 166.
54. M. E. Yapp, *Strategies of British India, Britain, Iran and Afghanistan 1798–1850* (Oxford, 1980).

Lord Curzon and Secret Intelligence*

KEITH JEFFERY AND ALAN SHARP

The modern British intelligence community effectively came into being during the First World War and the years immediately following it. The functional distinction in foreign political intelligence-gathering between human intelligence and signals intelligence was institutionalised with the emergence of the Secret Intelligence Service (SIS) and the Government Code and Cypher School (GC&CS), the forerunner of today's Government Communications Head-Quarters. Lord Curzon's time at the Foreign Office—October 1919 to January 1924—is therefore an apposite period for an examination of secret intelligence and its influence on the conduct and formulation of British foreign policy. It is additionally suitable for study since a considerable volume of evidence about intelligence activity has survived in accessible archives, in marked contrast to later peace-time years.

The single most important development in Britain's intelligence organisation at this time—as Curzon particularly recognised—was the emergence of a specialised signals intelligence agency, GC&CS, which provided a novel and valuable source of information for the Foreign Office. From the point of view of the historian attempting to trace the impact of intelligence on policy-making, moreover, the product of signals intelligence is comparatively easy to follow through the bureaucratic machine. Intercepts constitute a more specifically tangible form of intelligence than the frequently generalised

* We would particularly like to thank the following people for assistance and encouragement in the preparation of this essay: Christopher Andrew, David Dilks, Tom Fraser, Richard Bingle, David Wenden and John Ferris. Quotations from the Rumbold Papers are made by permission of Sir H. J. S. Rumbold, and from the Wilson Papers by permission of the Trustees of the Imperial War Museum. Crown Copyright material is reproduced by permission of the Controller of Her Majesty's Stationery Office.

kinds of political information collected and collated by the Secret Intelligence Service. This essay concentrates primarily on an aspect of Britain's foreign relations in which sigint played an important role: policy towards the Near East, culminating with the Lausanne Conference of 1922–23.

For most of the century before the First World War British intelligence-gathering with regard to foreign countries had generally been the preserve of the armed forces. Following the war, however, during the period that Lord Curzon was Foreign Secretary, the administration of British secret intelligence was largely concentrated under the Foreign Office.[1] SIS, for example, which had originated as the Foreign Section of the Secret Service Bureau in 1909 and had at times variously been the responsibility of both the War Office and the Admiralty, came under Foreign Office control towards the end of the war. In 1919 the Cabinet appointed a Secret Service Committee, chaired by Curzon, to review post-war arrangements and on its recommendation in 1921 the Foreign Office was confirmed as the controlling department.

The intended function of SIS, nevertheless, was to provide information for any relevant government department—civil or military—as required. The Service did not apparently take much initiative in ordering the priorities of its information-gathering efforts and it engaged in very little analysis or interpretation of intelligence. Material was sent to the departments which had requested it or which SIS considered would be most interested. In all cases, however, confirming that department's centrality in the intelligence scheme, it seems to have circulated a copy of each report to the Foreign Office.[2] While the Foreign Office itself did not exercise a very close supervision over SIS,[3] it was certainly the most dominant of the government departments with which the intelligence community had to deal.

The signals intelligence organisation had a similar brief to supply information to a range of departments, GC&CS was created in 1919 by the amalgamation of Room 40 and MI1 (b), the sigint and cryptanalytical branches of the Admiralty and War Office respectively. The interception and decoding of enemy wireless and cable messages, especially by Room 40, had proved to be a most valuable new source of information during the war.[4] After hostilities had ceased Curzon argued that the Foreign Office was 'the proper place for the new school to be housed'.[5] Sir Hugh Sinclair, the Director of Naval Intelligence, disagreed. The school, he maintained, should be located in the Admiralty since the fighting services possessed the required expertise and 'all the arrangements as regards decyphering messages' were 'already in existence in the Admiralty building'. Sinclair's case was not merely based on convenience.

Without wishing to disparage the Foreign Office in the least [he continued], it is considered that the atmosphere of calm deliberation which characterizes that Department is not suited to an organisation such as the proposed Code and Cypher School, which, above all things, must be a 'live' undertaking, especially in connection with the 'breaking' of codes and cyphers, where it is a question of working against time in order that the de-cyphers, may be of value.[6]

On 29 April 1919 a conference, comprising the Foreign Secretary, the Secretary for War, the First Lord of the Admiralty and senior intelligence officers, met at the Foreign Office to settle the question. Curzon, although in the chair, failed to persuade the conference that the school should be housed in his department. Sinclair and the First Lord, Walter Long, were strongly opposed and it was agreed to place GC&CS in the Admiralty. Curzon, however, did not leave the meeting empty-handed. He secured the valuable power of controlling the information produced by GC&CS. It was decided that in the first instance he, as Foreign Secretary, should receive all intercepted telegrams and be responsible for passing them on 'to the Prime Minister or other Cabinet Ministers concerned when they were of sufficient importance'.[7]

When in February 1921 Walter Long, who was interested in intelligence matters, was replaced by Lord Lee, who was not, Curzon began to press for the transfer of GC&CS to the Foreign Office.[8] This time he succeeded. In May Lee agreed[9] and from 1 April 1922 the Foreign Office took over responsibility for the school.[10] As it turned out, this arrangement did not suit the service ministries who lodged a vigorous complaint in April 1923, claiming that GC&CS under Foreign Office domination had 'entirely lost its interdepartmental character'.[11] The row simmered on until November when Sir Eyre Crowe, permanent under-secretary at the Foreign Office, devised a compromise whereby the school was placed under the general authority of Admiral Sinclair, by now head of SIS. Although Sinclair, in turn, was answerable to Curzon, he was personally acceptable to the service intelligence chiefs.[12] Like SIS, GC&CS was charged with providing information for all government departments which required it. Yet, also like SIS, its closest relationship was with the Foreign Office.

In the immediate postwar years the Foreign Office was challenged, especially by the Prime Minister and the Cabinet secretariat, as the sole exponent of British foreign policy. Curzon's keenness to secure control of GC&CS was undoubtedly pointed by his desire to reassert the Foreign Office position within the decision-making process.[13] His views as to the value of the signals intelligence organisation are clearly set out in a 'most secret' Cabinet memorandum he wrote during the summer of 1921 in response to a suggestion that GC&CS be moved away from the Whitehall area to 'distant quarters in Queen's Gate'.[14] In May 1921 the Cabinet, exercised by the high cost of accommodation in central London, appointed a committee under Sir Eric Geddes, the Minister of Transport, to consider the extent to which government offices 'now accommodated centrally might be transferred to outlying areas'.[15] Among Geddes's money-saving proposals was the relocation of GC&CS. Curzon was appalled and solemnly declared to his colleagues that such a move would 'gravely affect' what he described as 'by far the most important branch of our confidential work'. The duties of GC&CS, he wrote, were twofold:

(1) The collection, decyphering and distribution of the telegrams of foreign Governments; and
(2) The construction of codes and cyphers for all British government departments, who require them, and the training in their proper use of the staff employed upon them by those Depts [sic].

It is, perhaps, significant that these functions as set out by Curzon differ somewhat from those officially laid down by the government. The publicly-announced function of GC&CS was 'to advise as to the security of codes and cyphers used by all Government departments and to assist in their provision'—that is to say effectively the same as Curzon's second duty. But there was also a secret instruction 'to study the methods of cypher communications used by foreign powers'.[16] Curzon, however, did not express himself quite so euphemistically in what he regarded as the first duty of GC&CS. Although the protection of the British government's own communications was self-evidently important—in 1922, indeed, a Foreign Office official asserted that through the exertions of GC&CS 'Imperial communications' had 'incomparably greater security' than before the war[17]—Curzon boldly declared that 'the decyphered telegrams of foreign Govts. [sic] are without doubt the most valuable source of our secret information respecting their policy and actions. They provide the most accurate and, withal, intrinsically the cheapest, means of obtaining secret political information that exists'. The Foreign Secretary, however, added that two important factors governed the practical use of this information. The first was the rapidity with which it could be made available, and the second concerned 'the successful and accurate interpretation of the messages' which required 'constant intercommunication' between the staff of GC&CS and the political departments of the Foreign Office. Curzon noted that 'in the ordinary process of their duty at least 16 different members of the School visit Govt. Depts. [sic] in the Whitehall district over 3 times a week each, which alone works out at an average of 8 visits a day. . . . The time occupied by these visits', he added, 'is, in the majority of cases, so much time lost to the decyphering of telegrams, and it is obviously desirable that the distance to be traversed should be as small as possible'.

A further consideration was that of secrecy. 'It is important', he wote, 'to leave this part of our activity in the deepest possible obscurity'. Curzon described how part of the School's work consisted 'in the daily discharge from Government vans of numerous sacks of cables which must be hastily copied and returned to the Cable Companies within 24 hours of delivery'. This procedure had already led to 'much suspicion and some ill will' on the part of the Companies who were obliged to co-operate with the government, and also 'complaints and criticisms in America'.[18] He observed that the constant activity which would be generated by GC&CS in Queen's Gate, a 'quiet and respectable neighbourhood' (the converse presumably being true of Whitehall), such as the unloading of sacks of telegrams and the continual arrival and departure of motor vehicles carrying officials between the School and the Foreign Office, 'could not fail to provoke curiosity and enquiry which it would be difficult to satisfy'.

Curzon argued that any savings which might be achieved by relocating GC&CS would far be outweighed by the extra expense involved in 'highly skilled and highly paid officials' spending 'a large proportion of every week on the road between Kensington and Central London'. However compelling—financially or otherwise—might be the case for decentralising government departments in general, the work of GC&CS, especially 'the importance attaching to the combination of accuracy, speed and secrecy', was of an 'altogether exceptional character'. This distinguished the School from every other branch of the public service. It was, he averred, 'the most secret and confidential aspect of Government work in any part of the world'. Sadly, Curzon's trenchant eloquence did not prevail in the face of Geddes's—and the Cabinet's—hard-nosed quest for economy. GC&CS was exiled to the distant charms of Kensington and remained there until 1926 when the School returned to the security of S.W.1, at Broadway Buildings in Tothill Street, which also housed the headquarters of SIS.[19]

As Curzon's Cabinet memorandum suggests, GC&CS handled a considerable volume of cable traffic. British signals intelligence was in a strong position to intercept the telegrams of foreign governments since British concerns dominated the world's cable communications network.[20] Diplomatic traffic in and out of London certainly seems to have been intercepted as a matter of routine. Much of the sigint material was evidently passed on to SIS for incorporation into general intelligence reviews.[21] Individual intercepts, however, were also from time to time circulated to ministers.[22] From the original intercepts which have survived it is possible to hazard some tentative conclusions regarding the volume and efficiency of GC&CS's operation.[23] Decrypted intercepts were numbered sequentially as they were issued by GC&CS and it appears that between mid-June 1920 and mid-January 1924 the School issued 12,600 intercepted signals, an average of approximately 290 per month. Over this period the volume of intercepts fell from over 300 per month in 1920 to 250 per month in 1922–23. They seem to have been processed comparatively quickly. Of the ten signals between Paris and the French embassy in London which have been examined, seven had been deciphered and distributed within five days of having been despatched.[24]

GC&CS was not the only supplier of intercepted signals to the British government. From the end of the war until 1923 an important sigint operation was run by the British occupying forces at Constantinople. Although this seems initially to have been set up by Military Intelligence in order to catch Bolshevik communications in south Russia, it was also used extensively to read Turkish, Greek, French and other traffic, both military and diplomatic.[25] This operation, possibly due to the simplicity of Turkish codes, appears to have processed its material more rapidly than GC&CS. Of seventeen original intercepts examined, thirteen were deciphered and distributed within five days.[26] Sigint was also provided by the Indian military authorities. There was, for example, an important station at Peshawar on the North-West Frontier directed towards Soviet wireless traffic in central Asia. In December 1920 this provided 'all that is now passing between Kabul and Tashkent regarding Bolshevic [sic] aspirations and methods'. There was, moreover, 'a first class cipher expert . . . who has so far been able to interpret every message even though they change their cipher every fortnight or so'.[27]

The use of secret intelligence concerning the Near East is sufficiently well-documented to permit an assessment of its importance as a factor in policy-making. Intercepts provided by GC&CS, and also from Constantinople, gave Lord Curzon and his colleagues reliable information about Greek, nationalist Turk and French policy in the region. During the Lausanne conference of November 1922 to February 1923, moreover, the British delegation had the distinct advantage of being able to read a large proportion of the Turkish delegation's private correspondence. More embarrassingly, as shown by intercepted Greek messages in 1921, secret intelligence also provided Curzon with confirmation of Lloyd George's independent (and in this case strikingly pro-Greek) approach to foreign policy.

The peace treaty signed at Sèvres in August 1920 with the Constantinople Turkish government, was remarkably short-lived.[28] By the beginning of 1921 it was abundantly clear that the settlement would not stick. The nationalist Turks under Mustafa Kemal, *de facto* ruler of Anatolia, refused to submit to its terms. Even the Sultan in Constantinople avoided ratifying it. The Greeks, although they had been awarded a zone in Asia Minor around Smyrna, had extended their control over a substantial portion of western Turkey and under Lloyd George's patronage seemed set to dominate the whole region.[29]

In February 1921 a conference was held in London under the presidency of the British Prime Minister to consider revising the Sèvres agreement, but it broke down partly because the nationalist Turk representatives, led by their Foreign Minister, Bakir-Sami, wanted a complete abrogation of the peace treaty, and partly because the Greeks desired even more than they had been awarded at Sèvres. In this they were secretly egged on by Lloyd George, as Curzon discovered when he saw intercepts provided by GC&CS. Using his private secretary, Philip Kerr, as an intermediary, Lloyd George advised the Greek delegation to break with the conference over the proposal to conduct an enquiry into rival Greek and Turkish claims in Smyrna and Thrace. At a meeting on 1 March Kerr added the tactical advice that while the Greeks 'ought not to hesitate to refuse, it would be desirable if the Turks should be the first to decline to submit to the decision of the conference'. He also indicated that the British government would look favourably on a renewed Greek military offensive against the Kemalists.[30] Just over a fortnight later Sir Maurice Hankey noted that Curzon, having read the Greek signal describing Kerr's meeting with them, was 'much upset at the P.M.'s permission to the Greeks to attack in Smyrna'.[31] Curzon complained to the Prime Minister who responded merely by allowing a warning to be given to the Turks that the Greeks might resume active hostilities. Despite Curzon's protests, moreover, Lloyd George subsequently hinted to the Greeks that Britain might be able to provide financial aid to support their military efforts in Asia Minor. Once again the Greek signal reporting this was intercepted by GC&CS and passed on to Curzon.[32]

Apart from the Prime Minister's underhand support for the Greeks, French manoeuvres at the conference also weakened the Allied unity which Curzon believed was essential. Facing Arab resistance to their mandate in Syria, the French were anxious to retrench in the region and withdraw the expensive garrison of 80,000 troops in Cilicia, who had already come under attack from the Turkish nationalists. During the conference, therefore, Briand, the French premier, made a separate agreement with Bakir-Sami by which the French promised to evacuate Cilicia and revise the Turkish-Syrian frontier. The French in return were to be granted various concessions within Turkey.[33] Although Curzon deplored this unilateral action, the British government made no formal objection at the time. It marked, however, the growing divergence of British and French policy towards the nationalist Turks. While Britain continued to support the Greeks, deal with the Constantinople government (which was rapidly becoming an irrelevance) and hope that some parts of the Sèvres settlement might be saved—all of which was anathema to the Kemalists—the French grew increasingly conciliatory towards the nationalist leadership in Angora. Although the French desire to come to an accommodation with the nationalists was openly known, British intelligence was able to provide detailed evidence of France's efforts to that end.

Largely because of the concessions offered to the French, the London agreement was rejected by Angora and in June 1921 Bakir-Sami arrived in Paris to renegotiate its terms. In July intercepts secured in Constantinople of signals from Paris to Turkey had begun to disturb the British general commanding the Allied occupation forces, Sir Tim Harington. Among the information gleaned by military intelligence was the suggestion that France might make a separate peace with Kemal.[34] Rattigan, temporarily acting British High Commissioner, passed on to London Harington's concern about his position if the French withdrew their troops from his command and noted that the British military authorities had 'unassailable proof' that the French were continuing to negotiate secretly with Angora.[35] Curzon, however, had already got wind of this. Referring to 'the various reports which have from time to time appeared in the press regarding the conversations in progress', and convinced of 'the supreme importance of complete inter-Allied solidarity', he sought reassurance from Briand that the French were not about to conclude a unilateral agreement with the Turkish nationalists.[36] Briand replied that the negotiations were merely 'local' and were concerned only with the problem of Turkish nationalist attacks on the frontier of Syria and Cilicia. Curzon was assured that the French government 'have constantly reserved [the] general question of peace between allies and Turkey'.[37]

Suspicions, however, lingered regarding the precise intentons of French policy towards the Kemalists. These were fuelled by the arrival in Angora of the well-known Turcophil Senator Henri Franklin-Bouillon. The French High Commission at Constantinople, reported Rattigan, maintained that

Franklin-Bouillon was 'entirely unofficial but they have been secretive about his movements. He is said to be (?personal) friend of Monsieur Briand's'.[38] In August Harington reported that 'Boiling Frankie' was allegedly seeking trade concessions from the nationalists and that there was 'plenty of dirty work going on, as our intercepts show'.[39] The following month Sir Horace Rumbold, the British High Commissioner at Constantinople, informed Curzon that Franklin-Bouillon had recently passed through *en route* to Angora. It was believed that his talks there concerned the exchange of prisoners. 'I learn confidentially . . .', wrote Rumbold

> that a certain person called on one of the chiefs of the French Military Intelligence Service and asked the latter if he could give him any information about the convention between M. Franklin-Bouillon and the Nationalists. The French officer, who thought that his visitor had called on behalf of the American Associated Press, asked him not to press the point as any statement he might make might have an injurious effect on Anglo-French relations . . . There is little doubt in my mind that M. Franklin-Bouillon's negotiations cover a wider ground than the exchange of prisoners.[40]

Drawing on a mixture of hard information, secret intelligence and surmise, Curzon on several occasions enquired of the French as to Franklin-Bouillon's true role. In June Briand told him that Franklin-Bouillon had no official mission, 'but had gone as a French journalist to report upon the situation'.[41] In September the French premier admitted an official role for the Senator, but denied that it covered 'the larger questions of peace'. It simply concerned the problem of French prisoners and the evacuation of Cilicia. 'Relying on these categorical assurances,' observed Curzon in November 1921, 'I had taken no further steps in the matter'.[42] But by this stage he had learned of Franklin-Bouillon's 'treacherous'[43] treaty with Kemal of 20 October 1921. The agreement ended the state of war between France and Angora, and effectively constituted formal French recognition of the nationalist administration as the government of Turkey.[44]

Despite his disappointment with France's independent, and to his mind overly friendly, policy towards the Kemalists, Curzon still hoped to achieve a general settlement drawing together Britain, France and Italy as allies, with the Greeks and the Constantinople government, as well as Angora. The need for some agreement was accentuated by the progressive collapse of the Greek position in Asia Minor from its high point in September 1921. Lloyd George, however, refused to abandon them entirely. The French, by contrast, moved closer and closer to Kemal. In February 1922 Rumbold told Curzon that in an 'account obtained from very secret source'[45] of an interview between the nationalist Foreign Minister and the French High Commisioner in Constantinople, the latter stated 'that France would be the advocate of Turkey against Great Britain who is supporting Greece. . . It is evident', added Rumbold, 'that French are entirely unscrupulous in their attempts to (?curry) favour with Nationalists and that their proceedings will greatly increase the difficulty of a settlement'.[46]

Loath to abandon all possibility of a general Near Eastern settlement, Curzon pressed on. In March 1922 the British, French and Italian Foreign Ministers met in Paris and examined the problem in exhaustive detail.[47] They jointly agreed proposals—drafted by Curzon—'for the final conclusion of Peace between the Allied Powers and Turkey', and pressed for an immediate armistice between the Greek and Turkish armies.[48] If Curzon really believed that the French were now committed to a common policy with Britain, an intercepted Turkish diplomatic signal soon disabused him of the notion. The Turkish representative in Paris reported that Poincaré (who had become both Premier and Foreign Minister in January 1922) had assured him, in direct contradiction to Curzon's stated view, that the Paris proposals were not necessarily final.[49] Curzon was infuriated by this information, Poincaré was 'a treacherous creature'. 'Even allowing for Turkish exaggeration,' the intercept showed that 'the moment the Paris conference was over he went and stabbed us in the back. My dear Charlie', he wrote to Lord Hardinge, 'I have no idea how to deal with such people . . . Here is Poincaré telling the Turks to tear up the agreement on which his signature is still wet. And these are our allies . . .'.[50] Hardinge was not at all surprised by Poincaré's 'dastardly behaviour . . . I regard him', he told Curzon, 'as a dirty dog, a man of very mean character'. It all simply went to show 'what very loose ideas of honesty these foreign statesmen have'.[51]

But what could Curzon do with this shocking revelation? Although the intercepted Turkish telegram, which had been sent on 4 April, was not circulated until a month later, it is clear that the British were already aware of France's attitude towards the Paris proposals. By this time Angora had issued a cool response to them.[52] On 23 April, moreover, the Turks indicated their view that the proposals were negotiable and suggested that a conference be convened at Ismid in Asia Minor.[53] Rumbold warned that 'in view of what we know of French dealings with nationalists since Paris conference, I trust any French draft rejoinder will be carefully scrutinised'.[54] While Curzon (with Italian acquiescence) was reluctant to accept the Turkish suggestion, Poincaré, by contrast, welcomed the idea of a new conference and responded favourably. In a minute of 25 May Curzon argued that 'what M. Poincaré is really after is a rupture, the responsibility for which can be laid upon us'. This was clearly the case 'when we know, as we do, that M. Poincaré is secretly promising the Turks his assistance and telling them the Paris terms will never be enforced'.[55] Curzon, however, made no public protest about France's *sub rosa* activities. In any case, by this stage he had been laid low with a nasty attack of phlebitis and Lord Balfour took temporary charge of the Foreign Office for two and a half months in mid-1922.[56]

A lobby in the Foreign Office, nevertheless, was anxious to take the French to task. In a memorandum reviewing the current state of Allied policy towards the Near East (which was to be communicated to Poincaré) London proposed the following sharp observation: 'The apparent alacrity with which M. Poincaré, at the bidding of the Angora Government, is prepared to abandon that [Paris] agreement, which His Majesty's Government on their part had looked upon as definite, has caused them the most painful surprise'. Hardinge, who after all had to deliver the memorandum, thought this was 'unnecessarily provocative . . . It can serve no useful purpose to put Poincaré's back up,' he argued. 'He is difficult enough to deal with as it is'. Thus, in the final version, the British government merely expressed astonishment 'at what appears at first sight to be a readiness on the part of the French Government to accept the breach of that agreement implied in the Angora proposal'.[57] During the summer of 1922 the Foreign Office were also troubled by suspicions that both the French and the Italians might be releasing arms held by the Allied occupation forces to the Anatolian nationalists. In July the War Office reported that they had 'no difficulty in obtaining absolutely clear and unimpeachable evidence against the French' and supplied the Foreign Office with a detailed list of arms and ammunition 'despatched to Anatolian ports from depots under Allied supervision' during May 1922. They warned, however, that 'by far the greater portion of this evidence is derived from a very secret source and must not, therefore, in any circumstances be communicated to a foreign Government'. Precisely because the information came from secret sources, presumably intecepts, Balfour did not press the point with the French.[58] In August reports were received from Sir Harry Lamb (the official British representative at Smyrna) that some Italians who had been supplying aeroplanes to Angora had said 'openly' that the French were 'pouring war material up to the Kemalists'. In London this was thought not to be sufficiently good or impartial enough a source 'to justify enquiries at Paris'.[59] Towards the end of the month the British High Commissioner in Baghdad reported that the French were supplying arms to the Kemalists for possible use against British troops in Iraq. Curzon, now back at his desk, passed this information on to Hardinge in Paris and asked him to tackle Poincaré with the Iraq aspect of arms supply. Frustratingly, however, the Foreign Secretary was still unable to tax the French with all of his suspicions. 'His Majesty's Government', he wrote,

> have no irrefutable evidence of the actual handing over of munitions by the French Government, as distinct from French private firms, although there is abundant proof from sources which cannot be divulged, that the French authorities at Constantinople have been facilitating, if not actually transacting, the leakage to the Kemalists of munitions from the Turkish stores under their guard.[60]

Unsurprisingly, when Hardinge took the matter up with Poincaré, the charges were categorically denied.[61]

The secret information, therefore, which London had of France's dealings with the nationalist Turks was not of much practical use. 'Our gallant Allies', wrote Rumbold, 'are always "playing the dirty" on us—to use a vulgar expression and if we could reveal some of the things we know about the French—for instance—the world would be more than astonished'.[62] In Lord Curzon's case it seems above all to have fuelled his frustration with the French, and particularly his exasperation with the pedantic and intransigent Poincaré. As Christopher Andrew has suggested, Curzon's (in any case acute) sense of outrage with Poincaré as exacerbated by secret intelligence may have been a contributory factor leading to the celebrated stormy meeting on 19 September 1922 when Curzon was led weeping from the room and refused to return until Poincaré apologised.[63] The chief point, nevertheless, over which the two statesmen fell out was the withdrawal of French troops from the Asiatic side of the Dardanelles, which Curzon bitterly described as 'abandonment' and 'desertion'. Even without the cumulative intelligence evidence of apparent French duplicity, Paris's breaking of Allied ranks in the midst of the Chanak crisis was surely on its own enough to explain Curzon's explosion at the meeting with Poincaré.

Despite the incident, Curzon clearly remained utterly convinced that the Allies should still mount a concerted effort to secure peace in the Near East. The clear emergence of the Kemalists as the only credible power in Turkey, however, lent irresistible force to the French insistence that a conciliatory approach was necessary towards Angora. Curzon appreciated this and was able to act upon it. The fall of Lloyd George's government not only enhanced his political position but also freed him from the constraints of the former Prime Minister's pro-Greek prejudices. After the immediate crisis at Chanak had passed, the Allies agreed to convene a new peace conference with the nationalist Turks at Lausanne.

The Lausanne conference, which was held in two sessions from 20 November 1922 to 4 February 1923 and from 23 April until 24 July

1923, represents one of the most interesting case studies of the use and value of secret intelligence. At its conclusion Sir Horace Rumbold, who accompanied Curzon for the first session and then replaced him as chief British negotiator for the second, observed that 'the information we obtained at the psychological moments from secret sources was invaluable to us, and put us in the position of a man who is playing Bridge and knows the cards in his adversary's hand'.[64]

The analogy is an apt one.[65] The information, which was obtained mainly from the British wireless intercept operation in Constantinople, did not guarantee that the British negotiators would be successful in obtaining all their objectives, but it did mean that on certain occasions they could cut their losses and know when not to push the conference to a breach. Rumbold, for example, was prepared to argue against, and eventually convince Curzon that the claims of the Turkish Petroleum Company should not be included in the final protocol. He did this because he attached great weight to the Angora government's intercepted instructions to Ismet (the chief Turkish negotiator) which demanded that he stand firm on the issue.[66] Similarly Rumbold could produce evidence to warn Curzon of difficulties relating to a new draft convention on legal arrangements for foreigners in Turkey. Although the Allies had drawn up a text, Rumbold was cautious:

> I feel that Ismet's hands are tied in this matter by instructions from Angora and you will have seen from secret sources that if we insist on going beyond the Montagna formula, he is instructed to break off negotiations and leave the Conference. In fact this is the one question on which the Conference may break down . . . We will do our best here to get some safeguards for our nationals, but I do not know whether our public opinion would understand a rupture over this business.[67]

Curzon again modified his position in the face of Rumbold's arguments.[68]

Curzon and Rumbold did not occupy a very powerful position at Lausanne. They faced a successful, resurgent Turkey backed by Soviet assistance in the wake of the crisis at Chanak which had exposed the isolation of Britain, not only from her supposed allies, France and Italy, but also, with minor exceptions, from her own Dominions. Nor was Curzon happy about the extent to which the British government, and particularly the Prime Minister, Bonar Law, was prepared to offer him support and backing. 'I found Bonar longing to clear out of Mosul, the Straits and Constantinople, willing to give up anything and everything rather than have a row . . .' , he wrote from Paris to his wife on 1 January 1923. 'He has not the clear grasp of Foreign Affairs. No instinct for Oriental diplomacy . . . I was really very much staggered at his flabbiness and want of grip.'[69]

In these circumstances the information gleaned from the BJs, Black Elephants or Ben Jamin (as correspondents variously described them) must have provided a welcome boost to the morale of the British delegation. The negotiations were certainly hard going. 'Sisyphus and his stone', remarked Curzon at one stage, 'were tame performers compared to my daily task'.[70] But there were lighter moments too. In November 1922 Henderson sent Rumbold 'a rather amusing wire from Angora which was intercepted by our control at the Ottoman telegraph office'. The telegram, apparently from 'The Major', contained the results of the 'Khalifate Selling Plate'. Mejid had won by 148 lengths, with 'also ran' Selim and Abdul Rahman, respectively 3 and 2 lengths behind. The Starting Prices were: Mejid, '7 to 4 on'; Selim, '100 to 7'; and Abdul Rahman, 'No quotation. Anything taken'. Curzon and Rumbold were very amused. 'Surely this is a fake', suggested the latter.[71]

Indeed one might go so far as to say that intercept material was the one ace in Curzon's hand. From the intercepts he learned of the difficulties facing Ismet in Lausanne and the Nationalist government in Angora. Ismet's position, caught between the terms acceptable to the Conference and those desired by his masters, was well known to Curzon and his associates. Reflecting on Ismet's opening speech, Henderson was 'convinced' that it had been 'largely concocted at Angora before he left. Ever since he made it the BJs have been full of telegrams complaining that Angora has not received the full text of that speech . . . I should not be surprised if Ismet watered down what he had been told to say'.[72] In February 1923 an intelligence report on the 'prospects of peace' summarised the 'difficult internal situation' in Turkey which had led to a temporary rupture in the negotiations. 'S.I.S. information' about Ismet's attitude, it noted, 'has indicated that he has been personally in favour of a moderate policy'.[73] The Turkish delegate's situation, caught between the Lausanne anvil and the Angora hammer, did not improve. 'You will have noticed from the usual secret sources', wrote Rumbold to Curzon on 2 June 1923, 'that Ismet's position with his own government is becoming more and more difficult'.[74]

From about Christmas 1922 the negotiators at Lausanne faced the very real possibility of the conference breaking down. On 25 December Henderson, the chargé in Constantinople, telegraphed to Curzon some information gleaned from 'usual secret sources'. Ismet, he said, had told Angora that the Allies were pressing matters to a conclusion and making impossible demands on Turkey.[75] Curzon sharply retorted that this was 'palpably untrue' since the matters complained of[76] were still under discussion. He observed that the Turkish attitude had stiffened and was 'becoming increasingly hostile and even insolent'.[77] Rumbold, too, was concerned with the progress of the conference. 'I am not very optimistic', he wrote on Boxing Day, 'and I think the odds now are rather against the success of the conference. But you know what the Turks are like. Over and over again at Constantinople we have thought that the breaking point has been reached and yet somehow or other we have not got through our difficulties'.[78] This view was confirmed by the confused Turkish attitudes revealed by secret information forwarded by Harington. The Allies, reported Ismet on 23 December

> are extremely tiresome and annoying and by their method of discussion they wish to cow down the Turk and on the other hand drag him gradually into a quagmire by throwing him into the discussions over rotten and insolent demands. [In the margin at this point an exclamation mark was added by a Foreign Office official.] In almost every question we have our backs to the wall. Either they will bring us to our knees and conclude another form of Sèvres Treaty or we will bring them to theirs. We are determined to conclude a peace like every other civilised and independent nation

This was dismissed in the Foreign Office as 'delusion & fanaticism' against which nothing could avail but 'force or fear'.[80]

The intercepts revealed that Ismet's perception of the Allied position differed markedly from Curzon's. 'The relations between French and British', maintained the Turkish negotiator, 'are reported good. There is little chance of these men foregoing their old confidence in one another'.[81] At the same time there was also evidence to confirm Curzon's worst suspicions. On 20 December Angora reported to Ismet that the Soviet ambassador was seeking a united Turco-Russian front during the Lausanne conference. They also revealed that the Soviets were 'extremely keen on coming to an understanding with [the] French'.[82] Furthermore, an intercept of 18 December clearly indicated that France was privately offering concessions to the Kamalists.[83] Curzon commented on the conference file which gathered together these telegrams: 'All this information points to rupture'.[84]

By early January the immediate threat of breakdown had passed and Curzon was complaining about the 'stagnation which seemed to have settled down on everything here' and he was seeking to 'bring matters to a head within [a] reasonable period of time'.[85] He even asserted that the delay was partially attributable to 'the Turks, who receive an exorbitant entertainment allowance, [and] greatly prefer the flesh pots of Lausanne to the austerities of Angora'.[86] The British position was not improved by the breakdown of the reparations conference in Paris. The subsequent French invasion of the Ruhr left Paris even more anxious to reach a settlement in the Near East. 'It is clear to me,' remarked Rumbold on 16 January 1923, 'that the deeper the French get into the mire of the Ruhr the more keen they are to get out of the Turkish mire'.[87] This was confirmed when Poincaré confidentially informed Angora that he did not regard the draft treaty, so painfully assembled by Curzon, as in any way final.[88]

The Foreign Secretary, however, must have been reassured to learn that the Turks were anxious to make peace and that, despite the unreliability of his allies, the real question confronting the Turks was their relationship with Great Britain. 'If they really want peace, as is clear from all the secret telegrams,' wrote Leo Amery to Curzon on 2 February, 'it is peace with us they want'.[89] Furthermore, as Rumbold pointed out to Henderson,

> We know that the Turks are very worried and consider that they have sustained a failure. In any event their personal position is none too rosy for if they return with what the Grand National Assembly will consider a bad treaty they would get dropped on, whereas if they return without having signed anything at all they will be accused of having wasted nearly three months and much money. So they are going to get it in the neck anyway. I cannot say I am sorry for them as I have never run up against such a lot of pig-headed, stupid and irritating people in my life.[90]

Nonetheless, the information received was not comprehensive or conclusive. In the final analysis it depended upon interpretation and judgment. As the crisis of the first session approached, Harington, supported by Henderson, advised the evacuation of Constantinople and Ismid and the withdrawal of British forces to the Gallipoli Peninsula.[91] In London the Cabinet agreed, unless Curzon had serious objections.[92] Curzon and Rumbold, however, disagreed. On 30 January Curzon telegraphed urgently to the Foreign Office to advise against Harington's proposal. 'We have', he declared, 'reason to believe that Ismet is much perturbed as to situation into which mistaken tactics of his Delegation have forced him, and it may very well be that before I leave on Friday night [2 February] the situation may change'.[93] Rumbold wrote to Constantinople that Curzon, Sir Eyre Crowe and he had very carefully considered the position and had been 'unanimous in deciding that there could be no question of evacuating Constantinople in present circumstances'. He added, for Henderson's eyes only, that 'our impression from your . . . telegrams was that Harington and [Admiral] Brock [CinC Mediterranean] had got cold feet'.[94]

Curzon and Rumbold reached their conclusion before they received Henderson's telegram of 30 January which contained information, learned 'from a sometimes well-informed source', that 'after final secret session held yesterday morning Grand National Assembly decided that war must at all costs be avoided'. Ismet, moreover, had 'been instructed to ask for adjournment rather than accept rupture of conference and to give undertaking if necessary to refrain from military action of any sort during adjournment'.[95] Curzon's judgment certainly may have been helped by the intelligence gleaned from the Turkish telegraph traffic, but Harington and Henderson saw the same information, and, indeed, saw it before Curzon. At this point experience told. As Leo Amery had reminded Curzon the previous December: 'There is always a moment in buying a carpet from a Turk when you have to leave the shop. If that moment is rightly judged, you will find that before you have got 50 yards the Turk has caught you up and agreed to your price, accompanied by a porter carrying the carpet!'[96] In the end the Curzon view, reinforced by Henderson's later information, prevailed and the Cabinet on 6 February (a meeting attended by Rumbold) reversed its previous decision.[97] The British troops remained in Constantinople and the conference was adjourned until 23 April.

One problem concerning secret intelligence thrown up during the first session of the conference was that of conveying the intelligence gathered by the sigint operation at Constantinople to the delegation at Lausanne. Curzon could not always rely on receiving the information in good time. This was principally because, although Harington sent some paraphrases of secret intelligence direct to Lausanne, the intercepts themselves were in the first instance sent to the War Office and only subsequently forwarded to the Foreign Office, thence to Switzerland. On 26 December 1922 Curzon complained[98] that he had not received copies of two intercepts referred to by Harington in a telegram of 25 December.[99] Although the War Office had received the intercepts on 25 December, they did not reach the Foreign Office until two days later and Curzon only saw them on 28 December.[100] The military in Constantinople were aware of the difficulty. 'I am afraid', apologised Harington to Curzon, 'these secret intercepts take a long time to reach you owing to the fact that I am not allowed to send them direct'.[101] On 23 January 1923 another officer wrote in similar vein to Rumbold:

> I am sorry that we are not allowed to send Ben Jamin's notes direct to Lausanne. Several items of interest to us, but only of real importance and value to Lord Curzon and yourself, and then only if communicated to you at once, have appeared and I have urged their immediate repetition to you, but apparently the War Office instructions on this point are categoric and our hands are tied.
>
> I found on investigation that the two messages from Harington to Troopers [the War Office] to which Lord Curzon in a telegram to the Foreign Office referred some weeks ago, saying how valuable they would have been to him, were both messages the direct repetition of which was forbidden under the above instructions.[102]

The position improved markedly during the second phase of the conference when important intercepts were sent direct to Sir Horace Rumbold at

Lausanne.[103] Towards the end of the negotiations Rumbold wrote apprecia-tively to Henderson: 'Your secret telegrams have been most useful and all arrived at the psychological moment, thereby being of immense assistance to us. It is a case of admirable liaison work between the Constantinople Embassy and this delegation and does you the greatest credit'.[104]

As was the case with the Soviet diplomatic traffic and the intelligence about French activities in the Near East, the British delegation at Lausanne had to be careful to conceal the sources of their information, particularly to their unreliable allies. 'The only matter which worries me at the present moment', confided Rumbold to Curzon in June, 'is the knowledge of Ismet's own position vis-à-vis his Government. I cannot, of course, let my colleagues into my confidence, and so I am obliged to confine myself to telling them that we must be careful to avoid a repetition of the Bekir Sami incident'.[105] Despite these problems, secret intelligence materially contributed to the success of the Lausanne conference and even provided the Foreign Office with evidence that the settlement was the best possible in the circumstances. 'On the whole the treaty has by no means a bad press and the skill and patience of our delegation is fully recognised. There is no reason to suppose we could have got better terms, judging by Ismet's telegrams from Angora'.[106]

In contrast to the positive value of intercepts at the Lausanne Conference, towards the end of his time as Foreign Secretary Curzon was troubled by more evidence of French intrigues. In October 1923 intercepted messages between Poincaré and the Comte de St Aulaire (Ambassador in London) uncovered an attempt to 'make mischief' between the Prime Minister, Baldwin, and Curzon. 'This is the worst thing I have come across in my public life', wrote Curzon to Crewe (British Ambassador in Paris), '& it will render it absolutely impossible for me ever to treat St Aulaire with the slightest confidence again'. Yet because of the source of the information, the Foreign Secretary was powerless to confront the Ambassador. 'It is a pity that I cannot have it out with him'.[107] All he could do was complain to Baldwin who agreed that the French attempts to go behind Curzon's back were 'perfectly futile; but they are very annoying and make our dealing with the French more difficult'.[108] When in December intercepts revealed further underhand dealings by the 'arch intriguer' St Aulaire, Curzon, who had 'declined to see him on some excuse or other for nearly 2 months', threatened that 'some day before I retire I shall have a few candid words with him without giving away my sources of information'.[109]

Christopher Andrew has suggested that Curzon, having been suddenly introduced to sigint in the later stages of his career, 'was emotionally incapable of coping with it'. He cites the evidence of the meeting with Poincaré in September 1922 and also Curzon's reaction to the French intercepts of 1923.[110] Yet the implication that Curzon was to some degree unbalanced by the kinds of information reaching him from the intelligence community seems unfair. We know how highly he regarded the work of GC&CS, and he certainly used intercept information to good effect during the Lausanne Conference. His excited reaction to some of the secret intelligence he received was in keeping with his normal demeanour. Lord Ronaldshay asserted that Curzon's emotions were 'always powerful and clamorous for expression',[111] and he responded temperamentally to matters both great and small. He was noted for a 'deficient sense of proportion',[112] which cannot have been helped by his general sense of insecurity in office, especially while Lloyd George was Prime Minister.[113]

Yet, despite his outbursts against Poincaré and the French, Curzon did not for long let his outrage cloud a sensible appreciation of the overriding requirement to secure a general settlement in the Near East which would draw in the French. The Poincaré-St Aulaire telegrams in 1923 never drove him to any irreversible break. Indeed, Curzon complained about his inability to tackle the Ambassador about the matter. The noteworthy fact is not that Curzon was unable to cope with the perfidy revealed by the intercepts, but that, on the whole, when it mattered he contained his personal feelings perfectly well. His reaction to intercepts was governed not so much by the sensational or disturbing nature of secret intelligence *per se* as by the particular issue involved; he was influenced more by the message than the medium. Thus his fervent, and perhaps disproportionate anti-Bolshevism led him into the idiocies of the diplomatic notes to Moscow in the autumn of 1921 and the early summer of 1923, which revealed the British interception of Soviet signals.[114] He was, moreover, perhaps lulled into over-confidence and a false sense of security by the apparent ease with which GC&CS were able to break the Soviet ciphers. The violent row with Poincaré in September 1922 was even patched up sufficiently for France and Great Britain to enter the conference chamber at Lausanne more or less united, so much so that the impression gained by Ismet was one of close harmony. Curzon's expostulations to his colleagues may well have been simply a means of venting frustration. In any case those around him made allowances for his intermittent outbursts. 'I do not think you need be worried about Lord Curzon's telegram No. 54', Rumbold advised Henderson in January 1923. 'I think he was annoyed with the sort of information which Ismet was sending from Lausanne'.[115]

Lord Curzon's experience with secret intelligence demonstrates many of the difficulties associated with using such material. Nevertheless, considering that sigint on the scale provided by GC&CS was a novel diplomatic tool, the record so far as it has been examined, reveals a remarkable degree of care, confidence and even deftness in its use. For an 'old buffer', as he once described himself,[116] Curzon was, for the most part, well able to handle the substantial volume of signals intelligence with which the British government were blessed during his time as Foreign Secretary.

Notes

1. The post-war reorganisation is covered in F. H. Hinsley *et al.*, *British Intelligence in the Second World War*, I (London 1979), chapter 1, and Christopher Andrew, *Secret Service: the Making of the British Intelligence Community* (London, 1985), chapter 9.

2. See, for example, the distribution of SIS's regular 'Eastern Summary'. No. 968 (22 November 1922), 'The Turkish attitude at the Lausanne Conference', was distributed quite widely, to the Foreign Office (Eastern, Northern, Central European and Western Departments), the War Office (MI1c—the War Office branch which formed part of SIS's head-quarters staff), the Admiralty, the Air Ministry, the India Office and the Colonial Office. No. 1086 (19 February 1923), 'Franco–Turkish relations', went to the same customers with the exception of the Foreign Office Central European Department and the India Office. Parts of No. 1180 (15 June 1923), a general political report on Turkey, were separately circulated. The section on 'Pan-Islamic policy' went to the Foreign Office (Eastern Department), the India Office and the Colonial Office, while a section on Turkish army involvement with the National Defence Committee was only sent to the Foreign Office Eastern Department and the War Office (MI1c). PRO FO 371/7964 E13341, 371/9121 E1979 and 371/9122 E6329.

3. Hinsley, *British Intelligence*, pp. 17–18.

4. See Patrick Beesley, *Room 40*, (London, 1982).

5. Curzon to Walter Long (First Lord of the Admiralty), 24 March 1919, PRO ADM 1/8637/55. We are especially grateful to John Ferris of King's College, London, for drawing our attention to this important Admiralty file.

6. Minute by Sinclair, 28 March 1919, ibid.

7. Minutes of Conference held at the Foreign Office, 29 April 1919, ibid.

8. See Curzon to Lee, 25 April 1921, and minute by Lee, 2 May 1921, ibid.

9. Lee to Curzon, 23 May 1921, ibid.

10. Details of the transfer are in PRO FO 366/800. Christopher Andrew, drawing on W. F. Clarke's account of GC&CS, says that the Foreign Office were 'embarrassed into taking over direct responsibility' for the School 'after its codebreakers had decrypted a telegram from the French ambassador in London reporting that Curzon had severely criticised Cabinet policy'. Andrew, *Secret Service*, p. 260 (amended in paperback edition, 1986).

11. Report of Inter-Service Directorate Committee, 9 April 1923, PRO WO 32/4897, no. 13A.

12. See correspondence in PRO WO 32/4897.

13. See Alan Sharp, 'Lord Curzon and the Foreign Office', in Roger Bullen (ed.), *The Foreign Office 1782–1982* (Frederick, Maryland, 1984), pp. 66–84.

14. GC&CS at this time occupied Watergate House, Adelphi. Queen's Gate was slightly over two miles away from Whitehall. Curzon's Cabinet memo is available in the Curzon Papers (India Office Library and Reccords) MSS Eur. F.112/302. It is numbered 'C.P. 3105', which in the PRO calendars is marked 'not yet circulated'. PRO CAB 24/126.

15. For the terms of reference of Geddes's committee see the Preliminary report of the Committee on the Decentralisation of the Housing of Government Staffs, 20 June 1921, PRO CAB 24/125 C.P. 3051.

16. A. G. Denniston, 'The Government Code and Cypher School Between the Wars', *Intelligence and National Security*, I (1986), p. 49. See also Hinsley, *British Intelligence* p. 20.

17. Memo on Code and Cypher School by C. Howard Smith, 10 August 1922, PRO FO 366/802.

18. The problem of British 'eavesdropping' on American cable traffic was brought up in Senate hearings in 1921. James Bamford, *The Puzzle Palace* (London, 1983), pp. 13 and 388.

19. See PRO FO 366/838 for details regarding the lease of Broadway Buildings.

20. This problem worried the Americans. See Bamford, *Puzzle Palace*, p. 13.

21. Intercepts are referred to or quoted in, for example, 'S.I.S. (Constantinople Branch) Summary of Intelligence Reports for week ending 16 December 1920'; 'Turkey: Prospects of Peace', S.I.S. Misc/26, 21 February 1923; and 'Memorandum on Russo–Turkish relations'. S.I.S. Misc/29, 27 June 1923; PRO FO 406/45 p. 40; FO 371/9121 E2083; and FO 371/9122 E6748.

22. An intercept of 22 September 1921 has distribution marked as follows: Prime Minister, Lord Privy Seal, S. of S. for the Colonies, India Office, Director of Naval Intelligence, Director of Military Intelligence and Sir Basil Thomson (Home Office).

23. There are a large number of original 'flimsies' of intercepts in the Lloyd George Papers, House of Lords Records Office, F/203/1 and F/209/3. Additionally, twelve flimsies as issued by GC&CS between 30 December 1920 and 17 January 1924 survive in the Curzon, Crewe and Hardinge Papers. Mr John Ferris of King's College London, who has examined a large number of intercepts dating from 1919 to 1928, confirms the findings which follow.

24. The time taken for the other three to be processed was: 8, 11 and 17 days.

25. See Keith Jeffery, 'British Military Intelligence following the First World War', in K. G. Robertson (ed.), *What is Intelligence? British and American Approaches* (forthcoming).

26. The other four took 7, 9, 28 and 32 days respectively. Constantinople intercepts may be found in the Hardinge papers and the PRO FO 371 series.

27. The cipher expert's name was Jeffery (no relation). Lord Rawlinson (CinC India) to Sir Henry Wilson (Chief of the Imperial General Staff), 3 and 23 December 1920, Wilson MSS (Imperial War Museum), HHW 2/13C/3 and 9.

28. The information in this section owes much to the excellent account of the Near Eastern peace settlement in Michael L. Dockrill and J. Douglas Goold, *Peace without Promise: Britain and the Peace conferences 1919–23* (London, 1981), chapter 5.

29. Strategic aspects of British Near Eastern policy are discussed in Keith Jeffery, *The British Army and the Crisis of Empire, 1918–1922* (Manchester, 1984), pp. 40–4.

30. Calogeropoulos, London, to Minister for Foreign Affairs, Athens, 1 March 1921 (intercept), Curzon Papers, MSS. Eur. F.112/319. At the Prime Minister's bidding, the Cabinet Secretary, Sir Maurice Hankey, delivered a similar message to the Greek delegation on 9 March. Stephen Roskill, *Hankey: Man of Secrets*, II (London, 1972), p. 222.

31. Roskill, ibid., p. 223.

32. Dockrill and Goold, *Peace without Promise*, pp. 219–21.

33. Christopher Andrew and A. S. Kanya-Forstner, *France overseas: the Great War and the climax of French imperial expansion* (London, 1981), p. 223.

34. Harington to Sir Henry Wilson, 13 July 1921, in Keith Jeffery (ed.), *The Military Correspondence of Field Marshal Sir Henry Wilson 1918–1922* (London, 1985), p. 285.

35. Rattigan to Curzon, 14 July 1921, *Documents on British Foreign Policy 1919–39*, First Series (henceforth *DBFP*), XVII, no. 305.

36. Sir Milne Cheetham (Paris) to M. Briand, 10 July 1921, ibid., no. 298.

37. Cheetham to Curzon, 16 July 1921, ibid., no. 309.

38. Rattigan to Curzon, 14 June 1921, ibid., no. 228.

39. Harington to Wilson, 4 August 1921, Wilson Papers (Imperial War Museum) HHW 2/46B/20.

40. Rumbold to Curzon, 20 September 1921, *DBFP*, XVII, no. 388.

41. Curzon to Hardinge, 30 September 1921, *DBFP*, XVII no. 398.

42. Curzon to Hardinge, 3 November 1921, *DBFP*, XVII, no.432.

43. Curzon's description: H. A. L. Fisher diary, 1 November 1921, Fisher MSS (Bodleian Library, Oxford).

44. Andrew and Kanya-Forstner, *France Overseas* p. 223; Curzon reviewed the treaty in a letter to Hardinge, 3 November 1921, *DBFP*, XVII, no. 432.

45. Most probably an intercepted message between Constantinople and Angora.

46. Rumbold to Curzon, 21 February 1922, *DBFP* XVII, no. 540.

47. The Paris meetings are covered in *DBFP*, XVII, chapter IV.

48. Curzon to Hardinge, 10 May 1922, *DBFP*, XVII, no. 627

49. Curzon to Hardinge, 2 May 1922, enclosing intercept of Ferid, Paris, to Minister of Foreign Affairs, Constantinople, 4 April 1922, Hardinge Papers (Cambridge University Library) vol. 45.

50. Ibid.

51. Hardinge to Curzon, 5 May 1922, Ibid., vol. 45. Curzon also believed that the Italians were about to make a separate treaty with Kemal.

52. Rumbold to Curzon, 5 April 1922, *DBFP*, XVII, no. 583. The timing of the Turkish response may have been related to the receipt of Poincaré's assurance on 4 April.

53. Rumbold to Curzon, 23 April 1922, *DBFP*, XVII, no. 603.

54. Ibid., no. 604.

55. Curzon minute, *DBFP*, XVII, no. 639 n. 7.

56. From 25 May until 10 August 1922.

57. Balfour to Hardinge, 7 June 1922, *DBFP*, XVII, no. 645.

58. Mr Oliphant (Foreign Office) to the Secretary to the Army Council, 13 July 1922, with references to Foreign Office letter of 27 May and Army Council reply of 5 July, *DBFP*, XVII, no. 684.

59. Rumbold to Curzon, 21 August 1922, *DBFP*, XVII, no. 738. The Foreign Office were also constrained by the fact that British companies were supplying war materials to the Greeks.

60. Curzon to Hardinge, 29 August 1922, *DBFP*, XVII, no. 746.

61. Hardinge to Curzon, 20 August 1922, ibid., no. 750.

62. Rumbold to 'Dear Mamma' (stepmother), 20 September 1922, Rumbold MSS (Bodleian Library, Oxford) Dep. 30.

63. J. Douglas Goold has gathered together the various accounts of this incident in his 'Lord Hardinge as Ambassador to France, and the Anglo-French dilemma over Germany and the Near East, 1920–1922', *The Historical Journal*, vol. 21 (1978), pp. 932–3.

64. Rumbold to Oliphant, 18 July 1923, Rumbold MSS Dep. 30.

65. Others have followed this analogy, for example: 'The Marquess [Curzon] played a Yarboro with dignity—some said brilliance—while Turkey took the tricks'. Lord Vansittart, *The Mist Procession* (London, 1958), p. 298.

66. Rumbold to Curzon, 19 July 1923, and Foreign Office telegrams of 16 and 20 July 1923, *DBFP*, XVIII, no. 680, and nn. 3 and 7.

67. Rumbold to Curzon, 12 May 1923, Rumbold MSS, Dep. 31.

68. Foreign Office telegram of 30 May 1923, *DBFP*, XVIII, no. 570 n. 5.

69. Curzon to Grace Curzon, 1 January 1923, Curzon Papers MSS Eur. F.112/797. Bonar Law had written to Curzon on 7 December 1922; 'As regards the position in Mesopotamia of course what I would like is some method of getting out of it altogether'. Ibid., F.112/282.

70. Curzon to Sir Eyre Crowe, 12 January 1923, *DBFP*, XVIII, no. 323.

71. Henderson to Rumbold, and reply, 21 and 28 November 1922, Rumbold MSS Dep. 30. On 19 November Henderson had reported that 'after prolonged secret session, in which apparently only 162 Deputies participated, telegrams from Angora state that Grand National Assembly elected Crown Prince Abdul Majid by 148 votes, Selim getting three and Abdul Raham two'. *DBFP*, XVIII, no. 214.

72. Henderson to Rumbold, 5 December 1922, Rumbold MSS Dep. 30.

73. Secret Political Report, S.I.S. Misc/26, 21 February 1923. Curzon initialled the file containing this report on 23 February. PRO FO 371/9121 E2083.

74. Rumbold to Curzon, 2 June 1923, Rumbold MSS Dep. 31.

75. Henderson to Curzon, 25 December 1922, *DBFP*, XVIII, no. 291.

76. These principally concerned the control of the Straits and the position of foreign minorities within Turkey.

77. Curzon to Crowe, 26 December 1922, PRO FO 371/7967 E14392; also *DBFP*, XVIII, no. 292.

78. Rumbold to Henderson, 26 December 1922, Rumbold MSS Dep. 30.

79. GHQ, Constantinople, to War Office no. 3310, 25 December 1922, enclosing intercept Ismet to Angora (23 December), PRO FO 371/7967 E14392.

80. Minute by Mr Lindsay, 27 December 1922, ibid.

81. GHQ, Constantinople, to War Office no. 3307, 25 December 1922, enclosing intercept Ismet to Angora (23 December), ibid.

82. GHQ, Constantinople, to War Office no. 3276, 22 December 1922, enclosing intercept Angora to Ismet (20 December), ibid.

83. GHQ, Constantinople, to War Office no. 3313, 25 December 1922, enclosing intercept Ismet to Angora (18 December), ibid.

84. Minute by Curzon, 28 December 1922, ibid.

85. Curzon to Crowe, 5 January 1923, *DBFP*, XVIII, no. 311.

86. Curzon to Crowe, 13 January 1923, ibid., no. 326.

87. Rumbold to Henderson, 16 January 1923, Rumbold MSS Dep. 30.

88. Curzon to Lindsay, 1 February 1923, and to Crewe, 23 February 1923, *DBFP*, XVIII, nos. 358 and 362.

89. Amery to Curzon, 2 February 1923, Curzon Papers MSS Eur F.112/282. Amery received intercepts by virtue of being Colonial Secretary.

90. Rumbold to Henderson, 30 January 1923, Rumbold MSS Dep. 30.

91. Harington telegram of 28 January 1923 and Henderson to Curzon, 28 January 1923, *DBFP*, XVIII, n. 348 and n. 1.

92. Cabinet minutes 30 January 1923, PRO CAB 23/45/4(23).

93. Curzon to Lindsay, 30 January 1923, *DBFP*, XVIII, no. 353.

94. Rumbold to Henderson, 30 January 1923, Rumbold MSS Dep. 30.

95. Henderson to Lindsay, 30 January 1923, *DBFP*, XVIII, no. 354.

96. Amery to Curzon, 15 December 1922, Curzon Papers, MSS Eur F.112/282.

97. Cabinet minutes, 6 February 1923, PRO CAB 23/45/7(23).

98. Curzon to Crowe, 26 December 1922, *DBFP*, XVIII, no. 292.

99. Harington to War Office, repeated Lausanne, PRO WO 106/1430; also *DBFP*, XVIII, no. 291 n. 3.

100. See cover for 'Conference File 79' in PRO FO 371/7967 E14392.

101. Harington to Curzon, 13 January 1923, Curzon Papers MSS Eur. F.112/283.

102. Colonel A. W. F. Baird (military attaché, Constantinople embassy) to Rumbold, 23 January 1923, Rumbold MSS Dep. 30.

103. See, for example, *DBFP*, XVIII, nos. 571 n. 3, 580 n. 4, 581 n. 15.

104. Rumbold to Henderson, 17 July 1923, Rumbold MSS Dep. 31.

105. Rumbold to Curzon, 2 June 1923, ibid.

106. Minute by Mr Osborne, 25 July 1923, *DBFP*, XVIII, no. 683 n. 5.

107. Curzon to Crewe, 13 October 1923, Crewe MSS (Cambridge University Library) C/12.

108. Baldwin to Curzon, 12 November 1923, Curzon Papers MSS Eur F.112/320.

109. Curzon to Crewe, 12 December 1923, Crewe MSS C/12.

110. Christopher Andrew, 'Codebreakers and Foreign Offices: the French, British and American experience', in Christopher Andrew and David Dilks (eds), *The Missing Dimension* (London, 1984), p. 46.

111. Lord Ronaldshay, *The Life of Lord Curzon* III (London, 1928), p. 368.

112. In Harold Nicolson, *Curzon: the Last Phase* (London, 1934), there is an entry in the index under 'Curzon's personality' for 'lack of acute sense of proportion'.

113. See Alan Sharp, 'The Foreign Office in Eclipse 1919–22', *History*, 61 (1976), pp. 198–211.

114. The profligate publication of secret intelligence material relating to Soviet Russia is discussed in detail in Christopher Andrew, 'The British Secret Service and Anglo–Soviet relations in the 1920s', *The Historical Journal*, 20 (1977), pp. 673–706.

115. Rumbold to Henderson, 8 January 1923, Rumbold MSS Dep. 30.

116. Quoted in Harold Nicolson, *Some People* (London, 1947), p. 167.

Japanese Intelligence, 1894–1922

IAN NISH

Much writing on intelligence is, as we should expect, in invisible ink. This is certainly true of Japan. Academic studies published in Japan about her own intelligence are few in number and largely devoted to the role of intelligence in the war of 1941–5. This neglect is probably due to the burning of military documents in Japan in 1945 and to the fact that such documents as remained were taken thereafter to Washington, though they were subsequently returned. In view of the recent worldwide interest in intelligence matters, there is a fresh enthusiasm for the subject in Japan and scholars will be producing the basic studies before long.[1]

The organization of intelligence in Japan could not be placed on a systematic basis until 1907, the year that the Imperial Defence Plan (*teikoku kokubō hōshin*) was accepted. There had of course been *ad hoc* arrangements for information-gathering and analysis at an earlier date. But it was understood after 1907 that the 'enemy contemplated' by the army would be Russia, while that contemplated by the navy would be the United States. This made the task much easier for the general staffs in both services who were responsible for intelligence matters rather than the ministries. The army general staff through its Second Bureau (*Dai-ni-bu*) concentrated on Russia, while it tended to neglect the United States. The general staff of the navy which was more of a technical service developed wide-ranging information sources on the United States but was correspondingly ill-informed about Russia. There was in our period no effective liaison body to coordinate intelligence between the two general staffs in peacetime. On the more specialized aspect of codes, the navy established a department to deal with them during the Russo–Japanese war but it lapsed with the return of peace. There was also an office devoted to code matters (*fugō jimu*) within the telegraphic section of the Foreign Ministry from the the end of our period.

That ministry had also a *Jōhōbu* though this was probably more concerned with information from overt sources than with secret intelligence.

Our account of the Japanese intelligence community will range over five wars. Three of these wars—the Sino–Japanese war of 1894–5, the Boxer expedition of 1900 and the land campaigns of the 1914 war—were fought on Chinese soil, while the other two were fought with Russia in 1904–5 and 1918–22. In all these contests Japan believed that she had to compensate for her lack of manpower and resources by other means. One of these means was intelligence. The Japanese justified their efforts to obtain information by covert means because of the basic weakness of the state. Nowadays we are more familiar with the opposite argument: that the great powers, especially the superpowers, maintain the most elaborate intelligence services because it is a mark of the strength of the state. Japan, however, felt herself to be unequal to Russia and the other powers around the turn of the century.

Are the Japanese good at intelligence? There are various factors which suggest that they should be. By the late nineteenth century, the Japanese had a good standard of general education at all levels of society, in addition to their traditional reputation for observation and analysis. They had become intrepid travellers and showed themselves to be full of energy and curiosity, their high sense of loyalty to their state and community made them reticent, reserved and perhaps secretive; and remarkably few secrets of state leaked out. We may illustrate this with the words of Sir Robert Craigie, the British ambassador to Japan, who addressed the Foreign Office on 22 October 1941 as follows:

> It would be unsafe to assume too confidently that Japan does not want a campaign in the South at present. The Japanese have a genius for secrecy.[2]

This remark was really addressed through the Foreign Office to Winston Churchill who seemed to Craigie to be taking a remarkably favourable view of the Japanese and their ambitions. The fact that Craigie's language was so guarded suggests that a major military secret of the Japanese had been well kept until very late in the day.

The Japanese are best at intelligence operations on their home ground. It used to be the case that only a minority of Japanese were good at European languages. So the Japanese sphere of intelligence interest tended to be Asia and the Pacific. Within that broad area Japanese are naturally at an advantage in China, Korea, the frontier regions of the north-east of Asia and in Vietnam, and the countries of south-east Asia. There they had the ability to merge with the countryside and avoid ready detection. This article covers the period of the Shina Rōnin, agents who wandered around China making contacts, picking up information and often stirring up trouble for the government.[3]

I have spent some time investigating the origins of secret intelligence in Japan. My initial suspicion was that intelligence was something learnt by the Japanese army and navy from their foreign instructors, Germany and Britain respectively. Major Jacob Meckel went to Japan in January 1885 for three years to teach at the military academy, to instruct groups of senior officers and to attend manoeuvres. It would appear that Meckel and his French predecessors did not follow a curriculum which schooled the Japanese in intelligence. Meckel himself was the author of manuals on tactics and his teaching method emphasized that side of the military art.[4] The explanation may be that the German army at the time did not dwell very much on information-gathering and that the Japanese officers did not have much to learn from European instructors. This is probably true of the British naval teaching mission as well. In 1873 Commander Archibald Douglas with 33 other officers and men led a mission to the Imperial Naval College in Tokyo. But the British team, we are told, were concerned with seafaring and training at sea, not to say encouraging sports and insisting on good mess manners.[5] So intelligence would not appear to have been one of the conspicuous imports of Japan in the nineteenth century. Its origins probably have to be looked for in something indigenous. It may well have arisen naturally from the customs and practices which developed over the war-torn feudal centuries: there was always the need for spies, for information-gatherers and for purveyors of secrets. After their long experience of feudal rule, the Japanese had enough native cunning and enough organizations so that they needed little instruction from foreigners about intelligence methods.

After these introductory speculations, let us turn to case-studies, based on the wars Japan fought for the security of her empire.

THE SINO-JAPANESE WAR 1894-5

In 1894-5 Japan entered the war with China without a great deal of confidence. Her diffidence was shared by the powers whose sympathies were with Peking and who did not in the main foresee that China's defeat would be of such catastrophic proportions in both the land and sea campaigns. The Japanese felt that they had to make up for their inferiority in numbers in comparison with China's army estimated at 720,000 men (wartime strength) by exploiting the lessons of intelligence. The 'father of Japanese intelligence', General Fukushima Yasumasa, was active in the China field. He had himself been posted to China as a young attaché. After his return from a spell in Germany in 1892 he arranged for many scouting expeditions in China. In June 1894, just before the outbreak of war, Fukushima, then an officer on the general staff, was travelling in Korea collecting up-to-date information. His concern was not only with the narrow problem of China but also with the likelihood of intervention by the powers. Fukushima's view was that Russia's military strength was weak and that it was beyond her ability to intervene militarily in the peninsula. On the other hand, he informed his master, General Yamagata Aritomo, that the government of China was very weak and flabby and liable to be browbeaten by outside powers. Fukushima was to act as chief of staff of the First Army during the war and was insistent on the need for a detailed assessment of the weak points of Japan's gigantic neighbour.[6] It would appear that in the lead-up to the China war and during its course a number of secret societies which interested themselves in Japan's role in Asia, were collecting intelligence. For example, Miyazaki Tōten had been active in China as well as south-east Asia since the early 1880s, probably with subventions of funds from the government. He was certainly active in information-gathering and cultivating relationships with disaffected elements in China. It is impossible to say what weight his reports carried with the authorities. But, if an unlikely character like Miyazaki could do this, how many more were active as civilian information-gatherers?[7]

It was of course Korea, the independent kingdom which had a tributary relationship with China and where Japan and China had struggled since the early 1880s, that was the cause of the trouble. If fighting were to take place, it would be in the Korean peninsula. One of the key officials during the war, General Kawakami Sōroku (1848–99), who was to serve as deputy chief of the general staff, made an intelligence ride in Korea in the spring of 1893 and allegedly came back with the conviction that Japan must have security in the peninsula. He was to be followed by other intelligence officers. The result was that Japan was able to do accurate advance planning:

> Every road in Korea and the adjacent portions of China had been mapped by intelligence agents long before the war and necessary material assembled down to the most Prussian detail.[8]

This is probably not an exaggerated assessment of the degree of Japan's preparedness for a military campaign.

The reports of the intelligence officers were a vital factor in Japan's decision for war, which was a hotly disputed issue during the months of June and July. The Japanese had in the main decided that, if China were to increase the number of her troops in the peninsula, they would match the force sent. Opinions differed on how aggressive China's mood was at that time. The naval attaché, First Lieutenant (*taii*) Takigawa Tomokazu, posted mainly in Tientsin, took the view that the Chinese leaders wanted to avoid a clash with Japan and did not wish to send a large force. The navy in Tokyo was, therefore, reluctant to see an excessive force sent over to Chinese waters. The military attaché at the Japanese legation in Peking, who was more senior, took a different line. He was Major Kamio Mitsuomi (1855–1927), who appears later in this essay as commanding general for the force which gained the surrender of Tsingtao in 1914. His reports played up China's desire to send increased forces to Korea and to open hostilities there with Japan. Kamio's messages were music to the ear of Kawakami who was able to present them in their entirety to the emperor in his position as deputy chief of the general staff.[9] It appears however that he withheld all these materials from the prime minister and foreign minister and showed them only materials which indicated the necessity for war. The result was that the members of the cabinet formed an appreciation of the situation on the basis of information (*jōhō*) supplied by the general staff which was slanted, if not positively in error. The emperor was in possession of more comprehensive and accurate intelligence in his capacity as commander-in-chief than his ministers.

Japanese scholars are inclined to conclude that the naval intelligence officers gave a more accurate appraisal of China's intentions and that their army counterparts were inclined to supply reports heavily weighted in favour of war. It goes beyond the scope of this article to assess which was closer to China's true feelings. But enough has been said to indicate the suspicions entertained about the accuracy of some of the telegrams which were received from intelligence officers in the field. Even at the Tokyo end, intelligence material was distributed in such a way as to secure the success of one or other party, the pro-war lobby or the strong foreign policy group (*taigaikōha*), and to achieve a predictable outcome.

It should not be a surprise that the army line should differ from the navy line. The navy which was still regarded in 1894 as the junior service, was always anxious to show that it could not be taken for granted. Whenever, as in the case of the Sino–Japanese war, an expeditionary force had to be sent overseas, the navy could prove to be difficult. In order to overcome this, the army minister called for the creation of the wartime Imperial Headquarters (*senji Dai-Hon'ei*) and this was done on 5 June, almost two months before the start of the war on 1 August. It was a means of coordinating the activities of the army and navy in the field of operations and intelligence, this being the first occasion on which the institution was used.[10] But even after it came into being, there were devasting criticisms of the army by the navy. Thus, at the end of June, an admiral claimed that the army had demanded far too many ships to be sent to Inchon, the port of Seoul, and that this had made it seem to world opinion like an actual war.[11]

General Yamagata, one of the makers of the new model army in Japan, shows the influence of intelligence in one of his writings. In an unusual English language source, his article on the Japanese army in the publication *Japan by the Japanese*, he writes as follows:

> It was owing to the accurate knowledge which I had obtained as to the conditions of affairs in North China that it was possible to lay the plans of the campaign as to surely and safely bring about the complete victory of our forces.

He discovered inter alia the great difference between the reported strength of the Chinese army and its actual strength in the field.

> The Chinese army was divided into *yees*, or battalions, which were supposed to consist of 500 men. In reality, however, they rarely ever consisted of more than 300 or 350 men. The commander of the *yee*, or camp, was in this way enabled to pocket the pay of 200 or 150 of his soldiers from the Government grants.[12]

Japanese intelligence had discovered not just the military weaknesses of China in this way but equally her political weaknesses. In a sense it was the intelligence they had received that gave the Japanese confidence to take up arms against the vastness of China.

The war was followed by three-power (*Dreibund*) intervention. After the treaty of Shimonoseki on 17 April 1895, Russia, France and Germany pressed Japan to return to China the Liaotung peninsula which she had acquired by the treaty. This gave rise to an emergency intelligence operation of a different kind from those directed earlier at China. The Japanese fleet was at the time still in the south capturing the Pescadores islands, though it was swiftly recalled and reached Sasebo base on 5 May, badly in need of re-fitting. It was a matter of urgency, therefore, for Japan to find out the location of the fleets of the powers, especially the Russian fleet.[13]

Efforts were made at Vladivostok, at Kobe and at Chefoo to find out what the Russian ships' movements were. Since it was the custom for Russian men of war to dock in Japanese ports, the Japanese set out to intercept the orders which their commanders were given. They did indeed discover that the men of war were under orders to leave port at twenty-four hours notice. At all events the intercepts looked sufficiently menacing for the Japanese government to give in on 4 May, the day before her squadron returned. Thus hostilities were avoided.

For the Japanese this was unquestionably a humiliating defeat, all the more serious and disappointing after her resounding victory over China. Why did the Japanese nerve crack in the face of threats from the three powers? The answer is that it did not, Japan handled the crisis in a cool and calculating manner, parrying the 'friendly advice' of the three powers with partial concessions. Her eventual capitulation was the result of a lot of intelligence work conducted systematically: her estimate of the positioning to the ships of Russia, France and Germany and her assessment of the likely consequences if Japan refused the demands. While it is still possible to speculate that Japan might have successfully called the bluff of the three powers and got away with it if she had continued to prevaricate, her leaders decided quite logically and rationally in favour of concessions to China's Great Power protectors, even though they were determined not to show their weakness to China herself.[14]

THE RUSSO–JAPANESE WAR, 1904–5

With the defeat of China in 1895, the military problem of the Far East changed from Japan. It was no longer the menace of China but the menace of Russia that was uppermost in the minds of her statesmen. General Yanagata passes over the Boxer Rebellion of 1900 which rocked Europe at the time with these remarks:

> Even as late as the Boxer disturbances, this state of corruption in the Chinese army did not seem to be known clearly to the world, although it was vital as creating an important difference between the paper and actual strength of the Chinese forces.[15]

In other words, Japanese intelligence concluded that China's army was less alarming and less menacing than Western intelligence allowed. Still Japan did take part in the international expedition which relieved the Peking legations.

After the humiliation of China in 1900, there developed a struggle between Japan and Russia over Korea and Manchuria. In that struggle, Russia seemed to the Japanese to hold the master card, a railway network linking the area with Europe. This was vital in an age when railways were the key to military success. An earlier generation had seen the problem of Korea as 'a dagger to the heart of Japan'. With the opening of the Chinese Eastern railway to traffic in 1902, the dagger carried the extra thrust from the railway artery which gave it strength. In other words, the Russians could from 1902 onwards bring troops from European bases relatively quickly (say, in two weeks) to Mukden, Port Arthur or Vladivostok. While this did not give them the capacity to send troops quickly to Korea, the primary area of territorial dispute at the time, it did greatly improve Russia's security in Manchuria. The pool of troops on which the Russian military authorities might draw was estimated at just over one million (in peacetime) and about 4,600,000 men (in wartime). When these figures are set alongside the strength of the Japanese army of 632,000 in total mobilisation, the extent of Japan's intelligence problem can be readily seen.

Even more than in 1894, the Japanese leaders felt unequal to the struggle which was inevitably developing with Russia. The general staff concluded that the only approach for Japan was to gain command of the seas between Japan and the Asian mainland, send the main part of her forces quickly to the Korean front, and thence move to annihilate Russia's forces before her main troops in Europe could be concentrated on the east Asian front. It was the task of naval intelligence to assess how close Japan was to command of the seas at a time when Russia was increasing her west Pacific squadrons. As in 1895 much could be learnt about Russian naval movements because they were still dependent for wintering on ports like Nagasaki. The Japanese took heart from the fact that the Russian Pacific squadron appeared to be widely scattered on the eve of the war and to have made little attempt at concentration in the area of likely hostilities.[16]

In 1904–5 Japanese intelligence was not restricted as in 1894–5 to east Asia; its activities extended also to Europe. At the European end, it had taken pains from 1898 onwards to train army and navy experts, who returned to Japan in 1903 to plan the campaigns against Russia. Others like Colonel Akashi, the military attaché in St Petersburg, tried to support the movements in Finland and Poland for independence from Russia and continued to do this from Stockholm after the Japanese legation was evacuated from the Russian capital. This was a bold and sophisticated initiative which sought to attack the flabby under-belly of Russia. How far it detained crack troops in Europe and prevented them joining an expeditionary force to the far east in the initial stages of the war is less easy to say. But this was a dominant political issue over which the tsarist regime was very sensitive and it may well have made them reluctant to consign large numbers of first-rate troops to the east when war broke out.[17]

There was also a sophisticated information-gathering network in China, Korea and Manchuria. At the Chinese capital there was the notorious Major Aoki Nobuzumi, the official side of military intelligence with widespread units for spying under him. More important for the war with Russia were conditions in Manchuria where the exploits of Ishimitsu Makiyo are probably representative of individual efforts. He moved around as trader, laundryman, photographer and barber and managed to insinuate his way into the goodwill of the Russians from time to time.[18] The result was that the Japanese army at the start of the war had a not inaccurate notion of the number of troops which the Russians were bringing, and could bring, along their strategic single-track line. The British thought that the Japanese had agents at every railway station in Manchuria and were complimentary about their proficiency.

As in the Sino-Japanese war, the material which came in from agents abroad seems to have been used fairly unscrupulously by those who favoured the coming of an early war with Russia. In a famous episode Colonel Tanaka in the General Staff deliberately distorted the number of trains—and hence the number of troops—that Russia could bring from Europe to the east. The selective use of this secret material was on this occasion less significant since the overwhelming weight of Japanese opinion was in favour of risking war against the Russians.[19]

ENTRACTE BETWEEN THE WARS

In 1907, Japan for the first time laid down a National Defence Policy. It contained no mention of intelligence. Its objective was to encourage a coordinated approach to military planning. It was a considerable innovation though its objective of integrating the policies and attitudes of the scarce resources continued and reached a peak of fury around 1912–13 when the navy came into the ascendant though it lost public credibility and support soon after because of the serious Siemens shipbuilding bribery scandal. The Defence Policy defined the focal point for the army as Russia, which was still expected in some Japanese circles to contemplate a war of revenge against Japan, and for the navy as the United States. Because of the Russian fears, much of the intelligence activity in the decade following the Russo–Japanese war still took place in Manchuria, Mongolia and the frontiers of Siberia.[20]

After Japan defeated Russia, she enjoyed a wave of popularity and admiration in Asia. Many of the more adventurous Asian families in seeking higher education for their sons looked to Japan. This applied to Chinese, Indians and Vietnamese who came in significant numbers to Japanese universities and in some cases military academies. Since these men were often destined to become key figures in their countries' nationalist movements, many Japanese, though rarely the Japanese government, chose to associate with them privately. The relationship was established through individuals (like Uchida Ryōhei and Kita Ikki), through patriotic societies like the Kokuryūkai (Amur river society) or through the army. In the case of Indochina, this affected Cuong De, a member of the Vietnamese royal family, who stayed in Japan between 1906 and 1909 and joined the movements there. He remained pro-Japanese for the rest of his career. Thanks to the cooperation of Japanese intelligence officers in China after 1937, he was to establish a group for associating Vietnamese émigrés with China and Thailand.[21] Important figures in Chinese politics also associated themselves with the Japanese in their struggle to rid themselves of the Ching dynasty. These included Dr Sun Yat-sen and Liang Chi'i-ch'ao on the political side and Tsao Ju-lin on the financial side.[22]

As a result of the contacts thus forged, Japan—and especially Japanese military intelligence—found herself drawn into the politics of Asia. Japanese official policy was to maintain the status quo in Asia; but many unofficial Japanese became involved in the politics of European colonies there and more were involved in the revolutionary outbreaks in China in 1911 and 1913. These activities were nominally unofficial but the main organizers were not too remote from Japanese government leaders. There were three important intelligence officers: Colonel (later General) Aoki Nobuzumi, military attaché at the Peking legation who was active before and during the Russo–Japanese war; Colonel (later General) Banzai, Richachirō, one-time military adviser to the Chinese republic who gave his name to 'Banzai Mansion', an intelligence training-point for Japanese in China which operated on a semi-official basis; and, a pupil and associate of Banzai, Colonel (later General) Doihara Kenji, who came to specialize in Manchuria. All three gave disbursements to pro-Japanese elements and possibly also arms and ammunition. They all enjoyed long periods of China service.[23]

Naturally these activities were not popular with the law and order authorities of China or of European colonies. In China the Ching dynasty and the republic under Yuan looked on Japan as subversive. In the European colonies in south-east Asia Japanese came under close police and immigration scrutiny. In Australia where Japanese subversion was linked with the problem of immigration, there were many rumours of far-reaching Japanese plans. When a Japanese touring party visited Queensland with their cameras in 1907 and photographed all manner of things, there was consternation and official complaint.[24]

An interesting source on Japanese military intelligence for this period which happens to be available in the United Kingdom is the set of reports entitled *Kaigai jōhō* (intelligence overseas). These are available in the library of the School of Oriental and African Studies, University of London, for the years 1907–8. They form part of an ongoing series issued by the Army General Staff. *Kaigai jōhō* was a monthly periodical in printed form which was not published but circulated on a confidential basis for the purpose of reference and teaching at military academies, staff colleges etc. It was marked '*hi*' (secret) and therefore comes relatively low in the scale of confidentiality for intelligence material. It was nonetheless a detailed and significant production: it ran from 100 to 150 pages per month and the reports could extend from one page to fifty pages.

The reports themselves cover army developments and relevant political and economic trends in all the countries of the world. The tendency is to emphasize the countries of Europe, especially Russia and Japan's ally, Britain, and the United States, and to focus on their colonial territories in east Asia. Thus there are large enquiries into fortifications in the Philippines, Russian railway building in Asia, developments on the north-west frontier of India, political changes in Thailand and perhaps most detailed on French Indochina. It would appear that these reports emanated from countries where there were Japanese military attachés or officers assigned for special language duties. They are unsigned, except for an enquiry by Colonel Shiba Gōrō, the military attaché at the London embassy, into local military manoeuvres in the United Kingdom. At a time when so much intelligence effort was being made in China and Asia generally, it is striking that much interest was also being shown in the affairs of the wider world. Even the Balkan problems which might be considered to be remote from Japan's national interests, receives fairly detailed coverage. There is also a particular supplement, published in 1908, which was devoted to military prospects in south American countries, connected with the special 'visit of inspection' by Major Itami. It covered Guiana, Venezuela, Colombia, Ecuador, Peru, Bolivia, Chile, Paraguay and Brazil.

THE JAPANESE–GERMAN WAR, 1914–18

The war on which Japan embarked in August 1914 was not a first-class war. '*Nichi-Doku sensō*' (Japan's war with Germany) is how the Japanese—or at least the Japanese army—commonly described it. The war of 1914 did not stand comparison with the Russo–Japanese war or the Sino–Japanese war. The Japanese did not see the necessity to set up an Imperial Headquarters (*Dai-Hon'ei*) as had been done without question in 1904 and 1894. This was a mark of the lesser significance which Japan attached to events outside the Pacific perimeter at that time.

For Japan the war consisted of land campaigns against the German leased territory in China (Kiaochow-Tsingtao) and various sea campaigns in the Pacific ocean, extending later into the Indian Ocean and the Mediterranean. Intelligence did not play a great part in any of them. Unlike 1894 and 1904 when intelligence preparations had been under way well in advance of the war, the decision of August 1914 in favour of war seems to have been an afterthought—a last-minute attempt to seize a convenient opportunity—and there is little evidence of advance intelligence work. Since German strength in the area was slight, the Japanese did not have to compensate for inferiority by using subversion or other methods of political intelligence.

So far as the land campaign against Tsingtao is concerned, the official army history makes little mention of intelligence. Indeed the campaign was not waged in ideal conditions and was not a spectacular success. But, after the German base of Tsingtao surrendered to General Kamio on 7 November, there was the problem of occupying the former German territory which Japan determined to retain till the end of the war. For this period, the official history writes of a limited use of intelligence work: Japan had to set up the *Santō tetsudō teisatsutai* (reconnaisance units for the Shantung railway). This was not of course to be an anti-German unit, but a group to protect the new Japanese-occupied railway against sabotage by the Chinese.[25]

The sea campaign against the German Pacific squadron has been criticized for the poor use of intelligence. The German squadron under Admiral von Spee which was based on Tsingtao boldly escaped from its haven and sailed around the central Pacific. Falk writes:

> German naval interference should have been eliminated more quickly than it was. . . . The Japanese omitted to shadow [the escaping German squadron], even by intelligence reports, during July 1914. When war broke out, Spee was lost to allied contact in the Carolines.[26]

This criticism pre-supposes that Japan was committed to active involvement on the side of the allies well before the outbreak of war. This was not so. At the same time it was a telling failure for Britain and Japan alike that the German squadron was able to escape.

While the Imperial Japanese Navy did take part in the European sector of the First World War in its last stages, the Japanese army did not. It declined to send troops to the Western Front—or indeed the Eastern Front—during the war years. Because it did not take up the various invitations received from the allies, it did not pick up the new skills which develop so fast under war conditions. So, as the late Captain Malcolm Kennedy who went from the Western Front to witness Japanese manoeuvres in 1917 observed, the

Japanese had fallen progressively behind military developments in the west.[27] This does not mean that the Japanese services were unrepresented at the battles in Europe. There were intelligence missions, which, if they were few, were of high quality and tended to consist of high-flyers. This is a controversial point. Some Western experts hold that these military observers on the Western Front were very ineffective, others feel that they made a substantial contribution to later developments in their services. Professor Peattie writes:

> . . . the army began to be aware of the need to grasp the new military technology. In 1917 a research division (*gunji chōsabu*) had been established in the War Ministry to cull information from the European combat theater and by 1920, after the comprehensive reports and commentaries by Japanese observers of the war had been assimilated, the research section of the Infantry School at Chiba had launched a serious study of the tactical lessons involved. To those younger officers who had seen modern war at first hand from their positions as military observers or attachés in Europe, and who were disturbed at the growing obsolescence of the Japanese army, such initiatives gave hope for a modernization effort. . . .[28]

The purpose of these observers was not just to learn the lessons of the allies but also to observe the shortcomings of the German army on which their own forces had in large measure been patterned. It has to be said that the modernization which was dreamt of was limited by the military retrenchment policies of Japanese governments of the 1920s.

Soon after the armistice was announced, the Japanese army general staff (*sambō hombu*) intimated that it wanted to send an intelligence mission to Germany. This mission of inspection (*gunji shisatsudan*) was evidently something which the other powers had not intended. When approached, they raised no objections, though they were not too pleased at Japan jumping the gun. The mission was made up of military officers but was guided by the Foreign Ministry official, Tōgō Shigenori, later to be foreign minister at two critical times in the 1940s. The mission reached Berlin on 17 April 1919 and laid its objectives before the German Foreign Ministry: to arrange for the release of Japanese prisoners of war who were in captivity in Germany and to assess the political situation there. Since there were no Japanese prisoners of war in Germany, the first item lapsed. On the second, the German side offered full cooperation to the inspection party which duly reported to Tokyo.[29]

SIBERIAN INTERVENTION, 1918–22

The Bolshevik revolution supplied the Japanese military with a positive outlet for their intelligence skills. Since the Russo–Japanese war, the Japanese had a network of information-gathering in Manchuria, Korea,

China and Siberia. There is no doubt that the Japanese wanted to prevent the contagion of Bolshevism spreading to Japan or their colony in Korea. Since developments in Vladivostok were serious from the end of 1917, they foresaw that it might require a full-scale expeditionary force if the tide of Bolshevism was to be turned back. It was necessary therefore to make advance preparations in the intelligence field. To this end, the general staff, under the influence of General Tanaka Giichi, its vice-chief, decided to send Major-General Nakajima Masatake, its intelligence chief, to Vladivostok with a view to establishing a ring of pro-Japanese and anti-Bolshevik sympathizers. Nakajima, a Russian linguist, had just returned from assignment in Petrograd, from which he had been observing the Russian war effort. He built up a team of officers, including Major Ishimitsu Makiyo, who wandered around Vladivostok, Blagovestchensk and Harbin, making contacts with right-wing leaders who were ready to dam the currents from the west. To this end the Japanese offered arms, cash and technical advice but they steered clear of sending forces. This was because of the known opposition of the United States to a Japanese expedition and the division within the ranks of policy-makers in Japan herself. In this period down to August 1918 there was plenty of activity, of negotiation with the resistance leaders like Semenov, Khorvat and Kolchak, but there was little tangible result to show for it.

After August the allied intervention took place and the intelligence problem changed. It was no longer aimed against the Bolsheviks but also against the Chinese, the Koreans and the 'allies'. The war years had left a legacy of distrust; and Japan was anxious to know what the various allies were up to in Siberia, an anxiety which was fully reciprocated.

An interesting and revealing source is the history of the Japanese military police in the Siberian intervention. The military police in Japan as elsewhere inevitably had an intelligence role to perform. The history defines their various duties and devotes a section to their intelligence activities. It states that intelligence (*chōhō*) in the Siberian Expeditionary force was the responsibility of army *tokumu kikan* (special service units) in every area. Among the officers attached to these *kikan* and the general staff at the headquarters there were those who had lived in European Russia, Siberia etc and were familiar with Russain conditions. For intelligence connected with the governance of Korea, Japan already had specialists in Harbin and Vladivostok in normal times. So far as military intelligence and miscellaneous intelligence about revolutionaries and disaffected Koreans are concerned, this was well provided by the various *kikan*. It is clear, the statement concludes, that for the military police which is the instrument (*kikan*) for enforcing law and order, the duty of collecting intelligence is an essential, if incidental, task.[31] The history proceeds to give the instructions sent on 18 June 1918, two months before the allied agreement on the joint expeditionary force to Vladivostok, Major-general Yui, to the deputy commander of the military police unit in that city, Major Fujimura. We need only say that the study of intelligence in Siberia is regarded as critical. Among the tasks to be specially investigated is to obtain intelligence about bandits; movements of the allied armies; matters relating to communications; distribution of raw materials and matters necessary for operations and defence. The *tokumu kikan* were expected to acquire information about the conditions of the people and the state of politics. Enough has been said to indicate that the intelligence activities of the military police had a very wide remit. They lacked a clear focus. The 'enemy' who was to come under observation was at once the Bolsheviks, the anti-Japanese Koreans and the 'allies'. Their work was to be not only political but also economic.[32]

The Siberian intervention was both a success and a failure for Japan. At one level, it succeeded in preventing the spread of Bolshevism to the Japanese home islands and also to Japanese colonies like Korea. To that extent the 'intelligence control' of which the instructions spoke had been effective. Japan had a positive interest in the results of bolshevik expansion which was not shared by other participants in the Siberian intervention. At other levels, Japan was left on her own in the Russian far east. Her weakness was exposed during the Nikolaievsk affair of May 1920. Eventually she was forced to announce the withdrawal of her forces towards the end of 1922. But intelligence was of great importance throughout the Siberian adventure which was perhaps more political than military.

Intelligence organizations in Japan in our period seem to have had their resemblances to those in the West as well as their differences. The similarity is that Japan used the ordinary techniques of information-gathering as did other countries which were colonial powers. Special features which seem to stand out in the Japanese experience are, firstly the independent role accorded to the military police (*kempeitai*) which we have documented for the Siberian intervention and also the ordinary civilian police, though this is harder to document in my period. Secondly, there were the individual efforts of *ad hoc* civilian societies and those who funded them. These societies can be variously described as 'right-wing', 'patriotic', 'pan-Asian', 'liberationist' or 'expansionist' (according to taste). But basically they were responding to two factors in Asia: imperialism and revolutionary nationalism. Their function was to observe, assist, finance, and report about, nationalist movements in China and elsewhere, while at the same time making things difficult for the imperialists, especially Russia, but also Britain and the United States. In China the Japanese were assisted by the research activities of the South Manchurian railway. It was the army which showed most interest in Russia, while the navy concentrated on the United States and the British empire.

There are doubts about the reputation enjoyed by Japan's intelligence agencies. There had been a number of failures: the failure to foresee the *Dreibund* in 1895; the failure to intercept the German Pacific fleet in 1914; the failures in Siberia. Perhaps for that reason, it would appear that, in considering candidates for promotion, the services placed a higher premium on command in the field. At the same time it has to be said that most of the generals in the run-up to the war in 1941 had served in intelligence either as head of the intelligence bureau of the army general staff—the so-called Second Bureau (*dai-ni-bu*)—or as attaché at an embassy overseas. These included (at random) Generals Homma Masaharu, Ishiwara Kanji, Sugiyama Hajime, Suzuki Sōsaku and Tōjō Hideki. In the upper echelons of the navy Admirals Itō Seiichi, Yamamoto Isoroku, Nomura Kichisaburō, Yonai Mitsumasa, Nagano Osami and Inoue Shigeyoshi were among those who had had intelligence experience. It would appear, therefore, that the reputation of intelligence was such that past experience in that field was not a disqualification for the attainment of high rank, even if command experience was the critical factor.

In the period covered by this article Japan argued that she had to use intelligence to compensate for deficiencies. These might be lack of manpower or lack of railways. The senior Japanese statesman, Count Ōkuma, said in 1913 that what was needed in east Asia was 'Western money and Japanese brains'. This may supply a clue to the high value Japan was to set on intelligence. Her intelligence officers were not senior wranglers or members of Mensa. They were on the whole simple men, who had been through the Japanese education system, War College and Staff College. They were practising the arts of military—and naval—intelligence: acute obervation, information-gathering, reporting and information-processing.

Notes

1. I refer especially to the works of Professor Iwashima Hiasao: *Kishū no kenkyū: jōhō to senryaku no mekanismu* (The Study of Surprise Attack: Mechanisms of Intelligence and Strategy) (Tokyo, 1984); and *Jōhōsen ni kanpai shita Nihon: Rikugun angō no hōkai* (Japan's utter defeat in the Intelligence war: the failure of the army codes) (Tokyo, 1984). A useful work is Michael A. Barnhart, 'Japanese Intelligence before the Second World War' in E. R. May (ed.), *Knowing One's Enemies: Intelligence Assessment before the Two World Wars* (Princeton, 1984), pp. 424–55.

2. Craigie to Foreign Office, 22 October 1941 in British Foreign Office Correspondence 371/27884. [F 11231/12/23].

3. Etō Shinkichi and M. B. Jansen (trans.), *My 33 Years' Dream: The Autobiography of Miyazaki Tōten* (Princeton, 1982). While Japanese were reputed to be able to pass themselves off as Chinese, Sun Yat-sen claimed that he could pass as a Japanese.

4. G. Kerst, *Jacob Meckel: sein Leben, sein Wirken in Deutschland und Japan* (Gottingen, 1970), pp. 52–67.

5. Ikeda Kiyoshi, *Kaigun to Nihon* (Tokyo, 1981), pp. 148–52.

6. I. H. Nish, 'Japanese Intelligence and the Approach of the Russo–Japanese War' in C. Andrew and D. N. Dilks (eds). *The Missing Dimension* (London, 1984), pp. 19–21.

7. Etō and Jansen, *Miyazaki*, chs. 17, 18, 19; F. H. Conroy, *The Japanese Seizure of Korea, 1868–1910* (Philadelphia, 1960), p. 242; Fujimura Michio, *Nisshin sensō*, Tokyo, 1973, p. 63.

8. E. A. Falk, *Togo and the Rise of Japanese Sea Power* (New York, 1936), p. 206; on Kawakami, see Fujimura, p. 67.

9. R. F. Hackett, *Yamagata Aritomo in the Rise of Modern Japan, 1838–1922* (Cambridge, Mass.), pp. 160–1; Fujimura, pp. 66–7.

10. Senshi Sōsho, *Dai-Hon'ei Kaigunbu · Rengō Kantai*, 2 vols, (Tokyo, 1975), I, pp. 51–5.

11. Conroy, pp. 241–2.

12. Yamagata Aritomo, 'The army' in Alfred Stead (ed.) *Japan by the Japanese* (London, 1904), p. 108.

13. I. H. Nish, 'The Three-Power Intervention of 1895' in A. R. Davis and A. D. Stefanowska, *Austrina* (Sydney, 1982), pp. 204–25.

14. G. M. Berger (ed.), *Kenkenroku: A diplomatic record of the Sino-Japanese war, 1894–5 (Tokyo, 1982), pp. 217–20.*

15. Yamagata, 'The Army' in Stead, p. 108.

16. I. H. Nish, *The Origins of the Russo–Japanese War* (London, 1985), pp. 198–9.

17. Nish in Andrew and Dilks, pp. 24–7. Another example was First Lieutenant Akiyama Saneyuki who reported from the United States on its 'high standards of naval training' in Ikeda, *Kaigun to Nihon*, p. 153.

18. I have written an article on Major Ishimitsu Makiyo for *Proceedings of the British Association of Japanese Studies, 1985.*

19. *Tanaka Giichi denki*, 3 vols, Tokyo, 1958, I, pp. 232–3.

20. Senshi Sōsho, *Dai-Hon'ei Kaigunbu*, I, 112–19.

21. Shiraishi Masaya, 'Vietnam' in LSE STICERD pamphlets, 1985/II, *1945 in South-east Asia.*

22. E. P. Young, 'Chinese Leaders and Japanese Aid in the Early Republic' in Akira Iriye, *The Chinese and the Japanese* (Princeton, 1980), ch. 7.

23. Madeleine Chi, 'Tsao Ju-lin' in Iriye, *Chinese and Japanese*, pp. 145–7.

24. E. L. Woodward (ed.), *Documents on British Foreign Policy, 1919–39*, first series, VI, no. 695.

25. Japan General Staff, *Nichi-Doku sensō*, 2 vols, I.

26. Falk, *Togo*, p. 441.

27. M. D. Kennedy, *The Estrangement between Great Britain and Japan* (Manchester, 1969), p. 20.

28. M. R. Peattie, *Ishiwara Kanji and Japan's Confrontation with the West* (Princeton, 1975), p. 12.

29. Hagihara Nobutoshi, *Tōgō Shigenori* (Tokyo, 1985), pp. 75–9

30. J. W. Morley, *The Japanese Thrust into Siberia, 1918* (New York, 1957), pp. 67–82.

31. Kempe Shireibu, *Shiberiya Shuppei Kempeishi*, 2 vols (Tokyo, 1976), p. 435.

32. Ibid, p. 436.

Japanese Intelligence, 1918–1945: A Suitable Case for Treatment*

J. W. M. CHAPMAN

When considering the role and effectiveness of Japanese intelligence activity in the period from 1918 to 1945, it should be remembered that Japan has always been seen as just about the most remote society in existence for most other societies, whether in a geographical sense or in terms of psychological distance, even from their nearest neighbours in North-East Asia. It is extremely difficult for any society that has insulated itself in such a determined and ferocious fashion for three whole centuries to adjust quickly and successfully under external pressure to alien systems and values. Non-Japanese value systems are automatically alien and have to be treated with suspicion because they are tied to fundamental identity. If there were no national myths to emphasise the uniqueness of Japanese culture, then manifestly they would have to be invented.[1] Perhaps the only difference now lies in the need to try to back up the claims of uniqueness and specialness with some kind of 'scientific' evidence: we can observe this in claims that Japanese physiology is different from that of Westerners, and this results in Japanese hearing with the opposite side of the brain to Westerners, or on a more mundane level, that Japanese are more prone to the effects of alcohol.[2]

---

* A substantial part of the research for this paper was carried out while the author was attached to the National Diet Library in Tokyo. The help of the Diet Librarian, Mr Arai Masahiro, and of Mr Ninomiya Saburō and Mr Miyawaki Mineo, in the best traditions of international scholarly co-operation, is gratefully acknowledged, together with the financial support of the British Academy and *Nihon Gakujutsu Shinkōkai* (JSPS). Japanese names are cited according to Japanese practice with the family name first.

The Japanese crisis of identity is, perhaps, much more acute at the present time than in the period with which this chapter is concerned, for the information era (*jōhō epokku*) threatens values much more directly than any previous threat to the defence or economic system that manifested itself at various points between 1853 and 1945.[3]

Even before Meiji times, close attention was paid to significant developments in the outside world via information reaching an isolated Japan from the Dutch trading station at Dejima (*rangaku*). But after 1868, the Japanese elite decided that it would finance efforts to seek out significant knowledge in the outside world by sending out some of its most intellectually able young people. But since Japan was so far away and seemed to have rather little of value to offer in return, the rest of the world did not exactly beat a path to Japan's door. Although this pattern may appear to have begun to change in more recent times, in practice the more widespread becomes the belief of Japanese society in the myth of its own innate superiority, the more likely it is that polarisation between Japan and the rest of the world will occur and that there will be a reversion to isolationism. In other words, there appears—to date at least—to be a cycle in which Japanese assiduously learn about those aspects of their environment that they deem to be essential to a maintenance of domestic harmony, engage in a hard-headed, rational and painstaking analysis of external conditions, but sacrifice its conclusions on the altar of national sentiment and on judgements of what other, unconsulted parties will tolerate.

INTELLIGENCE AND DEFENCE ORGANISATION

The organisation of defence and national security in Japan prior to 1945 did not undergo the same structural changes as in the other major powers, which have subsequently been introduced with the establishment of the Defence Agency (*Bōei-chō*) in the 1950s. Most powers introduced independent air forces, whereas the Japanese retained the two traditional services on to which separate air forces were grafted. In the course of time, co-ordination of the activities of the armed forces was managed elsewhere by the establishment of defence ministries, whereas in Japan such co-ordination normally took place in times of crisis and war through the institution of an 'Imperial Headquarters' (*daihonei*), with separate Army (*Rikugun-bu*) and Navy (*Kaigun-bu*) sections, and then only very loosely. Both services had the right of direct access to the Emperor (*iaku jōsō*) on the pre-1918 German model. Liaison with the civilian hierarchies and bureaucracy was channelled via such bodies as the Privy Council, the Cabinet and the liaison conference system, primarily among the War, Navy and Foreign Ministries.

There was no formal combined intelligence structure, either for overt defence intelligence (*jōhō*) or for covert activities (*chōhō*). The General Staff (*sambō-hombu*) had a separate Intelligence Section, which was responsible for both overt and covert data. Covert intelligence activity included subversion and sabotage, but military counter-intelligence remained the responsibility of the military police (*kempei*), in conjunction with the civil police run by the Home Ministry (*Naimushō*). Signals intelligence came mainly within the province of the Inspectorate of Military Training and the War Ministry, aerial reconnaissance within that of the Inspectorate of Air Force training. But the various functional aspects of intelligence were inevitably reflected in the territorial and field units of the Army and in the activities of military attachés abroad. In field units facing target or enemy states, special service units (*tokumu kikan*) were established to engage in covert operations, employing both Japanese and foreign nationals. Agent training was not begun in any systematic way until the establishment of the Nakano School in 1938, a model not emulated by the Navy.[4]

Although Navy manpower was far smaller than that of the Army, the strength of the Navy lay in its rapid ability to concentrate the units of the fleet in particular locations in accordance with central decision-making. The differences and frictions between central Army agencies and field units that tended to emerge more clearly in the 1930s were partly a product of the geographical diffusion of the Army's resources and of a tradition of defiance of superior orders (*gekokujō*), though not confined to the Army alone. However, tensions existed not only between the Naval Staff and the Navy Ministry, but also between the Naval Staff and the Combined Fleet. Naval intelligence, overt and covert, was assembled in the 3rd Section of the Naval Staff, signals intelligence in the 4th Section. But the Combined Fleet, responsible for the execution of operations at sea, had its own staff and carrier-borne reconnaissance aircraft at its disposal. Naval posts and bases close to foreign territory could establish their own special service sections (*tokumu kyoku*) comparable to those of the Army, while naval missions such as those in Shanghai and attaché posts abroad were the main source of strategic intelligence estimates.

Attachés abroad were provided with budgets to employ secret agents and could engage in sabotage and subversive activities. The activities of Colonel Akashi Motojiro in the Russo–Japanese War, for example, were legendary for Army officers and this example was continued in the inter-war period by military attachés in Europe who employed former Tsarist officers and maintained links with White Russian exile groups, and representatives of minority groups living outside the Soviet Union. Although the naval attachés in the United States employed paid agents before 1941, access to information about US naval developments, particularly on the technical side, was not too difficult to come by, especially where funds were available.[5] Attachés also worked closely with Japanese business and technical representatives abroad as language officers or for special study and attached, usually without diplomatic privileges, to the bureaux of attachés abroad. Occasionally, officers were planted in Japanese consular offices and the Kwantung Army appears to have made particular use of the diplomatic and consular posts of the Manchukuo government in the few countries where this was recognised. The Army tried to exploit the Japanese consular network in the Soviet Union for gathering intelligence about military movements and developments in Central Asia and Siberia.[6] In 1936, the Russians ordered the closure of Japanese consular offices and this effectively limited the activities of Army officers to observations made by people travelling between Japan and Europe via the Trans-Siberian railway. The Navy also relied on reports from Japanese consulates in the Mediterranean, the Indian Ocean, and North and Central America for details of the movement of warships and troop transports that were thought to have significance for Japanese national security.[7]

Alongside the military and naval networks, the Foreign Ministry (*Gaimushō*) maintained a political intelligence service in areas of particular significance to current policymaking. This service appears to have relied heavily on Japanese journalists and their contacts, representatives of semi-official agencies, Japanese utilities and trading firms abroad.[8] The *Gaimushō* also had a section in Tokyo engaged in efforts to intercept and decode foreign diplomatic and consular traffic, which by 1941 was decoding numerous State Department and Foreign Office cables. By November 1941, however, the Foreign Office began sending many information telegrams to Tokyo in clear language as part of efforts to dissuade the Japanese from entering the European war, and evidently had little faith in Japanese decryption agencies to process encoded materials rapidly enough. It is evident, however, that even though the information being passed on in this way was accurate, it was perceived in the Japanese Naval Staff as deliberately intended to have a disruptive impact on Japan's relations with its allies. From the evidence available about British policy toward Japan between 1934 and 1941, it would be hard to contest the accuracy of such a perception and, in order to assess the effectiveness of Japanese intelligence, the signals intelligence dimension is one that merits closer attention.

JAPAN IN THE SECRET WAR OF SIGNALS INTELLIGENCE

Of the three principal Japanese foreign intelligence-gathering agencies, the Japanese Army was perhaps the most successful in the signals intelligence field in the sense that it managed to protect the security of its signals the most effectively, and to decipher at least Soviet, Chinese and US signals at various times.[9] The earliest recorded Japanese Army deciphering success came in the Siberian Expedition, when wireless codes in use by the Red Army were resolved or captured in 1918 or 1919. These were evidently simple 'Caesar alphabet' substitution codes, but were passed on by the Japanese Army to the Poles in 1920 and provided vital clues in accomplishing the defeat of Soviet armies threatening to encircle Warsaw during the Soviet-Polish war.[10] As a mark of their gratitude for the Japanese gesture, the Polish General Staff despatched Captain Jan Kowalewski to Japan in 1921 to instruct the Japanese Army in the organisation of more secure, modern enciphering systems.[11] It was as a result of this Polish assistance that Japanese Army wireless signals in the Maritime Provinces ceased to be read by the American decryption team under Herbert Yardley, who first revealed this in the course of 1931 in a series of articles in the *Saturday Evening Post*.[12] Apparently, too, these signals were also being anxiously monitored until then by the Japanese Navy, which had been instumental in landing the first Japanese units at Vladivostock, but which had become increasingly worried about the dangers of an open-ended commitment on the Asian mainland.[13]

The revelations of Herbert Yardley in 1931 about US reading of Japanese military and diplomatic signals up to the Washington Treaties of 1922 contributed in no small way to the feeling in Japan that the United States had forced Japan into treaties as unequal as those under which Germany, the Soviet Union and China had suffered after Versailles or Brest-Litovsk.[14] Even if it now seems unlikely that Yardley's revelations were the result of Stimson's moralising on the habits of gentlemen, the State Department long remained a byword of cryptologic incompetence for Army and Navy experts who, no doubt, savoured the delicious ironies surrounding the whole affair.[15] Just as post-1919 revelations of the compromise of the German Navy's codes by Room 40 forced the Germans into a reappraisal of their code and cipher systems, so the Japanese were prompted after 1931 to accelerate their efforts to shift to machine ciphers.[16] Japanese agencies studied the various models available on the market but developed their own systems. The Japanese Army continued to co-operate directly with the Polish General Staff in this field during the 1930s. It is known that the diplomatic code in use by the Chinese mission in Tokyo was being effectively penetrated during the 1930s by the Japanese Army, along with some State Department telegrams in traffic with US diplomatic posts in the Far East, but it appears that it did not have similar success with either Soviet or British codes before 1941.[17] The ciphers employed by Japanese military attachés abroad were not penetrated until the summer of 1943.[18]

On the other hand, there is firm evidence that Japanese diplomatic bags despatched between Europe and Tokyo via Moscow were being systematically opened by the Soviet internal security authorities and resealed after a scrutiny of their contents at least until 1936.[19] It was as a result of this that the correspondence of the Japanese military attaché in Berlin, Major-General Ōshima Hiroshi, concerning the negotiation of the agreements with Ribbentrop, Canaris and Himmler in 1935–6 for collaboration against the USSR was compromised. This fact would appear to confirm suspected Soviet decipherment of Japanese diplomatic traffic in the 1930s.

From at least the spring of 1936, it is certain that the German Foreign Ministry and Navy had been regularly decoding the cable traffic among Japanese diplomatic missions in Europe and between Japanese legations and the *Gaimushō*.[20] The Foreign Office in London also received from GC&CS decrypts of Japanese traffic in Europe at least from 1936 and was particularly well informed about Japanese diplomatic moves in 1938–9, when Ribbentrop pressed the Japanese to sign a tripartite alliance with Germany and Italy.[21] In the autumn of 1940, William Friedman resolved the principal code in use between embassies abroad and the *Gaimushō*, and three items of decoding equipment were supplied by the United States to Britain. By April 1941, claims about 'Anglo-American inroads ' into Japanese code and cipher systems were known in Berlin, but by the summer of 1942, German decryption specialists appear not yet to have succeeded in resolving 'Purple' code material, only 'Red'.[22]

In the case of the signals systems of the Japanese Navy, American , British and Dutch traffic analysts and decryption specialists had been actively keeping these under close surveillance in the 1920s and 1930s. Since at least 1931, the British, French and Dutch authorities had been engaged in an exchange of intelligence about Comintern threats to colonial rule. The British-run police in the International Settlement at Shanghai, for instance, had passed on a copy of the code materials of the Comintern agent, 'Noulens', to the authorities in the Dutch East Indies.[23] In 1935, a British combined intelligence organisation, the Far Eastern Combined Bureau, had been established at Hong Kong, which was subsequently transferred to Singapore in August 1939, then to Kilindini in Kenya before the fall of Singapore. The FECB had a Navy head and most of its information came from Navy listening posts in the Far East, which obtained fixes of Japanese fleet units and deciphered many Japanese naval, diplomatic and consular signals during the inter-war period. There was an MI6 intelligence bureau at Shanghai with paid agents in China and Japan, a combined information bureau in Japan which relied heavily on the work of British consular posts and of shipping agents and business people in Japanese fleet units were photographed during operations in China and British submarines were kept intermittently on station off the Japanese coast, apparently being refuelled by Glen Line steamers at sea north of Taiwan, and penetrating anchorages used by units of the Japanese Combined Fleet.[25]

From the summer of 1940, combined British, Dutch and American efforts were made to maintain regular air reconnaissance surveillance to warn of any impending Japanese fleet movements. Japanese fleet manoeuvres were closely studied by the signals monitoring services of all three navies, though the US Navy's activities in this sphere are those most accessible to the historian.[26] According to one account, the Royal Navy was particularly reliant on the supply of decrypt material by the US monitoring post at Corregidor on the Philippines from late 1939.[27] Another account insists that the FECB was the source of the first decrypts of the main Japanese Navy cipher, designated JN25, which was introduced in 1938 and that the keys were passed on to Corregidor via the US Navy liaison representative at Singapore in 1940.[28] Yet other accounts refer to the longstanding work undertaken by Dutch cryptanalysts and to the liaison between Dutch agencies in the East Indies and the FECB.[29] During the Pacific War, Australian involvement with British and US agencies increased, but it would appear that inter-allied collaboration in the signals intelligence field in the Pacific area left a great deal to be desired. The US Army, which dominated the set-up at Brisbane after the spring of 1942, sought to exclude British involvement as far as possible and claimed after the war that its successes owed nothing—unlike other US agencies—to Allied contributions.[30] By contrast, the US Navy had a much more positive relationship with the Royal Navy and the Royal Australian and New Zealand Navies. But even here, individuals like Commander Rochefort, when based with CINCPAC at Hawaii in 1942, were aghast at the actions of Washington in briefing the Australian Prime Minister about cryptanalytical progress with Japanese naval ciphers at the most critical stage in the naval war in the Pacific.[31]

However much historians complain about not being given freedom to scrutinise NSA and GCHQ holdings of signals intelligence material prior to 1945, the written evidence that is available is incomparably greater than anything that appears to have survived on the Japanese side. Allied holdings provide very substantial insights into detailed traffic and hindsight confirms that much of the interpretation of that traffic reflected only a very crude representation of the real situation and relationships under examination, which in fact probably helped disguise the scale of Allied foreknowledge of enemy operations and helped prevent their enemies from coming to unambivalent conclusions about cipher compromise. One of the most surprising aspects of Japan's relations with its allies was that the latter were apprised of the compromise of Japanese signals traffic from the end of 1940, yet appear not to have warned the Japanese of this even after the Japanese entry into the war. The German Navy, for example, instructed that any information obtained by the decryption of enemy signals was not to be passed on directly to Japanese naval attachés abroad, but should be relayed to the German Naval Attaché in Tokyo using German Navy ciphers exclusively for submission to the Japanese Naval Staff.[32] Most such messages were sent by cable to Tokyo using the DJ Enigma cipher tables introduced early in January 1940, which meant that they were not being intercepted by Allied listening posts round the world. This picture changed from May 1942, when the German surface blockade-runner, 'Tannenfels', arrived in the Far East with a complete long-range transmitter and group of operators equipped with 'M Bertok' cipher tables. Some of this radio traffic was deciphered in 1942, mostly retrospectively, but it was not until the later years of the war that it was regularly decrypted.[33] It is not clear, however, from available material whether or not its decryption finally convinced the British authorities in 1943 of the extent of German inroads into British code and cipher systems.

A communications agreement was signed between the German and Japanese navies in September 1942, which was principally concerned to regulate signalling arrangements between ships of the two navies, mainly bringing into effect a special signal table (codenamed 'Togo') for the exchange of recognition signals. Members of the Japanese naval mission to Europe in 1941 had been told in general of the importance of traffic analysis for naval operations at sea, but it was not until 1942 and 1943 that supplies of Enigma cipher machines were handed over by the German Air Force and Navy to the Japanese services, and offers were made to train Japanese personnel in direction-finding, radio interception and decryption techniques. When the German Navy was approached in the autumn of 1942 to monitor weather signals transmission from the Australian station at Belconnen near Sydney early in the fighting in the Solomon Islands, this was interpreted as evidence of the primitive state of the Japanese Navy's radio monitoring system and techniques. The German Navy's view, however, was also coloured by the many frustrations experienced in trying to gain Japanese support for direct radio transmissions to Europe and to establish its own local stations in South-East Asia for communication with U-boats operating in the Indian Ocean from the end of 1942. Similar frustrations attended efforts by the German Embassy in Tokyo to transmit directly to Europe after the outbreak of the Pacific War, when the Japanese Army began broadcasting on the same wavelength and demanded to have detailed information about the embassy transmitter. Similar demands were put forward by the Japanese occupation forces in China, where the War Organisation of the Secret Military Intelligance Service (*Abwehr*) and the Information Service of the Foreign Ministry (*Deutsche Informationsstelle*) operated a number of transmitters.[35]

At the end of 1940, the Japanese military attaché in Berlin, Major-General Okamoto Seifuku, approached the German Army's Signals Corps with a request for an exchange of intercepted Soviet cryptographic materials. It is not known if this request was met before the outbreak of war between Germany and the Soviet Union, though it is clear that exchanges did take place from the autumn of 1941. German analyses of Soviet radio networks were regularly passed on in the course of the war to the Japanese Army, while captured Soviet and Anglo-American radio and electronic equipment was frequently inspected by the staff of the Japanese military attaché in Berlin. Details of the German cryptanalytical successes in the early years of the war were finally revealed to the Japanese Navy only in the summer of 1944, by which date it was believed to be virtually out of the question that such successes could ever be repeated again. On the other hand, it appears that information had been provided from 1942 onward about the Anglo-American arrangements for communications with merchant shipping (BAMS).[36] In post-war interrogations, Commander Miyazaki stated:

> One of your greatest mistakes, and one of the greatest sources of information for us, was your constant communication with the Merchant Marine. This is the BAMS system. The frequency of communications was followed from area to area. One could follow movements from Hawaii to Wake by following the volume of communications from Hawaii to Wake.[37]

Similar traffic analysis of signals exchanged with reconnaissance and fighter aircraft squadrons revealed the movements of fleet units, while the adjustment of radio frequencies by aircraft, even if the actual content of the coded signals could not be decrypted, portended major attacks and made it possible to take advance precautions.

> Call-signs were analyzed, volume of traffic and routing of traffic was studied, and radio direction-finding was used.[38]

That Japanese radio-direction finding techniques were by no means as primitive as the Germans believed them to be can be confirmed from US Navy monitoring of Japanese naval signals. It was conceded by the US Navy that it did not approach the Japanese numbers or quality of operations in the Far East until 1939. In fact, using high frequency D/F equipment in 1940, the Japanese tracked the movements of three US cruisers secretly despatched from Pearl Harbor to Singapore and correctly predicted the date of their arrival there.[39] Much of the information available to the 4th Section of the Japanese Naval Staff about US Pacific Fleet dispositions prior to the Pearl Harbor attack came from the monitoring of local radio which revealed to Japanese vessels off the Hawaiian Islands and to the Japanese Consulate at Honolulu the names of the US warships in port several days before the Combined Fleet attack.[40] Through intensive study of US Pacific Fleet manoeuvers in the 1920s and 1930s, the Japanese Navy arrived at quite an accurate assessment of its likely dispositions and strategy in the event of war. 'War Plan Orange' was altered after study of the Japanese Navy's fleet manoeuvres of 1931 had led to the conclusion that the Japanese had a good grasp of American war plans already rehearsed in earlier years at the War and Navy Colleges. Japanese conclusions were that the US Navy would despatch forces for the relief of the Philippines and sought to whittle down the size of the American forces as they crossed the Pacific before bringing it to a decisive battle on more even terms and preferably on ground of Japanese choosing.[41] By 1940, the Japanese Navy had built up a network of radio monitoring stations and air reconnaissance squadrons in the central Pacific to a pitch where they were able to boast to their German allies that no American force could move undetected into the western Pacific. However, it was also recognised by the spring of 1941 that it was highly unlikely that the Americans would split up their naval forces by despatching sizeable units to Singapore or the Indian Ocean. There was an awareness, and a fear, that the United States would simply retain its core fleet at Hawaii and despatch only cruisers, submarines and aircraft to the Far East to engage in protracted warfare against Japanese north-south lines of naval communication and avoid the kind of decisive fleet engagement envisaged in Japanese war planning assumptions.[42]

OPERATIONAL INTELLIGENCE

Faced with the prospect of war, both the British and German navies had already examined and established operational intelligence centres as the best means of co-ordinating information of direct relevance to naval operations. Defence intelligence agencies for co-ordination of strategic intelligence among all services were also perfected in the course of the war. Only rather rudimentary equivalents were developed on the Japanese side and within the Japanese Navy, for example, information from the 4th Section of the Naval Staff was distributed to the 1st (Operations) Section and to the First Committee (*daiichi iinkai*) in the Navy Ministry, but there was little liaison with either the Naval Aviation Bureau or with intelligence officers of the Combined Fleet, and certainly 'no organised exchange of information' with the Army and Army Aviation Bureau, except through the liaison meetings of the War, Navy and Foreign Ministries or the fuller meetings involving the chiefs of staff, often presided over by the Emperor. Combined Fleet Headquarters had a single intelligence officer responsible for both communications and regular intelligence, but mainly in charge of a small team of junior officers and ratings engaged in radio interception. Each of the five fleets that made up the Combined Fleet disposed of a single intelligence officer, but they received no systematic reports from the Combined Fleet intelligence officer and it was rare for any flag officer in command of a squadron to have an intelligence officer attached to it. The intelligence function was ordinarily part of the duties of the ship's captain and signals officer on individual ships, which were expected to supply information about sightings of the enemy rather than to receive it.[43]

While naval operations went smoothly, the flow of communications and of intelligence was also relatively smooth. But even in 1932, when the Japanese Navy intervened at Shanghai, it was estimated that marine landing forces could easily overcome the local opposition, but soon found themselves bogged down when they encountered a more spirited resistance than expected from the Chinese 19th Army.[44] A similar underestimate of US marines on Guadalcanal had even more far-reaching consequences. Aerial reconnaissance up to the middle of 1942 was extremely good because of the high quality of manpower and equipment. But when this advantage was reduced or removed, communications became 'progressively more difficult' until the bombing of the home islands disrupted communcations among the different headquarters units and it became 'very difficult to gather together information rapidly and completely'. This mirrored perfectly the situation of the ABDA Command in the opening stages of the Pacific War, when although efforts had been made to promote inter-allied communication in advance of operations, this was regularly interdicted by larger and more efficient Japanese forces.

FECB correctly estimated, from an analysis of Japanese shipping movements, the assembly of the task force headed by the commander of the 2nd Fleet, Admiral Kondō Nobutake, and its progress across the Gulf of

Siam. A Catalina reconnaissance aircraft spotted the task force on its way and reported its observations before being shot down on 6 December 1941. The information was duly passed on to Washington and helped draw attention toward South-East Asia as the central *locus belli* and away from Pearl Harbor, where Admiral Kimmel and his staff were apparently being starved of 'Magic' intercepts.[45] British plans to move into southern Thailand (Operation 'Matador'), had they been implemented, could certainly have made initial Japanese operations in Malaya rather more difficult and would have delayed considerably the early cut-off of aircraft reinforcements from Burma and India.[46] A better tactical starting-point for operations, however, had to be weighed against strategic considerations: firstly, was it more important to hold the Middle East than to defend the Far East and therefore to allocate available resources, made more scarce as a result of assistance to the Soviet Union? The Americans argued that the Far East could be lost and regained, while the Germans were hoping and planned for the British to divide their forces to cope with a Japanese attack.[47] Secondly, the War Cabinet in London was concerned lest any pre-emptive tactical move in Thailand, or even at sea, might prejudice British claims to be clear victims of Japanese aggression. Life would have been extremely difficult in a situation where the Japanese attacked British or Dutch possessions without touching the Philippines and the strategic initiative had long since been resigned to the United States, for Churchill seems to have believed until very late in 1941 that a Japanese attack would constitute an irrational act.[48] However well-informed the British and Dutch may have been about the movements of the Combined Fleet, as has been argued, they could take no effective initiative to counter these beyond informing the Americans. But in terms of resources and preparations at the points that mattered, and especially in the Hawaiian Naval District, as Commander Rochefort has pointed out, the local Elint, Sigint and Comint set-up was extremely deficient and was not properly integrated into the command and control system as a whole until the spring of 1942.[49]

DOCUMENTARY INTELLIGENCE

Next to information derived from broadcasts and signals transmissions, the Intelligence Division of the Japanese Naval Staff (*gunreibu sambō-hombu*) regarded documentary evidence, and to a much lesser extent prisoner-of-war interrogations, as the most valuable contributions to their knowledge. In peacetime, however, the opportunities for acquisition of windfalls resulting from operational moves hardly exist, though it should be recalled that East Asia was not the most peaceful area in the world between 1918 and 1941.

Operations were conducted in North-East Asia between 1918 and 1923 and again between 1936 and 1939 against Soviet forces by the Japanese Army, for example, not to mention the operations in China from 1931 onward. The US Navy in its appraisal of the Japanese Navy's secret operational codebook of 1918, was struck by the enormous number of very detailed locations in China for which code groups existed. The Japanese Navy was frequently called on to send warships to various points on the Chinese coast to rescue Japanese citizens or protect business interests and property in the course of the interminable internal upheavals that characterised the society before 1949. On the other hand, the Japanese authorities were as willing as those of the other powers to extend their privileges, if need be at the expense of the others, and there is no doubt that the Japanese had a strong feeling that they had greater proprietorial rights in East and later South-East Asia than foreign powers from the other side of the world. This feeling was exacerbated by Japan's almost complete lack of the resources essential for building an advanced industrial economy and also by dependence on the same powers for the technical know-how entailed. The aggressiveness of Japanese business representatives contributed in no small way to the alienation of foreign firms and, following World War I, first US, then British, then even German firms reacted hostilely to Japanese methods of technology transfer and to what they viewed as 'an exaggerated nationalism'.[50] In industries involving defence applications in particular, reaction was accompanied by strong claims about Japanese commercial and military espionage which constricted technology flows even further and made resort to espionage and corruption that much more likely. Faced with such restrictions after 1922 and again after 1931, Japanese perceptions of being involved in a struggle for survival heightened and the greatest sensitivity tended to be manifested whenever moves were made by the foreign powers in the China area.

Japanese political and military intelligence tended to be focussed, consequently, on events in China or along its borders and every threatening move provoked very sharp signals of alarm or pain. The Bolshevik Revolution had very significant economic consequences for Japan as a major supplier of Russian war needs, and the nature of the ideology threatened to undermine the foundations of Japanese imperialism, especially after Lenin shifted the focus of Comintern activities from Europe to Asia in 1919. The viciousness of the struggle in the Russian Far East until 1923, and later against the Chinese Communist and Nationalist Parties, was based in large part on a Japanese recognition of their investments in Manchuria and the coastal areas of China being seized without compensation. In the mid-1920s, they were far from averse to a situation where Britain was the main target of Chinese nationalism and.there are some suspicions that the Japanese in China were even partially instrumental in deflecting Chinese passions away from themselves.[51] There was alarm over the deal between Chiang Kai-shek and the Anglo–American Powers in 1927, but much greater apprehension about the reintegration of Manchuria in a unified Chinese state and in 1929 about the inability of the Chinese to handle their dispute with the Soviet Union without provoking armed Soviet incursion across the frontier. The adjustment of the equilibrium in East Asia could be handled by an input of resources as well as of diplomatic and military organisations to provide information about the regional environment.

The handling of the strategic environment, however, was a rather different matter. Regional freedom of manoeuvre was partly contingent on the support of one or other of the major powers in world politics, so that it was also of considerable importance for Japan to make wise choices of partner at the global level. But such choices were influenced not only by calculations of national self-interest: there were always complicated domestic political and economic or military ties and considerations. The alliance with Britain against Russia in 1902, for example, was by no means a foregone conclusion since Germany was put forward as a more suitable alternative, and kept on being advanced in 1911, 1914 and 1918 by powerful factional interests. Fear of Bolshevism and resentment at US interference in China added to the strains long apparent in the Anglo–Japanese alliance and precipitated a shift toward an alignment with France which lasted until 1931, when a Franco-Soviet *rapprochement* left Japan virtually isolated and this isolation became highly visible following the unilateral moves of 1931–32 against the Chinese. From 1931 to 1936, the only countries still friendly toward Japan were the small states of Eastern Europe and the small, independent states of Asia such as Turkey, Afghanistan and Thailand.

We have seen that the Japanese Army benefited particularly from the special relationship with Poland in the inter-war period. Not only were the Poles highly skilled in areas such as cryptology and signals intelligence, but they developed to a fine art the acquisition of documentary intelligence through theft, calculated break-ins and subterfuge. An outstanding example of the last variety was revealed with the arrest in Germany of Jerzy von Sosnowski, a dashing cavalry officer who was financed by the Polish General Staff as an international show-jumper between 1925 and 1933. This provided him with the kind of cover that gave him an entrée into high society and the opportunity to seduce several secretaries in the German Defence Ministry from aristocratic families that had found themselves rather down on their luck as a result of the war and post-war hyperinflation.[52] The Japanese Army was an important beneficiary of intelligence obtained from such sources and relied heavily on the assistance of Polish experts to make the most of the many Soviet citizens who defected, especially during the period of the purges in the 1930s.[53] But it was already understood in Tokyo by the summer of 1931 at the very latest that, however useful such services were, they did not make up for previous relationships with stronger powers which could make effective use of available intelligence, or were endowed with capabilities on a scale that made good intelligence dispensable. This was also one of the reasons why the Japanese Navy looked back even more nostalgically to the old relationship with Britain, and for such a long time.

One of the reasons why relations with Britain began to worsen from 1935 onward lay in the efforts of Sir Frederick Leith-Ross, supported by Chamberlain as Chancellor of the Exchequer, to stabilise the Chinese currency at the very moment when the Japanese government was expecting financial weakness to bring Chiang Kai-shek on his knees asking the Japanese to come to his rescue. Even though this regime was also being supported by big business, the military and the conservative bureaucracy in Germany, the old charge of 'perfidious Albion' stuck, and there were even rumours circulating in Japan to the effect that Britain was prepared to provide finance to the Soviet Union. Such moves and apprehensions could scarcely help but alienate the Japanese Army, but there was also the refusal of the Western Powers to accept the fact that nothing short of equality would be acceptable to the Japanese Navy in the naval arms talks of 1934 to 1936. The position was also complicated by the internal factional rivalries within the Japanese Navy officer corps, the history of which goes back at least to before World War I and was intertwined with debate about whether or not Britain or Germany was the more valuable partner for Japan.[54] Admiral Yamamoto Isoroku, who headed the Japanese Navy delegation to London in 1934, was regarded as someone sympathetic to the Anglo-American point of view and criticised as a compromiser by his opponents, whose leading protagonist was Admiral Nagano Osami, who headed the 1935 delegation to London.

Yamamoto was approached by Ribbentrop to have talks on his way home from London via Berlin, but was advised against this by Ambassador Matsudaira in London and by Ambassador Mushakoji in Berlin. General Ōshima Hiroshi, the Military Attaché in Berlin, who was then engaged in discussions with Ribbentrop, General von Blomberg and Admiral Canaris about a military convention between the two countries, informed Canaris on 12 November 1935 that Nagano had asked that it be made known to Ribbentrop and Raeder that he was prepared to 'range far beyond his instructions' and speak his mind openly to them on his way to London, if the Germans would do the same.[55] Aside from a few handwritten notes for an agenda for discussion at a dinner held at Raeder's house on 1 December 1935 we do not know for certain precisely what was said to Nagano, but it is not without significance that the same file contains a translated copy of Captain Vivian's lengthy report of February 1935 on the efficiency of the Japanese Navy in which he characterised the Japanese Navy as 'second-rate' and which had secretly been photographed and sent to Berlin by Captain Wenneker in the summer of 1935.[56] It is hard to believe that in a free and frank discussion with Admiral Nagano this piece of documentation would not have been utilised, especially as so much British and French diplomatic traffic was already being deciphered by German and Italian agencies at this point in time.[57] By 1939, decryption had extended to five major British cipher systems employed by military as well as diplomatic agencies, and the German and Italian decryption agencies had organised a division of labour which maximised the coverage and penetration achieved. Since so much of the traffic with the Far East was radioed by the late 1920s, ample opportunities were provided for the logging of sufficient material to unravel the recode and recipher tables employed with the basic codebooks, with the result that the Germans and Italians were in an excellent position to anticipate Anglo-French moves pretty well all along the line in the Far East as well as Europe.[58]

The position was little altered by the outbreak of war, as the rate of decryption was estimated to be well above the percentage that could normally be expected in wartime. Recode and recipher tables were brought in at shorter intervals in time, but several basic codebooks appear to have been seized during German operations in Scandinavia and the Low Countries.[59] At sea, too, there were many seizures of Allied merchant ships which generally yielded low-level code materials and confidential books, but on occasion provided unexpected surprises. One of the most spectacular of these was the haul of the raider *Atlantis* when it captured the Blue Funnel liner *Automedon* just west of Singapore on 11 November 1940. Its mail room contained the whole of the top secret mail from London for the new British C-in-C, Far East, Sir Robert Brooke-Popham and for the service commanders at Singapore. The vessel was also scheduled to sail on to Hong Kong and Shanghai and also carried post for military and Secret Service agencies there, as well as for attachés in Japan. A whole trunk full of material was relayed to Japan and then by courier to Berlin, where it arrived at the end of December. A large part of this material was destroyed by the Germans themselves before the end of the war and much of the evidence that came into British hands was apparently weeded and not returned to West Germany after 1958. Odd and mostly inconspicuous small items stayed lodged in some US-held archival materials, but the principal evidence was not released until the late 1970s, although some official British historians, notably Captain Roskill, noted that 'valuable intelligence' was lost. Because the lost material included cipher and SIS material, such categories of archival material in the British records remain closed for 50 or 75 years or more, as a general principle.

However, what is known for certain is that Captain Rogge of the *Atlantis* recognised the significance of a British Chiefs of Staff memorandum on the situation in the Far East were Japan to enter the war. This was produced on 15 August 1940 and submitted to the War Cabinet for approval. Rogge arranged for it to be sent direct to Japan into the hands of the German Naval Attaché, Rear-Admiral Paul Wenneker, who retained a copy, wired a summary to Berlin, and asked permission to hand it to the Japanese Naval Staff, especially as he had been urging his superiors only two weeks earlier to provide firm guidance about encouraging Japan to seize Singapore and help bring the war to an end.[60] Since this view coincided with that of Grand-Admiral Raeder who was 'diametrically opposed' to Hitler's plans to attack the Soviet Union before finishing off the war against Britain, permission to hand over the document was granted on 12 December even before its full text had been seen in Berlin.[61] The document was handed into officers of the *gunreibu sambō-hombu* in the morning and Wenneker was summoned to meet the vice-chief of staff, Admiral Kondō Nobutake, who repeatedly expressed his thanks for such a document, without which the Japanese would never have guessed just how weak and overstretched the defences of the British Empire were from outward appearances.

From the admittedly patchy surviving Japanese documentation, it can be seen that the summary of the COS memorandum sent from Captain Yokoi in Berlin would have gone automatically to the Navy Ministry as well as the Naval Staff. The Navy Minister, Admiral Oikawa Koshirō, made a statement to a liaison conference held in Tokyo on 27 December 1940 which referred to information obtained from 'documentary secret intelligence' (*bunshō chōhō*), revealing that Britain would definitely go to war with Japan over the Dutch East Indies, but not over French Indochina. The original document in the hands of the Naval Staff emphasised that this appraisal was based on then current circumstances, but expressed the hope that successful operations in the Mediterranean would make it possible to despatch a strong naval force to Singapore, and asked for a tactical appraisal of the situation in the Far East by the service chiefs at Singapore. We do not know if a Japanese translation was circulated to the Navy Ministry and the Combined Fleet Headquarters, but Admiral Yamamoto would certainly have been able to cope with the original memorandum. Some of his correspondence for this period has survived and it is clear from a letter he wrote to Admiral Shimada Shigetarō on 10 December that he had not yet made the fundamental decision to incorporate the Pearl Harbor attack plan in fleet war plans, which were due for annual revision at this date. From two letters written a year later, on 19 December 1941, to Admiral Takahashi Sankichi and Harada Kumao, he indicates quite conclusively that the basic decision was taken 'in December of last year', and this is borne out by a surviving letter of 7 January 1941 to Admiral Oikawa.[62] The well-known Japanese naval historian, Professor Ikeda Kiyoshi, has observed:

> I have always wondered why Yamamoto changes his mind about the surprise attack on Pearl Harbor in the winter of 1940–1. The captured chiefs-of-staff report appears to explain it.[63]

The importance of a document of this kind is that it is an authentic statement from the highest levels of a target state. Only in his wildest fantasies could a top commander imagine being privy to the calculations of his opponents under normal circumstances. This document, it should also be emphasised, was only one item—though certainly the most outstanding—among many known to have been transmitted to the Japanese armed forces between 1935 and 1945 by the Germans and Italians. Partly because the most secret intelligence material is often destroyed by the agencies collecting it and partly because Allied intelligence and counter-intelligence agencies combed through the captured archives pretty systematically and conducted interrogations of enemy intelligence personnel, many of whom were taken into Allied employment after 1945, only some superficial pieces of the jigsaw can be spotted in the publicly available data. An exchange of secret intelligence data about the Soviet Union between the Japanese and German armed forces was more formally initiated in 1935 by Admiral Canaris and General Ōshima and then extended to include Captain Kojima, the Japanese Naval Attaché in Berlin in May 1937. A written agreement was signed in 1938 and the agreement was extended to cover the Western Powers after Munich, when an annual exchange of data was held in alternate years in Tokyo and Berlin. But inevitably, when particularly interesting material is obtained, efforts are made to use such data to further the ambitions of individual officers or to influence the policies of the other partners to the agreement, usually via the individuals and agencies who are most receptive and who, it is hoped, will be able to maximise the impact of the message through their own credibility and influence.

Between 1935 and 1939, Captains Lietzmann and Wenneker had been in close touch with members of the Japanese naval officer corps amenable to closer relations with Germany, but it is striking that it was not until after Admiral Nagano returned from London and was appointed Navy Minister that Britain came to be targetted as a potential enemy for the first time since 1922 and Germany and Italy seen as potential allies against Britain in the future. Rear-Admiral Nomura Naokuni, when chief of staff of the Combined Fleet in 1936, urged Captain Wenneker to avoid at all costs allowing knowledge of such a change to reach British ears. The fact that the Japanese Navy was the one element that 'showed little or no sign of wishing for closer relations' with Britain was noted by the British Ambassador, Sir Robert Clive, in March 1937.[64] But it was not until the outbreak of the War in China that a widespread belief in British support for China as being the principal obstacle to Japanese victory took hold, all the more so when, contrary to the predictions of the Foreign Office, the Germans agreed to withdraw their support from Chiang Kai-shek.[65] When the British authorities sought to draw Japanese attention to the fact that the Germans continued to supply arms and equipment to Chiang Kai-shek despite their assurances to the contrary, the truth was discounted as firmly as British warnings to Stalin in 1941.[66]

The Japanese Army and Navy had extensive organisations in China which kept an eye on foreign establishments and agents. The head of the Japanese Navy mission in Shanghai in 1939–40 was Admiral Nomura Naokuni, a former Japanese Naval Attaché in Berlin, who was used as a channel of communication with Captain Lietzmann to express the Japanese Navy's satisfaction with the shift in German policy to one of détente with the Soviet Union and its desire to see a settlement in the rear with the Soviet Union that would enable the Navy to concentrate its efforts in a southward direction. A raid by the Hong Kong police in 1939 led to the discovery of British official documents in the hands of a certain David Kung, illegal radio transmitters were also traced, and there was even suspicion of an itinerant Chinese beggar spotted in the vicinity of British naval dockyards between 1938 and 1940 in metropolitan Britain.[67] As early as the spring of 1940, the Japanese counter-espionage authorities requested the Gestapo to send a representative to Shanghai to keep the European emigré community and British intelligence agencies under surveillance. Heydrich duly obliged with the despatch of a detective named Kahner in the summer of 1940, as well as of a much more senior investigator, Sepp Meisinger, in March 1941, whose precise brief still remains something of a mystery.[68] Japanese agents were able to procure a number of low-level British documents such as aircraft recognition manuals issued to the China Station, but these could easily have been items in a trade-off with hostile agents, especially as Shanghai remained a centre of international espionage up to 1949.

The intelligence networks of the Japanese armed forces spread out into South-East Asia during the 1930s, operating from Army and Navy advance posts and kept separate from the networks built up within the consular and diplomatic services. Captain Roskill noted in 1969 that 'their Intelligence service, especially in the Far East was extremely efficient, and we had much trouble with it in Malaya'. Agent networks were played down in significance by Navy officers interrogated after the war, as they rarely added much to what could be observed by retired military personnel located in consular missions or working for commercial firms such as Mitsui and Mitsubishi abroad. Military and naval attachés were provided with secret funds to purchase information of a technical or strategic nature or to finance subversive propaganda or sedition. There have been persistent stories about the acquisition of documentary intelligence in the form of blueprints of warships or construction of defence networks and bases at locations such as Pearl Harbor and Singapore. There is some evidence of successes of this kind with individual warships in both Britain and the United States, and certainly such data were swapped with Germany and Italy prior to 1941, but it is not always easy to pinpoint the source of such successses. A great deal could be learned simply by observation of defence sites and targets. On the plans of the Singapore base, one story has it that information was leaked by Captain Baillie-Stewart of the Seaforth Highlanders who served as ADC to the Governor prior to 1933, was cashiered and imprisoned and subsequently gave up British nationality.[69] Another story has it that the opportunity was given to Japanese agents in Singapore to photograph the plans of the base for £50,000, but this account lacks even circumstantial credibility.[70] One of the first discussions of a Japanese attack on Singapore comes in suggestions put forward by Ambassador Ōshima during the visit of General Terauchi to Germany in September 1939, and information about Singapore was certainly handed over by the *Abwehr* to Rear-Admiral Endō, the Japanese Naval Attaché in Berlin, in the winter of 1939 in more than usual conditions of secrecy.[71] Information about the British bases at Gibraltar and Malta was found in the archives of the French Navy at Brest, and it may have been that data about Singapore from French sources was also available, since a great deal of top-level French and Inter-Allied information was seized by the Germans in 1940.[72] It has also not to be forgotten that much information was available via the Italian armed forces, who were very free with the supply of such data to their German allies from an early date. Allied decryption data covering Italian signals traffic has not been released in any quantity, mainly because such data was primarily the responsibility of the British agencies concerned, so that the extent of intelligence collaboration between the Italians and Japanese remains murky to say the least.

For the Japanese, however, Rome remained a highly important overseas centre and it is not without significance that the naval attaché there, Captain Mitsunobu, was the son-in-law of navy minister Shimada. Mitsunobu worked after 1941 with Admiral Abe Katsuo, a former head of the Naval Affairs Bureau, who became head of the Navy Mission in Italy and had a standing brief to pay particular attention to a situation in the Mediterranean that might lead to the redeployment of substantial British forces east of Suez. Mitsunobu regularly provided information from Tokyo about US strategic intentions that his German colleague could never decide was Mitsunobu's own opinion or represented the authentic views of the Navy Ministry. On one occasion, Mitsunobu predicted the arrival of cruisers and the carrier HMS 'Hermes' in the Indian Ocean, based on 'an absolutely certain, but very secret, source', a form of words that suggests either decryption or HF/DF detection.[73] Mitsunobu collated data provided by consular posts in the Mediterranean, round the coasts of Africa and the Indian Ocean which appears to have been more efficient than that available by way of the central agencies in Tokyo and the direct Berlin-Tokyo circuits, but reports from consular posts in British-controlled areas, such as Cairo, still had to go first to Tokyo and then on from there to Rome. The mission at Lisbon was also important as it was fed by Japanese consular posts in the Portuguese colonies, as well as by those in Latin America. These last links were also assisted by the provision of a radio link between Lisbon and Madrid, installed by the *Abwehr* which trained Japanese operators to man it. A similar service was performed to maintain a radio link between Teheran and Berlin in 1941 and the Japanese, in return, permitted use of their courier services via Turkey and Iran to assist German-supported units of Georgian and Azerbaijanian special forces which were intended initially in 1942 to go in behind Soviet lines to prevent the destruction of installations in the Baku oilfields, but were later prepared for sabotage operations in this area in 1943 and 1944.[74]

Strategic information was also collected for the Japanese Army by various posts in Europe: Lisbon was important for US intentions, Stockholm and, to a lesser extent, Sofia and Istanbul, were important for Soviet intentions, Major-General Onodera struck the Germans in 1941 and 1942 as unusually well-informed compared to most of his colleagues in Europe, but later it was decided that the bulk of his information about the Soviet Union was coming from suspect Polish sources. Onodera himself conceded that it was not always possible to rely on Polish information about the Middle East and India in exchanges with Tokyo, but complained that, even when his Polish informants supplied quite truthful information about German–Soviet relations and the like, his colleagues in Berlin sought to discredit him. Much of what was supplied to Tokyo from all the European posts was dependent on information derived from Allied journals and newspapers. This was certainly particularly true of Stockholm, which was supplied by Mosquito flights from London and by sea from the few Swedish vessels allowed to trade with the Americas.[75] Undoubtedly, however, Polish contacts in such locations as Lisbon and Stockholm were feeding misinformation from the spring of 1943 about the willingness of the Japanese Army to reach a tacit deal with the Soviet Union which would permit the withdrawal of Japanese forces to the Pacific front and of Soviet forces to the European front. Since the Japanese Navy had been informally sounding out the Germans about possible Japanese mediation in the German-Soviet conflict ever since October 1941, and since private opinion both within the military and the Nazi Party itself was very divided about the wisdom of Hitler's attack on the Soviet Union, it was an area of possible contention and friction between the Axis allies about which both the Soviet Union and the Anglo–American powers had some inside information.[76] Further disinformation was fed in through the *Abwehr* organisation in China in the autumn of 1943 which convinced Ribbentrop that the Japanese were closing their eyes to the transfer of no fewer than one million Soviet troops from Siberia. These suggestions were angrily rejected by Ambassador Ōshima and by the general staff in Tokyo in October and November 1943, much to the discomfiture and irritation of all concerned.

Both the German general staff and the naval war staff, on the basis of the quality of most of the information they received from the Japanese armed forces in the early months of the Pacific War and in the year that preceded it, did not have a very high estimation of the Japanese military intelligence services. Most of what was passed on about Japanese battlefield experiences was often little better than the propaganda issued for domestic consumption in Japan, and the Germans who felt more charitably than others suggested that the lack of frankness and accuracy was more the result of what the central agencies in Tokyo were withholding than of any reservations or ill-will on the part of their messengers. Hitler, on the other hand, after Stalingrad regarded the Japanese as utterly cynical and moved entirely by their own self-interest, but seems to have resigned himself to the Japanese view that the only hope lay in achieving a stalemate in separate wars of attrition. Hitler wanted essentially to win his own war, just as Yamamoto wanted a separate triumph against the United States, and neither wanted to fight a joint war in which victorious honours would be shared. The Japanese were always looking over their shoulders, fearful lest Hitler should spring another surprise on them right up until the eve of Pearl Harbor. The vague operational zones between the Axis allies were deliberately kept as vague as possible, and the Japanese always seemed to prefer an outcome where there would be a weakened Soviet Union and a weakened British Empire between them and their German allies, far more than an outright Axis victory. These sentiments were amply mirrored in the range of opinions within the membership of the Japanese Embassy in Berlin, which was undoubtedly being 'tapped' and 'bugged' by the *Forschungsamt* and the *Gestapo*, early in 1942.[77]

This divergence of strategic aims can be traced back to the differing interpretations placed by Germans and Japanese on the meaning and implications of the captured British COS memorandum in December 1940. For Yamamoto, it provided the basic information on which calculations could be relied upon for the distribution of Japanese offensive capabilities as between Pearl Harbor and South-East Asia; for Hitler, it was possible to determine how many units would suffice to keep the British and Americans at bay long enough to launch the surprise attack that would destroy the Stalinist system. The Japanese might be needed to provide the additional constraints on the Anglo-American Powers in the medium-term, though he discovered, too, by the end of 1940 that he needed them in the short-term to supply the vital amounts of natural rubber required for the conduct of Operation 'Barbarossa'. To make sure that they did not interfere with his plans, he would not allow the Japanese to be told of the impending attack on the Soviet Union until after he knew that the ships transporting the rubber to Europe were well on their way. The deception measures adopted to convince the Soviet Union that the attack would really be launched at the British Isles were almost as important to deceive the Japanese and make them more willing to release the vital strategic materials.[78] These were so important that Hitler was prepared to allow a very far-reaching handover of technical information and details of German experience in warfare against Britain, which Raeder saw as tantamount to a total sell-out of German know-how. General Yamashita Hōbun, who had fought with the 4th division at Nomonhan and implemented many of the recommendations of the Army Commission of Enquiry in his few months as inspector-general of the Army Air Force, was sent as head of the Japanese military mission to Germany. On his return to Japan, he judged on the basis of what he had learned that in view of the out-of-date equipment of the Japanese Army, the last thing Japan should contemplate was the initiation of war against the United States, Britain or the Soviet Union. 'Japan should accordingly,' he recommended on 1 July 1941, 'exercise patience in avoiding the outbreak of war, meanwhile concentrating all her strength on the modernisation of her military material.'[79]

This was essentially the position adopted by Admiral Yamamoto within the Navy, but despite this the Japanese government was stampeded into the decision of 2 July 1941 to occupy southern Indochina, acting on the premiss revealed in the British COS report that Japan could proceed to occupy Thailand or French Indochina without precipitating war. By this date, however, this piece of documentary intelligence was no longer the benchmark by which to judge the reactions in Washington, to which the intiative in responding to Japanese expansionism had already shifted. This error of judgement was probably compounded by miscalculation in Washington of the time it was likely to take before economic sanctions would begin to bite hard.[80] Separate British and US estimates of the Japanese fuel reserves generally provided only the roughest of crude, global estimates. They could not, and did not, provide the precision of Japanese figures for different kinds of oil fuel required, or for other strategic raw materials. The Cabinet Planning Board's estimate of 29 July 1941 showed that, while there was enough aviation fuel to last for fifteen months, the position for light, machine and heavy oil ranged between 10 and 75 days only. The position for gasoline and crude oil varied between 3½ and 6 months, while that for strategic materials such as nickel and manganese varied between two and four months.[81] While these were inevitably approximations of the real positions, further calculations in October were little more reassuring and all the indications from projections up to the end of 1942 pointed to November and December as the optimum launching date.[82]

CONCLUSION

It is interesting that so many of the Japanese calculations, strategic and economic, of this period appear to be based on the concrete framework of the East Asian regional system in which Japan inevitably played the dominant role. If the extra-regional actors could be persuaded to withdraw themselves voluntarily or otherwise to the boundaries of the system, everything would be resolved. The more perceptive members of the élite recognised that such a framework was a product of wishful thinking, but this seems to be why the Doolittle Raid of April 1942 and the Soviet entry into the Pacific War were so shattering in the collective national consciousness. Somehow, the extra-regional environment is to be exploited for the advantages it can confer at the regional level, but at the same time the environment should remain passive and remote, even when it is manifest that the whole environment is considerably larger and more significant than the part represented by the regional system.

The proximity of Soviet territory to the Japanese main islands and the capacity of the Soviet air forces to inflict a high cost on Japanese centres of industrial production in Manchuria and Honshu, coupled with a calculation of a low economic return from any military successes, provided a powerful motivation for limiting conflict in North-East Asia. Japan's severe lack of indigenous resources, coupled with contemporary geopolitical theorising about the crude equation between territorial control and national security and fuelled by Japan's immediate historical experience that wars were profitable, propelled the society into conflict with neighbours who could offer least resistance. But since that resistance continued interminably, it was judged that it was some external cause rather than mistaken assumptions, policies and actions by the Japanese élite that must account for the confounding of initial expectations. The conjoining of Japanese expansionist aspirations with those of Germany and Italy confirmed the fears of the dominant states in the external environment about a concerted plan to overthrow the prevailing system. There was an awareness on the part of the major powers of the inherent dangers of confrontation with the rampant fanaticism of Japanese nationalism, but Japanese awareness of gaps and short-term flaws in their counter-strategy provided what appeared to be a rational basis for belief that an outside chance of success existed. In practice Yamamoto's calculation of a massive blow delivered by surprise and modelled on the defeat of France proved to be as flawed as Hitler's dream of a Soviet disintegration, not least because the throw-weight of the blow was nowhere large enough in relation to the target to achieve the results desired.

In Japan's case, it is clear that the outstanding military commanders were only too aware of the dangers inherent in clashes with powers that possessed superior technologies and resources. Japanese opportunities to maintain a channel of access to German technology were contingent on the Soviet Union, just as German designs on the Soviet Union depended crucially on Japanese supply of raw material resources. The Germans, however, supplied the Japanese with only a part of the inside information available to them, and withheld information not only about joint enemies, but also about their own intentions. This coincided in time with the precise period at which their enemies were beginning to acquire a fuller degree of knowledge about their strategic plans and intentions. Their enemies by contrast, were prepared to share their knowledge with fewer mutual reservations, so that when the physical resources available to them became ready for use, these were used to far more effect. Perhaps the profoundest irony of the World War II era was that, after having benefited so signally from German and Italian exploitation of Allied communication weaknesses, the Japanese themselves were a principal source of Allied knowledge of Hitler's strategic intentions and arrangements for continental European defence. But, to cap it all, the weakness of Japanese signals security was known to German agencies well before Pearl Harbor, but for reasons that are still unclear, these agencies either gave perfunctory or vague warnings or were not prepared to reveal precise information to each other. What is particularly bizarre is that Hitler himself seems either not to have been warned about the dangers of compromise through talking to Ōshima or chose to ignore any such warnings.[83]

Whatever the explanation, Allied penetration of Japanese and Axis communication systems developed and expanded after 1941 and yielded not only insights into the areas where mutual frictions and unspoken differences existed, but also into the cleavages that had been temporarily covered up during the festive days of unbroken victories. These differences and internal divisions showed up all the more clearly in defeat because someone had to be blamed when things went wrong. In the case of Japan, the strains within the society were already evident to the perspicacious observer able to examine it at close range. On the one hand, Japanese intelligence specialists assured Allied interrogators that there was 'a tendency in Japan to look upon intelligence as synonymous with espionage' and argued that, so far as they as intelligence professionals were concerned, espionage actually produced little good intelligence.[84] Nevertheless, there appears to have been a paradoxically inveterate belief among senior Japanese officers that when the battle went against them, it was the result of treachery somewhere among the ranks, a version of the 'stab-in-the-back' theory that Japanese leaders had been known to condemn in the German militarists of World War I.[85] A good example can be highlighted in the replies of Rear-Admiral Tomioka Sadatoshi, who stated:

> We respected your intelligence—your reconnaissance, and any number of other sources. We also thought you had some Fifth Columnists or spies on Okinawa. We caught some suspects, but were not able to determine conclusively that they were your agents.[86]

We find precisely the same explanations forthcoming from the German Navy High Command when it simply refused to accept the reality of Allied decipherment of the U-boat cipher time after time after time. When the leaders blame the led, the ultimate in demoralisation has been reached. Yet, such a condition can be brought about, at least in part, by a skilful manipulation of the leaders by their enemies. The Gestapo had led the way in 1937 with its setting of the counter-intelligence community against the Army and the Party inside the Soviet system, which had still not quite recovered from a self-induced blood-letting before it was bludgeoned once again by the German armed forces in 1941.[87] Although the Soviet security authorities were probably already well primed about what was going on in Japanese and German circles in the Far East from the Sorge network, and also from the monitoring of foreign cable and telephone traffic via the Soviet Union, radio intercepts, hidden microphones in the specially prepared embassy compounds in Kuibyshev, and almost certainly from decryption of foreign signals, perhaps the greatest contribution to Japanese demoralisation was actually delivered by the behaviour of their agents after capture in October 1941. The prosecuting counsel in the Sorge Case recalled after the war that the one salient fact that emerged for him was that Sorge had done his very best to implicate the maximum number of people, both German and Japanese, in his freely given confession with the result that it proliferated the already profound suspicion not only about foreign espionage, but about domestic treachery in Japan, no matter how highly placed the individual suspect might be.[88]

Whatever measure of success or efficiency can be applied to the various dimensions of intelligence-gathering, evaluation and distribution in Japan in the period from 1918 to 1945, the one area that stands out as profoundly unbalanced and irrational to the point where it tended to render all the other areas ineffective was that of counter-espionage. A system, which began innocuously enough with the Peace Preservation Laws of 1925, where the police and military police came to have powers of arrest and repression of a quite untrammelled kind very soon ceases to operate by any system remotely based on 'objective' rules of evidence and proof, quickly loses sight of the rationale on which it was based in the first place and ceases to be able to discriminate between what is indispensable to protect national security and what is absurd even to begin to contemplate regarding as an official secret. A state in which the elite has even formulated the concept of 'the enemy within' has already taken itself well down the slippery slope toward the tragic Hegelian formula of pity, fear and waste.

This error was compounded by the fact that the Japanese either derided or feared their allies. They may have come to respect the intelligence of their enemies by the end of the war, but few among the military had any respect for it before the Pacific War began. Rather, as a result of the intelligence that came their way by their own efforts or those of their allies, they had come to believe that they knew far more about their enemies than they believed their enemies knew about them, and consistently spurned all information provided by their enemies, even when most of it was actually true. They more often than not preferred to accept the half-truths of their allies, who well understood how to supplant principle with expediency and exploited the envy, ambition and greed that masqueraded behind the facade of superpatriotism. There was little respect in Japan for the intelligence function: admiration was reserved for it only where it was conjoined with covert action that seemed to produce concrete or decisive outcomes. Caution and wisdom became terms of abuse among the headstrong middle and junior ranks of the officer corps because they were identified with the attitudes of their seniors. Knowledge of the world was subverted by staff officers who fell into the oldest of traps, that of doing the enemy's thinking for him. Inevitably, whether it was Russians or the Chinese or the British or the Americans, the enemy was perfectly capable of thinking for himself. The blows they rained on the Japanese, however, more often than not merely led to a redoubling of effort, fresh inputs of fanaticism and even more repressive harshness, which brought the population of Japan ever closer to despair and desperation, and convinced more and more of their enemies that the greatest kindness that could be done for the 'mad dog of Asia' was to put it down. The discovery of a rich vein of uranium ore in Indochina and the interception of this information in a cable of 22 January 1945 from Hanoi to Tokyo, combined with the subsequent evidence of nuclear-related materials being sent to Japan by U-boat in the spring of 1945, played no small part in making the American leadership feel increasingly justified in pressing ahead with the testing and dropping of the atomic bomb on Japan. Intelligence gained by their enemies from Japanese signals systems not only greatly facilitated the defeat of Japan's European allies, but brought Japanese society itself closer to total annihilation than any since Carthage.

Notes

1. Vice-President Mushakoji Kinhide of the UN University in Tokyo examined this question in some depth in an article, entitled 'From Fear of Dependence to Fear of Independence', *Japan Annual of International Affairs* (1961), pp. 77 ff., relating to the contemporary context of Japan's emergence from US post-war tutelage.

2. Foreigners have observed the low Japanese capacity for alcohol and sometimes sought to exploit it. For example, officers of the German General Staff who were under orders from Hitler in late July 1943 to learn as much as possible about Japanese planning and strategy seem to have made the Japanese military attaché in Berlin a target of such a tactic. It proved to have very little value. Cf. W. H. Forbis, *Japan Today*, p. 74, quoted in A. J. Marder, *Old Friends, New Enemies—The Royal Navy and the Imperial Japanese Navy, 1936–1941* (Oxford, 1981), p. 347 n. and the author's 'Commander Ross RN and the Ending of Anglo-Japanese Friendship 1933–1936', *International Studies* (1985/3), pp. 34–56.

3. Japanese writers, particularly on the political right, have been trying to explain the reasons for Japan's post-war economic success in terms of re-interpretations of history that would accord Japan a unique place: sometimes retrospectively backwards from the present, as in the case of Ishida Ichirō of Tokai University, or directed to the future in terms of the information society, as in the case of groups such as the *Jōhōshakai Kenkyūjō-chō*. New-found national self-confidence, however, was already being expressed by Mr Nakasone Yasuhiro when head of the Self-Defence Agency in the early 1970s, which attracted Soviet and Chinese criticism of 'the revival of militarism', or in the 'textbook controversy' where accusations were levelled at the Japanese Ministry of Education for rewriting the history of the present century in line with a more benign image of Japan's international role. Accusations about a revival of Japanese intelligence activities abroad and about a sinister interpretation to moves in the Japanese Diet by right-wing members of the ruling party for the adoption of an anti-espionage law covering the whole of the Japanese population have been regularly aired by members of the Opposition parties in the Diet: see *Akahata*, 5 May 1976 and *Japan Times*, 5 February 1986, for example.

4. See Louis Allen, 'The Nakano School', *BAJS Proceedings* 10 (1985), pp. 8–18.

5. Most attachés were supplied with funds for intelligence and covert activities in general. Information about the US naval building programme was generally quite easy to purchase prior to the spring of 1940, for example in the Brooklyn Navy Yard. Non-Japanese were usually employed as agents only in particularly difficult areas, when Japanese efforts to buy information locally ran into resistance. For example, areas like the Soviet Union where White Russians, Poles, Finns and Balts were often employed, or Italians and Germans in China, S.E. Asia and the United States in 1941. The late Captain Roskill cited the case of former Flight-Lieutenant F. J. Rutland said by the FBI to have been spying in the United States for the Japanese: letter of 24 September 1969 to Dr A. M. Le Q. Clayton, RMA, Sandhurst, cited with the latter's permission.

6. Army officers were planted in many of the more remote consular posts in Siberia and the Far East, mainly from the late 1920s onward. There were also reports of Japanese officers learning languages like Ukrainian and being posted to consular posts in European as well as Asiatic Russia. On the whole, however, the Japanese general staff tended to work mainly with Polish, Finnish, Rumanian and Baltic military agencies and established a co-ordination centre within the 2nd Section of the Polish general staff building in Warsaw during the 1930s to centralise and evaluate intelligence gathered from the European zone. The Polish agent Alfons Jakubianec, who worked closely with the Japanese consul at Kowno, Sugihara, was arrested by the Gestapo in Berlin in July 1941. Under torture, he claimed that the Japanese intelligence co-ordination centre working against the Soviet Union had been moved from Warsaw to Stockholm, where it was headed by Colonel Nishimura and Major-General Onodera Makoto. Onodera's closest Polish collaborator, Colonel Michal Rybikowski, has stated in a letter of 8 January 1986 to the author:

Japanese consul Sugihara had in his office (as secretary) a Gestapo man—by name Wolfgang Gudsche. That is the reason that I never worked closely with Sugihara and never met him.

One of the earliest accounts of Colonel Rybikowski's exploits was published in Sweden: see Jerzy Adamczyk: 'Hemlig Agent Avslöjade Militärkupp mot Stockholm', *Aftonbladet*, 11 June 1969 and Józef Lewandowski, *The Swedish Contribution to the Polish Resistance Movement, 1939–1942* (Uppsala, 1979). General Onodera's memoirs have recently been compiled by his wife, Yuriko, and published in Japan as *Baruto-Kai hotori-nite* (Tokyo, 1985). See also S. Strumph-Wojtkiewicz, *Tiergarten* (Warsaw, 1974) for a Polish account. Ther author is grateful also to Dr Jósef Garliński, and Mrs Halina Czarnoczka of the *Studium Polski Podziemnej* for their help and advice in consulting surviving records of the 6th Section of the Polish General Staff.

7. For example, when reports of European arms supplies began to circulate in the autumn of 1937 as heading for the Kuomintang regime in China, the Japanese consular network in the Mediterranean was activated to check the sources of supply. The consular posts in Egypt were particularly active because of the opportunities for obtaining information on cargoes passing through the Suez Canal. This appears to have become known as a result of the decipherment of Japanese consular traffic by a number of states. The network in Egypt was later to be useful in estimating British military and naval forces and their activities in North Africa and the Balkans in 1940/41.

8. Some of the most famous post-war journalists in Japan were stationed in Europe during World War II and their intelligence-gathering (not to speak of their amorous) activities were closely followed by German counter-espionage agencies. Some of these agencies' ciphers were also being read from 1941 by GC&CS and particular interest was paid in the Gestapo's intelligence activities by the Counterintelligence War Room in Britain, which interrogated such figures as Walter Schellenberg in great detail in the summer of 1945. A great deal of statistical material intercepted was closely studied and some of such data on the acute shortage of fuel in occupied Europe after the failure of the German offensive in the East was passed on *en clair* to Ambassador Craigie. This information was perfectly accurate, but the reaction of the Japanese naval staff (which was heavily influenced by pro-German officers) was to treat any information from British sources as highly suspect.

9. The earliest ciphers of the Japanese Army to be penetrated were those of the Sea Transport Section *(Rikugun Unyu-bu)* in the War Ministry about the beginning of 1943. For its deciphered signals, see National Archives, Washington DC, Record Group 457, Records of the National Security Agency, Series SRR. Citations from this archive will be abbreviated to NAW/RG457/SRR, with similar abbreviations from other groups and series.

10. These systems were evidently used throughout the 1920s and early 1930s by the Red Army, Air Force, *OGPU/MVD* and *kolkhoz* networks and among the few that were relatively easy to solve. There are detailed accounts of such systems in the quarterly reports of the decryption group in the Cipher Section of the German Ministry of Defence. See the author's 'No Final Solution', in C. M. Andrew (ed.), *Codebreaking and Signals Intelligence* (London, 1986), chapter 2.

11. The author is grateful to Professor John Erickson and Mrs Mary Pain for information relevant to Colonel Kowalewski, who was at different times Polish military attaché in Moscow and Bucharest in the inter-war period. The officer with perhaps the greatest knowledge of relations between the Polish and Japanese general staffs was Colonel Levittoux, who served in Tokyo from 1937 to 1941 and was unfortunately killed in Normandy in 1944. The interrogation of Lieut. General Wakamatsu Tadakazu in 1946 throws some further light on the relationship in the mid-1930s: NAW/RG331/IPS Case 453; and see the author's 'The Polish Labyrinth and the Soviet Maze', *International Studies*, 1982, pp. 66–87.

A telegram of the German Foreign Ministry to its mission in Japan, dated 28 April 1941, claimed that, according to information from the German Army C-inC, Colonel Levittoux's bureau in Tokyo was 'a dangerous espionage centre' working closely with the British Secret Service. When questioned about this in an interview with the author at Bad Godesburg in September 1982, the late General Gerhard Matzky, who had been German military attaché in Japan from 1938 until late 1940 and was chief of the Intelligence Division (*Chef O Qu IV*) at this date, could not recall his admittedly large department dealing with this issue. However, it is more likely than not that the information was derived from General Fellgiebel's department, the Army Signals Inspectorate, which was monitoring signals between the Polish government-in-exile and its outposts abroad, along with the *Forschungsamt*.

12. See Herbert Yardley, *The American Black Chamber* (New York, 1931) and the subsequent work by Ladislas Farago and David Kahn. Yardley's revelations first appeared in the April 1931 issue of the *Saturday Evening Post*. It appears that, although Yardley was given an *ex gratia* payment when the 'New York office' was closed in 1929, he had no pension rights and essentially published details to supplement his income. This was a common enough problem for the American unemployed at this date, and cuts were made in practically every secret service round the world, with the exception of the Soviet Union, on budgetary grounds. Even the US Office of Naval Intelligence (ONI), which had been given a secret 'slush' fund of $100,000 by President Wilson's Treasury Secretary at the end of World War I, had what was left of this taken away from it in 1931 when the acting head refused to take responsibility for it. NAW/RG457/SRH335.

    ONI had used some of its funds to arrange a break-in at the Japanese Consulate-General in New York, where the Japanese Navy's secret operational code-book of 1918 was extracted from the safe, photographed and returned unnoticed in 1921. Over the next six years, the material was translated and organised as the 'Red Book' (from the binding given to it by ONI), and it was fortunate that the basic codebook of 1918 remained in force until 30 November 1930. The radio traffic of the Japanese fleet, particularly during annual fleet manoeuvres, was monitored by a series of Navy and Marine Corps posts set up at Beijing, Shanghai and the Philippines in the period from 1925 to 1939, as well as by ships of the US Asiatic Fleet. Sufficient expertise was accumulated by 1930 for it to be possible to reconstruct the new codebook cryptanalytically and organise a new 'Blue Book'. The ONI lost out to MI-8 after 1918 to receive funds for a central decrypt agency, but after the War and State Departments closed down Yardley's operation in 1929, ONI and MID were able to compete on a more even basis in this field.

13. These points were among the findings of a group of former Japanese Navy officers, known as the *Shiryō Chōsa-Kai*, published in 1976. The standard history of the Japanese Navy is that by Ikeda Kiyoshi, *Kaigun to Nihon*, (Tokyo, 1981), and see also Toyama Saburō: *Nihon Kaigunshi* (Tokyo, 1980), the papers of Admiral Saito Makoto in the National Diet Library, Tokyo and the doctoral dissertation of I. T. M. Gow on Admiral Kato-Kanji, University of Sheffield, 1985. Then there are the naval volumes in the monumental official Japanese war history published by *Bōei-chō, Kenshūjo* (now *Kenkyūjō*), *Senshi-shitsu*, which were begun by the Demobilisation Bureau under Rear-Admiral Tomioka Sadatoshi and published by the G-2 Section of SCAP in the 1950s in translation. See also Iwashima Hisao, *Jōhō Sen ni mattai makeshita Nihon-Rikugun Angō 'shinwa' no Hōkai* (Tokyo, 1984) and *Kenkyū no Kishū*, (Tokyo, PHP Kenkyūjō, 1984).

14. This feeling was widespread among the US signals intelligence community at the time and this is summed up in a characteristic fashion by Commander Joseph J. Rochefort in the Oral History Series of the US Naval Institute at Annapolis in 1969. The author is grateful to Mr Paul Stillwell, and to Dr Dean Allard and Mr Mike Walker, US Navy Operational History Archive, Navy Yard, Washington DC for assistance with this and other materials, cited in subsequent footnotes in abbreviated form (USNI/OHP and USNOHA). Rochefort was involved in the radio interception programme in the Far East in the late 1920s and was in Tokyo as a language officer when the news of the Yardley revelations broke. He was subsequently the chief cryptanalyst at the 14th Naval District at Honolulu in 1941–42.

15. Stimson has been commonly ridiculed, and it is now suggested that President Hoover may have been behind the closure. This does not seem to square with Hoover's support in the early 1920s to radio communications development when secretary of commerce. Rochefort

(see n. 14 above) virtually denounces Yardley as a charlatan, and it is not without significance that William Friedman, who was brought in with 'Miss Aggie' to replace Yardley in 1929, had an uncompromisingly negative view of Yardley. The two could never have worked together. Yardley's operation had already been cut back before 1929 and its failure to deliver further Japanese decrypts at a time when the US Navy was making headway seems to have been the main reason for ending the relationship and substituting the Friedman team.

Rivalries of this kind between agencies and individuals recur in virtually all the countries involved in such activities at this date and it is interesting also to look at the virulent denunciation of the activities of a former US Navy chief engineer, E. K. Jett, of the Defense Communications Board by Captain L. S. Safford of Op-20-G in 1941 and 1943. Safford was not a cryptanalyst, but was involved throughout the US Navy's radio intercept and decryption process from the early 1920s in an administrative capacity and with a special interest in protecting the security of US Navy ciphers. NAW/RG457/SRH-355 and SRNM-007.

16. Most accounts argue that the shift by the Japanese Army to a machine cipher in 1932 and by the *Gaimushō* in 1934 stemmed from the Yardley revelations. This theory has doubt thrown on it by Captain Holtwick USN in his study of 1971, though mainly, it would appear, as a result of there not being any early response of such a kind from the Japanese Navy. The latter, of course, did not have the kind of collaboration that the Army had from the Poles in cryptography: we are not quite sure yet if the Poles were working together with the Japanese Army on decrypting Soviet signals, or whether the Poles simply—like the Germans later—passed on to the Japanese intelligence derived from the analysis of communications, without specifically spelling out its exact origins. There is certainly no evidence to suggest that the Poles revealed to the Japanese Army what they revealed to the French and British later. The Poles certainly brought with them to France members of the deciphering team that worked on Soviet ciphers as well as on the 'Enigma'.

It appears that the Japanese acquired at least commercial 'Enigma', as did the US Army and GC&CS in Britain, but the military versions were not evidently acquired before 1942, and 'Enigma' systems were not apparently incorporated in Japanese equipment (as Winterbotham alleged in 1974). The US Navy sent Commander (later Rear-Admiral) J. N. Wenger to Europe to study the O'Brien machine in Britain, the Belin machine in France and the 'Enigma' in Germany in 1934. The US naval attaché in Berlin evidently apprised the German Navy in advance of Wenger's intentions and it obstructed his access to the commercial firm manufacturing it. In addition to developing the M134a (SIGABA), the US Army ordered cipher machines from the Swedish inventor Hagelin, who also sold his equipment to the French and the Italians. In 1936, Hagelin was given introductions to cryptographic specialists in the German defence establishment by their naval attaché in Sweden, Rear-Admiral Steffan. The Hagelin system, however, was rejected by the Germans, who used tabulating machines during World War II to decrypt Italian and US ciphers using the Hagelin system. It was partly as a result of such tests that the German faith in the security of the 'Enigma' system was reaffirmed.

17. Harada Kumao in the spring of 1936 noted an altercation between Colonel Kagesa of the Japanese War Ministry and *Gaimushō* officials after Army cryptanalysts solved messages from the Chinese minister in Tokyo to Nanking and took offence at what were regarded as slanderous statements by Japanese officials to the Chinese envoy about the Army's China policy. In 1931, the Chinese were reported to be employing commercial codes for transmitting information from missions in Europe to Nanking, according to German traffic analysts. Since the Germans were involved in supplying military assistance and equipment to Chiang Kai-shek's forces, it is presumed that the secure operational ciphers used to communicate between the Chinese forces in the field and headquarters at Nanking in the early 1930s were of German origin. The East Germans had claimed credit for Richard Sorge and his network obtaining photographs of such cipher tables from the German radio

engineer Stölzner, though the claims, as published, lack the same kind of documentary evidence that is available from Soviet archives for Sorge's activities in Japan. See Julius Marder, *Dr. Sorge-Report* (Berlin, 1984), pp. 94–5, quoting only the memoirs of Otto Braun. See also Allen, op. cit., p. 12.

18. Following a brief break in late 1942, the main cipher used by Japanese military attachés abroad was broken in the early summer of 1943. According to information from General Onodera in 1982, he also had an additional special cipher that he believed to have been secure. NAW/RG457/SRA Series.

19. For details, see the author's article, 'The Polish Labyrinth and the Soviet Maze', op. cit.

20. The German Foreign Ministry and Navy were reading 'Red' signals from Japanese legations in Europe from at least the beginning of 1936 and there are signs of attempts by the Foreign Ministry to read Berlin-Tokyo traffic as far back as 1925. By the summer of 1942, Ribbentrop was complaining that his Cypher Section (*Pers.Z*) was still unable to resolve 'Purple' signals because he was keen to know what Ambassador Ōshima was saying to *Gaimushō*. Weber (*BRAM*) minute of 5 May and Schauffler (*Pers.Z*) reply of 6 May 1942 in: *Auswärtiges Amt, Politisches Archiv: Handakten von Loesch: Akte M 30: 'Japan'*. The German Navy archives contain a top secret decrypt of a Japanese radio signal dated 9 January 1943: *Oberkommando der 'Kriegsmarine: 1 Skl.: 'Kriegstagebuch, Teil C, Heft XVII: 'Haltung der USA, (1941–4)*. It should be noted that, as a result of individual file designations employed in different archives where German records are held, citations seek to identify the original user agency designations.

21. An example of GC&CS decipherment of Japanese signals in the 1930s can be found in the relay of the text of the Secret Supplementary Protocol to the Anti-Comintern Pact to the Far Eastern Department of the Foreign Office on 4 December 1936: Public Record Office, Kew, FO371/F7504/303/23. The Russians also had the text and had also been apprised that the German embassy in Japan had not been informed. Dr Sorge probably supplied the latter information, but it is possible that it came from decodes of German traffic. The US Army Signals Intelligence Service is also rather coy about disclosing anything about decrypts of German diplomatic traffic. See the 'sanitised' section of the report by Brig. General W. P. Cordeman of 20 February 1946: NAW/RG457/SRH-349, pp. 30–31. Such omissions are more often than not based on prior Anglo-American consultation, and there are some signs in German archival materials of British insights into German diplomatic traffic, but they do not indicate more than temporary losses in communications security. The German military, however, believed that their Foreign Ministry's 'minor' code (used in legation traffic) was insecure in 1940: *OKM/2.Skl.:'Kriegstagebuch' (1940)*, memorandum of 2 November 1940. Concern about a loss of security indirectly via the Italians, however, was seen as a much greater headache, especially from the end of 1940, when German agencies began to decipher a number of more important British ciphers.

22. The German embassy in Washington reported US decipherment of Japanese diplomatic codes in April 1941, and specific warnings were sent by the German Navy High Command to naval command posts where Japanese naval officers might make approaches after the outbreak of the Pacific War not to pass on any information based on the decipherment of British signals so as not to risk such knowledge getting back to the British in view of 'Anglo-American inroads into Japanese code materials'. All such information based on radio intercepts and decrypts was only to be relayed direct to the Japanese naval staff via the 'DJ' version of the 'Enigma' machine in use from January 1940 to June 1942 on the Berlin-Tokyo circuit. Virtually all of these signals were sent by postal cable via the USSR. East German historians have claimed that Captain Lietzmann, the German naval attaché in Japan from 1937 to 1940, 'brought his diary and the German naval code to Dr Sorge's knowledge': Mader, op. cit., p. 362. If so, it is not made specific whether it was the hand cipher (Code A) in operation from 1937 to the end of 1939 or the 'DJ' machine cipher, the tables for which were changed every three months. Lietzmann was replaced by Rear-Admiral Wenneker at the end of the first change of 'DJ' keys in March 1940. He appears

not to have been made privy to the most secret exchanges between the *Abwehr* and the Japanese naval attaché in Berlin. See the author's *The Price of Admiralty—The War Diary of the German Naval Attaché in Japan, 1939–1943,* I (Ripe, 1982).

If Soviet decrypts were made of this traffic, then they are certainly not available to scholars in the way that Ultra decrypts of the radio traffic between Berlin and Tokyo between June 1942 and May 1945 are: NAW/RG457/SRGL Series. These signals were mainly in 'M Bertok' or 'Seahorse' cipher and most appear to have been deciphered retrospectively in the autumn of 1945.

23. German police and military decipher experts who had encountered Comintern and *GRU* agent signals since the early 1920s appear not to have had much successs with the book-based reciphers they employed. Acting on a tip-off from the French police about a PCF representative, Serge Lefranc, the mainly British-run International Settlement Police at Shanghai arrested several Chinese Communists and raided the house of 'Hilaire Noulens' (Paul Ruegg) of the Pan-Pacific Trade Union Secretariat. A meticulous examination of his correspondence and papers revealed that correspondence had been coded with the German Mosse Code, then recyphered using pages from the book by P. Oppenheim, *The Lion and the Lamb.* A copy of the ISP memorandum was found in the Netherlands Consulate-General (Shanghai) Report No. 3106/211 of 11 September 1931 in: *Ministerie van Buitlandse Zaken, s'Gravenhage:* 'Archief Consulat Generaal Shanghai,' *(1874–1951), Doos S.III.* See also the account in: Marder, op. cit., pp. 107–9.

24. A file on the work of British consular officers in the Far East in 1941 is marked as 'closed for 75 years': PRO/F0371/28033, as is the file PREM 252/5. A central bureau for the exchange of intelligence with the dominions was established in London in 1939: FO371/23966 & 23994, and an information bureau in Tokyo: FO371/23967. There are references to SIS and MI-6 activity in the Far East in the author's 'Commander Ross RN,' op. cit. For further information on the FECB, see Marder, op. cit., pp. 356 ff., and 'Notes on the Far East,' dated 12 March 1942 in: Brooke-Popham Papers, Folio v/9/5/2, Liddell-Hart Centre for Military Archives, King's College, London; D. Horner, *High Command—Australia and Allied Strategy, 1939–1945* (Canberra, 1982), chapter 10. The author is also grateful to Mr William Symon, a former member of OIC, Eastern fleet, for information received.

25. Marder, op. cit., p. 356 & n. Descriptions of reconnaissance missions in anchorage areas used by units of the Combined Fleet suggest that Special Boat Sections of the type used in the Falklands in 1982 were despatched from British submarines based at Hong Kong. An Italian intelligence report of 1941 relayed to Berlin by the German Naval Attaché in Rome in *B.Nr.GKdos 1322/41* of 12 August 1941 contained information obtained from two British prisoners in North Africa who claimed to belong to a commando unit headed by Colonel Lang which infiltrated Italian ports and attached limpet mines to supply vessels. Infiltration was achieved by small sections delivered by submarines which were receiving information about the movements and location of Axis transports by radio from a transmitter near Derby. *OKM: 1. Skl. Lagezimmer:* 'Attaché-Meldungen,' *(1939–1941).*

According to Mr Symon, the establishment near Derby was located at Stratton-under-Fosse; it engaged in operational traffic analysis and decryption and was more significant than the Bletchley Park set-up. He recalls being attached to the establishment at a point in time when a Japanese air-to-ground code was unravelled when an alert young lady intercepting and transcribing signals stayed on the same wavelength after a signal was intercepted and overheard a further plain-language conversation by the Japanese radio operators which was helpful for resolution of cipher signals.

A German agent who frequented bars used by Allied sailors in Japan was told that Blue Funnel and Glen Line steamers were being used to refuel warships from the China Station outside Japanese territorial limits to enable them to keep continuously on station. This was reported to Berlin on 1 March 1940 and a general circular was issued by the German Navy in mid-September to report on the movements of steamers belonging to these particular lines. This suggests that warships may well have been instructed to pay particular attention to the same vessels and may be why the raider *Atlantis* singled out the *Automedon* in November 1940. It is also quite likely that information about the Glen Line steamers off Japan was passed on to the Japanese Navy, but it is not known if this was connected with the reported loss of H.M. Submarine *Regulus* on 6 December 1940. See *The Price of Admiralty*, op. cit., vol. 1, p. 99 and vol. 2, p. 366 & n., Marder, op. cit., and fn. 60 infra.

26. The Royal Navy's chain of HF/DF stations was rapidly expanded in 1940/41 and was believed by the Germans to be equipped to deal with both 'short signals' (*Kurzsignale*) and high-speed signals. When, as a result of the early breaks in the U-boat cipher traffic in 1941, Allied vessels began to be re-routed to take them out of the areas in which U-boat groups were known to be located, Admiral Doenitz expressed worries about the loss of cipher security and was reassured by the head of the *B-Stelle*, Teubner, at Lorient in June 1941 that the HF/DF network's efficiency was the source of the problem. Information about the network was obtained from an analysis of papers found on board H.M. Submarine *Seal* captured in the Baltic, which ought not to have been kept on board the vessel. See *3.Skl.B 530/41 gKdos* of 21 February 1941: NAW/RG457/*B-Bericht 1940, Bd.4* and Tim Mulligan, 'The German Navy Evaluates Its Cryptographic Security, October 1941'. *Military Affairs* XLVIV 1985, pp. 75–79. The author is grateful to Mr R. M. Coppock, Ministry of Defence, London and to Mr Harry Rilley and Mr John E. Taylor, National Archives, Washington D.C. for help with these and other points. For information on US monitoring of Japanese naval and diplomatic traffic from 1924, see: NAW/RG457/SRH-178/179/222/223/206/320/355. In peacetime, it was much less likely that information on such activities would be given away. Under wartime operational conditions, it was more difficult to conceal prior knowledge of enemy intentions, but it was more difficult to conceal prior knowledge of enemy intentions, but it was always possible to find some other explanation than cryptanalysis. The Germans noted, for example, that the Italians had been taken by surprise in the Battle of Cape Matapan and could put it down to the weakness of Italian ciphers or other inefficiencies that Italian commanders often assured the Germans would never happen in German units: see NAW/RG457/ *B-Bericht 13/41* of 4 April 1941. The Germans complained that, although the movements of convoys could be learned from the decryption of signals in traffic with merchant vessels, it was rare for them to be able to decipher signals relaying HF/DF bearings because these were sent in warship ciphers. The occasional signal intercepted by 'chance' may well have been part of the deliberate deception arrangements employed to disguise Ultra intelligence: *Chef MND (B) 1584/41 gKdos* of 19 June 1941.

27. Gordon Prange, *At Dawn We Slept* (New York, 1982), chapter 9.

28. Horner, op. cit., p. 225.

29. Most of the files of the Dutch agencies involved in decrypting Japanese signals in the East Indies were destroyed prior to the Japanese takeover in 1942 and a good deal of controversy surrounds claims of warnings sent to the United States about the meaning and significance of the 'Winds' message and also of Japanese Combined Fleet movements in the early days of December 1941. See Robert Haslach, *Nishi no Kaze, Hare* (Weesp, 1985); R. Pineau & J. Costello, *I Was There*: (New York, 1985); J. C. Bijkerk, *Waarwel, tot Betere Tijden:* (Franeker, 1974); Rear-Admiral J. F. W. Nuboer, 'A History of Afdeling I (Intelligence), Naval Staff, Batavia . . .,'. *The Cryptogram* XLVII 1978, pp. 1–8. The author is grateful for this information to Mr. J. E. S. Rusbridger. For information on Anglo-Dutch co-operation, see PRO/ADM 199, War Diary of the C-in-C, China Fleet. The main War Diary (Naval) of the Admiralty, Vol. 48 contains a C-in-C, China signal 1403/14 of 14 March 1941 to Admiralty requesting permission for Anglo-Dutch codebooks locally produced at Singapore to be handed over to US Asiatic Fleet. Some Dutch code material appears to have been compromised in 1941, when a Dutch radio operator defected to the Germans in the Far East, asking to be rapatriated to the Netherlands.

In March 1940, when the Germans were planning to organise a break-out of some of their 19 merchantmen in Dutch East Indies waters to Vladivostock, these vessels were shadowed on the orders of the Dutch C-in-C. The German move was cancelled when it became clear that information about it had been apparently revealed by British sources at Singapore and relayed to Tokyo by Japanese press correspondents. Commander F. C. van Oosten (*Ministerie van Defensie/Marine/Afdeling Maritime Historie*) to the author, 17 January 1983; see also files of the Netherlands Consulaat Generaal, Shanghai for 1940–41 on Germans interned in the East Indies and on German propaganda in: *Ministerie van Buitlandse Zaaken*, s'Gravenhage. The author is grateful for the assistance of Miss W. M. E. Bruseker of the Central Mail & Filing Division.

30. Horner, op. cit., chapter 10; Cordeman memorandum: NAW/RG457/ SRH-349, p. 19. It is claimed by Cordeman that the US Army was responsible for developing the electronic equipment deployed against four-wheel 'Enigma' but accepts that CBB in Brisbane simultaneously achieved the first breaks in the Japanese Army's Sea Transport cipher in April 1943 and that the British-run Wireless Experimental Unit in India contributed to resolution of addresses in Japanese radio traffic.

31. Marder, op. cit., p. 357 n. states: 'For reasons unknown the FECB records are apparently no longer extant.' For information on co-operation between the Royal Australian Navy and the US Navy, see: NAW/RG457/ SRNM-006; Rochefort interview: USNI/OHP. Australian co-operation with FECB and Bletchley is discussed in Horner, op. cit.

32. *AA/PA/Büro St.S.: 'Japan,' Bd.3, (1941); 1.Skl.I op a 2937/41 g.Kdos to Marine Gruppe Süd*, 19 December 1941. The German Naval Attaché in Tokyo asked in cipher *Tel.Nr.1360/ 41 gKdos* of 19 December 1941 if his earlier DJ telegrams dealing with the most sensitive reports on the naval situation were secure, as he was being constantly pressed by Ambassador Ott to utilise Foreign Ministry codes. In view of the constant reiteration of the need for security by the Japanese Navy, he had refused these requests. After consultation with his superiors, Commander Hibsch of the German Navy Signals Division (*MND/Nba*) was told that Wenneker was 'to stick in principle to our own circuits and our own cipher material at all costs'. *O.K.M.: 1.Skl.: Akte X.I: 'Zusammenarbeit Deutschland-Japan,' (1941–1943)*, pp. 17, 27 & 29; communication from Rear-Admiral Helmut Neuss, 13 December 1982.

33. See NAW/RG457/SRGL Series; PRO/ADM223/4 & 6–7. The author is grateful to Mr Ralph Erskine for supplementary information. The British files are not nearly as compact as those of NSA, but from internal evidence some 'sanitisation' has occurred and some signals were monitored by British interception posts and not by US ones. The author is grateful to Dr Carmen Blacker and Dr Michael Loewe for information on work done on Far Eastern Ultra at Bletchley Park.

34. 'Seahorse' traffic of August 1942 resolved in September and October 1943 includes references of messages emanating from the *B-Leitstelle*, the central decryption agency of the German Navy: PRO/ADM 223/4. The text of the German–Japanese Naval Communications Agreement of September 1942 is in: *O.K.M.: 1.Skl.: 'KTB Teil C, Heft XV: Zusammenarbeit mit Japan,' Bd.2, (1942–1944)* and intercepts of subsequent amendments are in: PRO/ADM 223/7.

35. Ott (Tokyo) Tel. No. 2872 of 23 December 1941 to Minister Selchow in: *AA/PA/Büro St.S.: 'Japan,' Bd.4, (1941–1942)*; Stahmer (Shanghai) Tel. No. 634 of 24 July 1942 in: *ibid.*, but *'China,' Bd.1, (1939–1942)*.

36. Entry in Halder Diary referring to discussion with General Fellgiebel, 4 December 1940; *Genst.d.H./O Qu IV/Attaché-Abteilung Nr.759/42g* of 4 February 1942 to Admiral Groos refers to discussions in August 1941 between Fellgiebel and Japanese Army officers; *O.K.H.: Genst.d.H.: Atttaché-Abteilung VIII: 'KTB,' (1942–1944)*; Kupfer-Taniguchi discussions on 6 July 1944 in: *O.K.M.: 1.Skl.: 'KTB, Teil B, Heft VI: Nachrichtendienst, B-Dienst,' (1944–1945)*.

37. 'Japanese Naval Intelligence,' *ONI Review* (July 1946): pp. 36–40: USNOHA. The map of BAMS radio zones compiled from captured material is reproduced on page 190 from an enclosure to *Skl./ Chef MND III Nr. 3325/42 g.Kdos* of 20 August 1942: NAW/RG457/*B-Berichte 1942*. Information picked up by the *B-Dienst* about the movement of Allied shipping in Japanese areas of operations was relayed to Tokyo intermittently, and information already in the hands of the Naval Attaché's monitoring group, mainly about the United States, was handed over at the outbreak of war. The German Navy made very little headway with US cipher traffic because machine ciphers were distributed all at once to military units, starting on 1 January 1942, creating a virtual blackout. Only when code tables or books were obtained was it possible, briefly, to obtain insights. Merchant ship code material continued to be seized by the Germans in the Auantic and Indian Oceans during 1942, and the Mersigs Code was acquired in late 1942 and in 1943.

38. *ONI Review* (July 1946), p. 38.

39. NAW/RG457/SRH-355, p. 122.

40. USSBS Interrogation No. 355; SCAP/ATIS Report No. 3543B: USNOHA: Prange, op. cit., chapter 8.

41. NAW/RG457/SRH-178/180, 222/5. 320

42. Wenneker conversations with Admiral Nagano Osami and Vice-Admiral Kondō Nobutake (Chief and Vice-Chief of Japanese Naval Staff) on 15 and 16 April 1941 in: *O.K.M.: M Att: 'Japan—Mobilmachung,' Bd. 4, (1941)* with translated text in: *The Price of Admiralty*, op. cit., vol. 2.

43. *ONI Review* (July 1946), pp, 36 & 38–9.

44. For a detailed report by a German-American correspondent of the fighting in Shanghai in 1932, see the memorandum *Abwehr Vb Nr.60/32 g.Kdos* of 14 April 1932 in: *O.K.M. 1. Skl.Ic.1: 'Marinepolitische Angelegenheiten, 'Heft 2, (1929–1935)*: see also Mader, op. cit., pp. 115–6, which contains no information about the small number of *Abwehr* contacts being built up in China at the same time as the network of the *GRU*.

45. 'Magic' intercepts, based on *Gaimushō* sources, only gave clues to the timing of the break in relations between Japan and the Western Powers. Messages accumulated thick and fast the closer it came to the operational deadline and there were often insufficient numbers of personnel to process and translate the intercepts and decrypts quickly enough, or to single out the really important signals from the less and least significant. The whole point of the elaborate Japanese exercise was to maximise surprise and deception about where precisely the blows would fall and in what order of priority.

Ambassador Ōshima declared to Hitler on 2 January 1942 that the US Ambassador in Japan had been deceived by the people with whom he had consorted in Japan and had received a false impression of Japan's true intentions. Japan had also chosen the right people in Nomura Kichisaburō and Kurusu Saburō because they had negotiated as though Japan were actually willing to reach an agreement. He also expressed the opinion that 'if the British and American diplomats in Japan had really kept their eyes open, they could not have failed to spot the preparations and mobilisation of the Combined Fleet'. *Auswärtiges Amt* memorandum *Füh.2/42 g.Rs* of 3 January 1942 in: *AA/PA/BRAM: 'Handakten von Loesch'* and see NAW/RG457/SRDJ Series. See also R. A. Theobald, *The Final Secret of Pearl Harbor* (New York,1954); Prange op. cit.

46. C. C. Ong: 'Churchill, Japan and Singapore Defence, 1940–1941,' *International Studies* 1985, pp. 57–72 argues that the British C-in-C, Far East, Air Chief Marshal Brooke-Popham, was so badly affected by his dismissal a month earlier that he lacked the necessary fearlessness to launch 'Matador', even though Churchill had given him the necessary go-ahead on 5 December. Up until then, however, London had repeatedly stressed the need to avoid any provocation of the Japanese and had not been prepared to give the field commander the slightest encouragement to take the initiative. Three days in which to reverse the habits of the previous year were scarcely the right prelude to adjustment to an

opposite mode of behaviour, nor was it absolutely certain that the Japanese Army would actually land in the Kra Isthmus. It cannot by any means be assumed that either the British or the Dutch commanders were any more prescient about what would happen on Hawaii than were the US President and his military advisers.

However, there can be no doubt about his conclusion that Churchill must take full responsibility for the loss of Singapore, and also for the inconsistencies in the policies that preceded it. Marder, op. cit., p. 361 saw a common failure in the US, British and Dutch leadership to take the Japanese seriously, with exceptions such as Admirals Dreyer and Layton on the side of the Royal Navy. He took as standard the set of attitudes embodied in the report by Captain Vivian, the British naval attaché in Japan from 1932 to 1936, on 'The Efficiency of the Japanese Navy' (PRO/ADM/116/3862) dated 18 February 1935. He did not, however, take into consideration the fact that a copy of this report was seen and secretly photographed by the German naval attaché, Captain Wenneker, who viewed it rather critically without saying so to Vivian, and almost certainly used it against the British in his subsequent dealings with the Japanese Navy officer corps. Cf. 'Commander Ross RN,' op. cit., p. 41 fn. 20 and *The Price of Admiralty*, op. cit., vol. 1, Introduction.

In a forthcoming book, *Thailand and the Fall of Singapore*, N. J. Brailey of the University of Bristol explores the ideas that Pearl Harbor was only a sideshow from the Japanese standpoint and that the attack on Kota Bharu was only a sideshow for attacking Thailand. A new monograph due to appear in 1986 by Dr Anthony Clayton, entitled *The British Empire as a Superpower. 1919–1939*, uses a most interesting study by Admiral Sommerville of November 1938 on the strategic possibilities arising from a Japanese intervention in a European war and the response of Admiral Backhouse, which showed up many of the inherent problems in efforts to defend S.E. Asia. Captain Roskill already argued in his letter of 1969: 'I think it is right to say that there was a very considerable failure of Intelligence regarding the Japanese Navy.' This is echoed for the Japanese Army, too, in a note by a former British assistant military attaché in Japan, Colonel G. T. Wards, 7 December 1965 which says about Japanese skills in combined operations:

> A similar evaluation, stressing the high standard of efficiency of the Japanese armed forces in combined operations was included in a report I submitted to the War Office at this time. The General Staff at the War Office considered that I had overrated the Japanese army and much of my report was not passed on to commanders or units in the field. As we were soon to find out, in 1941–42 in Malaya and Hong Kong, our commanders and troops were completely surprised, outwitted, out-generalled and out-fought.

47. The planning for Operation 'Barbarossa' was steadily pushed ahead from early August 1940, even within the German Navy, where it was opposed by Raeder in particular: we can see preparations for the return of coastal defence equipment to the Baltic from the West in the period from 21 August to 7 October, when orders were issued to expand the Swinemünde base to take account of the 'possible hostility of Russia': *O.K.M.: 1.Skl.: Akte Barbarossa V.7: 'Ost-Aufrüstung,' Bd.1, (August 1940–März 1941)*. Raeder consistently pursued the argument about the need to finish the war with Britain first, especially as the flow of arms from the United States was beginning to grow sharply in late 1940 onward, which began to create an increased likelihood of a British intervention on the European mainland as Italian weakness in North Africa became glaringly evident. See *O.K.M.: 'Ob.d.M. Persönlich: Grossadmiral Raeder, Heft 2, (1940–1941)*.

48. On 5 November 1941, when Admiral Wenneker reported the view of a 'senior naval officer' that any prospect of an improvement in Japan-US relations was being regarded in Tokyo as 'hopeless' and that the government had as good as decided on war with the United States, the German Navy chief of staff Admiral Schniewind minuted that he did not regard this as 'wholly authentic'. When the report went on to mention Japanese plans for the occupation of the Philippines, Schniewind noted: 'Manila, in my opinion, is an error', i.e. on

Wenneker's part. *O.K.M.: 1.Skl.: 'KTB Teil C, Heft XV: Zusammenarbeit mit Japan,' Bd.1, (1941)*.

For Churchill's view, see Ong, op. cit., and P. C. Lowe, *Great Britain and the Origins of the Pacific War, 1937–1941*: (Oxford, 1977).

49. Rochefort interview: USNI/OHP.

50. This was contained in an impassioned diatribe by Commander Wilhelm Canaris, the subsequent head of the German Secret Military Intelligence Service, who was sent to Japan in the summer of 1924 to discuss the future of technical co-operation between the German and Japanese navies. See the author's 'The Transfer of German Underwater Weapons Technology to Japan, 1919–1976,' in: C. J. Dunn & I. H. Nish, eds., *European Studies on Japan* (Tenterden, 1979).

51. Boyé (Minister in China) Report No. 2416 of 3 August 1926 to German Foreign Ministry on Japanese policy in China claims that, while the Japanese outwardly displayed solidarity with the rest of the consular corps during the Shanghai disturbances, considerable sums were secretly paid by Japanese undercover agents to militant student and strike committees in cities all over China to ensure that Japanese interests were not made specific targets of boycott and agitation tactics. *AA/PA/Abt.IVb/Akte Po.1/'Allgemeine Auswärtige Politik Japans,' Bd.1, (1920–1928)*.

52. This was the explanation given in a circular about the case issued by the Abwehr to units of the armed forces. Sosnowski was exchanged in a major swap of German and Polish agents in 1936, but apparently rearrested after the German occupation of Poland. See *AA/PA/ Abt.IV Polen/Akte Po.15g: 'Austausch,' (1935–36)*.

53. Hundreds of defectors crossed the Korean and Manchurian frontiers. One of the most important of these was the NKVD General H. S. Lyushkov, who was debriefed by Polish officials and officers in the summer of 1938 because of his detailed knowledge of the situation in the Ukraine as well as the Far East. Subsequently, German intelligence personnel were allowed access and he was interrogated by a Colonel Greiling of *Abwehr III* following an offer put by General Ōshima to Foreign Minister von Ribbentrop that was linked to a German acceptance of a formal agreement between Ōshima and the German War Ministry for an exchange of intelligence about the Soviet Union, for which Ōshima had been agitating since 1935. Senior Soviet officers employed as military advisers in China who were captured on the Eastern Front were interrogated in depth by the Germans and facilities made available to Japanese Army officers involved in covert intelligence activities, such as Colonel Yamamoto Bin and Major Saigō Yūgō, to study these at *Abwehr Stab Walli* in Bialystok and in General Gehlen's organisation (*Abteilung Fremde Heere Ost*). Cf. Allen, op. cit., p. 11 on Yamamoto, who worked closely with Subhas Chandra Bose, and PRO/FO371/22162 & 23515.

54. See fn. 50 *supra*.

55. Canaris memorandum *Abwehr-Abteilung (Chef) Nr.30/35 g.Kdos* of 12 November 1935 to Naval Command in: *O.K.M.: M–IV: 'Attaché–und Asulandsangelegenheiten,' Bd.1, (1934– 1936)*, pp. 302–3. Dr. Gerhard Krebs has argued in the *Nachrichten* of the *OAG* in Tokyo, on the basis of Ambassador Mushakoji's post-war memoirs, that Yamamoto met Ribbentrop in Berlin. This is quite likely to have occurred at receptions during Yamamoto's brief visit, but the point documented here is that he avoided being drawn into any political discussion. This is quite consistent with the views of Ambassador Mushakoji, as confirmed to the author by his son, Mushakoji Kinhide, in an interview in Tokyo in 1974. The reversal of position by Admiral Nagano underlines the difference in approach by the two leading officers that was of major significance in the Anglo-German-Japanese triangular relationship, but also illustrates personal and factional differences within the Japanese Navy. When Nagano became Navy Minister, he tried to have Yamamoto retired early, but this roused a storm of protest and had to be abandoned.

56. See note 46.

57. See citation in note 10.
58. Ibid, and see the German Navy memorandum *A I op 47/39 g.Kdos.Chefs.* of 28 April 1939 dealing with a division of labour agreement between Commander Teubner of the *B-Dienst* and Commanders Galetti and del Mestre of the Italian Navy. An appendix lists French and British ciphers being analysed. British ciphers included the Naval Cypher (officer and rating variants, and those used for the relay of intercepts of Italian signals to DNI from Malta and Gibralter), RAF Code & Decode, Small Ships' Recypher Table, Government Telegraph Code, General Signalling Instructions and Training Procedures. The Italians relayed decrypts of signals from the British C-in-C, China Station, Sir Percy Noble, to Berlin later in the summer of 1939. See *O.K.M.: 1.Skl.I op: Akte 29–1: 'Zusammenarbeit Deutschland-Italien-Spanien-Japan-Russland-Ungarn-Rumanien,' (1938–1941).*
59. See Donald Maclachlan, *Room 39* (London, Weidenfeld, 1969), p. 406; Henry M. Denham, *Inside the Nazi Ring* (London, 1984). The author is grateful to Captain Denham, British naval attaché in Copenhagen and Stockholm from 1940 to 1945, Sir Peter Tennant, press attaché in Stockholm, and Mrs Elizabeth Murray-Clark, cipher clerk in Stockholm, for more detailed information received, as well as to Mr R. M. Coppock, Ministry of Defence, London for help in identifying signals publications from Admiralty Fleet Orders, and to Lord David Cecil for points about security lapses in British diplomatic missions in the 1930s.
60. For details of the *Automedon* seizure, referred to in fn.25 *supra*, see *The Price of Admiralty*, op. cit., vol. 2, pp. 317 *et seq.* and articles in the *BAJS Proceedings*, Vols. IV (1979) and V (1980). The British COS report cited is COS (40) 592 and there are summaries of it and subsequent papers relevant to the Far East in: S. W. Kirby *et al.: The War against Japan*: (London, HMSO, 1957), vol. I, pp. 33 ff. This makes no reference to correspondence with Brooke-Popham, who died in 1953, about the fact that the COS paper had been seized, which Brooke-Popham had raised in his comments on Kirby's draft on 1952. Nor does it allude to the loss already identified in S. W. Roskill, *The War at Sea, 1939–1945* I (London, 1954), p. 282.

    Discussion of the significance of the British COS report for Japanese strategy at a research seminar in the Research Division of Japanese Self-Defence Agency in the winter of 1985 led to the view being expressed that the British authorities deliberately allowed the document to fall into enemy hands. Such an argument, which is somewhat akin to the Pearl Harbor conspiracy theory, can be shown to be absurd in several ways. Firstly, the Foreign Office Index for 1940 includes a directive covering the period when the *Automedon* sailed from Liverpool (24 September 1940) instructing 'all secret mail to be sent by sea, not air' as it coincided in time with the Battle of Britain. Secondly, the Germans need not have handed the report over to the Japanese. After all, it seems to have been the only document from a very large haul of material that was actually handed over. They handed over British cipher material to the Italians from the haul, but there is no evidence that the German Navy, at any rate, was prepared to do the same for Japan before 1943. If there is any conspiracy, it was a German one because it fitted in extremely expediently with Hitler's policy so soon after the Italian defeat in North Africa. The author is grateful to Iwashima Hisao, Chief, 1st Research Section, *Bōei-chō Kenkyūjō Senshi-shitsu*, Tokyo for information received.
61. A translation of Wenneker's letter to Schniewind may be seen in *The Price of Admiralty*, op. cit., 2, pp. 511–13. Raeder's discussion of the matter with Hitler took place on 27 December, the minutes of which are in the memorandum *1.Skl.I Op 2/41 Chefs* (p. 514) which called for a study of an activation of Japan in the war. This study, *1.Skl.I Op 46/41 Chefs* of 14 January 1941 (pp. 514–521) was filed with Wenneker's letter (*1.Skl.I Op 45/41 Chefs*) and was not completed before Raeder's next meetings with Hitler on 8 and 9 January. Copies were sent to General Jodl (*Chef WFSt*) and Admiral Groos (*Chef Sonderstab HWK*) apparently only on 8 February following Raeder's discussion with Hitler on 4 February 1941.

Courier mail from Tokyo, enclosing the haul of materials from the *Automedon* left on 6 December 1940 and arrived in Berlin on 30 or 31 December 1940. It reached the Operations Section of the Naval War Staff and the Signals Section at 1600 hours on 2 January 1941, presumably after the different materials had been sorted out in the Naval Attaché Section and the Intelligence Section of the Naval War Staff (*3.Skl.*) beforehand, The part of the War Diary describing the Japanese reaction to receipt of the COS report was received about 8 January and read by Admiral Schniewind on 28 January.

62. Prange, op. cit.; NAW/RG457/SRN-0020; Sugiyama memorandum of the second liaison conference at the *daihonei* on 27 December 1940.

63. BBC2 Television, 'Timewatch' programme, 1 January 1986 (Producer: Jonathan Dent; Presenter: Christopher Andrew).

64. Wenneker (Tokyo) *B.Nr.237/36g* of June 1936 to the German Naval Command in: *Reichskriegsministerium: Marineleitung: M Att: 'Attaché-Berichte Tokio 1936';* Clive (Tokyo) report of 17 March 1937 to Foreign Office: PRO/FO371/F2116/414/23.

65. See the comment of Rear-Admiral Inagaki in the summer of 1938, for example, that the Sino-Japanese War would have been over long before had it not been for British interference: *The Price of Admiralty*, op. cit., 1, p. xxiv. General Ōshima had had to threaten a Japanese withdrawal from the Anti-Comintern Pact in October 1937 in order to impress on Hitler and Ribbentrop the need to take a positive stance in support of Japan.

66. Ibid., p. xxiii and see John Erickson, *The Road to Stalingrad* (London, 1985), p. 110 on Stalin's perceptions of 'English provocation'.

67. PRO/FO371/23520, 23571, 27719; Dr Clayton, communication of January 1986.

68. See *AA/PA/Inl.IIg: 'SD-Leute Shanghai'.* Kahner was subsequently moved to Kobe to keep an eye on alleged Soviet observation of the movements of German blockade-runners to Europe. Meisinger, described variously as a favourite of Heydrich and Kaltenbrunner, had investigated senior Party and state officials and claimed that *Gauleiter* Koch of East Prussia had used his influence with Goering to have him, in effect, exiled to Japan for having pursued his investigations too close to the top Party leadership. Although said to have a prodigious memory, Meisinger's early interrogations reveal conflicting accounts of the dates and purposes of his whereabouts and activities between November 1940 and February 1941 and his interrogator stated that they had to prise information from him.

Meisinger spent most of his first six months in the Far East in Shanghai, evidently mainly in a counter-intelligence investigation and this may tie in with his statement of November 1945 that he was attached to *RSHA/Amt VI*, headed by Walter Schellenberg and responsible for intelligence and counter-intelligence matters. Shanghai was one of several locations at this date where Heydrich was keen to post police attachés. The stated objectives were to counter British and Allied espionage, subversion and sabotage, but since they were also locations where *Abwehr* posts had been established, it is not unreasonable to suppose that police attachés (especially ones with investigative experience such as Meisinger) had instructions to keep the activities of *Abwehr* personnel under close scrutiny.

Having served in Poland, it is possible that Meisinger was apprised of the decryption of Polish signals by the *Forschungsamt* and of warnings that later came from the Italian secret service about Polish links with Japan and with Britain (cf. note 11). Meisinger wrote that his duties in Warsaw were terminated on 31 December 1940, at which date it is known that the *Forschungsamt* was concentrating on the British Interdepartmental Cipher, used by British attachés and intelligence posts abroad. Some signals in this cipher were decrypted by the Navy's *B-Dienst* on 15 January 1941 for the first time, which suggests that it had had sufficient time to examine either cipher material captured from the *Automedon* or to compare intercept material with copies of original signals as a means of penetrating the cipher. Cipher signals from British military, naval or air attachés in places as far apart as Stockholm and Rio appear to have been regularly decrypted between January and August 1941, when one-time pads were introduced on these circuits. There was time for Meisinger to be apprised of such evidence and to study British SIS documentaion relevant to the Far East before he left for the Far East on 16 March 1941. This appears to be a good enough reason for the US Counterintelligence War Room to make repeated requests between September 1945 and February 1946 for Meisinger to be brought to Europe for detailed interrogation by BAOR, and to fill in gaps emerging from the interrogation of Schellenberg from 26 June to 12 July 1945. Copies of the Schellenberg interrogation or of Meisinger's interrogation in Europe, prior to his extradition to Poland, are unobtainable: see NAW letter of 12 February 1986, and NAW/RG59/SD File 862.20294/1–145, which is a cover letter inclosing a USFET/G-2 copy of an interrogation of 25 May 1946, but the enclosure is missing. Meisinger was tried for war crimes in Poland and executed on 3 March 1947. An account of the trial is in Sawicki-Cyprian, *Siedem procesów przed Najwyzszym Trybunalem Narodowym* (Poznan, Instytut Zachodni, 1962).

69. This is based on a communication to the author from Mr William Symon, who says that he was told about it by Commander Alan Hillgarth, his superior at OIC in Ceylon, who had earlier served in NID4. Baillie-Stewart was apparently funded by the Italians but could not be tried for treason because he had changed nationality. Some of the people who co-operated with the Germans appear to have been accused of being British undercover agents, and this included people of Indian, Iranian and Arab origin. But it was complicated by the fact that Germans, Italians and Japanese were competing with each other and there were factional rivalries among their collaborators. There is no doubt, too, that the Japanese intelligence groups were involved in 1941 and 1942 in drawing up questionnaires for their contacts aimed at learning more about German intentions in the event of a breakthrough, for example, in the Caucausus. A discreet veil tended to be drawn about precisely where the boundaries between the German and Japanese spheres of influence would eventually be drawn. Ambassador Ōshima also complained to Foreign Minister von Ribbentrop about the involvement of Colonel Erwin Scholl, appointed as German military attaché at Bangkok in July 1941, in dealings with the Indian prisoners-of-war of the Japanese Army in South-East Asia. German submarines were occasionally employed to land some of these people as Japanese agents in India and there were various schemes where Scholl worked both with Japanese Navy *tokumu kyoku* and Army *tokumu kikan*, including the well-known *Fujiwara Kikan* and *Iwaguro Kikan*. There is also the interesting case of John Amery who made propaganda broadcasts about India.

70. The story is based on the statements of Professors Momo and Kageyama of Nihon University to Captain Kurt Fricke, a subsequent head of the Operations Section of the German Naval War Staff (*Chef 1.Skl.*), while travelling between Capetown and Europe in the autumn of 1936. The loss was alleged to have occured about January 1936, but the details of the story do not even begin to tally with information kindly provided to the author by Mr A. H. P. Humphrey, who was private secretary to the Governor of Singapore, Sir Shenton Thomas, from May 1936 onward, but who arrived in Singapore in 1934. See Fricke memorandum of 25 September 1936 in: *O.K.M.: 1.Skl.Ic.5: 'Verschiedenes,' Bd.1, (1933–1939)*, pp. 120–126.

71. Terauchi, who was later appointed C-in-C of the Japanese Southern Army, had originally been invited to attend the Nazi Party Rally in September 1939. On its cancellation following the outbreak of war, Ambassador Ōshima pressed for him to be allowed to inspect the German frontlines and he met Hitler and Ribbentrop at the end of September 1939: see *AA/PA/Büro St.S./'Japan,' Bd.1, (1938–1940)*. The *Abwehr* exchanged 'valuable material about England and in particular about Singapore in Berlin' with Admiral Endō on 20 October 1939: see *The Price of Admiralty*, op. cit., vol. 1, pp. 45 & 70.

72. Cf. reference to the document *OKW/Ausl.VIIIc 1605/41g* of 12 June 1941, from the files of the German General Staff (*Genst.d.H./O Qu IV/Abt.FHW*) which was destroyed in February 1945 in the final German retreat: NAW/RG1027/T-78/451. This file also records receipt of *OKW/Ausl.IIIa 00237/40 gKdos* containing a memorandum on a 'captured British

report on the situation in the Far East' on 23 December 1940, references to a top secret request of *FHW IV* of subsequent date for the Army's radio intercept organisation (*Chef HNW/Horchleitstelle*) to despatch intercepted British radio signals, and copies of decrypts of telegrams from the British air and military attachés in Berne to London of 29 March 1941 relayed by the German Navy's *B-Dienst*. The author is grateful to Professor Dr Herbert Franke of the University of Munich for information on the history of the archives of this unit, with which he served during World War II.

French copies of the minutes of the Inter-Allied Supreme Council, the diary of Prime Minister Reynaud, the war diary of the French naval attaché in London and much else were captured in June 1940 and later. There was much argument about which of the German intelligence agencies had primary rights of control over captured material, including Colonel Liss (*FHW*), Colonel von Bentivegni (*Abwehr III*), even *Sonderkommando Künsberg* attached to the Foreign Ministry. Cf. Paul Paillole, *Notre Espion chez Hitler* (Paris, 1985).

73. See *O.K.M.: 1.Skl.Lagezimmer: 'Attaché-Meldungen,' (1939–1941)*.

74. Lahousen *Nr.992/42 g.Kdos.Abw.II (L.A.)* of 1 May 1942: NAW/RG1026/T-77/902.

75. See fn. 59 *supra*.

76. Counterintelligence War Room, London questionnaire for Colonel Kurt Meisinger, (Item 11 a) on agent 'Boris'; Misc. Report No.9, *Espionage, Sabotage, Conspiracy:* USNOHA. Agent 'Boris' was suspected by the Gestapo early in 1945 to have been a Hitler Youth leader working in the Shanghai/Nanking area of China and to have been filtering information fed by the Soviet secret services. Similar suspicions exist about the Russian Fascist Party leader, Rodzhayevskii, in Manchukuo and about the Harbin area *Ortsgruppenleiter* of the Nazi Party, Adalbert E. Schulze, who was married to a Russian. On 22 August 1935, Karl Knoll of the German Foreign Ministry was told by a man named Foellner of the Nazi Party's Foreign Division that it did not have confidence in Schulze and planned to remove him from his post at the earliest available opportunity. Schulze appears to have intrigued against Knoll with Party officials and Rosenberg called on Hitler to have matters investigated by Himmler. In the course of this investigation, Hitler threatened to have Knoll and Karl Ritter, the head of the Trade Policy Section in the Foreign Ministry, sent to a concentration camp. It is uncertain if these investigations were conducted by Meisinger or not, but in February 1942 Schulze was informing against other members of the German comunity in Manchuria to Meisinger, which resulted in arrests and torture of a number of German citizens by the *kempei*.

77. The Japanese embassy seems to have been wired up during the 1930s, as a memorandum of 1942 giving background information on Tōgō Shigenori in the archives of the German Foreign Ministry indicates that among the sources on which it was based in 1938–39 was the *Forschungsamt*. See Hagihara Nobutoshi: *Tōgō Shigenori:* (Tokyo, 1985), vol. 2 and *AA/PA/Inl.IIg: 'SD-Berichte, Irland/Japan,' (1940–1942)*.

78. Admiral Canaris was put in charge of the deception measures for 'Barbarossa' with instructions to circulate rumours via neutral countries, supplying the pieces of a fake mosaic that could lead to the desired deductions. See *OKW/WFSt/Abt.L I op Nr.44142/41 g.Kdos.Chefs.* of 15 February 1941 in: *O.K.M.: 1.Skl.: Akte V,5:' "Barbarossa"-Weisungen des OKW und Zeittafel,' Bd.1, (1940–1941)*. Japanese Navy personnel in Berlin in mid-March 1941 indicated repeatedly that an early Japanese intervention in the war was contingent on the expected German invasion of the British Isles. In order to persuade the Japanese authorities to facilitate the docking and loading of German rubber transports (first indicated on 7 February 1941), Admiral Wenneker said he 'had to employ the most powerful means available' to him. *The Price of Admiralty*, op. cit., 2, pp. 414 & 539–541.

79. See *Bōei-chō, Kenkyū-jō Senshi-shitsu: 'Nomonhan Jihen Kenkyū Hōkoku, 'Riku Man Himitsu Dai Nikki* (1939), vol. 18 and (1940), vol. VI, no. 50; *Manshū Dai Nikki* (1939), vol. 18; *'Yamashita Shisatsudan Hōkoku,' (1941): Gunji Gyōsei Sonota 87*, Parts I & II; *O.K.M.: 1.Skl.: 'Japan-Kommission.' (1941)*.

80. Using the knowledge gained from the Germans about British military weakness, Japan intervened in a longstanding boundary dispute between Siam and Indochina in January 1941, which demonstrated Japanese dominance in the region. The decision to proceed with the occupation of southern Indochina on 2 July followed closely on the heels of the German invasion of the Soviet Union, which created a principal precondition for a Japanese southward advance. Interestingly, this idea had been discussed in 1925 at the time of the Soviet-Japanese initiation of diplomatic relations: see Solf (Tokyo) Reports J.No. 3657 and No. 3691 of 13 and 14 November 1925: source as fn. 51 *supra*. On 15 July 1941, Admiral Wenneker reported to Berlin:

> Occupation of Indochina expected soon in connection with the supply of raw materials. Serious repercussions on the part of Britain and America not anticipated.

The Price of Admiralty, op. cit., 2, p. 476. For background to the US reaction, see I. H. Anderson, Jr. *The Standard-Vacuum Oil Company and United States' Asian Policy, 1933–1941* (Princeton, 1975), and see also the author's 'Oil, Deviance & the Traditional World Order,' in: P. G. O'Neill, ed.: *Tradition and Modern Japan* (Tenterden, 1981), pp. 130–50.

81. Admiral Wenneker, who himself had been actively searching for supplies of fuel in the Pacific Basin area for German naval operations, was already encountering considerable difficulties in obtaining the relatively small amounts he needed. He estimated the Japanese Navy's supply of fuel at 9–12 months in the autumn of 1940, but by the spring of 1941 he had put a more favourable figure of 12–18 months' supply as generally applicable to the Japanese economic position. However, on 26 July, he spoke of a 'permanent shortage of foodstuffs' in the area and on 4 August saw the oil procurement position for his own needs 'hopeless'. On 22 August, Wenneker referred to the Japanese having an 'urgent problem of raw material supply'.

   Even before 'Barbarossa', the German Naval War Staff had warned of the problems that would arise for the conduct of the war against Britain if imports of oil were cut off from the Soviet Union. As in the Japanese case, the oil problem was complicated by the types of fuel and mixtures of oil required for different users; for example, the heavy surface units burned furnace oil and U-boats diesel. Even before the attack on the Soviet Union, the German Navy decided that it would have to respond to urgent calls from the Italian fleet for furnace oil in order to keep the Italians in the war against Britain Hitler refused to sanction the transfer of fuel to the Italians and Raeder made the decision on his own responsibility, but it meant that after the 'Bismarck' operation in May 1941 the German surface warships could only go to sea if enough fuel was available. See unnumbered memorandum by Commander Junge of 11 December 1940: source as note 78, and see *O.K.M.: 1.Skl.: 'Kriegstagebuch Teil C, Heft IX: Versorgungsfragen,' (1939–1942)*.

   On the basis of statistical studies, it was estimated in Britain that Germany would need to turn eastwards in pursuit of oil: see the paper presented to the Cabinet meeting of 31 October 1940, CAB 69/8 DO (40) referred to in F. H. Hinsley, vol. I, *British Intelligence in the Second World War* (London, 1979), p. 432 n. On 26 November 1941, after news had been received from Washington about the deadlock in talks with the United States, Captain Maeda Tadashi informed Admiral Wenneker that the British were resorting to a new method of propaganda:

> In the last few days, a number of lengthy telegrams had been sent *en clair* by Foreign Secretary Eden to Ambassador Craigie here. The telegrams are primarily concerned with the 'hopeless' situation of Germany. They contain, in particular precise statistics about an alleged oil crisis. In Maeda's opinion, they are intended to have a deterrent effect on Japan.

The Price of Admiralty, op. cit., vol. 3, entry for 26 November 1941. The Japanese Navy drew up a list of its material requirements to cope with the new strategic situation in the second half of financial year 1940/41 on 27 August 1940. These figures appear to have been the basis for the budget demands put forward by the Navy on 1 September as its precondition for acceptance of the Tripartite Pact. The first stage of the programme was expected to cost ¥1,7 billion, the second stage ¥3.1 billion. See *Gendai-shi Shiryō* (Tokyo, Misuzu Shōbō, 1973), vol. 10, pp. 497–503, and pp. 545–7 for the Cabinet Planning Board's computations of 29 July 1941; Tsunōda Jun (ed.), *Taiheiyō Sensō e no Michi* (Tokyo, 1962), vol. 7. pp. 53 ff.

82. Cabinet Planning Board assessments of civilian fuel and transport requirements for various materials essential to the national economy, dated 22 October 1941 are in: *Gendai-shi Shiryō*, vol. 10, pp. 568–601.

83. Hitler usually contrasted the discreetness of the Japanese with the indiscretions of the Italians and warnings were frequently circulated during 1941 in German diplomatic and military channels about the insecurity of Italian ciphers. Rumours about leaks from the Japanese embassy in Washington in the spring of 1941 traceable to a decipherment of the mission's signals were passed on to the German Foreign Ministry, the information apparently relayed to Ambassador Ōshima and the *Gaimushō* informed. The German cable from Washington was by no means specific about the source of its information and it appears that the inference drawn in Tokyo was that it was mainly a question of tightening up security in the Washington mission, especially given that a non-career diplomat, Admiral Nomura Kichisaburō, was in charge. In general the Foreign Ministry received only limited information about military operations and was more likely to send especially confidential information by courier or special messenger rather than by cable. Information derived from *Gaimushō* traffic about Japanese intentions was generally rather indirect and only of limited value for pinpointing the targets of military attacks. It was only when Japanese diplomats and attachés came to report specific observations or relayed information back to Tokyo that Allied monitoring of this traffic came into its own.

Ōshima insisted to Ribbentrop and Hitler on 2 and 3 January 1942 that he alone was the authentic channel of communication with the central agencies in Tokyo on strategic matters: the military and naval missions and attaché bureaux were there for technical and not political questions. Hitler accepted this and confided to Ōshima alone his strategic intentions, particularly about the war with the Soviet Union. Since the attaché ciphers were not continuously resolved until the summer of 1943, Ōshima's traffic was among the most valuable for the Allies between early 1941 and 1943. But even after that, it remained significant: for example, the detailed descriptions of German defences in northern France resulting from a long tour of the area in October 1943 were of great value in preparing for 'Overlord', while an interview with Albert Speer in late 1944 provided information from the horse's mouth about the latest efforts and products of the German war industries. Japanese military attachés were described as 'the best secret agents of the United Nations on conditions inside occupied Europe': NAW/RG457/SRH-349.

84. *ONI Review* (July 1946), p. 37.

85. Takahashi Korekiyo as premier and finance minister used German militarism as a stick with which to beat the budgetary demands of the military in Japan until he was assassinated in February 1936. See Solf (Tokyo) Report J.No. 68 of 9 January 1922 to the German Foreign Ministry in: *AA/PA/Abt.IVb/Akte Po.1: 'Politische Beziehungen Japans zu Deutschland,' Bd.2, (1922–1924),* and the article by Professor Mitani in *BAJS Proceedings* V (1980).

86. USSBS Interrogation Report No. 355 of 15 November 1945: USNOHA.

87. See Louis Hagen, ed., *The Schellenberg Memoirs* (London, 1956); Erickson, op. cit.

88. See Tanaka Azusa: 'Iwayura Zoruge-shosei ni tsuite: e no gaiyō to sankō bunken no shōkai', *Sankōsho-shi Kenkyū* 24 (1982), pp. 1–29; Marder, op. cit.; M. Kolesnikov, *Takim Biyl Richard Sorge* (Moscow, Defence Ministry, 1965).

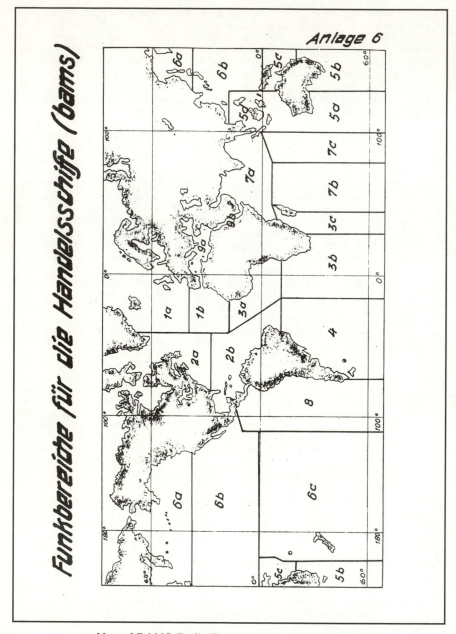

Map of BAMS Radio Zones (see note 37, page 181).

French Military Intelligence and the Coming of War, 1935–1939[1]

ANTHONY ADAMTHWAITE

Assessing the influence of intelligence on French policymaking on the eve of the Second World War is an intelligence operation in itself. Sources are a fundamental obstacle. Many secret papers were lost or destroyed during the war, others remain closed.[2] There is no official history of French intelligence. The history of intelligence work has not attracted the same attention in France as in Britain and the United States.[3] The memoirs of former intelligence chiefs require careful handling because they are apologias, written to exculpate themselves from any blame for the defeat of 1940.[4] The aim of this study is to test the claim that Intelligence was blameless and gave accurate and timely notice of external threats. The focus is on the army's intelligence service, the *Deuxième Bureau*, in particular its perceptions of Germany and the Soviet Union.

How was intelligence organised? The *Deuxième Bureau* has been dubbed 'a sort of dirty tricks department', synonymous with intelligence.[5] In fact six independent intelligence organs flourished. The army, navy and air force operated separate services and from 1937 the ministry of colonies had its own intelligence apparatus, In addition the *Sûreté nationale* and Paris prefecture of police supervised home intelligence and counter-intelligence in metropolitan France. Unlike the British Foreign Office, the French foreign ministry had no special responsibility for any of these agencies nor did it have a service of its own.[6] It did however maintain a *cabinet noir* for the interception of diplomatic communications. Of the six services the most important and best known was the intelligence division of the army general staff. It had two sections, the *Service de Renseignements* (SR), and the *Deuxième Bureau*. The Service de Renseignements gathered intelligence which the *Deuxième Bureau* evaluated and forwarded to the general staff.

How accurate and reliable was the evaluation of the German menace? The claim that the general staff and government always received full and ample warning of Germany's designs does not stand up to close scrutiny. The *Deuxième Bureau* reported on the evolution of Germany's strategic and tactical doctrine, especially the revolutionary role of tanks and aircraft, but its criteria were the defensive assumptions of the general staff. For example a 1938 study on the use of tanks and aircraft in Spain concluded: 'in general terms we are finding nothing which would cause us to renounce the basic ideas which we have held up to now'.[7] An early 1939 report suggested that in the light of the Spanish Civil War German officers were wondering whether tanks were really worth their cost.

As for German army strength, fear impelled French leaders to exaggerate it.[8] In April 1935 General Maurice Gamelin, chief of the general staff, spoke of a German army of 32 divisions, perhaps doubling itself by the end of the year, reinforced by 50 divisions of frontier troops, culminating in a programme of 120 divisions. Against which the French metropolitan army had only 31 divisions. Gamelin took it for granted that in a long war—the only kind he envisaged—Germany had the advantage. Where he got his figures is not known but *Deuxième Bureau* estimates were different. In March 1936, on the eve of the Rhineland reoccupation, French army intelligence put German strength at 29 divisions (a figure confirmed by recent German studies). This force, it was stressed, had a crippling weakness in the severe shortage of trained officers. Accordingly, the *Deuxième Bureau* discounted the huge paramilitary formations in Germany because they could not be effectively mobilised without officers.

Two years later the *Deuxième Bureau* made two serious overestimates—the strength of the Siegfried Line and the number of German divisions available for immediate mobilisation. Colonel Maurice-Henri Gauché, head of the *Deuxième Bureau* from 1935–40, stated that the Siegfried Line in September 1938, although unfinished, could be utilised and constituted a formidable barrier.[9] On 27 September, two days before Munich Gauché advised the general staff that Germany could mobilise 120 divisions and was ready for 'general war'.[10] In official discussions with ministers Gamelin exploited this overestimate of German fortifications. Officially he cited it as a reason for not fighting for France's ally, Czechoslovakia; privately he admitted that 'another year or even more would be necessary to make the Siegfried Line really formidable'.[11]

From arms to the man. How accurately did French intelligence predict Hitler's coups? The reintroduction of conscription on 16 March 1935 came well in advance of the *Deuxième Bureau* forecast of October 1935.[12] From late 1935 the likelihood of a Rhineland remilitarisation in 1936 was publicly debated but the timing of the event on 7 March 1936 surprised the French government. In February the *Deuxième Bureau* had warned that parliamentary ratification of the Franco-Soviet pact on 27 February would provide a pretext for reoccupation but no date was given.[13] Similarly, from late 1937 an *Anschluss* was widely predicted for 1938. At the beginning of March 1938 a coup was reported imminent: 'the operation will be sudden and all will be settled within a few hours'.[14] Again, however, no date. Did imminent mean in a few days or a few weeks? For Czechoslovakia in 1938 and Poland in 1939 dates for German aggression were forthcoming—in both crises prediction was relatively easy since gradual German mobilisation could not be concealed. By contrast, without access to Hitler's entourage, accurate prediction of the Rhineland and *Anschluss* was extremely difficult, if not impossible.

A key event in Hitler's decision making was the secret conference of 5 November 1937 when he informed advisers of his resolve to annex Austria and Czechoslovakia at the first favourable opportunity. Paul Paillole, an officer of the *Service de Renseignements* in the 1930s, claims that France's master spy, Hans-Thilo Schmidt, supplied full particulars of the conference.[15] Thus French intelligence scored a major triumph. Alas, the claim is not convincing. According to Paillole, on 6 November 1937 Schmidt reported through an intermediary to the French embassy in Berlin. The ambassador André François-Poncet alerted Paris by telegram and sent a full account by courier. Deeply troubled, Colonel Louis Rivet, chief of the *Service de Renseignements* from 1934–44, saw war minister Edouard Daladier on 12 November and Schmidt's revelations provoked a meeting of the top-level defence policy committee, *Comité Permanent de la Défense Nationale*, on 8 December 1937. So much for Paillole's story. François-Poncet did indeed wire Paris on 6 November that a secret conference had taken place the previous day but his brief telegram (immediately decoded by the Germans) said: 'it is difficult to know what was the subject of this conference'—if it concerned problems of raw materials and iron and steel allocation—'it is surprising . . . that so many senior officers were called to the chancellery'.[16] This message gives the lie to Paillole's claim that the ambassador had seen a full report of the conference. The other pieces of evidence cited by Paillole are also unconvincing. Rivet's diary, quoted by Paillole, confirms the interview of 12 November but states 'the minister hardly alluded to H.E's information' ('HE' was the codename for Schmidt). It hardly seems consistent, therefore, in the light of Daladier's reaction on 12 November that he should have summoned a meeting of the *Comité*

Permanent for 8 December. The minutes of that meeting make it plain that the reason for its convocation was not central Europe but the government's preoccupation with the Mediterranean.[17]

The problem in Paris was not so much knowing one's enemy as knowing oneself. Until April 1939 there was no will to stop Hitler by force. Well before the Rhineland coup the general staff had decided to do nothing. Gamelin, although accurately informed by the *Deuxième Bureau* of German strength in the Rhineland, gave his political masters vastly inflated estimates.[18] Two years later the month long build-up of tension over Austria allowed the Government ample opportunity to decide its policy. But France had no government on 12 March and no one wanted to fight for Austria. Likewise in the Czech crisis the *Deuxième Bureau* from 8 April alerted the general staff that Germany was preparing an attack and on 25 August gave the operation date as 25 September. It was 'quite exceptional for an intelligence officer to be able to predict with such confidence and without qualification', Gauché boasted.[19] But all the intelligence in the world could not save Czechoslovakia without the will to fight. And Gauché admitted 'Of course, there will not be a European war since we are not going to fight'.[20]

The *Deuxième Bureau's* performance in the Munich to Prague winter is very difficult to assess because the available evidence is scanty and open to different interpretations. Three points call for comment. Firstly, an allegation needs to be refuted.[21] There is no evidence that in December 1938 and January 1939 the *Deuxième Bureau* deliberately fed British Intelligence secret false information about an imminent German attack in the west. Secondly, perceptions both of Hitler's intentions and state of military preparedness changed considerably within a few months. Thirdly, the claim that from 6 March Paris knew of Hitler's plan to occupy Prague needs substantial qualification.

On the first point, no evidence has been produced to corroborate the disinformation accusation. In January 1939 German opposition groups were responsible for feeding alarmist reports to London.[22] British fears about supposed German plans for an attack on Holland and London conflicted with the French view that 'the more probable point of danger was Rumania'.[23] Initially, Paris viewed the Ukraine as Hitler's number one target. French intelligence had no knowledge of Hitler's 21 October 1938 directive for the destruction of the remainder of Czechoslovakia. On 19 December the *Deuxième Bureau* forwarded to the general staff the reported opinions of one of Hitler's familiars.[24] Germany's targets in order of priority were Poland, Rumania and the USSR. Poland would be destabilised by encouraging a separatist movement in the Polish Ukraine and then Germany would demand the Polish Corridor and Upper Silesia. Thereafter Germany might turn to the west against France or continue eastwards at the expense of the Soviet Union. But how much time did France have before Hitler might attack? On this crucial point the oracle was silent and the *Deuxième Bureau* disagreed with its main Berlin source, the French military attaché, General Didelet.[25] On 12 December Didelet argued that Hitler would not be ready for general war until 1942 and would not risk a conflict with France before that date. In the interim Germany might expand in one of three directions—Poland, Rumania or the Soviet Ukraine. Didelet's opinion of German preparedness contradicted Gauché's own view expressed in September 1938 that Germany was ready for 'general war'. Was the French general staff and government misled by Didelet? For some weeks his views may have prevailed in Paris. Gauché states in his memoirs that Didelet's analysis was not accepted and the attaché was cautioned for being too categorical. Unfortunately no date is given for the admonition. Gamelin writing to Daladier on 19 December 1938 commended the attaché's report. By 10 January Didelet had decided that Rumania was most menaced and he repeated his opinion that in the west 'Germany will not be ready militarily, economically or psychologically to run the risk of world war in 1939'. What of Czechoslovakia? The ambassador in Berlin, Robert Coulondre, successor to François-Poncet, has been praised because, unlike his military attaché, he alerted Paris to Czechoslovakia.[26] While it is true that from late January Coulondre believed Czechoslovakia was next on Hitler's list, his main anxiety was to preserve the Franco-German Declaration of 6 December 1938. Indeed neither the Berlin embassy nor Paris showed any great concern for Czechoslovakia.

This indifference to the fate of central Europe was confirmed by the failure to exploit information received on 6 March from the *Deuxième Bureau's* prime secret source MAD that Hitler planned to seize Prague on 15 March. The memoirs cite this advance information to support the argument that the general staff and government were always fully alerted to German coups. In fact no effort seems to have been made to utilise the 6 March scoop. One obvious reason for inaction was that French intelligence shared the general view that Czechoslovakia was a lost cause. It is also likely that the value of 6 March source was not recognised until the coup took place. A 9 March *Deuxième Bureau* report to the general staff said nothing of 6 March information and concluded that no imminent threat existed.[27] The same day General Dentz, deputy chief of the general staff, spoke of increasing German pressure on Prague but his tone was conjectural and devoid of any sense of urgency: 'He was wondering whether Hitler's success for 1939 was not to be the final destruction of Czecho-Slovakia . . . and he thought it was quite possible that the end of the year might see the reduction of the country to the status of a German protectorate'.[28] Yet Paris had confirmation of its 6 March source from Czech intelligence. General Moravec, head of Czech intelligence, heard on 3 March from his master spy A-54 of Hitler's designs. In vain he tried to alert the French.[29] At a meeting of the *Conseil supérieur de la Guerre* on 13 March Gamelin did not refer to the secret information. He thought that a crisis might still be avoided. That evening he even denied that there had been 'any form of German mobilisation'.[30] On 15 March Hitler occupied Prague. Gauché confided to the British military attaché that the occupation 'had been foreseen by the French general staff even to the date . . . ten days ago'.[31] Perhaps he was already drafting his memoirs.

In their apologias intelligence chiefs skated over post-Prague alarms and excursions because the confused intelligence signals of March-April 1939 belied the thesis of an omniscient *Deuxième Bureau*. Paradoxically it was in this period when intelligence was worst informed that it probably exercised most influence on ministers. By stressing the imminence of war intelligence appreciations injected a new firmness and decisiveness into French policy. On 16 March the prime minister and war minister Daladier was advised that Prague 'can be the start of a very serious crisis in the near future menacing France directly'.[32] Joint German-Italian action, he was told, might develop 'in a very short time . . . April is the leit-motiv in most of the information received'. The most likely option was German action against Holland, together with Italian operations from Libya. On 23 March Hitler occupied Memel. More alarms and confusion followed. From MAD, the secret source who had predicted 15 March for the Prague coup, came the warning 'The Danzig affair will be settled on 1 April or 2nd at the latest . . . Germany intends to reorganise the Rumanian army and make it a vassel force'.[33] But MAD's own informant considered 'that there will be no war for a year at least'. On the morning of 9 April Gauché forwarded first-class information from an excellent source whose sincerity cannot be doubted'.[34] War was 'inevitable and very near; the delay will not last beyond 20 April'. The conflict would begin with a massive air attack on Paris and London accompanied by the seizure of Rumanian oil fields. Gauché believed that 'unity of views' had now been established between the three dictators, Hitler, Mussolini and Franco. That afternoon ministers and service chiefs decided on immediate and far reaching measures, including mobilisation of the fleet and putting the air force on alert. After Prague, Memel and Albania French leaders believed the worst.

Perhaps the greatest single shortcoming of French intelligence was the underestimate of the Soviet alliance and the failure to secure information on German-Soviet relations in the summer of 1939. Conjecture and prejudice prevailed. No sustained attempt was made to reach a balanced appraisal of Soviet military power.[35] The 1935 Franco-Soviet pact, like the 1924 Franco-Czech alliance, had not been cemented by a military accord. Perceptions both of Soviet intentions and preparedness were almost completely pessimistic in the years 1936–9. Before and after the Franco-Soviet pact the *Deuxième Bureau* expressed sharp disapproval: 'We shall without a doubt bring to this alliance more than we shall receive with such an uncertain partner, who could lead us into an adventuristic undertaking and then abandon us'.[36] Needless to say, army intelligence counselled against a military alliance. What most concerned the *Deuxième Bureau* in 1935–6 were the political consequences of the pact. Germany might use the threat of encirclement as a pretext for action and Poland, it was argued, was the preferred ally: 'The Polish alliance . . . must take precedence over the Russian alliance from the political point of view'.[37] In particular the *Deuxième Bureau* apprehended British disapproval. France's security, it was pointed out, depended on the entente and 'in the event of conflict English support outweighs in power, in certainty, and in constancy that which the USSR can give us'.[38] But these were political judgements which were outside the *Bureau's* competence. 'The *Deuxième* would do better to devote itself to gathering military information', censured war minister Daladier.[39]

The role of political prejudice in shaping military assessments of the Soviet Union is exemplified by the Loizeau and Schweisguth missions of 1935 and 1936. Within a year two separate French general staff missions visited the Soviet Union and reached contradictory conclusions. Impressed by Soviet strength General Loizeau urged further contacts. Paris, he counselled, should not wait too long before responding to Soviet advances for 'the USSR will certainly not accept an equivocal or dilatory attitude'.[40] General Colson, deputy chief of the general staff, blocked Loizeau's report and ensured that neither Gamelin nor the war minister saw it. The Rhineland coup did not soften *Deuxième Bureau* attitudes. Rapprochements with Poland, Czechoslovakia and Italy were recommended but Moscow was anathema—'its help can only be limited, late and uncertain'.[41] In September 1936 General Schweisguth attended Red Army manoeuvres and advised against any military alliance. Moscow was castigated because it seemed 'to be seeking ever greater cooperation . . . in order to force France into a confrontation with Germany'[42] Thus the USSR would 'become the arbiter in an exhausted Europe'. So set was the *Deuxième Bureau* on keeping Stalin at arm's length that it disregarded one of its principal sources of information, the French embassy in Moscow. Both the ambassador, Robert Coulondre, and his military attaché, Colonel Palasse, tried to break down the barriers of mistrust and ignorance.[43] Three major reasons—ideological mistrust, the Soviet purges, fears of alienating Poland, Rumania and Britain—combined to ensure the failure of Franco-Soviet military talks in 1937. By autumn 1938 army intelligence believed that 'militarily' the Soviet Union was 'entirely impotent'.[44]

The lengthy and frustrating Moscow negotiations of April-August 1939 allowed Hitler and Stalin ample time to reach agreement. Arguably the course of events would have been different had French leaders been briefed on the progress of German-Soviet talks. Despite two warnings (7 and 22 May) from the French embassy in Berlin,[45] French intelligence failed to discover what was afoot. On 10 May the *Deuxième Bureau* speculated briefly on the dismissal of foreign minister Litvinov. The possibility that his removal meant Stalin wanted to conclude a secret pact with Hitler was rejected—'such a reversal of Soviet policy' seemed 'difficult to reconcile' with a newly-negotiated Soviet-Turkish accord.[46] By 24 May the possibility was taken seriously. A weekly armed forces and foreign ministry liaison meeting minuted the urgency of reaching agreement with Moscow since Soviet-German contacts had been signalled.[47] A month later the *Deuxième Bureau* had reached the conclusion that 'German diplomacy is actively engaged in sabotaging the Moscow negotiations and even in preparing a German-Soviet entente which could be very rapidly negotiated'.[48] By the end of May therefore French intelligence clearly recognised the danger of a German-Soviet pact but no systematic effort appears to have been made to monitor the progress of Moscow-Berlin exchanges. Thus on 5 July prime minister and war minister Daladier admitted that he 'had no specific information' about German-Soviet negotiations but 'feared that they might be most serious'.[49] When news reached Paris that a Nazi-Soviet pact was to be signed, Daladier reminded the American ambassador, William Bullitt, that 'at least six times since last January' the envoy 'had warned him that most serious negotiation were under way'.[50] Daladier 'told all the French government services to attempt to verify' Bullitt's warnings 'but had been reassured that there were no negotiations other than the commercial negotiations in progress between Germany and the Soviet Union'. Thanks to the German diplomat in Moscow, Johnnie von Herwath, the United States was well-informed on the German-Soviet contacts. But Washington kept Paris in the dark and von Herwath did not confide in his French or British colleagues.[51]

The Nazi-Soviet pact of 23 August rendered war inevitable. The Soviet Union's benevolent neutrality freed Hitler from the danger of a two front war. Poland could be attacked in safety. The threat of imminent war concentrated the minds of French leaders wonderfully. Their public voice was much more determined than in 1938. Intelligence contributed significantly to this firmness. During the summer patient, methodical investigation revealed the full picture of German mobilisation against Poland. There was no doubting Hitler's intent. On 19 August Gauché confidently predicted that Germany would be ready to attack by the end of the month—'It was not humanly possible to get closer to the truth'.[52] But the truth was now too close. Desperately ministers and officials clutched at reports of flagging German morale and indecision in high places. In the last week of August hopes of German bluff flickered into life. On 31 August Mussolini proposed a conference. Convinced that Germany and Italy were waging a war of nerves senior foreign ministry officials utilised Italian intercepts to convince an irresolute Daladier that the proposal was a snare and delusion. Firmness, they counselled, was the only answer to Axis manoeuvres.

Most of the reports on Germany came from ambassador Coulondre in Berlin. From 27 August the embassy signalled public discontent, divided leadership, military unreadiness, a hesitant Hitler. The messages culminated on 30 August with a private letter to Daladier:

> the attack on Poland was fixed for the night of 25–26 August . . . I have learnt from a reliable source that for the past five days Hitler has been hesitating. Irresolution has gripped the heart of the Nazi Party. Reports indicate a growing discontent among the people . . .[53]

Read out to a bitterly divided Cabinet on 31 August, Coulondre's letter reinforced Daladier and like-minded colleagues in their opposition to Mussolini's conference proposal. The advice was the more telling because before the Cabinet met Daladier had been shown a foreign ministry memorandum which argued from Italian intercepts that Italy was playing Germany's game.[54] The conference proposal was a trap.

How reliable was the government's information on Germany and Italy? On Germany, Coulondre's reporting was largely wishful thinking, derived from consular reports, Berlin diplomatic gossip and personal impressions. He was particularly swayed by an interview with the writer and francophile Friedrich Sieburg who told of a divided party and wavering Führer. But Paul Stehlin, assistant air attaché, disagreed with the ambassador and complained at not being consulted about the letter to Daladier. However Coulondre was not alone in his views. Reports from other sources reaching both the *Deuxième Bureau* and Quai d'Orsay told a similar story.[55] As for the Italian intercepts shown to Daladier on 31 August, Dr Paul Stafford argues that they were fabricated by Quai d'Orsay officials, fearful lest the wobbling prime minister might join his foreign minister Georges Bonnet in supporting Mussolini's conference proposal.[56] The suggestion is unconvincing. Although it would not have been difficult for the foreign ministry's *cabinet noir* to concoct the intercepts (Italian diplomatic ciphers had been read since 1938), it is most improbable that cautious leading functionaries like Alexis Léger, secretary general, and Emile Charvériat, political director, would risk both careers and a first-class political scandal in such a reckless ploy.[57] Even supposing that they had been momentarily tempted, the memory of the storm caused by the pre-1914 intercepts, *les verts*, would have been sufficient deterrent.

How successful was French intelligence in cryptography and the discovery of enemy secrets? The great pre-war scoop was the recruitment in 1931 of a master spy, Hans-Thilo Schmidt, codenamed Asche or HE, employed first in the German army cipher section and later in the *Forschungsamt*, Göring's intelligence communications agency. From Schmidt the *Service de Renseignements* secured operating instructions and keys for the German military Enigma cipher machine. Between 1931 and 1939 Schmidt supplied not only further Enigma material but top-secret political and military information. Sadly, Schmidt was much less of a success story for French intelligence than he should have been. Possession of the Enigma documents should have given France a strong lead in breaking German codes. Unluckily the potential advantage was lost to the Poles.

Exaggerated and misleading claims have been made for France's contribution to the breaking of Enigma.[58] By July 1939, it was asserted, France, with allied help, had succeeded both in replicating and reading Enigma. In point of fact the French role, although vital to the Enigma solution, brought no tangible benefit to French intelligence in the approach to war. Before 1939 France did not attempt to replicate or read Enigma. In November 1931 Gustave Bertrand, head of the cryptography section of the *Service de Renseignements*, handed the enigma material received from Schmidt to the cipher section of the general staff. He was told that Enigma could not be broken. Since British Intelligence was lukewarm Bertrand approached France's Polish ally. Polish Intelligence which had been working on Enigma since the late 1920s welcomed French help. The resulting Polish success in breaking Enigma—by 1933 they had rebuilt it and were reading intercepts—was the fruit of French intelligence work and Polish mathematical and technological skills. The French contribution was indispensable.[59] However the Poles kept their success to themselves and Paris-Warsaw co-operation was one way traffic only. The French continued to feed Enigma keys received from Schmidt without getting anything in return. At a French-British-Polish intelligence conference in Paris in early January 1939 the Poles still kept quiet about their achievement, although recent German modifications to Enigma were making decipherment increasingly difficult. The final wartime breakthrough was a joint Anglo-Franco-Polish effort. The first results came in France in December 1939 but it was not until March 1940 that Enigma began to yield secrets in any quantity.

Given will and resources there was no reason why from 1931 France should not have exploited the Enigma material and achieved as much, if not more, than Poland. Unhappily, instead of stealing a march on friends and foes, France found herself outflanked in the intelligence battle. The consequences for her diplomacy were most grievous. The crumbs of comfort—on the eve of war the codes of 12 countries, including Italy, were being read[60]—were nullified by two disasters. In April 1939 the *Service de Renseignements* discovered that for some time Rome had been reading French diplomatic and naval codes and delivering them to Berlin.[61] The Quai d'Orsay insisted that its Rome diplomats were above suspicion. Only after several months of enquiry was the source of the leak identified—the French embassy safe in Rome, like the British, was being regularly burgled. But by far the most serious blow was Schmidt's revelation in April 1938 that Germany was intercepting Paris-Prague and Prague-London traffic. In addition Germany was reading the codes of fourteen French posts.[62] French diplomacy lost its credibility. The fact that Paris was speaking with two voices in the Czech crisis—publicly promising support for Prague while privately pressurising the Czechs to carry conciliation to the limit—was fully known to Hitler. Rivet warned Daladier personally of the eavesdropping but to no effect. Nor were Berlin and Rome the only eavesdroppers. Captain André Beaufre, a member of France's military mission to Moscow in 1939, believed that telegrams from the French military attaché in Warsaw on 19 August, analysing the breakdown of Anglo-French efforts to persuade the Poles to offer transit to Soviet forces, were read in Moscow and helped to confirm Stalin in his decision to ally with Hitler.[63] Amid so many broken codes it would have been small consolation for the French to have known that after 1935 their secrets were safe at least from the British.[64]

'Never in her history would France enter a war in such initial unfavourable conditions', Gauché warned the general staff on 1 September 1939.[65] The *Deuxième Bureau* and *Service de Renseignements* must share some responsibility for France's plight. Although German designs against the Rhineland,

Austria, Czechoslovakia and Poland were foreseen, German military strength in 1938 was seriously overestimated, Soviet strength underestimated. Blinkered by the prevailing defensive outlook military intelligence did not see the full implications of German innovations in armour and air power. Alerting government to the possibility of a German-Soviet rapprochement, as both diplomats and *Deuxième Bureau* did from October 1938,[66] was one thing, supplying hard information on its realisation was another. On the nitty-gritty of German-Soviet negotiations in 1939 intelligence drew a blank. The record on codebreaking and signals intelligence was especially poor. The failure to break Enigma unaided and the extensive compromising of French codes seriously disadvantaged foreign policy-making.

The explanation of these failures is part administrative, part political and psychological. Intelligence laboured under severe constraints. There was no machinery for the co-ordination and centralisation of intelligence.[67] France lacked an economic intelligence section comparable to the Industrial Intelligence Centre in Britain. Intelligence work was handicapped by the rivalries between the general staff, foreign ministry and interior ministry. The general staff and Quai d'Orsay were deeply suspicious of each other.[68] Grudging co-operation in the First World War ended in 1922 when prime minister and foreign minister Raymond Poincaré stopped the distribution of foreign ministry decrypts to the war ministry.[69] In 1935 the *Service de Renseignements* complained that although they delivered diplomatic decrypts to the Quai d'Orsay they got nothing back.[70] Army intelligence was something of a Cinderella, starved of resources. The *Service de Renseignments* budget for 1938 was the same in real terms as in 1918. There was no money for a printing press and outside contractors had to be used for the printing of secret documents. Pay and conditions were poor. A regular visitor to *Deuxième Bureau* headquarters recalled 'a few bare wooden huts . . . trestle tables, hard wooden chairs'. His visits were welcomed as the signal for 'a slap-up lunch on the expense account'.[71] Within the general staff *Deuxième Bureau* service was not highly regarded; able and ambitious officers avoided it. Inadequate resources and even a certain amateurishness were additional handicaps. Neither the *Service de Renseignements* nor the general staff cipher section had the expertise to tackle Enigma. Sidney Cotton, the British pilot who flew several aerial photography missions for the *Deuxième Bureau*, was critical of his partners.[72]

Once gathered and analysed, intelligence had to be put into the hands of the decision makers. Almost nothing is known as to how frequently or infrequently ministers and service chiefs discussed intelligence. What is certain is that neither Gauché nor Rivet of army intelligence had the regular access to policymakers that Quex Sinclair of SIS enjoyed in Britain. The confusion engendered by a weak and unstable executive did not make for effective use of intelligence appreciations. In theory the Cabinet provided co-ordination of political and military leadership but the ephemeral administrations of the period had neither the time nor energy to do justice to the issues.[73] When in 1936 the foreign ministry wanted to know what the army would do about a Rhineland remilitarisation its only means of finding out was a lengthy formal correspondence. Below the Cabinet the top defence policy body was the *Comité permanent de la défense nationale* but it met infrequently—13 times in three years. Briefly in 1936–7 Léon Blum, Popular Front prime minister, chaired weekly meetings with Gamelin and intelligence chiefs. From 30 March 1938 a weekly interministerial liaison committee of deputy chiefs of staff and senior diplomats met at the Quai d'Orsay but minutes show no trace of intelligence papers. The *Deuxième Bureau* had a daily liaison arrangement with the foreign ministry. In addition the general staff had a liaison officer attached to the Quai d'Orsay. But complaints about inadequate liaison and consultation suggest that at critical moments intelligence analyses may never have reached policymakers. Even Gamelin in 1938–9 had difficulty in getting access to Daladier. On 12 March 1938 Léger, secretary general of the foreign ministry, complained to Gamelin that the war ministry had not kept him sufficiently informed of German moves against Austria. The same day Rivet noted in his diary 'summoned by the war minister's *cabinet* . . . to explain "the inconceivable suddenness" of the operation'.[74] Between 1934–39 prime ministers consulted Rivet only four times.[75]

The decisive failure was political and psychological. 'Damned if we do, damned if we don't' describes the dilemma of French decision makers. To fight made war certain and defeat likely; not to fight invited demoralisation, decline and probable collapse. This quandary eroded the will to resist Germany. Filtered through the defensive assumptions of Gauché and the general staff the impact of intelligence was deadened before it reached ministers. Those representatives who challenged the received wisdom on the Soviet Union, Czechoslovakia and Italy—Palasse in Moscow, General Faucher in Prague, General Parisot in Rome—were cold-shouldered.[76] Assessments of German military might had a paralysing effect on military and political leaders already convinced of French inferiority. In an official climate of pessimism, procrastination and vacillation the pursuit of intelligence became an end in itself, intelligence for intelligence's sake. The exercise of intellectual rigour and painstaking analysis offered escape from impending doom. All unfolded like a classical French tragedy—issues and information were discussed and dissected from all angles but action shunned. Internal upheaval undermined intelligence work. Anxiety about the ideological enemy within distracted attention from the enemy without. At a meeting with war minister Daladier on 12 November 1937 to discuss the latest secret intelligence from Schmidt, Rivet was dismayed to find that Daladier hardly mentioned Schmidt and was interested only in German intelligence activities in France and the presence of Spanish Nationalists and Republicans.[77] Moreover the domestic turmoil bred indifference, scepticism and distrust of intelligence.[78] Everyone eavesdropped on each other, secrets were bandied about, spies were everywhere. Even the lorry drivers who dropped off mailbags at *Deuxième Bureau* headquarters would shout: '*Voilà pour les espions*'.

Notes

1. I am grateful to Monsieur Gilbert Bloch, Dr J. W. M. Chapman, Professor Jean Stengers and Professor Jürgen Rohwer for help and advice. My thanks are due also to the Leeds Literary and Philosophical Society for a travel grant which enabled me to consult French archives.

2. For the state of the archives see Robert J. Young, 'French Military Intelligence and Nazi Germany, 1938–1939', in Ernest R. May (ed.), *Knowing One's Enemies: Intelligence Assessment Before the Two World Wars* (Princeton, NJ, 1984), p. 271, n. I. The main sources for this study are *Deuxième Bureau* files at the Service Historique de l'Armée de Terre (hereafter SHA) Vincennes; French foreign ministry archives. I am grateful to Monsieur Degros, *conservateur en chef honoraire des archives*, for permission to consult the proofs of the final volume of *Documents Diplomatiques Français* (hereafter DDF), *1932–1939*, 2ᵉ Série (1936–1939), XIX (to be published in 1986).

3. For example, Gustave Bertrand's *Enigma ou la plus grande énigme de la guerre 1939–1945* (Paris, 1973), was hardly noticed in France when it appeared in 1973 and was not reviewed in any important periodical. Although French historians (notably Maurice Vaïsse, Patrice Buffotot, Antoine Marès and Elisabeth du Réau) have analysed a number of themes— Franco-Soviet relations, the role of military attachés, decision making and the perception of German power—no substantial French work on the *Deuxième Bureau* has appeared since Georges Castellan's *Le Réarmement Clandestin du Reich, 1930–1935* (Paris, 1953). Michel Garder, *La Guerre Secrète des Services Spéciaux français (1935–1945)* (Paris, 1967) is dated and full of errors. Marc Bloch's reflections on the *Deuxième Bureau* in 1939–40 are illuminating (*L'Etrange Défaite* Paris 1946). The most recent monograph is Wolfgang Ferner, *Das Deuxième Bureau der französischen Armee: subsidiäres Überwachungsorgan der Reichswehr 1919–1923* (Frankfurt am Main, 1982). The only general study in English is Philip John Stead, *Second Bureau* (London, 1959). It is very slight and mostly based on Castellan and the memoirs of General Gauché, head of the Bureau from 1935–40. Major-General Sir Kenneth Strong's *Men of Intelligence* (London, 1971), has a chapter on the *Deuxième Bureau*, based largely on Gauché's memoirs. The most recent scholarship in English is represented by Christopher Andrew, 'Déchiffrement et Diplomatie: Le Cabinet noir du Quai d'Orsay sous la Troisième République', *Relations Internationales*, 5, 1976, pp. 37–64; 'France and the German Menace', in May, op. cit., pp. 127–49; 'Codebreakers and Foreign Offices: The French, British and American Experience', in Christopher

Andrew and David Dilks (eds), *The Missing Dimension: Governments and Intelligence Communities in the Twentieth Century* (London, 1984), pp. 33–53; Robert J. Young, 'French Military Intelligence and Nazi Germany, 1938–1939' in May, op. cit.; 'Soldiers and Diplomats: The French Embassy and Franco-Italian Relations 1935–6', *Journal of Strategic Studies*, 7, (1984), pp. 74–91; 'French Military Intelligence and the Franco-Italian Alliance, 1933–1939', *The Historical Journal*, 28, (1985), pp. 143–68.

4. The main memoirs are General Gauché, *Le Deuxième Bureau au travail, 1935–1940* (Paris, 1953); Paul Paillole, *Services Spéciaux, 1935–1940* (Paris, 1975); Gustave Bertrand, *Enigma ou la plus grande énigme de la guerre 1939–1945* (Paris, 1973); Henry Navarre, *Le Service des Renseignements 1871–1944* (Paris, 1978); *Le Temps des Vérités* (Paris, 1979); Paul Paillole, *Notre Espion Chez Hitler* (Paris, 1985). For the claims made for French intelligence see Gauché, op. cit., pp. 106, 159–60; Navarre, *Service des Renseignements*, pp. 81–2.

5. The phrase is Douglas Johnson's in 'The French View', Roy Douglas (ed.), *1939: A Retrospect Forty Years After* (London, 1983), p. 58.

6. In April 1939 the Quai d'Orsay proposed to set up its own 'Service de Renseignements'. The *Deuxième Bureau* agreed to provide initial training and additional financial credits were allocated but nothing was done before the outbreak of war (7N2524, *SHA*).

7. Robert J. Young, 'French Military Intelligence and Nazi Germany', May, op. cit., p. 202. See also Patrice Buffotot, 'La Perception du réarmement allemand par les organismes de renseignement français de 1936 à 1939', *Revue Historique des Armées*, 3 (1979), 173–84; 'Le réarmement aerien allemand et l'approche de la guerre vus par le IIe, Bureau Air Français, 1936–1939', in K. Hildebrand (ed.), *Deutschland und Frankreich, 1936–1939* (Munich, 1981).

8. For this paragraph see J-B. Duroselle, *La Décadence 1932–1939* (Paris, 1979), p. 167.

9. Gauché, op. cit., p. 141; Gerhard L. Weinberg, *The Foreign Policy of Hitler's Germany: Starting World War II, 1937–1939* (Chicago, 1980), p. 324.

10. Gauché, op. cit., pp. 71 and 138.

11. For the off the record admission see *Documents on British Foreign Policy, 1919–1939* (hereafter *DBFP*), E. L. Woodward and Rohan Butler (eds), Third Series, II (London HMSO 1949), no. 807; for Gamelin's official advice see *Servir*, II, *Le Prologue du Drame, 1930–1939* (Paris, 1946), pp. 324, 334, 345. German strength in September 1938 was 77 divisions (48 active-duty, 29 reserve and Landwehr). But Landwehr divisions might have taken 2–3 weeks to mobilise. (Williamson Murray, *The Change in the European Balance of Power, 1938–1939* (Princeton, NJ, 1984), pp. 220–1).

12. Georges Castellan, 'Le réarmement clandestin de l'Allemagne dans l'entre-deux guerres', in *Les Relations Franco-Allemandes 1933–1939* (Paris, 1976), p. 286.

13. Gauché, op. cit., pp. 42–3; Navarre, *Service de Renseignements*, p. 78; Duroselle, op. cit., p. 161.

14. Gauché, op. cit., p. 57; Navarre, op. cit., p. 79.

15. Paillole, *Notre Espion Chez Hitler*, pp. 107–15.

16. *DDF*, 2 serie, VII (1972), no. 196.

17. Ibid., no. 325.

18. Duroselle, op. cit., pp. 167–8.

19. Gauché, op. cit., p. 71.

20. *DBFP*, no. 1012 (Enclosure)

21. Douglas Johnson's allegation, op. cit., p. 58.

22. For discussion of these reports see D. Cameron Watt, 'Misinformation, Misconception, Mistrust: Episodes in British Policy and the Approach of War, 1938–39', in Michael Bentley and John Stevenson (eds), *High and Low Politics in Modern Britain: Ten Studies* (Oxford, 1983), pp. 225–6; 'British Intelligence and the Coming of the Second World War in Europe', in May, op. cit., p. 263.

23. *DBFP*, IV, no. 44.
24. Gauché, op. cit., pp. 82–3.
25. Gauché, op. cit., pp. 96–7. For Didelet see Duroselle, op. cit., pp. 401–2, Robert J. Young, 'French military intelligence and Nazi Germany, pp. 294–6.
26. This is Duroselle's argument, op. cit., p. 402. But Coulondre's report of 26 February 1939 while recognising that Czechoslovakia was threatened concluded that appeasement should continue: 'Let us indicate, *without delay*, our willingness to collaborate by achieving some concrete results in economic co-operation' (*DDF*), XIV (1980) no. 218).
27. 'Note pour le Commandement sur la situation en Europe Centrale', 9 Mars 1939, 7N2524, *SHA*.
28. *DBFP*, no. 201.
29. *Master of Spies: The Memoirs of General Frantisek Moravec* (London, 1975), pp. 154–5.
30. *DBFP*, IV, no. 234.
31. Ibid., no. 268. Rivet's diary for 12 and 14 March 1939 mentions the 6 March information but the tone is curiously detached and offers no clues as to whether the *Service de Renseignements* and *Deuxième Bureau* tried to initiate action (Paillole, *Notre Espion Chez Hitler*, pp. 143 ff.).
32. 'Note sur la situation crée par la disparition de la Tchécoslovaquie' 16 Mars 1939, 7N2524, *SHA*.
33. 'Renseignement', 31 Mars 1939, 7N 2524, *SHA*.
34. 'Situation', 9 April 1939, 7N2524, *SHA*.
35. For the *Deuxième Bureau* and Franco-Soviet relations see Maurice Vaïsse 'La Perception de la Puissance Soviétique par les militaires français en 1938', *Revue historique des Armées*, (1983), pp. 18–25; 'Les militaires français et l'alliance franco-sovietique au cours des années 1930', *Forces Armées et Systèmes d'Alliance: Colloque International d'Historie Militaire*, II (Les cahiers de la Fondation pour les études de défense nationale, Montpellier, 1983) pp. 689–703; Patrice Buffotot, 'The French High Command and the Franco-Soviet Alliance, 1933–1939', *The Journal of Strategic Studies*, 5 (1982) pp. 46–59.
36. Buffotot, op. cit., p. 548.
37. Ibid., p. 549.
38. Ibid.
39. Ibid.
40. Ibid., p. 550.
41. Ibid.
42. Ibid., p. 551.
43. For Colonel Palasse and the 1937 military exchanges see Vaïsse, 'Les militaires français et l'alliance franco-soviétique au cours des années 1930'.
44. *DBFP*, III, no. 529.
45. For the warnings see *DDF*, XVI, nos. 100, 251.
46. 'Bulletin de renseignements', 10 May 1939, 7N2524 *SHA*.
47. 'Liaison hebdomadaire', 24 Mai 1939, 7N 2525 *SHA*. On 20 May French leaders in talks with the British foreign secretary, Lord Halifax, still spoke only of rumours of German-Soviet talks and did not press the point. It was a possibility to be reckoned with but no more (*DDF*), XVI, no. 243).
48. 'Evénements de la période du 19 au 26 juin 1939', 7N2524 *SHA*.
49. *Foreign Relations of the United States: Diplomatic Papers* (hereafter *FRUS*) *1939*, I (Washington, 1956), p. 281.
50. Ibid., p. 302.
51. Johnnie von Herwarth, *Against Two Evils* (London, 1981), pp. 153–61. When Bullitt requested information on German-Soviet contacts Washington replied on 7 July 'We have

not been informed of any development of importance' (*FRUS*, I, 1939, p. 281, n. 20). Herwarth's leaks to Chips Bohlen of the United States embassy began on 16 May and continued into August. In this period he tried on one occasion only to alert a member of the French embassy.

52. Gauché, op. cit., p. 101.

53. *DDF*, XIX, no. 235. For previous messages see nos 81,131,150,179,180,182,229,255.

54. 'La manoeuvre italienne du 22 au 31 août pour amorcer une conférence de revision des traités', Daladier Papers (Fondation Nationale des Sciences Politiques) 2DA7 Dr 5, sdr a.

55. For *Deuxième Bureau* see Gauché's 'Note sur l'état d'esprit en Allemagne', undated but almost certainly of 31 August (Gamelin, op. cit., p. 455); for Quai d'Orsay see 'Etat d'esprit de la population en Allemagne', 31 August 1939, *DDF*, XIX, no. 285.

56. 'The French Government and the Danzig Crisis: The Italian Dimension', *The International History Review*, 6 (1984), pp. 48–87.

57. For Léger's conviction that the proposal was a trap see *DDF*, XIX, no, 280. According to Pertinax (Andre Géraud) the *Deuxième Bureau* 'had for ten days informed the Quai d'Orsay' that the conference proposal 'was in the making' (*The Gravediggers of France* (New York 1944), p. 409). One of the few surviving French officials of the period, Count Etienne de Crouy-Chanel (Léger's private secretary until April 1939) utterly rejects Dr Stafford's thesis (Interview, 27 September 1985).

58. See Garder, op. cit., p. 77; Paillole, *Services Spéciaux* p. 64, 167.

59. For the most recent research on the French contribution see Jean Stengers, 'Enigma, the French, the Poles and the British, 1931–1940', in Andrew and Dilks, op. cit., pp. 126–137; Gilbert Bloch, 'La contribution française à la reconstitution et au décryptement de l'Enigma militaire allemande en 1931–1932', *Revue historique des Armées*, 4,1985, pp. 17–25. Paillole's *Notre Espion Chez Hitler* adds further details to the story of Hans-Thilo Schmidt's delivery of Enigma material revealed in Bertrand, op. cit.,

60. Bertrand, op. cit., p. 54.

61. Bertrand, op. cit., pp. 17–18; Paillole, *Services Spéciaux*, p. 133; Navarre, *Service de Renseignements* pp. 92–3.

62. Bertrand (p. 35), Navarre (p. 80) mention only Prague-London traffic but O. A. Pernikoff says Paris-Prague communications were intercepted (*Faisons le Point*, Paris, 1950) and Paillole, *Notre Espion Chez Hitler* (pp. 133–4) confirms and amplifies this point. According to Paillole, the Quai d'Orsay appear to have taken little or no action to protect their codes (p. 142).

63. General André Beaufre, *1940: The Fall of France* (London, 1967), pp. 125–6.

64. A. G. Denniston, 'The Government Code and Cypher School Between the Wars', *Intelligence and National Security*, I (1986), p. 55.

65. Gauché, op. cit., p. 104.

66. See *Deuxième Bureau* report of 20 October 1938, *DDF*, XII, no. 188.

67. In May 1939 the need for central co-ordination of intelligence was mentioned but with no sense of urgency, 7N2524 *SHA*.

68. For allegations of Quai d'Orsay obstructionism see Navarre, *Service de Renseignements* pp. 46–7; *Temps des Vérités*, p. 49.

69. General M. Givierge, *Au Service du Chiffre: 18 ans de souvenirs'* II (Amiens, 1930) Bibliothèque Nationale, 17575 NAF, p. 975.

70. 'Note pour le 3 ème Bureau de l'Etat-Major de l'Armée', 28 October 1935, 7N 2492 *SHA*.

71. F. W. Winterbottom, *The Nazi Connection* (London, 1978), p. 116; *Secret and Personal* (London, 1969), pp. 69–70.

72. Ralph Barker, *Aviator Extraordinary: The Sidney Cotton Story* (London, 1969), pp. 105–13.

73. For military-diplomatic co-ordination see Jean Baptiste Duroselle, *Tout Empire Périra* (2ᵉ edn, Paris 1982), pp. 65, 76–7, 81–3; for decision-making see Elisabeth du Réau, 'L'information du "décideur" et l'élaboration de la décision diplomatique française dans les dernières années de la III République', *Relations Internationales*, 32 (1982), pp. 525–41.

74. Paillole, *Notre Espion*, p. 125, n. 2.

75. Navarre, *Service*, p. 46, n. I.

76. For the military attachés and the *Deuxième Bureau* see Claude Carré, 'Les Attachés militaires français, 1920–1945; rôle et influence, Memoire de Maîtrise', Paris, 1975–76 (SHA, Vincennes); Maurice Vaïsse, 'L'évolution de la fonction d'attaché militaire en France au XX siècle', *Relations internationales*, 32, 1982, 507–24; Antoine Marès, 'Les attachés militaires en Europe centrale et la notion de la puissance en 1938', *Revue historique des Armées*, I, 1983, pp. 60–72. For General Parisot, see Robert J. Young, 'French military intelligence and the Franco-Italian Alliance, 1933–1939; *The Historical Journal*, 28 (1985), 143–68.

77. Paillole, *Notre Espion*, p. iii.

78. Former *Service de Renseignments* officers argue strongly that government and high command were sceptical of intelligence work, Navarre, *Service*, pp. 45–6; Paillole, 'Le contre-espionnage s'est heurté au scepticisme du Commandement', *Le Crapouillot*, 52 (1979) pp. 49–57.

British Intelligence in the Second World War

F. H. HINSLEY

In the Second World War, if we leave aside the information they obtained by overt means from embassies, the press, the radio and other such channels, the British authorities got their intelligence from four sources. They were:

1. physical contact in the form of captured documents, the censorship of mail and the interrogation of prisoners;
2. espionage;
3. aerial reconnaissance, particularly aerial photographic reconnaissance (PR);
4. signals intelligence, Sigint for short.

About these four sources we should note two points. Essentially, each of them had always existed. There never was a time when governments did not avail themselves of captures, prisoners and spies; aerial reconnaissance was old-fashioned reconnaissance greatly extended by other means; Sigint, in the same way, was the product of the marriage of one of the most ancient of crafts—cryptanalysis—with the advent of wireless communication from the beginning of this century. In the second place and by the same token, all governments availed themselves of the same sources in World War Two or did their best to do so.

How, then, did the performance of British Intelligence in World War Two differ from that of other states, especially the enemy states, and why? The short answer is that the British were the most effective because they were more successful than the others in breaking the high grade ciphers on which states relied for their wireless communications.* Provided one could read the

---

* But note the important qualification that after the American entry into the war at the end of 1941 the British and US authorities created what was virtually a single organisation for cryptanalysis, as for intelligence as a whole.

ciphers, Sigint had become for the first time in history the most prolific as well as the most reliable of the sources, and the possession of it enabled one to maximise the efficiency of the others. To a far greater extent than the enemy states, the British came to enjoy these advantages. Leaving aside the decryption of tactical codes and ciphers—confining ourselves to the high-grade decrypts for which Whitehall used the cover-name Ultra—they were reading at the height of the war, in 1943, 90,000 German signals a month—3,000 a day—and a large though smaller volume of the Italian and Japanese traffic. Whereas to Germany, Italy and Japan the Allied ciphers were by then virtually invulnerable.

One should not conclude from the scale of this success that it was easy to achieve. On the contrary, it was monumentally difficult. It goes without saying that governments were not going to put a vast volume of communications on the air without taking steps to develop ciphers they judged to be impregnable. The ciphers of the First World War were all elementary as compared with those in use in the Second World War. In addition, the availability of radio had put a premium on speed in ciphering and deciphering in war-time. The outcome of these pressures was the resort in the 1930s to mechanical ciphers which gave speed together with, or so it seemed, invulnerability. This was particularly true of Germany. For most purposes, she went over almost exclusively to a single machine—the Enigma—distributing it to every warship, throughout the Army down to division level, to every airfield, and using it no less widely for other organisations, the railways, the police, the *Abwehr*. She did so in the belief that the machine would remain quite safe. In this belief she was mistaken. But she was very nearly right, as may be seen if I add a little more about the famous Enigma.

The Enigma may have been a single machine but it was the basis for many separate ciphers. The Army, the Navy, the Air Force, the other organisations, each used it with different arrangements and different procedures. Each of them used its own version, and did so with a great range of different keys which served its different commands for different purposes in different theatres. At no time after 1941 were there less than 50 keys in use concurrently. Each key was changed or re-set every 24 hours. Every 24 hours anyone not knowing the setting was faced with the problem of selecting from between many millions of possible solutions. When I add that for intelligence purposes it was not enough merely to find the daily settings—one had to find them without great delay—it can be seen that the German experts had good grounds for their confidence. They knew it did not help with this problem to be familiar with the way the machine worked, which had been common knowledge since the early 1930s, and they believed it would not help even if one came to know the wiring of the wheels, as one might do because in war-time the machine was liable to capture. As it seemed to the Germans, one had to be able to capture the settings; and as they issued settings only for short periods at a time and took good care to make their capture difficult, they were confident that except in the extremely unlikely event of repeated captures of settings for a wide range of keys the Enigma would remain safe against all but localised and temporary compromise.

The long and tangled story of the conquest of Enigma does indeed begin with the compromise of its settings. From 1932 to the autumn of 1938 the Poles solved Enigma keys by methods which involved great mathematical ingenuity but which, as the Poles have confirmed, were made possible only by the fact that in 1931 a German signals officer supplied operating instructions for the machine and settings for two months to the French, who passed them to the Poles. The French have recently asserted that the Poles received from this officer via Paris, in at least thirteen translations, settings for at least twenty-six months of the period from December 1931 to September 1938. There is as yet neither any confirmation for this claim from the Poles nor any information as to what extent, if at all, after their first break into the Enigma, the Poles depended on this further material for their continued success. There is no doubt, on the other hand, that the Poles ceased to be able to read the Enigma at the end of 1938 either wholly or in part as a result of the introduction by the Germans at that time of more secure ciphering procedures.

It is further testimony to the complexity of the problems presented by the Enigma that, though the work of the Poles made an invaluable contribution to the subsequent success of the British, to whom they handed their results in the summer of 1939, the Enigma was not broken again without a prolonged delay. Despite the fact that from the outbreak of war in September 1939 the Germans used it heavily in operational conditions, whereas they had previously used it sparsely and almost wholly for practice traffic, no Enigma key using the new procedures was fully solved after the end of 1938 until the general purpose key of the German Air Force was mastered—by which I mean brought to the point at which its settings could be found daily without much delay—from 20 May 1940. As a result of that first important war-time achievement, most of the specialised and regional Air Force keys were thereafter mastered soon after they were brought into force. But no naval keys were read regularly before May 1941 and no Army keys before the spring of 1942. It may be noted, moreover, that the mastery of the Naval Enigma depended critically on the capture of settings, and that captured settings played an important if less crucial part in the eventual success against the Army keys.

Delayed though they were, and at the outset dependent to this extent on the compromise of settings, it would nevertheless have been impossible for the British to achieve or to sustain these successes without the brilliant mathematics which created a novel high-speed calculating machine for the job—not the first computer, to which I will refer later on, but nevertheless machinery of a sophistication which the Germans had not allowed for. Even so, the successes, once achieved, could not be counted on to continue. Although not exactly precarious, they were subject to two threats. The first was that the Germans, who had made progressive improvements to the Enigma before the war, might continue to do so as a matter of ordinary precaution. The second was that they would improve or replace it from suspicion or conviction that it had been radically compromised. In the event, under the pressures of war and in view of the wide dispersal of their armed forces, they with one exception deferred a precautionary overhaul until after the middle of 1944, by which time the Allied grip was too strong to be shaken off. The exception was the U-boat command, which brought a separate key and virtually a new Enigma into force in February 1942. The introduction of the U-boat key, which defied Allied attacks from February to December 1942, was primarily a precautionary measure. Although it was prompted by the frustration of the U-boats in the Atlantic at the end of 1941 and by the suspicion that this was due to the fact that the U-boat Enigma had been compromised, an enquiry into the technical safety of the Enigma in war conditions gave it a clean bill of health. Thereafter the suspicion that it was fundamently insecure was laid aside. It re-surfaced from time to time, and not only in the U-boat command which had the best reasons for harbouring it; but it did not re-surface as often as the British feared it would and it was not until early in 1945, when the Enigma was in any case wide open to physical compromise, that the Germans became convinced that it was well-founded.

There is a not unnatural tendency to attribute this prolonged innocence to the fact that, to undue confidence in the invulnerability of the Enigma before the outbreak of war, the German signals and security authorities added incompetence and stupidity in the period after the Allies had established their grip on it. I have already suggested that their original confidence was not unreasonable; that to believe that it was stupid is to overlook the versatility of the Allied intelligence effort; that the only moral we can deduce, and *that* only with the aid of hindsight, is that it is not wise to be confident about anything, ever. In the same way, to believe that

Germans were subsequently incompetent would be to belittle the efficiency of the precautions the Allies took when making operational use of the intelligence that came from Ultra, in order to avoid enemy suspicions.

Receipt of Ultra and knowledge of its existence was strictly confined to selected people in Whitehall and Washington and at Command HQs. They were under strict instructions that no action was to be taken on it unless they could issue orders which did not refer to it and had provided cover for any action that might result. Let me give an example. At one stage in the war—as it happens, with the assistance of Italian machine decrypts, rather than of Enigma decrypts—the British were sinking 60 per cent of the Axis shipping that plied between the European Mediterranean ports and North Africa, but no Axis ship was attacked before the enemy had learned that it had been sighted by an aircraft or warship which, unknown to itself, had been put in a position to do the sighting. There were occasions on which, to the alarm of the Allied authorities, these regulations broke down. There were situations to which they did not apply. In the Atlantic, in particular, there was a long period in which the decrypts of the instructions to U-boats, though used to great effect, were used only passively or negatively, to route convoys out of the path of U-boats rather than to steer destroyers and escort carriers to where the U-boats were waiting or re-fuelling. But in such a situation, in which more and more U-boats made fewer and fewer sightings, the mere absence of sightings of convoys was bound to create enemy suspicions unless cover was found. Immense trouble had to be taken to lull these suspicions by finding cover from the extension of Allied air reconnaissance over the convoy routes and by propagating the rumour that the Allies possessed a miraculous radar, capable of detecting submerged U-boats over long distances.

Taken together with the fact that the enemy's intelligence was distinctly inferior, these precautions go far to explain why, in the fog of war, he failed to conclude that his ciphers were radically compromised. But other factors should also be bought into the account, two in particular. We must not forget the other intelligence sources. And then—a further consideration—I have to say that the influence which intelligence exerted on operations was not easily discerned by the outside observer because it was not so overwhelmingly decisive as has sometimes been claimed.

I have already explained that, on the scale on which the Allies possessed it, Sigint was incomparably more valuable than the other sources. I may now add that, from the beginning of 1943, the balance moved even further in favour of Sigint. In response partly to another technological advance and partly to the fact that her land-lines were being disrupted by Allied bombing,

Germany began transmitting a good deal of the communications between her high level HQs by radio signals based on teleprinter impulses that were ciphered and deciphered automatically. Largely by developing a super cryptanalytical machine—the Colossus, which *was* an approximation of the modern computer—the British broke this system without much delay. In the last two years of the war its decrypts made a contribution to the stock of intelligence that was greater in value, though not in volume, than that made by the Enigma. But even so there were always the parts which Sigint could not reach and for which the other sources had to be called on—large areas like the Reich itself and much of occupied western Europe where the enemy did not have to use wireless because he had landlines; and crucial developments in connection with which he did not have to communicate by wireless at all.

The earliest intelligence to the effect that Germany was developing the V-weapons was obtained by the espionage service from a Danish engineer, and agents and PR threw as much light as the Enigma on the development of these weapons. The first news of the development of a revolutionary new type of U-boat and of new aircraft, including the jets, came not from the Enigma but from prisoners. Eighty per cent of the information about the fixed defences Germany concentrated on the French coast against invasion was provided by PR, and over 50 per cent of the intelligence about the German Army order of battle in the West before the Normandy landings was obtained from captured documents or from the French, Belgian, Dutch and Polish underground movements; they had observers at every important rail centre and were supplied with means for communicating their information to London. But these sources were not only, or even mainly, useful for the intelligence they provided. Because the enemy was oblivious of the existence of Ultra but knew that the Allies possessed the other sources, those other sources could be cited in Allied orders, particularly in the course of operations, to give cover for the Sigint, which had to be kept secret from the Allied forces, and they could be appealed to by the enemy as explaining Allied action that in fact sprang from Sigint. I need not add that the Germans, fighting alongside unreliable allies in occupied countries with hostile populations, needed little prompting before attributing to captures, prisoners, spies or treachery the setbacks and surprises they encountered as a result of Sigint. When the U-boat command introduced a separate Enigma key for the U-boats it had accepted that the Engima was safe, but was for that reason all the more suspicious that the U-boats were failing because the plain texts of its signals were somehow reaching London through the agents of the French underground. When the Axis was suffering from extraordinary high shipping losses in the Mediterranean the Germans found the explanation in the combination of Allied air reconnaissance, the resources for which they greatly exaggerated, and the existence of treacherous or careless Italians in the major Italian ports.

It may seem that I dwell somewhat heavily on these episodes—on the frustration of the U-boats at the end of 1941, and the destruction of the Axis Mediterranean supply line—but the prominence I have given them illustrates my next point. They are outstanding among the operations on which intelligence exercised an absolutely decisive effect; and the number of such operations was by no means as large as is widely believed.

In the first place, although claims to the contrary have been made, there was virtually no intelligence of operational value before the summer of 1940. Matters improved slightly, and in fact Sigint exerted a considerable impact for the first time, during the winter of 1940–41. In the autumn Bletchley broke the key the German Air Force (GAF) used in connection with the navigational beams which directed its bombers during the Blitz on the UK. With this and other intelligence, notably POW and discoveries made from crashed aircraft, the air defence authorities were able somewhat to mitigate the ferocity of the Blitz—though not in time to save Coventry in November 1940—by anticipating the German raids, their times and targets, and by jamming the beams. Only one other campaign benefited from intelligence before the spring of 1941. In a different theatre and in a different form—as a result of temporary success in reading the high grade book ciphers of the Italian Army, Navy and Air Force—Sigint contributed substantially to the speed and economy of the British conquest of East Africa.

Between the spring of 1941 and the summer, the intelligence picture was transformed in one respect by the breaking of the Naval Enigma and of increasing numbers of GAF keys. But the immediate utility of intelligence did not increase dramatically during this phase. The British were faced with some situations in which they had massive knowledge but could put it to little use; this was true of Germany's preparations for the drive to the Balkans and Greece, and of the drive itself. They were faced with other situations in which they evaded disaster despite an almost total lack of intelligence; this was the case in the Atlantic and during Rommel's first drive against Egypt. Towards the end of this period, however, intelligence, almost always Sigint, began to affect to different extents the outcome of some operations. It contributed positively to the naval victory at Matapan and to the sinking of the Bismarck. In the Greek campaign it contributed heavily, though only negatively, by enabling the British forces to withdraw without great losses and to inflict a severe mauling on the German forces who invaded

Crete. But not even in those operations did it contribute so heavily as to give the enemy good ground for suspecting that his communications were now radically insecure. . . . It was in these few months, however, that the intelligence authorities acquired by research on the limited Sigint at their disposal a familiarity with enemy organisation, and especially with enemy signalling systems, that enabled them to read virtually all German wireless communications, and an important part of those of the Italians and the Japanese, from the autumn of 1941 to the end of the war.

Once this mastery had been achieved, it conferred a knowledge of the enemy's aims, methods, dispositions and resources which was so continuous and so extensive that one might well want to take the view that from the autumn of 1941 intelligence had a decisive impact on all operations; and it is indeed true that after the autumn of 1941 there were few individual battles or sizeable encounters in the European theatre, including the Atlantic, the Arctic, North Africa and the Mediterranean (but excluding the Soviet Front) to the understanding of which the existence of massive Allied intelligence is not indispensable. But in all cases intelligence was but one element in the equation. When one casts up the account one finds that it is necessary to consider much else besides the influence of intelligence on operational decisions. It is necessary to consider what else besides the decisions affected the outcome. Relative strengths were one such factor. In the first battle of Alamein in June–July 1942 intelligence was far from being plentiful, but it was crucial in enabling Auchinleck to prevent Rommel from breaking through to Cairo with his greatly superior armour. Before the second battle of Alamein in October 1942 intelligence was massive; but it was not decisive for Montgomery's victory over Rommel's greatly inferior forces. Bad or good luck could also be a factor. A great deal of intelligence was available when the convoy PQ 17 sailed in June 1942. But as luck would have it the convoy still ran into disaster. On the other hand, the sinking of the *Scharnhorst* in the Arctic at Christmas 1943 was almost wholly due to good intelligence combined with good fortune.

The impact of intelligence at dramatic moments, in individual operations, was thus quite variable, and taken together with the rigorous Allied precautions governing the use of Sigint in the field, this haphazardness was suficient to avert enemy suspicion for most of the time.

Unlike the direct impact of intelligence on operations, its long-term effects on the course of the war—its strategic as distinct from its tactical consequences—were far from haphazard. But they were indirect, and for that reason and also because his own intelligence was poor, the enemy was in no position to detect them. On the other hand, because they were indirect, and also cumulative, it is not easy to assess their contribution to the total influence of intelligence on the war.

Taking together both its effect on individual operations and the guidance it continually provided to Allied strategy after 1941, what, then, may we conclude about its total influence? I began my appraisal by saying that it is possible to pronounce firmly on only two points. First, intelligence did not come fully on stream before Germany invaded Russia in June 1941, and it was still not in full flood when the US entered the war the following December. Britain had hung on until then with next to no intelligence, and it was with next to no intelligence that Russia survived the first German offensive. By the same token we may safely conclude that intelligence did not of itself win the war. Given the Russian survival and the American entry, the Axis would have been defeated even if the western Allies had not acquired by the autumn of 1941 that superiority in intelligence which they retained during the remainder of the war.

The remainder of the war? Nearly four more years is a length of time which might suggest that, as well as not on its own securing the defeat of the Axis, intelligence made little contribution to it. That this was far from being the case, however, is the second point we may make without qualification. Only one major campaign, only one large sector of the war effort of the western Allies, benefited little, either positively or negatively, from the strategic impact of intelligence after the end of 1941: the area bombing offensive against German civilian morale and the German war economy. On every other front, both positively and negatively, the massive intelligence that was currently and continuously available enabled the Allies to achieve enormous economies in lives and resources for so long as the war lasted and to shorten the length of the war by adding enormously to the burden Germany had to carry and by assisting the Allies to pace their effort and adjust their plans.

By how much did it shorten it? But for intelligence the remainder ot the war would have taken a very different course; and if only for this reason it is not easy to be precise without indulging in hypotheses. But it is clear that at particular junctures it shortened the war to an extent that may be calculated with reasonable precision provided we assume that the Allies, having suffered the setbacks from which it saved them, would still have fought the war with the same strategy. By keeping the Axis out of Egypt, as it did, it brought forward the re-conquest of North Africa and the reopening of the Mediterranean to Allied shipping by at least a year, from 1944 to 1943. By preventing the U-boats from dominating the Atlantic in the winter of 1941–42, and by being directly instrumental in defeating them there in the spring of 1943, it probably saved the western Allies another two years.

If the Allies had not been spared these delays by their intelligence another hypothesis has to be considered. We cannot know whether the Germans would not have defeated the Russians before the western Allies could bring their forces to bear. But we can be fairly certain that since Germany's war production was rising throughout 1943 and 1944 despite the Allied bombing effort, and since she would have been free to devote most of her effort to the Russian front, the Russians would not have defeated the Germans—that the Western Allies would still have had to open a second front. And if it is not unreasonable to conclude that the issue in Europe would have remained undecided until such time as they were able to do this, then that time might not merely have come in 1947 instead of in 1944. It might have come after an even longer delay imposed by Germany's ability to use the delay to create further difficulties for the Allies by mounting an enormous V-weapons offensive against the United Kingdom, by deploying revolutionary new U-boats, by finishing the Atlantic Wall.

It might not be an exaggeration to say that the war would have been prolonged for longer than three years, and it is certain that in every year after 1944 the damage incurred by the Allies would have greatly increased. But of course the Allies would not themselves have been idle in those years and it is perhaps safer to conclude that, but for the superiority of their intelligence, they would have been celebrating the fortieth anniversary of VE day in 1988 or 1989 and not, as happened to be the case, in 1985.

The Evolution of the JIC System Up to and During World War II

EDWARD THOMAS

A reviewer of Vol. II of the official history of British Intelligence in the Second World War took the authors to task for taking the reader 'on a tour of the committees' before getting on with the story. But at least he did not repeat the charge of the American compiler of an 'Analytical Bibliography of Intelligence and Espionage' who wrote that the official history is 'strictly speaking not a history of intelligence' at all.[1]

The official historians have attempted to preserve a distinction between 'intelligence' and 'information'. Information is first gathered—or arrives unbidden as in the Thirties—from sources open and secret. That it comes from such secret sources as cryptanalysis and espionage does not *ipso facto* make it intelligence, though the term is often used of it. At this stage the terms 'source material' or 'the raw material of intelligence' are to be preferred. Properly speaking it becomes intelligence only after it has been sifted for relevance, weighed for value, collated with like or relevant information from the same or other sources—if good organisation and fortune has succeeded in providing it—and, finally, interpreted. Sometimes an item of information will prove to be unique. But this does not mean that it can escape the process of evaluation and interpretation. This may result in its rejection or qualification. If no information is to hand to meet a given need the lacuna may have to be filled by guesswork. It may, however, pass as intelligence if performed by those with appropriate background knowledge and skilled in the practice.

Since the official history is a history of intelligence in wartime, the context to which intelligence is related can be either operational or strategic. Day-to-day operational intelligence evolved through the stages just described

219

and resulted from the interpretation of short-term items of information against an extensive, if sometimes mundane, background of intelligence developed by departments or commands with the help of certain inter-departmental agencies. Operational planning also drew on this background, supplemented by economic and political intelligence from appropriate quarters. Much of the official history is taken up by operational intelligence which need detain us no further.

Much of the history is devoted to the provision of intelligence at the highest level—that needed for strategic policy making, planning and decision—and is of a different character from the simpler form needed for operations. It is here that one may be permitted to differ from the judgement of the 'analytical bibliographer'. One might indeed say that the provision of strategic intelligence—estimating the total capabilities of the enemy, making forecasts of his likely strategy and ability to carry it out, and assessing his likely reactions to the strategy of one's own side—represents the apogee of the intelligence process, accepting as it does inputs of evaluated and analysed intelligence from wherever in government it is produced and developing the synthesis required in a form useable by top decision-takers.

During the Second World War, strategic intelligence of this kind was worked out by the Joint Intelligence Committee (JIC) system. On the face of it, the idea of drawing intelligence contributions from departments and inter-departmental agencies and putting them together seems so sensible, not to say obvious, that it must cause surprise that it was evolved over so long a period and with such difficulty. Before and during the First World War there seems to have been little or no collaboration between such bodies as existed to do what is now called intelligence. There is no traceable evidence that there was any exchange between them of information, methods or opinions, let alone any attempt to assess enemy capabilities or strategy. This was done at the level of the Committee of Imperial Defence (CID) and continued to be done at the top until 1940, despite various moves in the 1930s to sort things out at a lower level.

In the aftermath of the First World War its experiences produced the first realisation that certain intelligence functions might be performed more economically, even efficiently, on an inter-departmental basis. But the moves that were then made, and made perhaps only because they were technical and largely uncontentious in character, took place in the field of the acquisition of information. The SIS, whose prototype had admittedly been set up on an inter-departmental basis before the First World War—only to have its functions completely gobbled up by MI and NID—was re-estab-lished in 1921 as the provider of information obtained by espionage to the three service departments and the Foreign Office. And by that date the wartime Room 40 and MI1(b) had already been combined in GC&CS for the provision to the same users of information obtained by cryptanalysis.

In the 1920s, it was more than once proposed that these and certain other secret activities should be combined under one head. This suggests the dawning of a sense that there might be a community of purpose between them which might be furthered by organisational contact. That these proposals came to nothing, that they sprang primarily from the desire to make economies, and that users of information strongly stressed their absolute right to interpret it and use it as they wished, does not invalidate this observation. Indeed, it was borne out in 1931 by a development of striking farsightedness.

In 1923 the CID had set up the so-called ATB Committee (its title is too long to spell out here) to study the potentialities of what later came to be called economic warfare. And, in 1929, they set up the FCI Sub-committee to study the industrial mobilisation of foreign countries. To help it with its work, which was of a detailed nature and unsusceptible to treatment at so august a level, the FCI set up in 1931 a small research staff whose functions were defined a little later, and with certain qualifications, as the collection, interpretation and distribution of industrial intelligence, and its coordination on behalf of the three services and the ATB Committee, on which the Foreign Office was strongly represented.

The Industrial Intelligence Centre (IIC) was a breakthrough on several fronts. It acknowledged that economic intelligence was a legitimate subject for study. It constituted an admission that research and interpretation by committees was largely impracticable. And it established the principle that departments as mighty and insular as the three services and the FO could depend for the evaulation and interpretation of a body of information of common concern, albeit in a limited sphere and with qualifications, on the work of independent analysts—and civilians at that. Needless to say its judgements were not uncontested. No one could claim that its head, Major (later Sir Desmond) Morton, however independent, was uncommitted. But that the concept could be put into practice at all, before even Hitler came to power, was remarkable. It owed much to the prescience, not to say ambition, of one who for many years had haunted the corridors of intelligence and yet retained faith in its potentialities. But at that time Major Morton's vision could not encompass two interrelated subjects which would ultimately have great inter-departmental significance and an important bearing on industrial intelligence. The application to strategy of science and technology, which had received so great a fillip in the First World War, was far from quiescent in the early 30s. Yet it would be another decade before another visionary compelled its acceptance as a legitimate subject for intelligence study. And, as ADC to Haig, Morton had already in the First World War detected the potentialities of a further specialised source, only in the earliest stages of re-birth in 1935, which would become second only to Sigint as an across-the-board provider of strategic information and the chief supplier of industrial information. But while it would be left to Morton's MI6 colleague, Winterbotham, to point air photographic reconnaissance (PR) in the right direction on the eve of war, its potentialities were earlier to help in an important advance towards the idea of inter-departmental assessment of intelligence.

In July 1935, the War Office's DMO&I, General John Dill, with the Deputy Director (Intelligence) of the Air Ministry (DDI)—posts we will come to later—a member of the FCI, drew attention to air target intelligence as 'an outstanding example of a case in which intelligence is received from a multiplicity of sources which necessitates careful and elaborate collation before it can be put to effective use'.[2] Thereafter—and still before the occupation of the Rhineland—two new and significant notes were struck. In the autumn of 1935 the DCOS noted that 'the intelligence which is now necessary to cover in time of peace in order to be prepared for the eventuality of war with any great power has been almost immeasurably extended and complicated by: (1) the extent to which modern war involves the whole resources of the nation; and (2) the vast extension of the zone of operations that has been brought about by the advance of aviation'.[3] And a month later, in January 1936, a report drawn up at the highest level and significantly entitled 'Central Machinery for the Co-ordination of Intelligence' recommended the establishment of an inter-service Air Targets Sub-Committee of the FCI responsible for coordinating all target intelligence including air photography. The necessary research and report writing devolved on the IIC and further accustomed the service 'I' branches to the idea that they had interests in common.

The Foreign Office played no part in this. Nor did they in a further step, also taken on Dill's initiative, proposed in the report on intelligence coordination. In his memorandum of July 1935 the DMO&I had also referred to 'the increasing tendency for certain specific aspects of intelligence to develop in which two or more separate departments are equally interested . . .'[4] He had, indeed, already discussed with the DNI in 1934 the need for collaboration between them on intelligence appreciations. Then it had come to nothing. But this time it did. In January 1936 the Chiefs of Staff (COS) and the CID approved the setting up of an Inter-Service

Intelligence Committee (ISIC) to consist of senior members of the three service intelligence branches.

While the ISIC has been called 'the first determined attempt to set up an organisation in which the three services could jointly undertake the administration and assessment of intelligence at a level of detail which had always been impracticable at the CID',[5] it nevertheless failed to leave any mark on the conduct of affairs in the six months before it was converted into the JIC. It failed for reasons which are among those which were responsible for the ineffectiveness of the JIC itself until 1940. In the War Office and Air Ministry intelligence had, since the First World War been a subordinate branch of the operations staff and, in 1936, was only just starting to feel its feet as a separate function. In the Air Ministry the rise of the German Air Force (GAF) was responsible for the creation in 1935 of the post of Deputy Director (Intelligence) (DDI) which placed him on a par with the DD (Ops): and in the War Office an intelligence deputy (DDMI) to the DDMO&I was created in 1936 after the occupation of the Rhineland. Neither department acquired a fully-fledged Director of Intelligence until the outbreak of war. The work of their branches, and that of the NID, had been of a factual and strictly single-service character. The terms of reference of the ISIC had put the emphasis on the study of factual matters of joint service concern, such as anti-aircraft and coastal defences, and apart from that had merely—and unhelpfully—called for the peparation of 'intelligence reports'. To have made something of this in the complex international situation of the mid-30s would have required men of greater initiative and imagination than were to be found in service intelligence appointments between the wars. Thinking or writing on matters beyond the single-service horizon was not part of their practice or training. Something might have come of it if the ISIC had been backed by a drafting staff comparable in ability and esteem to the Joint Planning Staff (JPS), founded in the early 20s, or by first-class military information. But neither SIS nor GC&CS was, for reasons given in the official history, able to provide such information. And imaginative projection was beyond the powers of such a committee.

The chance for a fresh start came in July 1936 after public pressure for improved defence arrangements had led to the creation of a Minister for the Coordination of Defence and a strengthened Joint Planning Staff (JPS). The ISIC was given a boost by being made a sub-committee of the COS, by being re-christened the JIC, and by being brought organisationally into closer contact with the JPS, no doubt in the hope that some of the realism and urgency, of their work would rub off onto the newcomer. For reasons not altogether clear the JPS made few demands on the JIC. No doubt, in the absence of first-class information, they felt that their own guesses, made on the basis of strategic possibilities, were as good as any one else's. And the JIC initiated no appreciations of their own, not even on the subjects of joint service character which were uppermost in people's minds in the late 30s—such as German rearmament or Blitzkrieg. Indeed, the War Office fluffed an opportunity to study the latter on the grounds that it was a political concept. Some limited studies were made and answers given on some military matters. But they carried no weight, or—when a specialist sub-committee they had set up concluded tentatively that Axis air power in Spain was primarily used in support of the ground forces—were disregarded.

If the JIC failed to produce broad appreciations of a long term character it is little wonder that they failed to assert themselves in the interpretation of short term source reports of military content. Arriving with ever greater fequency from 1936 onwards, such reports were wont to find their way to the top without evaluation or comment. Why, when the need for interpretation was as urgent as it was universally apparent, did the JIC not evolve to meet it? No further comment is needed on the lack of intellectual quality. This went hand in hand with a general aversion to what was dismissed as 'speculation', especially by the War Office which was sceptical—indeed, all at sea—about forms of warfare beyond its ken, and in any case deferred to French opinion in matters of continental warfare.

A more serious impediment to the production of meaningful appreciations at the JIC level was represented by the differing attitudes towards the central question of German intentions and capabilities adopted by the three services. Wesley Wark has written extremely well on this subject.[6] MI was in no doubt that the Germans would lead off with a major land campaign, probably eastwards, and that the GAF existed primarily to support the ground forces. This view was anathema to AI who followed the Air Ministry as a whole in propagating on every occasion that came its way its faith in the strategic bombing mission of the GAF (a mirror of its own). The Navy, anxious to uphold the assumptions underlying the Anglo-German Naval Agreement of 1935, long clung to the view that the German Navy was being shaped for operations in the Baltic. These beliefs, which owed little to intelligence, went hand in hand with the ingrainedly autonomous outlook of the three services.

More serious still were the differences, until the eleventh hour, between the COS and the Foreign Office. There were certain subjects which, had the pre-war JIC tackled them, would have lent themselves to purely military treatment. But the really urgent problems of the late 30s called for weighing of both military and political factors. For this the JIC was the appropriate forum as all, at the eleventh hour, came to see. But right from the committee's inception the Foreign Office, jealous of its prerogative to be the only source of political advice to the Government, stood apart. It reserved the right not only to have the last word in the assessment of all incoming political information, but to interpret the significance of military information also. Its high-flyers were critical of the stategic estimates prepared by the JPS and COS: but while it now and again put questions on military matters to the JIC, it did not offer to assist when the JIC was invited to offer appreciations in support of those estimates.

The Foreign Office, as always, was the direct recipient of information from a wider range of sources—official and non-official, open and secret—than was available to other departments; but, exercising its right to make autonomous use of this, and in the absence of machinery for joint evaluation and promulgation, the FO habitually circulated such reports in the raw state to other departments and the decision making bodies, notably the Foreign Policy Committee (FPC) whose difficulties were increased by the receipt of differing assesments from the FO and the COS.

In the wake of the Anschluss, information and opinions received direct from German military officers and civilians critical of Hitler's policies were increasingly referred upwards by the Foreign Office, who now no longer checked them against materials reaching them through the diplomatic channel. When, after the Munich crisis, such reports became increasingly alarmist, the DDMI proposed to the FO, as Professor Dilks reveals,[7] the formation of a Central Intelligence Bureau which would sift all such reports and pronounce upon them before they were circulated. This the FO resisted on the grounds that it was the sole 'repository of foreign political intelligence'.[8] The FO had, immediately before this approach, submitted to the FPC the alarming, yet unevaluated reports, about a German threat to Holland which led to the Cabinet's decision to undertake a continental commitment. The consultations which followed these and resulted in the declaration of support for Poland were initiated by unevaluated rumours from Berlin which the FO submitted direct to the Cabinet, this time by-passing the FPC.

These commitments at last removed what might be termed the major 'doctrinal' obstacle to collaboration between the FO and the Service departments in intelligence as in strategic planning. But it was not these developments that precipitated remedial action: it was the circumstance that the FO continued the circulation of unevaluated reports. In April 1939, barely two months after DDMI's *démarche*, they passed direct to departments unchecked warnings of U-boat patrols in the Channel and imminent German air attack on the Fleet. These reports, which led to publicly announced counter-measures, caused much embarrasment when they proved false. In fact both seem to have been 'planted'. At about the same time it transpired that warning of the Italian attack on Albania, which took Whitehall by surprise, had been received some days earlier by MI5 and, for want of a machine to feed it into, had not reached the COS. The COS thereupon insisted, with the Prime Minister's approval, that a body for sifting, evaluating and issuing such reports be set up forthwith. This body, known as the Situation Report Centre (SRC), consisted of representatives of the three service departments under FO chairmanship and effectively discharged its short-term commitment for a couple of months until, in July 1939, this illogical arrangement was terminated and the SRC amalgamated with the JIC. The FO, which approved the move, provided the chairman and thus gave the committee the form which it retained throughout the war. As well as continuation of SRC-type reporting it was charged with 'the assessment and coordination of intelligence received from abroad with the object of ensuring that any Government action which might have to be taken should be based on the most suitable and carefully coordinated information available'.[9] Its status *vis à vis* the departments was enhanced in that it was required to consider means of improving 'the intelligence organisation of the country as a whole'—a phrase that was now used for the first time.

Muddle and mischance had brought a potentially effective machine into being. It would take the shocks of war to make that machine truly effective. For many months after the outbreak of war the JIC, while continuing satisfactorily the relatively undemanding work of the SRC, yet failed to produce the forecasts and longer term appreciations called for by the new situation. Some of the reasons were the old ones. It was not until well into 1940 that the services could provide first-class men for intelligence work. And while sources improved, they remained inadequate for many months after the outbreak of war. Over and above this, the service I branches, naturally enough, became absorbed in supporting the operations of their own service and accumulating their own single-service background. This left them little time for thinking about broader issues. The JIC became immediately burdened with all manner of new administrative tasks such as the organisation of new sources, deception and security. A more serious impediment to work on the substantive issues of intelligence arose from the fact that the upper echelons of government called incessantly for more and more summaries of enemy operational, political and economic activities during the Phoney War period, no doubt in the hope that they could work out for themselves the trend of events. These summaries required the approval of the JIC who, between whiles, attempted to jot down, or dictate to their secretary, such thoughts about the enemy's position as they were able to improvise. Their quality may be judged from the occasion when, having enumerated certain rather obvious courses which the enemy might take in the spring of 1940 (which did not include an invasion of Scandinavia), they concluded that 'which of these courses the enemy will select will depend less on logical deduction than on the personal and unpredictable decision of the Fuehrer".[10] The lack of a drafting staff severely hampered the JIC at this time: it is little wonder that the JPS thought that they could do the job of strategic appreciation better themselves.

The countless summaries of this period bred bad habits. In retailing the enemy's operations at daily or weekly intervals each of the service I branches began to introduce, from its own limited perspective, thoughts about the enemy's capabilities and likely future intentions. The need for more consolidated appreciations was grasped by the forceful personality at the head of MI's German section (MI3(b)—later MI14). Expressing his belief that the only sure guide to German intentions was the whereabouts of their divisions, he started circulating weekly appreciations to the members of the JIC. MI3(b)'s performance as the German divisions withdrew from Poland and gathered in the west was impressive. But as regards Germany's probable intentions there, as later those in the east, MI's vision was clouded by preconceptions. There were as yet no reliable sources that were capable of correcting these.

In December 1939 MI3(b), whose attention at the time was mainly taken up by German intentions towards the Low Countries, mooted (on the strength of SIS reports of shipping concentrations) the possibility of a German invasion of Scandinavia. Between then and 9 April, the date of Germany's thrust northwards, reports from a wide range of sources kept this possibility, as well as that of a German offensive in the west, before the mind of Whitehall. From the beginning of April, reports pointing northwards came in thick and fast. Those concerning GAF preparations went to the Air Ministry and political pointers to the FO: army evidence went to two separate points in MI, and naval evidence to two separate points in NID. Each of these streams of evidence can be seen in retrospect to point clearly to the coming invasion. But they were not seen as such at the time. MI believed that the Germans would have to employ 36 divisions against Scandinavia, whereas the evidence pointed to the presence in north-west Germany of only six (which was, in fact, the number used). MI therefore ceased to credit the likelihood of a move northwards. In naval circles an invasion of Scandinavia was thought beyond Germany's powers in the face of British control of the sea; and when the first big ship movements were detected by PR they were interpreted as preparations for a breakout into the Atlantic. There was some limited exchange of information between departments, but nothing like full: nor was there any concerted consideration of the evidence. Even between the different points of receipt in the War Office and the NID there was no coordination. Had all the evidence been pooled, or had Ultra—as it was often to do later—shed its reliable light on the situation, there is little doubt that the German intention should have been twigged in good time and the Home Fleet sent to the right place. But the JIC remained silent and, on the very eve of the invasion, MI3(b) would do no more than credit the possibility of limited operations against Norway. Consequently there was neither strategic nor tactical warning. Of the German attack in the west a month later MI did, indeed, give strategic warning: but its vision clouded by the expectation that the German objective would be Holland (as a springboard for massive air attack on the United Kingdom), it could predict neither the time nor place of the attack. The Germans thus gained complete tactical surprise. The British Expeditionary Force, whose plans had been geared to the prevailing assumption about the German objective, was lucky to escape being outflanked. This situation corresponds to the German position before D-Day: they had adequate strategic warning, but none whatever of the actual time and place of the Allied landings.

On coming to power on 10 May 1940, Mr Churchill ordered an instant review of the system by which intelligence was related to the government's procedure for taking operational decisions. On 17 May the JIC was given new terms of reference which confirmed it as the central body for producing operational intelligence appreciations and for bringing them to the attention of the Prime Minister, the War Cabinet and the COS. The committee was directed to take the initiative at any time of day or night (a phrase used twice in the terms of reference), producing papers on any strategic development suggested by information reaching the FO or service departments. The point was made that the JIC was better placed than anyone else to assess the value of such information in the light of whatever other information might be available. Since this instruction implied that the FO and the other intelligence bodies should no longer report separately upwards on strategic questions—which was indeed the heart of the matter—the Ministry of

Economic Warfare (MEW), SIS and MI5 were made members of the committee.

The wording of these terms of reference strongly suggests that they were influenced by the advent of 'Enigma' which had come on stream during the Norwegian campaign. But this is unlikely for various reasons which we will not go into. Up to the overrunning of Scandinavia and France, information from embassies, the neutrals, SIS and private sources had been voluminous, if often of doubtful value. Most of this was lost after the fall of France. The implementation, from 17 May, of the JIC's new terms of reference did indeed coincide with the first current reading of an important 'Enigma' key. And PR greatly improved during the summer of 1940. But both sources still suffered from notable limitations and neither was able to answer certain supreme questions about German capabilities and intentions during the Battle of Britain and the watch on the German preparations for SEALION. Nor was JIC able to report satisfactorily on new strategic developments: for example, when 'Enigma' revealed the beginnings of the German penetration of Romania, it was for a long time uncertain exactly what was afoot. Nevertheless, during the summer months, the Sigint and PR enabled the service staffs to make great progress in building up the detailed background knowledge of the German forces, which in the not-too-distant future would inestimably benefit the conduct of operations and, through the improvement they brought about in the JIC's work of appraisal, the conduct of strategy.

But this was a long-term process and could not immediately bring about any significant improvement in the JIC's appreciations since, as the war got into gear, the committee became yet further encumbered with administration and the organisation of new sources and intelligence bodies. Furthermore as the pace of events quickened the number of summaries which it had to produce again started to increase.

This precipitated Mr Churchill's famous explosion of August 1940 when he revolted against the summaries and castigated the 'form of collective wisdom' represented by the committee's appreciations. It was on this occasion that he offered to do the appreciation himself if Major Morton would do the sifting. It is possible that the Prime Minister who had been sent his first 'Enigma' decrypts in June,[11] wished the JIC to reflect more of this very un-collective form of wisdom. At all events, after exchanges on the subject of intelligence organisation between the PM and the COS—who acknowledged that the JIC was overburdened—the JPS proposed in November 1940 the setting up of an altogether new staff within the COS organisation for the appraisal of intelligence. It should be equal in rank to, but independent of, the JIC and report direct to the COS who might, if they wished, seek the JIC's comments on the papers of the new body. Called the FOES (Future Operations (Enemy) Staff), its terms of reference were 'to watch continually on behalf of the COS the course of the war from the enemy's point of view, and, in particular, to prepare enemy appreciations and work out enemy plans under the general direction of the COS'.[12] Thus they were to be a parallel organisation to the JPS's own Future Operations Planning Staff (FOPS) which had been set up shortly beforehand. The FOES, which comprised three senior service officers of general's rank and an FO equivalent, were instructed to 'get into the skin of the Germans',[13] a task which they reckoned would take them three weeks to accomplish and hoped to acquit by drawing up their papers as OKW reports and subscribing them 'Heil Hitler!'.

This experiment, in which the appreciators were organisationally remote from the—now rapidly improving—raw materials of intelligence and the desk officers specialising in its analysis, lasted only three months. It had some successes, notably in guessing that Germany would invade Yugoslavia if Britain strongly reinforced Greece, but hopelessly duplicated the work of the JIC which had not been absolved from the task of preparing its own appreciations. Rather than call yet another staff into being to coordinate the sometimes differing conclusions of the FOES and JIC, in March 1941, the COS agreed to the disbandment of FOES.

But at least a step in the right direction had been taken. FOES was replaced by the Axis Planning Staff, of similar composition, but now instructed to report to the COS through the JIC. While this was intended to remove duplication, the APS were still as remote from the departmental analysts as had been the FOES. The prompt dissolution of the APS was probably brought about by the handling of intelligence about events in the Balkans in the spring. The big upsurge of Enigma from that area required the DMI and his desk man to appear several times before the CIGS and the COS so as to explain what was going on. Before this it had been almost unheard of for the Ds of I to meet the COS. It was almost certainly this that prompted further thoughts about the appraisal of intelligence and its presentation upwards. In May the APS was replaced by the Joint Intelligence Staff (JIS).

This was the reform that stuck. Within a short time the JIC was issuing appreciations of a very different stamp from what had gone before. The deliberations of the COS, the JPS and the higher echelons of government benefited accordingly. Complaints ceased, and by the end of the war the committee head earned the esteem of the COS and their earlier critic, the Prime Minister. This does not mean that their appreciations and forecasts were invariably accurate and realistic. But they were mostly so and stand up well to retrospective scrutiny, sometimes strangely suggesting official history written simultaneously with events. If the Allied leadership made the right decisions in their conduct of the war, then the JIC deserves some of the credit. Of course, there were failures—as, for example, when the committee predicted that the Germans would not seriously contest the Allied advance on Tunis after the 1942 landings, a conclusion which led to unpreparedness and six months costly campaigning. But successes enormously outnumber the failures and are less well known—as when the JIC correctly estimated that the Germans would not be able to muster the forces to invade Spain in 1942 or launch a counter-offensive against the Allies when Hitler decided to stand south of Rome after Salerno. On both these occasions the JIC/JIS stood up to the CIGS, as on subsequent occasions they resisted opinions of the US JIC which subsequently proved unfounded.

Credit for the successes must go the 'the intelligence organisation of the country as a whole', notably Bletchley Park. But the JIC was at the sharp end, had to gather all the bits together and take the responsibility. And much of the credit for the success of the committee's substantive work must go to the JIS. Why did its advent make such a difference, and so quickly? First, because its birth coincided with the start of the really productive period of Enigma breaking. This contributed decisively to the soundness of the departmental briefs to which the new drafting staff worked. Furthermore, the diplomatic decrypts were now beginning to throw an important light on German strategic thinking. It was Baron Oshima who, belatedly yet conclusively, revealed the nature of Hitler's intentions towards Russia and ended months of futile speculation. But the Sigint was not always as helpful as this. The Sigint, military and diplomatic, was always incomplete, allusive and suffering from other limitations. It seldom provided direct answers to the sort of question the JIC's appreciations were called upon to answer. But both in itself, and in the great help it gave to the evaluation of nearly all other sources, it went far to provide the foundation on which the JIS erected its superstructure of speculation and synthesis.

Secondly, the JIS was soundly organised. Fully integrated into the departmental intelligence machinery and that of the COS, it produced its drafts at the instance of, and for the approval of the JIC in whose name they went forward to the COS. After approval—or, with less frequency, amendment—at that level they were distributed as 'finals' to the War Cabinet and, if need be, to the departments represented thereon. The JIS comprised representatives of the three services, the FO and the MEW, all of them subordinate in rank—if in little else—to their masters on the JIC.

It has been said that one of the reasons for the success of the JIS was that its members were young, hand-picked for ability, and not too senior to strike attitudes. Their use of their material and the quality of their reasoning benefited not a little from the inclusion in their number of a barrister, a history don, and an advertising agent—all three thinly disguised as service officers. Their position in the hierarchy meant that they had easy access to the departmental analysts with whom they could discuss as equals the intelligence emerging at desk level and its implications. To facilitate this exchange they were given offices both in their departments and in the War Cabinet Offices. In the latter they were located next to the JPS who soon rejoiced at being able to discuss, at all hours of the day and night, with a staff of comparable ability to themselves which kept currently abreast of intelligence developments and pondered their significance. The JIS became the corporate memory of the entire intelligence establishment and were sometimes irreverently called 'the real JIC'. Their Ultra background and their painstaking deliberations enabled them to speak up with confidence to the JIC, the CCS, the Americans—and sometimes the Prime Minister. Though I would not go as far as McLachlan in saying that the prolonged debates of the JIS encouraged habits of objective thought, it is certainly true that they fostered an inter-service and inter-departmental outlook—though promotion prospects set a limit to this process. Perhaps it could be said that the JIS incorporated the principle of the search for truth through the medium of the seminar—a word little heard in Britain in those days—and in their case a seminar that sat permanently.

No system is without its disadvantages. What were those of the JIC/JIS system? McLachlan claims that its successes stemmed from the principle that three heads are better than one. This does not necessarily follow. It can give rise to compromise and weasel-wording, especially when the shape of major campaigns, big building programmes and important foreign policy decisions often depended on statements in JIC appreciations. Sometimes the JIC, before finalising a JIS draft, would attempt to dilute conclusions which seemed to be going too far. But while they sometimes succeeded, the combination of Ultra and prolonged exploration of every possibility would generally cause them to retreat. Sometimes indeed, the addition of a little water might have been beneficial. In August 1944, the newly appointed DMI was confronted by a euphoric draft predicting the collapse of Germany before the end of the year. He would have liked to water this down considerably. But he lacked the courage—and reproached himself thereafter literally to his dying day.

There is no doubt that a teamwork approach to drafting makes it less likely that a departmental representative who tries to tailor the evidence to suit his department's policy, or has a bee in his bonnet, will be allowed to get away with it. 'Unfortunately this cannot always be avoided. But there were very few cases where a member of the JIC dissented from the majority conclusion.

Christopher Andrew draws attention to a more serious potential weakness when he writes that 'this very process of assessment carries with it the danger that it will emphasise intelligence which conforms to the conventional wisdom of the time (which is invariably afterwards discovered to have contained at least some false assumptions) and exclude or underplay apparently eccentric information which points in other directions'.[14] This is, indeed, a danger. During the Second World War the availability of Ultra was a deterrent to the growth of a conventional wisdom out of line with objective facts which, in wartime, are generally easier to establish than in peace. The presence in the JIS of independent minds in the shape of civilians, however thinly disguised, who had spent most of their lives outside Whitehall, helped to ensure that problems would be looked at from many points of view. There was certainly no lack of heterodox opinions on the JIS in the Second World War. Perhaps the ideal is that intelligence should play a part in the moulding of the conventional wisdom. That wisdom is, after all, sometimes right. And this might help in that direction.

But, however great this danger, it must be conceded that there are worse ways of constructing a window on the world. In the final appreciation which the JIS prepared for the JIC during the war—an appreciation entitled 'Why the Germans lost the War'—one of the reasons given was the fragmented state of German intelligence and the fact that information was nowhere collated and appreciated below the level of head of state. The emergence of the JIC system at least steered us clear of that. But it is open to anyone, if he can, to suggest a better method.

Notes

1. G. C. Constantinides, *Intelligence and Espionage: An Analytical Bibliography* (Boulder, 1983), p. 235.
2. F. H. Hinsley, *British Intelligence in the Second World War* I (London, 1979), p. 26.
3. Ibid., p. 31.
4. Ibid., p. 34.
5. Ibid., p. 35.
6. C. Andrew and D. Dilks (eds), *The Missing Dimension. Governments and the Intelligence Communities in the Twentieth Century* (London, 1984), chapter 4.

 7. Ibid., p. 124.
 8. Ibid., p. 125.
 9. F. H. Hinsley, op. cit. p. 43.
10. Ibid., p. 95.
11. M. Gilbert, *Winston S. Churchill: The Finest Hour* VI (London, 1983), p. 609.
12. F. H. Hinsley, op. cit. p. 297.
13. Ibid., p. 297.
14. C. Andrew and D. Dilks (eds), op. cit. pp. 12–13.

Army Ultra in the Mediterranean Theatre: Darkness and Light

RALPH BENNETT

The simple metaphor of my title represents a feature of Ultra intelligence which deserves more attention than it has yet received. We still tend to speak of Ultra as if it were an abstract, uniform concept of unvarying consistency, instead of a bundle of awkward practical realities which varied both in quality and quantity of content and also over time. To think of it as a smooth unchanging abstraction is dangerous, for it can mislead interpretation and distort a historical judgement of Ultra's strategic worth. Those of us who helped to make Ultra what it became grew familiar through experience with the sometimes capricious and unpredictable variations in the material from which Ultra was compiled, and I doubt whether anyone who did not serve in Hut 3 at Bletchley Park could gain an equal familiarity now simply by studying the documents in the Public Record Office. Therein lies a certain risk that Ultra may in future be seen as a constant ingredient in intelligence rather than as the living and evolving creature which it really was.

Perhaps it would help if we were in the habit of speaking of Ultras not Ultra. The Ultra of the week in June 1944 which saw the capture of Rome and the D-Day landings was very different from the Ultra of the corresponding week in 1941, for instance, and any attempt to assess its influence on the war must take account of the difference. The change over the intervening three years in the quality and quantity of its content is fundamental to such an assessment; so too is the complete contrast between the ways in which Ultra intelligence was received, appreciated and utilised by operational commands at each of its two periods. In no field were these changes more marked than in that of army Ultra.

Attempting to explain the number and variety of Ultras to an unsophisticated audience, I have sometimes likened Wehrmacht Enigma keys to three sisters each with a brood of children. The naval sister was the least fertile; her first-born was long in gestation (no naval key was broken until August 1941) and never had many siblings, but one of them was the source of Ultra's single greatest contribution to victory: Ultra-based knowledge of U-boat movements combined with new means of locating and destroying them to win the battle of the Atlantic in May 1943. Luftwaffe Enigma was the first to lose its virginity (if I may labour my metaphor) and later became the most prolific bearer of children. The GAF general key yielded to the cryptographers early in 1940 and was decrypted almost every day for the rest of the war; in addition, progressively smaller and smaller air commands were given their own key, all of which were broken in due course, though not all of them all the time.

By contrast, Army Ultra was late to appear and smaller in volume. Its lateness (the first breaks were not unil September 1941, and thereafter Army keys were only read intermittently until April 1942, and even then somewhat discontinuously and often several days late) and its irregularity (the officers who used Army Enigma and the operators who enciphered their messages observed such strict security that their transmissions were hard to break) frequently posed problems of interpretation. The security-consciousness of the *Heeresnachrichtenwesen* was expressed in the warning its head, Fellgiebel, gave to his staff in 1939: *Funken ist Landesverrat [To use the radio is to commit treason]*, and strikingly demonstrated by the fact that scarcely one even of the cover-names for large military operations was mentioned in radio messages in army keys. These two features—drawbacks from our point of view—could not however prevent the weight of intelligence conveyed by Army Enigma and the authoritative provenance of so much of it from outstripping Luftwaffe Enigma in intelligence value once Army Ultra was available in quantity. This was partly, of course, because the Luftwaffe was in decline from mid-1942, though Tedder's and Coningham's tactics had wrested air superiority over the desert from *Fliegerfuehrer Afrika* much earlier—Siegfried Westphal, Rommel's operations officer, complained that even in 1941 the via Balbia was only safe at the RAF's mealtimes. But in any case a *Panzerlage* (a return of the number of tanks serviceable each day, the number under repair and the estimated length of their stay in the workshops, each head broken down under the several types of tank)[1] was worth more than *Fliegerfuehrer's* (or *Fliegerkorps II's* or *X's*) equivalent daily strength returns, which were more common, because it was *Panzerarmee Afrika* which captured Tobruk and had to be prevented from breaking through at Alamein, not any part of the German air force. For the same reason, but with a far higher intelligence rating, *Panzerarmee's Tagesabschlussmeldungen* were usually of greater value than *Luftflotte 2's* parallel evening reports of operations carried out and intentions for the following day.

Forty years ago, there was no difficulty in identifying Army Ultra—the difficulty was to decrypt it. Today things are different. There is now no absolutely certain way of knowing whether a particular signal in the Public Record Office was derived from Army Ultra or not. There are two reasons: in the first place, whereas the whole of the Naval Section's output came from naval Ultra, Hut 3 dealt in army and air material indifferently. Unless, therefore, a given signal bears unmistakeable marks of its origin upon its face ('Strength return *Fliegerfuehrer* tenth June', for instance, or 'Day report *Panzerarmee . . .*'), conclusive evidence to distinguish between army and air material is now lacking in a great many cases, and evidence to distinguish between keys in almost all. Common-sense suffices in a number (plainly, a tank return will not have been transmitted in a Luftwaffe key), and the lists in the appendices to *British Intelligence* in others; but while the lists prevent gross error by giving the dates of the first breaks of each key, they are not precise enough to elucidate individual instances. Secondly, the office copies of the teleprints underlying each signal carried a note of the key involved in each case, but we are not allowed to see the teleprints. This is another example of the extraordinary and seemingly indefensible security measures from which historians of the Second World War suffer: since we are allowed to talk openly about intercepts and decrypts today, why may we not trace each message to its source? Until we can do so, a historical analysis such as I am attempting here cannot be carried to a proper conclusion, and I am bound to admit this limitation upon what follows. (It is of course a matter for even greater regret that the publication of an official account of how the decrypting was done is still forbidden; this condemned the late Gordon Welchman to write *The Hut Six Story* from an inevitably faulty memory and without access to documents, with the natural but infinitely regrettable result that his book contains nearly as many errors as Winterbotham's does on the intelligence side, and probably more omissions).

To sum up: there is now no absolutely certain way of identifying particular signals as derived from Army Enigma. Past acquaintance with them may, I hope, serve to reduce my mistakes to a minimum. Having read all the signals when they were first issued and shared in the composition of many of them, and having now, forty years later, read all 100,000 of them again, I feel fairly sure of my ground. It seemed only right to admit, however, that I cannot be quite as confident as Professor Rohwer and Mr Beesly of the provenance of my material.

Some dates are now necessary. The general-purpose Luftwaffe key, and another air key for use in the Mediterranean, were both being read currently at the beginning of 1941. Rommel landed in Tripoli on 12 February, advanced into Cyrenaica early in April and reached the Egyptian frontier by the end of the month. Direct signalling from Hut 3 to Cairo (later to other headquarters as well) began on 13 March. No army decrypts were read until 17 September, and only irregularly to start with: for a few weeks until mid-October, again for most of November, but then no more until April 1942. Thus Rommel's spectacular drive across Cyrenaica, which outwitted his opponents and nullified all the gains of O'Connor's winter rout of the Italians, BREVITY and BATTLEAXE (the first two abortive British counter-attacks) and the latter part of CRUSADER, the British autumn offensive—all these passed without benefit of Army Ultra. Luftwaffe decrypts told what Froehlich's and Geissler's aircraft were up to, but Rommel's tanks were the danger, and there was no news of them at all. Army officers like myself, forced to sit idly by while our RAF colleagues composed signal after signal without any apparent influence on the fighting, were keenly aware of the prevailing imbalance in Ultra, but it seems to have passed unremarked elsewhere. Most importantly, it did not deter Churchill from goading first Wavell and later Auchinleck to the attack, although neither knew much of the enemy's situation and both professed themselves far from ready to take the initiative.

Churchill was Ultra's first and greatest friend, and nothing can detract from his wartime leadership, but in these months he was so anxious for a victory to set off against Dunkirk, Crete and Singapore that he overplayed his hand and inadvertently associated Ultra too closely with setbacks in the desert. He took one or two signals[2]—they showed that Rommel had been ordered to rest on his laurels or even draw back a little—at face value and ordered the generals to press on regardless. Disasters followed. There are several explanations; one in particular is relevant here. Neither Churchill nor anyone else seems to have realised that the virtues of the new intelligence tool, Ultra, were matched by corresponding vices: it was as yet unbalanced, for the reasons just given, and an understanding of it called for more than just a translation of the German words. Of course no one possessed all the requisite skills in 1941, but no one stopped even to wonder whether Ultra could really solve all problems so easily, whether there was not a catch somewhere. There was. Without Army Ultra, nothing could show whether or not Rommel had the resources to attack supposing, however improbably, that he chose to defy German military tradition and disobey the orders of Halder and OKH; but there seems to have been no attempt to estimate whether he had the petrol and tanks to push on if he were disposed to take the risk. It was not grasped that the encouraging (from the British point of view) evidence lacked a sufficient background against which it could be set in perspective and properly assessed. Still worse: throughout this period—it included the time of Force K's ascendancy in the central Mediterranean—air Ultra was providing evidence of German shortages and betraying the movements of convoys so frequently that the RAF and the navy were taking a heavy toll of Axis supplies. A lot was known about ships, but little about what they carried and nothing at all about that part of their cargoes consigned to the Afrika Korps. Ultra told nothing about the number of tanks reaching Libya or about the performance (it was excellent) of the tank repair workshops. Yet it was the tanks (and the 88s [88mm anti-tank guns] upon which I will not dwell, although there is much to say about them too) which mattered. They mattered supremely on one occasion. As Rommel slowly retreated in December, it was lightly concluded in Cairo that he had few tanks left. No one looked carefully at the hint—it was no more, but it was a plain hint—in Ultra that there might possibly have been tanks on the last ship to dock at Benghazi before the Germans evacuated the port. There were, and it was with them that Rommel counter-attacked on 21 January 1942, regaining in a few days what CRUSADER had stutteringly conquered in six weeks and at great cost. (The *Ankara*, the ship that carried the tanks, became a *bête-noire* to the British; she made countless transits of the Mediterranean and it took over a year to sink her).

The episode has another disquieting aspect. The whole British intelligence system was in a very poor way in 1939, as Dr Andrew has just shown in unprecedented but regrettably still incomplete (because of more inexplicable security black-outs) detail.[3] British army intelligence scarcely existed. It was given no prominence at Sandhurst or Camberley. The Intelligence Corps had been abolished after the First World War. Field Marshal Gerald Templer later had the well-deserved reputation of knowing a lot about military intelligence, but there is singularly little evidence in John Cloake's new biography to prove it for the pre-1939 period.[4] To stay long in intelligence imperilled an officer's chances of promotion and thus his whole career. Ill-founded optimism prevailed in Cairo at the time of CRUSADER, and in retrospect the mistake over the *Ankara* is unsurprising though still grievous. It follows that even if more Ultra had been available it is unlikely that it would have been used to much advantage. This is only speculation, but it may serve as a reminder that an army (or navy, or air force) is only as good as its commanders' intelligence (in both senses of the word) and armament when the two are put to combined use; a failure of either leads to ruin. By how little did 8th Army escape that ruin in 1941–2!

Shafts of light began to pierce the gloom during the spring of 1942—for instance, the first *Panzerlagen* were decrypted and soon became frequent enough to banish for good miscalculations like that of January—and they were not much dimmed even by the loss of Tobruk in June and the headlong retreat to Alamein, where a front was at last stabilised in late July. Changes of organisation and personnel at both ends of the Ultra delivery line made for improved drafting of signals and a fuller appreciation of them at the same time as new cryptographic successes were providing a greater depth and variety of intelligence and this was gradually being brought into a closer relationship with the direction of operations. It is important to stress the range of this development both at Bletchley and in the Cairo and desert headquarters during these months. Though beaten and temporarily discouraged, 8th Army was not demoralised but ready for another fight when Montgomery took over in mid-August, and this applied particularly to the intelligence staff.

With Rommel poised for the final push which would take him into the Delta and begin the dissolution of British authority in the Middle East, there was a crying need to know what he planned to do and still more how he planned to do it. Ultra was able to provide the answers in good time, and the intelligence officers whom Montgomery inherited were able to convince him of its value in a way their predecessors had never managed to convince his. Montgomery used Ultra with resounding success at once and thereby founded in the public mind (and, less fortunately perhaps, in his own as well) the legend that he alone had the secret of victory. Army Ultra came into its own in August 1942, and retained for the rest of the war the intimate connection with operations which it had lacked before and which it now thoroughly deserved.

Alamein at the end of October has been regarded as a turning point ever since Churchill's victory speech; from the intelligence angle, Alam Halfa, where Rommel shot his last bolt at the end of August, deserves the title even more. There are two extreme views of this battle, one represented by Mr Correlli Barnett's myopic determination to denigrate everything Montgomery did, even to the extent of mistakenly quoting Ultra as evidence for the prosecution, and the other by Mr Hamilton's account, which was written before criticism began occasionally to oust hero-worship from his narrative. Did or did not Montgomery take over an existing plan for the defence of the Alam Halfa ridge and steal the credit when he thwarted

Rommel's attack and forced him to turn tail for the first time? The argument has nothing to do with Ultra, but an appreciation addressed by Rommel to OKH and OKW, which was decrypted from an army key on 17 August,[5] sheds more light on one part of it than has yet been fully realised. Montgomery had taken certain actions on 13 August, the day he assumed command of 8th Army; he had not seen the existing plan when he did so, and his actions departed widely from the plan. Four days later—the time interval is important[6]—Ultra showed that these actions were absolutely correct, for they had provided a strong defence at the point where Rommel intended to attack. Armed with the confidence that his judgement was a hundred per cent right, Montgomery could relax and enjoy the crucial defensive battle, certain that the brave and inspiring words with which he had addressed 8th Army officers when he took over were about to be justified by events.

Ultra's chief contribution to victory at Alamein was to throttle Rommel's petrol supply line by what Italian historians have called 'the hecatomb of the tankers', but this was the work of Italian naval and German air force decrypts. Army material was for the moment necessarily tactical, like the whole battle (because there was no room for manoeuvre behind a short front with ends sharply defined by the sea and Qattara Depression; by contrast, Alam Halfa had strategic overtones) and tactics was Army Ultra's weakest point since it could seldom deliver its results in time to keep up with a fluid battle—here it differed markedly from naval Ultra at its best—and the Y Service was often quicker: Ultra reported the move north of 21 Panzer Division which created the opportunity for Montgomery's decisive thrust on 3 November,[7] but the Y Service had done so already.

After the brilliant intelligence successes of the past three months, it is sad that much good Ultra was wasted between Alamein and Tripoli, between November 1942 and January 1943. Ultra told how few weapons the Afrika Korps had carried away from the battlefield (eleven tanks and 29 anti-tank guns), and week by week throughout Rommel's retreat it showed how little petrol there was for his tanks and transport vehicles: only enough for 150 kilometres on the morrow of Alamein, so little that the Afrika Korps was delayed twenty-four hours in moving out of Benghazi, supply lorries stranded with empty tanks for days on end between Buerat and Tripoli.[8] Rommel called the situation 'catastrophic', partly because he knew that a TORCH had been lit behind him which might burn down the Tunisian refuge towards which he was straining with painful slowness before he could reach it. When on top of all this Ultra revealed that Rommel had told Hitler and Mussolini that they must 'face the probable annihilation of what was left of Panzer Army',[9] surely Montgomery should have cast aside his groundless fear that Rommel could still strike back and his apprehensions over the mutual distrust of infantry and armour, made light of the undoubted difficulties of a lengthening supply line, and risked a bold stroke to cut Panzer Army off and destroy it before it could reach Tunisia? Intelligence alone does not win battles, but here was as good a chance as any to find the exception to the rule.

Even the intelligence-directed battle of Medenine could not atone for this neglect. After the shock Rommel administered to the Americans, from Eisenhower down to the unfledged Combat Commands, at Kasserine in February, it was obvious that his next move would probably be to use his interior lines to throw the whole weight of his armour against the British 8th Army. He joined 10th Panzer Division from Tunisia with the old desert hands of 15th and 21st Panzer; 31,000 men and 135 tanks advanced eastwards, and Army Ultra followed their every move closely. Rommel's Chief Quartermaster let out the date on which they planned to attack— 6 March or sooner—and by the third the whole force was under orders to move along two thrust-lines which pointed directly at Medenine.[10] Amply forewarned, Montgomery dug 600 anti-tank guns into the ground and awaited developments with more than his usual equanimity. The German armour recoiled, and soon the ground was littered with burning tanks. 'The Marshal had made a balls of it. I shall write letters', said Montgomery when he saw them.[11] In fact, Rommel had not been there at all. His desert veterans were humiliated under the command of a mere Italian, General Messe. Rommel, a sick as well as a disappointed man, left Africa for good almost at once.

Army Ultra played a great part in the immediately succeeding battles of Mareth and the Wadi Akarit. It showed that Messe foresaw the shape of the coming British attack but got its timing wrong,[12] and that he was ready to retreat because he believed himself to be weaker than the Anglo-American forces converging on his escape route from two directions. It revealed the strength of the Mareth defences (in spite of which a costly frontal assault was made on them to distract attention from the New Zealanders' 'left hook' through the hills), was particularly up-to-date with exceptionally frequent tank strength returns, and betrayed von Arnim's cry to Kesselring on the morrow of defeat that the situation was desperate, so short was he of petrol and ammunition.[13] By mid-April the Axis bridgehead was no more than the outer defences of Tunis and Bizerta; in a relatively built-up area the Wehrmacht could use land–lines in preference to radio, and Ultra of all types diminished considerably in the last weeks before the surrender on Cape Bon on 13 May.

Inter-allied differences about closing down the Mediterranean theatre after the conquest of Tunisia were temporarily stilled at Casablanca in January 1943 by the decision to invade Sicily but not necessarily to go any further. The target was too obvious for comfort, and an attempt to throw dust in Axis eyes was made at the end of April by Operation MINCEMEAT ('The Man Who Never Was'), which suggested that the obvious was being used as a cover for genuine landings in Sardinia and the Balkans.

Deception plans, particularly plans as ingenious as MINCEMEAT, are fascinating and intellectually persuasive: but how to discover whether they are succeeding in their purpose of deluding the intended victim? The most skilful agent could hardly penetrate the highest councils of the enemy and send his report of their discussions out in time and without being detected. Here Ultra now performed a service which could scarcely have been thought of by those who broke Enigma in 1940. It performed a similar service to even greater effect a year later, when it proved that the elaborately structured illusion that the 'real' OVERLORD would hit the Pas de Calais in July was believed not only on D-Day, as intended, but for another month or more as well, with incalculable benefit to the invaders. On this occasion the critical intercept was the formal warning sent on 12 May by OKW to OB South and OB South-East.[14] It began: 'According to a source which may be regarded as absolutely reliable, large-scale landings in the eastern and western Mediterranean are projected in the near future . . . the cover-name is HUSKY', and it went on to specify points on the coasts of Greece and the Aegean islands which were particularly vulnerable and therefore in need of special protection. The two theatre commanders and their subordinates began at once to demand extra aircraft and troops to meet the supposed threat. The RAF's raids on Sardinian ports and airfields were interpreted as part of a softening-up process preceding the landing, the garrisons of Sardinia and Corsica were strengthened (notably by an SS Brigade) rather than that of Sicily, but the most convincing sign that MINCEMEAT was being swallowed was the immediate transfer of 1 Panzer Division (then probably the best armoured formation in the German army) from Brittany to Greece, where it arrived on 14 June, still almost a month before HUSKY struck Sicily. At least a hundred tanks, which could have thrown the landing parties off the Sicilian beaches, were thus shown by Ultra to have gone off elsewhere on a wild goose chase. This calmed the fears of Eisenhower, who had asked permission to call the assault off if he had reason to think that the garrison of Sicily had been strongly reinforced, and significantly contributed to the success of HUSKY, which was none too well planned (because the responsible commanders were still engaged in Tunisia at the planning stage and so scattered all over the Mediterranean that it had been difficult to bring them together to discuss ways and means) and none to well executed (because there had been too little time to train the troops in the novel techniques required for a combined operation on this scale).

The longer term importance of this intelligence was to confirm the view which the British Chiefs of Staff were to urge with increasing conviction throughout the next twelve months of debate—that pressure in the Mediterranean could and would relieve the Russians by attracting divisions away from the German eastern front and at the same time weaken the prospective opposition to OVERLORD, then still a year away. At no time was this more comprehensively manifested than in the third quarter of 1943 in a series of Army Ultra intercepts of outstanding value. There had already been vague hints that the Germans were taking advance precautions against the possibility that the Italians might desert the Axis, and the name of Rommel had been associated with them. Just after the middle of August—that is, soon after the fall of Mussolini on 25 July—the scope of these precautions was suddenly revealed. Army Group B, it appeared, commanded by Rommel, was controlling three corps and nine divisions (two of them armoured, one being the *Leibstandarte Adolf Hitler*, a recent expansion of the Fuehrer's bodyguard) and 200 tanks, half of them the new Tigers and Panthers with formidably thick armour and tremendous hitting power; its purpose was to keep open the Brenner supply route and secure control of northern Italy.[15] The likely maximum scale of the German reaction to an Italian surrender— which in the event was announced to coincide with the Salerno landing (AVALANCHE) on 9 September—was thus known well beforehand. It was followed by a series of reports by II SS Corps (one of the three corps in Army Group B) detailing over the next week or two the strong-arm methods by which Lombardy was being 'pacified'. The strategic significance of all this is beyond doubt: all that was missing was an Allied force strong enough to over-run the sketchy defence which was all the Germans had yet been able to prepare south of the Lombard Plain, and an inkling of Hitler's future intentions (he did not know them himself yet): would he fight for the whole peninsula or retire to the safety of the mountains in the north?

In view of Hitler's lengthening record of 'Stand fast' orders, it was to be expected that he would follow the same policy now, although plain strategic sense, backed by Rommel's reputation and persistent advocacy, suggested that it would be preferable to conserve resources by abandoning the Italian mainland in favour of a more easily and more economically defensible line either across the northern Apennines from Genoa to Rimini or along the Alpine foothills. Had Hitler accepted Rommel's advice (and the second alternative would have served also as the southern wall of the Alpine Redoubt of which later rumour spoke), he would of course have disappointed the Allied Chiefs of Staff, who counted on Italy to hold as many divisions as possible away from Normandy and Russia, but he would have avoided the compulsion to permit Army Group B's infantry (though not its panzers) to be drawn bit by bit into the cauldron of Cassino—to be followed by others from both the other theatres under the stress of later emergency—with nothing to show for his pains but a slight slowing down of the Allied advance towards the Lombard plain. The first sign that Hitler would once more settle for 'No retreat' came in early October with an order to Kesselring to that effect.[16] It was quickly followed by a series of moves south by Army Group B's divisions[17] and in the course of time by others from every corner of the overblown Reich. On the German side, therefore, the strategic decision that there was to be an Italian campaign was taken within a month of AVALANCHE, but Hitler dithered for a further month before appointing Kesselring *Oberbefehlshaber (OB) Südwest* and sending Rommel off to improve the Channel defences.

With the front static on the Winter Line, the Anzio landing (SHINGLE) was laid on in late January 1944 in the hope of breaking the deadlock. Army Ultra gave the undertaking a kind of blessing by demonstrating that 5th Army's immediately preceding offensive on the main front had drawn 3, 29 and 90 Panzergrenadier Divisions away from the landing area and down to the Garigliano[18] but a combination of insufficient force, imprecise orders and timid leadership ruled out the advance on Rome which was its ostensible but problematical purpose. A few weeks later, heroic resistance saved the constricted beachhead from Kesselring's set-piece counter-attack (FISCHFANG), and the defensive battle was materially assisted by Ultra-based foreknowledge not only of Kesselring's whole plan (with his boast that he could 'throw the Allies back into the sea') and its timing, but also of its likely strength in tanks and infantry.[19]

With the failure of FISCHFANG, Kesselring set out his alternative—a series of defensive lines to protect Rome.[20] Allied planning, which had already begun, for the DIADEM offensive in May could thus take account of these in good time, and it was further aided by a succession of tank returns which showed that Kesselring disposed of slightly more than 300 tanks and 600 anti-tank guns;[21] an additional bonus was that the returns were set out under divisional headings so that, since the air liaison officers reported (in a Luftwaffe key) the locations of their divisions and corps almost daily, it was usually possible to tell the distribution of heavy weapons over the whole front at a glance.

In a short sketch like this, the piling up of apparently repetitive detail may easily become tedious, but one or two examples of a rather different kind from those already cited may be of interest. Directly after the capture of Rome on 4 June 1944, Alexander's allied Armies in Italy, which had already lost several of their best divisions to OVERLORD, were milked of more in preparation for the ill-considered and militarily unnecessary ANVIL/DRAGOON landing in the south of France, and the Mediterranean was relegated to the status of the second-class theatre. This ought to have meant that well-fortified defence lines would serve the German purpose now even better than at Cassino, while conversely it seemed to present the Allies with a more difficult task than before if (as was the case) Alexander refused to accept second-class status but determined to continue the advance in spite of his diminished resources. How could Ultra help him to escape from a kind of poverty trap?

During his short tenure as GOC-in-C Army Group B, and as part of his advocacy of withdrawal from peninsular Italy, Rommel sent Hitler a map of a proposed 'Apennine position' and issued orders for the construction of defences in the Lower Alps.[22] No word of this reached the Allied commanders through Ultra until the New Year, when the establishment of a new authority, *Armeegruppe von Zangen*, was reported; its duty was 'to develop the Apennine position with the greatest energy'.[23] Precise details of the whereabouts of this 'Apennine position' and an insight into the nature of the defences under construction came in an extremely long report from Kesselring's Chief Engineer in mid-April.[24] It revealed that far more labour and materials were being devoted to the two coastal sectors (the Serchio valley in the west, and the Foglia valley down to Pesaro in the east) than to the mountain stretch between them, and that the Adriatic coastal plain— where 8th Army broke through the following autumn—was the less well protected of the two. Still later, at the end of June, a Hitler directive,[25] the purpose of which was to speed up construction, gave away information of the greatest significance. So little had been done to date, Hitler complained, that it was essential that the 'common misconception' that there already was a fortified Apennine position should be 'scotched once and for all', in spite of the fact that it was intended to be the final defence line to prevent the 'incalculable military and political consequences' of an Allied penetration into the plain of Lombardy. Unhappily, the long and at times bitter disputes about the desirability or otherwise of ANVIL had come to an end shortly before this illuminating piece of intelligence (which among other things finally killed the theory that the Germans might withdraw of their own volition) could be used to show that a powerful blow delivered at once in Italy might reach the Alps and open the Riviera approach to the Rhone valley more quickly and effectively than a landing on the coast of France. Alexander lost several more experienced divisions. But he nevertheless assaulted the Gothic Line in August, delivering his main stroke on the Adriatic, where Ultra had shown it to be weakest. A succession of river obstacles, the slower progress of 5th Army over the fearful obstacle of the mountains in the centre, and the lateness of the season unfortunately prevented the complete breakthrough which Hitler had feared.

Army Ultra paved the way for the final offensive in the spring 1945 and assisted materially in its execution. Eight tank returns, the last of them a conveniently short time before the offensive, showed that the wastage of the autumn and winter fighting was barely being made good, for the total number of Army Group C's tanks remained almost constant from January to March, without significant increase. The strictest economy in the use of ammunition was enjoined by OKW—only essential targets were to be engaged, and even the current ration of six (!) howitzer rounds a day could no longer be justified—and after Christmas OKH issued a warning that the February allocation would be reduced by 30 per cent. Petrol was just as short. Berlin threatened to cut the monthly quota if the situation on the eastern front deteriorated, and Jodl peremptorily ordered OB Southwest and OB Southeast to limit the scope of their operations 'ruthlessly' in view of the general fuel shortage.[26] The scarcity of petrol was shown up in other ways too. Because Allied air raids repeatedly blocked the Brenner route, it took 715th Division (on its way to help stem the Russian advance into Hungary) a whole month to cover the 150 miles from southern Lombardy to the Austrian side of the pass, but the constant breaks in rail communications also curtailed the inflow of petrol so drastically that Kesselring could not avoid stooping to complain to OKW that he had not received proper compensation for petrol used in moving this single division to railhead,[27] and in April his successor had to remind Berlin that his petrol supply would last scarcely a fortnight at current rates of consumption but for a far shorter time if he had to make tactical moves in such a hurry that 'improvised means (ox-drawn vehicles)' were ruled out.[28]

By careful attention to the time and place of real and simulated operations the Allied command exploited this tactical handicap to the full, taking advantage of the Germans' known nervousness on both flanks to lead their armoured and mechanised formations a sorry dance from side to side of the front to meet illusory threats, thus compelling them to burn up precious petrol which could have been put to better use and to wear out tank tracks, which were hard to replace. A small attack in the mountains, principally designed to improve 5th Army's start-line for its attack on Bologna, for instance, drew 29th *Panzergrenadier* (PG) away from Liguria (where it had gone to forestall a rumoured coastal landing which the Allies were not intending to make). Soon the division was lured right across to the east coast by the trick of playing on enemy fears (which Ultra had repeatedly disclosed in recent months) of a landing at the head of the Adriatic to join up with Tito's forces in Bosnia and Croatia. It was possible, through Ultra, to track 29th PG from its new position behind Bologna by stages through Mantua and Padua to the area north of Venice and on into Istria, whence it hurried back (minus several tanks) too late to stop British commandos round Lake Commachio from opening 8th Army's route to break through the Argenta gap and burst into the enemy's rear. Much the same story, but with less local colour, could be told of 90th PG and 26 Panzer Division. The bulk of the German armour and motor transport had long been confined to these three and only one or two other formations, which were thus first lured out of the way and then side-stepped when feigned operations gave way to real.

One of the longest messages ever intercepted (it ran to almost a thousand words in translation) gives a fine impression of what Army Ultra could do in the last year of the war, and at the same time it offers an unsurpassable tribute to the strategy of Alexander and Mark Clark, for it is an admission of defeat from the mouth of their principal opponent. On 14 April von Vietinghoff (who had become OB Southwest when Kesselring took over as OB West at the beginning of March) gloomily surveyed the first five days of 8th Army's offensive.[29] The fury of the Allied attack, especially from the air, he wrote, confirmed the Allies' intention to destroy the German armies in Italy before the end of hostilities in the rest of Europe. Severe damage to signals communications was making control of operations impossible, and every attempt at movement was smashed as it started. Four divisions had been almost completely wiped out, and every new line of defence was penetrated as soon as it was manned. Parts of the front would have to be given up voluntarily in order to free even the smallest reserves to meet the expected American attack west of Bologna. Unless the British could be halted north-west of Lake Commachio, they would break through to the Po. If OKW wished to keep the Allies away from the 'Reich fortress' for as long as possible, the Army Group would have to begin retiring towards the Ticino soon, for it would take a fortnight to execute so elaborate a movement.

Depleted though their strength had been through a political decision, their enemy recognised, three weeks before he surrendered, that the Allied armies in Italy had won a total victory.

In time of war it is essential to distinguish intelligence that is useful from that which is merely interesting and to classify it by source in so far as that helps to grade it by degree of reliability; but it is open to question whether, when peace has returned, it is profitable to separate the different elements and to scrutinise them a second time in isolation from each other, thus divorcing in the study items which in the field were treated as parts of a single though variegated whole. Again, military intelligence is by its nature ephemeral, a means to an end not an end in itself. The historian of intelligence dare not fall into the academicism of his colleagues in constitutional or economic history. By studying in minute detail the structure of government, society and wealth in fourteenth- and fifteenth-century England and France, for instance, the medieval historian may even now discover new clues to explain why Edward III and Henry V, ruling over a thinly-populated offshore island, were able to win Crécy, Poitiers and Agincourt and dominate a larger and wealthier country for so long. The significance of the battles themselves, however—and that of Alamein—remains quite unaffected by the most profound study of the intelligence which led up to them. We ought always to bear this in mind, lest we claim too much for our subject.

Is a study of Army Ultra on its own of little value, then, even though it was an important part of a larger whole which for more than half the 1939–1945 war provided almost all the Allies knew about the enemy and furnished information on a scale unapproached by any previous intelligence source? Manifestly, a study so artificially restricted cannot avoid distorting truth. There was no place in it for an examination of the damage done by aircraft and warships to trans-Mediterranean supply traffic in 1941 and 1942, for example, and for the tremendous strategic influence a shortage of petrol and ammunition excercised on the defeat of Rommel, for all the intelligence which made it possible came from air and naval keys. Yet its chief consequence was to limit the mobility and firepower of the Afrika Korps.

On the other hand, two advantages can certainly be claimed for such a study, though their value will diminish or disappear entirely when, in the course of time, the place of Ultra in the history of the Second World War becomes clearer and more precisely definable than it is today. The first drives home the point that Ultra was not a constant but that its content was subject to apparently random fluctuation from month to month, even from day to day. The case of the Gothic Line illustrates this. The information quoted above came from two very long messages, one in April and one in May. Neither was much more than a list of figures under a number of headings, therefore slow and tedious to encipher on a machine on which every figure had to be spelled out as a word. What accident caused them to be transmitted by radio in Enigma? Did chance bombs cut teleprinter lines, or was there a simple electrical failure? Why did the accidental interruption of more natural methods of communicating complex data about the construction of wire and concrete defences happen twice at an interval of five or six weeks, and never again?—for it is unthinkable that no more progress-reports were rendered between the end of May and the assault on the Gothic Line in August and September. These questions have no answer, but they are still worth asking if they induce a more realistic appraisal of the source and a better appreciation of the fortuitous way in which it imparted information even of the highest strategic significance.

Secondly, if a deliberate but momentary concentration on one aspect of intelligence throws its unpredictable variability into sharper relief, then it will usefully discourage hasty judgements on the contribution of Ultra to victory. We are indeed nearer a final verdict today than could have been foreseen ten years ago, but we have not yet got beyond the stage of establishing the facts and thereby agreeing on the foundations upon which a final verdict may one day be based.

Notes

A more complete set of references will be given in my forthcoming book *Ultra and Mediterranean Strategy*.

1. At some periods—the Tunisian campaign was one of them—the Y Service decrypted similar returns in lower-grade ciphers, but there seems to be no record of how regularly this was done.
2. OL 211. Ultra signals quoted in this paper were prefixed OL, MKA, QT, VM, ML, JP, VL, KV, BT, KO. All are in the Public Record Office.
3. C. Andrew: *Secret Service: The Making of the British Intelligence Community* (London, 1985).
4. John Cloake: *Templer, Tiger of Malaya* (London, 1985), esp. pp. 64–7.
5. MKAs 2094, 2095
6. Sir Edgar Williams, Montgomery's chief Intelligence Officer, has twice recently (Nigel Hamilton: *Monty, The Making of a General 1887–1942* (London, 1981), pp. 652–3; T. E. B. Howarth (ed.), *Monty at Close Quarters* (London, 1985), (pp. 21, 22) stated that it was on 15 or 16 August—i.e. before he could have seen Rommel's appreciation—that he gave Montgomery the decisive account of Ultra intelligence. He does not expressly refer to the 17 August signal, yet seems plainly to imply it.
7. QT 4958
8. QTs 5794, 5977, 5877, 5893, 5959, 6374, 9177, 9681.
9. QT 6859.
10. VMs 5605, 5620
11. N. Hamilton: *Monty, Master of the Battlefield 1942–44* (London, 1983), p. 169.
12. VM 6984
13. VMs 7823, 7841
14. ML 1955

15. JPs 1487, 1512, 2911, 2952, 3080
16. JP 6045
17. JPs 6545, 6578, etc.
18. VLs 4302, 4331, 4546
19. VLs 4559, 5359, 5449, 5594
20. VL 8072
21. VL 3190
22. Oberkommando der Wehrmacht, *Kriegstagebuch 1940–1945* ed. P. E. Schramm (Frankfurt, 1961–65), iii, p. 1141, iv, p. 591.
23. VLs 5359, 5381. The Apennine position became the 'Gothic Line' in April and was rechristened 'Green Line' in June. Fuller details about Ultra knowledge of the fortificatons may be found in a paper I presented to an international congress in Pesaro in 1984, the proceedings of which have been published under the title *Linea Gotica 1944* (Milan 1986). See pp. 125–42.
24. KV 1578
25. KV 9843
26. BTs 2635, 2879, 3367, 4854, 5510
27. BT 6125
28. KOs 555, 586, 588
29. KOs 496, 529

British Naval Intelligence in Two World Wars— Some Similarities and Differences

PATRICK BEESLY

Two World Wars or one? For British Naval intelligence (NID) a more appropriate title might be 'The Great German War', just as our ancestors referred to 'The Great French War'. Coalitions were formed and dissolved, allies were defeated or changed sides, a few remained constant, but one principal enemy dominated the scene throughout—Germany, just as France had done one hundred years earlier. I do not dismiss NID's contribution both before and after Pearl Harbor to the defeat of Japan—it was probably greater than is generally supposed—but for some forty years, except for an interlude in the twenties and early thirties, NID's sights were focussed on Germany and NID's successes not only made a major contribution to victory, but also profoundly affected the development and status of the nation's other Intelligence Services.

We have enjoyed forty years without a major war since 1945, a date already beginning to seem remote, while 1914 has receded into a past almost as distant as Trafalgar and Waterloo. It is, therefore, as well to remind ourselves that only twenty-one years elapsed between the cessation of fighting in 1918 and its renewal in 1939. It is not surprising that, at the opening of what I might call the Second Round, little seemed to have changed. Indeed, in many respects, it had not. A large proportion of the Royal Navy's ships had either served in or been designed during the First Round: officers of captain's rank and above had had personal experience, some of them in responsible positions, of war against Germany: the First Lord, from 3 September, was the same Winston Churchill who had presided

253

over the Board of Admiralty on 4 August 1914—the first person he asked for on again assuming office was the Director of Naval Intelligence (DNI). He had been well served by NID in 1914–15 and he expected that the same sort of information would immediately be available to him again!

There was, it is true, a good deal of '14–18' experience available. The DNI, Rear-Admiral John Godfrey, had not actually served in NID before, but he had much to do with Intelligence during his four years in the Mediterranean in the first conflict, and had seen something of the work of Room 40—the Admiralty's cryptanalysis section—on a visit to London in 1917.[1] Moreover, the great 'Blinker' Hall, DNI from 1914 to 1918, was still alive and able to give Godfrey a great deal of useful information and advice about his own experiences. The head of MI6, the Secret Service, was Admiral 'Quex' Sinclair, Hall's deputy in 1918 and successor as DNI in 1919. As 'C' he now controlled Room 40's successor: the Government Code and Cypher School (GC&CS) (Bletchley Park or BP as it came to be called) whose chief was Commander Alistair Denniston RNVR. Denniston had joined Room 40 in 1914 and was supported in GC&CS by a number of his old colleagues such as 'Nobby' Clarke, 'Dilly' Knox, that most brilliant of codebreakers, Fetterlein (who had come from the Imperial Russian Navy's Room 40 in 1918), and one or two more. They were joined, or rather re-joined, in 1939 by other old Room 40 hands such as Nigel de Grey (who had decrypted the Zimmermann Telegram in 1917), Frank Birch, who eventually became head of BP's Naval Section, Walter Bruford (who had worked on the German Madrid traffic in 1917) and quite a few more. The ex-naval contingent at BP was further strengthened by officers like M. G. Saunders and others with several years of experience between the wars and, of course, Commander Edward Travis, who took over control of the military side of BP in 1942.

In the Admiralty itself Godfrey had, by 3 September 1939, got his hands on other officers with 1914–18 NID experience. Serving as head of the Operational Intelligence Centre (OIC) was Captain 'Jock' Clayton (a retired rear-admiral who had been a watchkeeper in the War Room in 1917), while the head of OIC's Submarine Tracking Room was Paymaster Captain Ernest Thring who had occupied exactly the same position twenty odd years previously. Similarly, the senior naval representative on the interservice prisoner of war interrogation department was Colonel Trench, Royal Marines, whose experience of naval intelligence dated back to 1912 (when he had been arrested with Lieutenant Brandon RN by the Germans for spying on the defences of the Friesian coast).[2] He had been in charge of naval interrogation of prisoners from 1914 to 1918, so that it is scarcely surprising that the excellent reports he produced between 1939 and 1945 were identical in format even down to their red covers. Many of the lesser posts in Godfrey's NID were filled by men and women who had served under Hall, and if the senior positions, such as those of Deputy and Assistant Directors, were occupied by officers who had been at sea as midshipmen or sub-lieutenants in 1918, they had had war experience and were aware of the sort of information which the Fleet would expect from NID.

From the point of view of personnel, therefore, there was a definite linkage, both amateur and professional, between 1918 and 1939, even though Godfrey has suggested that the 'Hall tradition' had barely survived the lean years between. Let us now look at the similarities in organisation and administration. Some tenuous form of naval intelligence department had undoubtedly existed in the Admiralty during the Napoleonic Wars, but during the Balkan crisis of 1878 there was but a single clerk in the Admiralty's Military Branch responsible for studying such information about foreign naval powers as did trickle in to Whitehall. In 1882 the Foreign Intelligence Committee was formed under Captain William Hall (Blinker Hall's father) with instructions to 'collect, classify and record, with a complete index, all information which bears a naval character, or which may be of value during naval operations, to keep up our knowledge of progress made by foreign countries in naval matters and to preserve the information in a form readily available for reference'. In 1886 it was decided to create a Department of Naval Intelligence under a Rear-Admiral responsible not only for gathering and disseminating information but also for mobilisation and preparations of war plans. These latter responsibilities were later split off to another department, but NID was the first department of the Naval Staff to be formed, and it remained the senior division of that staff throughout its existence: its Director was the senior director with direct access to the First Sea Lord and First Lord, giving him prestige and authority which was recognised and acknowledged not only by his colleagues but by the whole Navy.[3]

By 1914, the Intelligence Department (it was not officially called a Division until about 1918), appears to have had a staff of around three dozen within the Admiralty, organized under a Director and Deputy Director and divided into small geographical sections covering the whole maritime world. its knowledge of foreign navies, the dispositions of their fleets and squadrons and of their capabilities and of their building programmes, of their bases and their defences, if not perfect, was more than adequate. The collection of information depended on reports from British warships visiting foreign ports, on a developing system of 'Reporting Officers' based on British consulates and vice-consulates in almost every port throughout the world and on the observation of an able band of naval attachés, supplemented by a careful study of the foreign press. All this was what one might call 'open' information and was more readily available then, than is the case today or even in the late 1930s. Two sources of information were conspicuously lacking: efficient espionage (the Secret Service had only been formed in 1909) and cryptanalysis—there was no organistion in existence to break enemy codes.* Plans existed for the creation of a censorship service and also for crippling Germany's overseas telegraph communications by cutting the undersea cables, but both of these measures seem to have had a defensive rather than an aggressive purpose—to prevent information about Britain reaching the enemy rather than to obtain information about Germany.[4] To sum up, British naval intelligence was, within limits and with one very important omission, efficiently organised and capable of fulfilling its function.

The one area where it was totally unprepared was in the collection and dissemination of Operational Intelligence—information about the movements and intentions of the enemy fleet once hostilities had begun. The time honoured method of close blockade with frigates 'looking into' enemy ports and shadowing and reporting any movement by the enemy had had to be abandoned—only in the nick of time—in the face of the threat from torpedo attack by destroyers and submarines. Neither light cruisers, submarines, still less aircraft, could, in 1914, replace the old frigates (indeed they were still incapable of doing so with complete reliability thirty years later), so that if enemy units did put to sea it was unlikely that their departure would be known and even more unlikely that their subsequent movements could be followed. Even the North Sea was a vast area and the chances of intercepting an enemy force at sea before it could achieve its objective were, to say the least, remote. 'Field Intelligence', to borrow an army term, was much more difficult than it was on land.

Before considering wartime developments in Intelligence, let us look briefly at the situation in 1939. Germany was again the principal opponent. NID, after twenty years of peacetime neglect, was being revitalised by the

---

* A recent book by Professor Santoni, of Rome University, appears to claim that the British were capable of decrypting German naval messages before the outbreak of war. Decrypted German signals for this period do exist in the Public Record Office, but all the evidence in my possession, and it is considerable, indicates that these signals were decrypted much later, perhaps not until after 1919, and that the information these messages provided was definitely not available at the time.

new DNI, John Godfrey. The Division was not much larger than it had been in 1914, its geographical sections organized on the same lines, its principal sources of information—naval attachés, reporting officers, the press and diplomatic telegrams, an inadequate Secret Service—very much the same. It was hoped that air reconnaissance would now replace the frigates for looking into enemy ports and reporting movements of enemy ships at sea, but this was a function which came a long way bottom of the RAF's priorities: there were no suitable photographic reconnaissance aircraft and the patrol aircraft of Coastal Command could not even reach the Norwegian coast. Although the German Navy was proportionately weaker vis-à-vis the Royal Navy than it had been in 1914, the latter's commitments were greater—three former allies were now at best hostile neutrals who might at any moment enter the war against us, while the British Fleet, compared with 1914, contained a greater proportion of obsolescent or even obsolete ships. Accurate Operational Intelligence was just as vital as it had been twenty-five years earlier but, in the absence of any major cryptanalytical ability, just as hard to obtain. Only in one respect was NID stronger than it had been in 1914. The problem of analysing and disseminating Operational Intelligence, if it could be secured, had been appreciated: the Operational Intelligence Centre had been created and would be in a position to meet the demands put upon it as soon as information, from any and every source, became available.

There were three very striking similarities between the two periods. Firstly, and perhaps inevitably, was the enormous expansion of the Division, both in the range of its activities and consequently in the numbers of its staff. On both occasions the additional personnel were largely recruited from civil life, mostly without any previous experience of naval matters let alone of naval intelligence. Initially at any rate, such recruitment was mainly through the 'old boy' network, by personal recommendation—and I do not know of a better method for a sudden expansion of an organisation dealing with matter of great secrecy. I do not know of the existence of any traitors in NID before the 1950s.

Secondly, this expansion was in both instances due to two exceptionally able and talented Directors of NID, Hall and Godfrey. I do not believe that either of them had their equal, during their periods of office among other heads of Intelligence departments, British or foreign, allied or enemy. These two men not only brought their own Division to a very high degree of efficiency but set the pace for, and greatly influenced the development of the country's other Intelligence Services. It is easy now, with hindsight, to criticise or even laugh at some of their ideas as amateurish and naïve—such as Hall's cruise of the *Sayonara*[5] (repeated unsuccessfully by Godfrey in 1939[6]) or Godfrey's flirtation with Hitler's alleged addiction to astrology[7] — but they at least showed an open mind and a desire to try to obtain indications of the enemy's thinking and possible plans by any and every means. Nor, particularly in Hall's time, was the opposition all that sophisticated. Neither man was content to rely on one single source for information: anything, no matter how far fetched, should, they thought, be investigated, and the results obtained compared with those from other sources. Reliance on a single source of information is almost always fatal. Both men were great innovators, Hall more so than Godfrey because he was confronted with practically virgin territory. There had been no major European maritime war for a hundred years. During this time scientific developments had revolutionised the naval and military scene quite as much as the domestic and international ones: strategy and tactics both on land and at sea had changed out of recognition even since 1900 but the new theories and practices had never been put to the test of full-scale war. Above all, wireless telegraphy had most recently and suddenly provided naval staffs with the means to exercise a degree of direct and immediate control over their fleets and squadrons at sea previously undreamed of. This centralized control in turn demanded centralized Intelligence—or was it perhaps the other way round? Did the amazing rapidity of the new methods of communication mean that Intelligence was now in a position, at least potentially, to influence, perhaps even to dominate, the Operational and Planning departments of the naval staffs?

It has been suggested that Hall ran the Government. No matter how exaggerated this claim may be, there can be little doubt that his power and influence extended far beyond the purely naval sphere: his handling of the Zimmerman Telegram is the best known and most obvious example of this, but many other instances can be quoted—his involvement in the resignation of Fisher and the dismissal of Churchill,[8] with the Arab Bureau in Cairo,[9] with counter-espionage and counter-sabotage in the still neutral United States,[10] with the Special Branch of Scotland Yard, with the Censorship, with the recall of Luxburg,[11] the German Minister in Buenos Aires and the trial of Cailleaux in France.[12] No doubt, if ever the British authorities were to release all the secret records of the period, a great deal more would emerge, including details of the world wide network of agents he built up apparently independently of the rather fumbling efforts of the Secret Service. Hall poked his nose into everybody's business, usually without being asked or authorised to do so, but it was on his own ground, in the handling of purely naval and specifically operational intelligence that he was least successful, at least until half way through 1917. I will return to this point later.

Despite the similarities in the outward situation which confronted Godfrey when he became DNI in February, 1939—the same enemy, lack of reliable information, twenty years of neglect of NID and so on—there were, in fact, considerable differences. The completely dominant postion of Hall's NID was now a thing of the past. Hall's Room 40, his cryptanalysis bureau, had become an inter-service organisation controlled by the Secret Service under the overlordship of the Foreign Office: the Army and Air Force Intelligence departments, although carrying less weight in the War Office and Air Ministry than did NID in the Admiralty, were well established, and rivals rather than colleagues with as yet no effective co-ordinating body over the three of them: other departments of state such as the Ministry of Economic Warfare, the Ministry of Information and, after nine months, SOE and PWE, dealing with matters in which Hall had dabbled and whose existence in many cases had been due to Hall's example and advice, certainly eased the burden on DNI but equally restricted his field of activity. Lessons— important lessons—had been learnt from the first conflict but the new arrangements were, in 1939, inevitably far from perfect. Churchill and the Sea Lords, with 1914–18 in mind, expected a great deal from NID but failed to appreciate, despite Godfrey's great efforts in the seven months up to September 1939, how much still needed to be done to rebuild the Division and to obtain from sources no longer under the DNI's direct control the information needed for success. Neither the Secret Service's agents, nor Bletchley Park's codebreakers nor the RAF's air reconnaissance could supply the information the Navy needed, and even when NID did produce very accurate figures of the total strength of the U-boat fleet, Churchill found them personally inconvenient and therefore unacceptable.[13] Nevertheless, Godfrey, following Hall's advice, had managed to establish excellent contracts in the City, with the Press and with Oxford and Cambridge. Hall had relied greatly on two talented personal assistants—Herschell and Serocold—and, again, Godfrey did likewise in recruiting Fleming and Merrett, who established and nurtured valuable links on a quiet and almost unofficial basis with other Government departments and with private institutions and individuals. Godfrey was the first to recognise that, if the situation vis-à-vis the enemy had not changed a great deal, that in Whitehall was very different and that the DNI could no longer act with the extraordinary independence that Hall had, taking advantage of a vacuum, swiftly established for himself. Godfrey played a leading part—he suggests the leading part[14] in involving the Foreign Office actively in the study and co-ordination of Intelligence by the establishment and development of the joint Intelligence Committee (JIC) and the Joint Intelligence Staff (JIS). It was Godfrey who created, from the tiny NID section, the Inter-Service Topographical Department.[15] It was Godfrey who, despite intense opposition from sections of the Air Staff, backed Sydney Cotton, that piratical character who pointed the way for the development of a prime source of Intelligence, the Photographic Reconnaissance Unit (PRU).[16] These were all major achievements—and there were others—which contributed greatly to the eventual superiority of British and Allied Intelligence to that of Germany and the Axis powers but they all involved persuading other departments and interests to accept ideas put forward by NID: they were concerned quite as much with using as with gathering information, and they had a marked affect on American as well as British Intelligence Services.

Godfrey never was responsible for a coup like the Zimmermann Telegram which, if not totally responsible for the US declaration of war on Germany in 1917, certainly ensured that it happened in April and not many months later with consequences that might well have been disastrous for the Western Allies. But Godfrey was one of the earliest and most persistent advocates of sharing British secrets with the Americans in order to create an identity of interest and foster personal relationships which would draw the United States ever closer to Britain.[17] Of course, he was not the only person with this sensible idea, but it is noticeable that he was advocating it when Churchill still thought that such exchanges should be on a strictly quid pro quo basis.

With the fall of France, of course, British horsetrading had to cease and Godfrey was officially permitted to disclose all NID's secrets to the US naval Attaché and the American DNI. Hall, too, had co-operated closely with the Americans but had been able, in those days, to do so on a 'Big Brother' basis, disclosing only such information as he considered advantageous to Britain. Although Hall gave the American Ambassador, Page, and his Second Secretary, Bell, an immense amount of information derived from decrypts, as he also did to Admiral Simms after America came into the war, he resolutely refused all requests to let our allies into Room 40's technical secrets to provide the expertise to enable Washington to establish its own cryptological bureau.[18] Twenty years later, the United States had expertise of her own in the shape of Magic and Purple: there was not only a quid pro quo, but Britain was now prepared to pay any price, which Hall had not been, to secure American good will and assistance. However, it is some indication of Godfrey's standing both with the British chiefs of staff and with influential individuals in Washington that he was despatched there in May

1941 to try to persuade the Americans to remedy what the British saw, with some justification, as grave weaknesses in the US Intelligence set-up. In the course of this mission he had dinner with President Roosevelt followed by more than an hour's private discussion with the great man.[19] Many other distinguished men, from Churchill downwards, were intent on achieving close and intimate co-operation between Britain and America but, in the Intelligence field much of the success was due to Godfrey. The post of Director of British Naval Intelligence still carried great weight on both sides of the Atlantic.

With such successes under his belt it may seem surprising that, in September 1942, on the very day when he was given the unprecedented promotion to Vice-Admiral on the Active List, Godfrey was summarily dismissed by the First Sea Lord, Admiral Sir Dudley Pound, on the grounds that 'co-operation among the members of the JIC which is important for its proper functioning was not possible as long as you were a member.' This dismissal has been roundly criticized by, amongst others, Stephen Roskill,[20] and contrasts with Hall's tenure of office right up to the Armistice, although he, too, was then abruptly dropped by the then First Sea Lord, Sir Rosslyn Wemyss. Both Godfrey and Hall were men of exceptional ability, innovators, individualists who were never afraid to act on their own responsibility, natural and instinctive intelligence chiefs. Both created highly successful departments under the stress of war, in Godfrey's case so well that it continued to function virtually without change even after his departure. Both, despite fits of blinding bad temper, won the loyalty and unstinted admiration of their staffs. Neither received any recognition from their own Service—Hall's KCMG was awarded on the recommendation of the Foreign Office while Godfrey was the only officer of his rank to receive no decoration whatsoever for his wartime successes. But in many ways they were very different characters. Hall was an extrovert who, although he made enemies, not least his immediate superior Oliver, Chief of the War Staff, also had great charm and won himself a host of friends. He could and did delegate, but on the whole he took good care that he personally should present important items of information to his superiors, usually after he had decided what course of action he wished them to take. He dealt direct with Oliver, with all the First Sea Lords under whom he served, with Prime Ministers Asquith and Lloyd George and with the Foreign Secretary Balfour. He played his cards close to his chest and his sources of information were so varied and some of them so far removed from the purely naval sphere, that one sometimes gets the feeling that he did, indeed, 'run the government'. Godfrey had just as far ranging and independent a mind, but he was perhaps more of an introvert and certainly more of an intellectual. Although often appearing harsh and overbearing, he was a shy man and did not have Hall's natural talent for making friends and suffered, at least in his early career, from a mild inferiority complex. He has confessed that he was not at his best when giving verbal appreciations of an Intelligence situation.[21] He rightly saw that his strongest qualities were not those of a 'day to day' Intelligence Officer, but as an administrator, as a creator of new departments to meet new needs, as a builder of intelligence machinery rather than as the chief operator of that machinery. The late Euan Montagu, whose testimony is all the more valuable because he did not like Godfrey personally, considered that he was a 'genius' and that, given the changed circumstances, Hall would not have solved the many problems which arose so successfully as did Godfrey.[22] On the other hand, Hall might have got his own way with his colleagues with less friction than his successor and, although I share Roskill's view that Godfrey's dismissal was unjust, it has to be admitted that his manners were often unnecessarily abrasive and that he took little trouble to conceal his impatience with some of his more pedestrian colleagues on the JIC. He might have made a very good intelligence 'Supremo' but such a post did not exist and the very idea was twenty years ahead of the times.

I must now return to the third of the striking similarities between Hall's and Godfrey's NID's—the absolutely vital part played by cryptanalysis and Sigint in general in their success. Effective wireless telegraphy (W/T) was only ten years old in 1914 and no power had anticipated the extent to which this new method of communication would enable naval staffs to control events at sea from on shore. Nor had the vast increase in W/T traffic, which central control and war conditions would produce, been foreseen. A prerequisite for Sigint is obviously the ability to intercept and record the enemy's coded W/T messages. The cutting by the British of the majority of German overseas telegraph cables on 5 August, 1914, which compelled the enemy to use W/T to a much greater extent than envisaged, seems to have been, as with the institution of censorship, a defensive rather than an offensive measure—to prevent information reaching Germany rather than to obtain information about Germany for Britain. It is therefore all the more to the Admiralty's credit that intercepting stations were so quickly established and a naval cryptanalysis section to try to decrypt the intercepted messages (Room 40) created from scratch within a month of the outbreak of war. Success did not come immediately. When it did, it was through the capture of the three principal German naval codes (the SKM from the *Magdeburg*, the HVB from Australia and the VB from the bottom of the North Sea). The first two did not reach Room 40 until October and the latter until December

1914, and it is quite clear to me, from the evidence of members of Room 40, that no worthwhile successes were achieved in Home Waters until December 1914 and overseas until well into 1915. Room 40's initial breakthroughs were entirely due to these lucky 'pinches', as was the subsequent penetration of German diplomatic codes and fresh naval codes when these were belatedly introduced by the Germans.[23] This does not mean that Room 40 did not develop great skills which enabled them to overcome changes in keys and even to reconstruct some codes (such as 0075 used for the Zimmerman Telegram) by purely cryptanalytical methods, but captures and German failures to recognise the inevitability of such losses and take swift remedial action enormously simplified Room 40's task.

There is an obvious parallel with 1939. At the outbreak of war no information from German naval Enigma was available. Intelligence derived from Luftwaffe Enigma did not become available until early 1940 and naval Enigma was not effectively broken until May 1941 and then, once again, thanks to timely 'pinches', but this time deliberately planned and skilfully executed.[24] Moreover, when the Germans introduced a fourth wheel in their naval Enigma for the benefit of their Atlantic U-boats, Bletchley Park was defeated until a further capture provided the necessary clues. Bletchley Park was not, as Room 40 had been, under the control of the Admiralty, who more than once pressed for greater effort to be devoted to breaking naval Enigma. One must, however, conclude that the centralization of all cryptanalysis was absolutely correct and that undivided control of naval codebreaking would not have produced results any quicker (probably the contrary) and would have been harmful overall.

What is indisputable is that when, on both occasions, German naval codes were cracked, the benefits for the Royal Navy were enormous. In 1914 the *Hochseeflotte*, although outnumbered by the Grand Fleet, was a very potent weapon, its bases better sited than those of the Royal Navy and its ability to choose its own moment for a sortie to spring a surprise on its opponent an immense advantage which might well have counterbalanced its numerical inferiority. Despite the gross failure of the British Naval Staff (in fact one man, Oliver) to make the best use of Room 40's priceless information, the British mastery of German naval communications robbed the *Hochseeflotte* of its greatest asset, surprise. Unsatisfactory, from the British point of view as the Scarborough Raid, the Dogger Bank and, above all, Jutland may have been, they would never have taken place at all but for the work of Room 40, and the results reinforced the views of the Kaiser and the *Admiralstab* that the *Hochseeflotte* must be preserved as a bargaining counter for the peace conference and could not be used as a weapon to bring Britain to her knees.

The corollary, of course, was unrestricted U-boat warfare which, in the end, was bound to bring America into the war on the side of the Western Powers. In this campaign, too, Room 40's expertise was of vital importance, although, again, this fact was not recognized soon enough—in fact only at the eleventh hour.

The impact of Bletchley Park's success with German naval Enigma in May 1941 was equally striking. Although Admiral Raeder had been confronted with war before he could complete his Z plan for the expansion of the German surface and U-boat fleet, the battleships and battlecruisers which he did possess outclassed their British rivals and the Royal Navy was now far more stretched than it had been in 1914 because of the loss of France as an ally, the active hostility of Italy and the potential and then actual hostility of Japan. Once again, the Germans had the advantages of being able to choose their moment for sorties of surface ships, and they demonstrated their ability to achieve surprise again and again up to the middle of 1941. It is true that the destruction of the *Bismarck* owed more to conventional Intelligence sources than to cryptanalysis,[25] but from that moment on the Admiralty were no longer without clues, often comprehensive ones, about the movements of German heavy units. Surprise was not impossible but it was much more difficult to achieve. This was perhaps a contributory factor in the almost total transference of German offensive effort to the U-boat war.

Room 40 had, from early 1915 onwards, an accurate and comprehensive knowledge of the size, composition and general disposition of the U-boat fleet. It knew, with few exceptions, when U-boats departed on patrol and when and if they returned, and hence the rate of loss. It was able to reconstruct, retrospectively, individual U-boat cruises and was able to check their often extravagant claims. It was in a position to estimate with a fair degree of accuracy, the likely weight of attack in any particular sea area. But, because U-boats were, until late 1917, operating independently and with a large degree of initiative left to their individual commanders, it was not often able to pin point a particular U-boat's position with the degree of accuracy needed by the British hunting forces to achieve a 'kill'.[26] Even when it could do so, the lack, until early 1918, of even moderately effective anti-submarine weapons and detection devices, rendered such information of little value. Only in one respect was Room 40 able to contribute to the Admiralty's mistaken reliance on offensive action to defeat the U-boats. This was the mining campaign whose effectiveness was delayed, again until 1917, by the ludicrous inefficiency of British mines. Despite this, mines were the greatest U-boat killer[27] and Room 40, by its detailed and always up to date knowledge of the German swept channels, did at least ensure that the mines were laid where they would do the most good. Of course, the obvious solution to the U-boat menace was the convoy system. One of the things that mystifies me most is that, in the light of Room 40's knowledge of the almost total failure of so-called offensive or seek-and-destroy patrolling up to May 1917, the Admiralty continued to proclaim that it was the only strategy holding out any prospects of success. When convoy was finally introduced, sinkings of ships *in* convoy dropped dramatically to the figure of one and a half to two per cent, which later statistical analysis was to show had been the rule in the age of sail and which was to be exactly repeated in 1939–45.[28] At last Room 40 was able to offer great assistance in evasive routing. It was a major contribution which would have been even more effective had the convoy system not been introduced with unpardonable slowness and had it been made universal even for coastal shipping.

At least, in 1939, the Admiralty immediately introduced convoy although, throughout the period, far too many ships were compelled to sail independently. The results, even without the benefit for one and a half years of cryptanalysis, were predictable. Losses of ships in convoy—that is excluding stragglers, rompers and independents—never in any period of three months exceeded one-and-a-half per cent. When, from mid-1941 to January 1942 and from mid-1943 until the end of the war, Bletchley Park was able to decrypt Atlantic U-boat traffic almost currently, convoys again proved not only an almost total defence but also provided the opportunity of offensive tactical action which sank more U-boats than any offensive, hunt and destroy patrols ever did. Even the RAF's Bay of Biscay offensive and the successful operation of the American hunter-killer groups in mid-Atlantic, dependent as they were for their success very largely on accurate decrypted information, could not rival the convoy's sea and air escorts.*

One major difference in the second Battle of the Atlantic was, of course, the German Wolf Pack tactics, which involved total control from the U-boat command ashore and consequently a vast amount of signalling both from and to U-boats. From June 1941 to the end of January 1942, and again from the middle of December 1942 until the end of the war, this traffic was, albeit with important delays at various times, read by the British with results which are impossible to quantify exactly but which were certainly of the very greatest significance. Even during the blackout in Atlantic U-boat traffic in 1942, the continued reading of the Home Water Enigma provided the

---

*Figures for aircraft kills were greatly swollen in the last weeks of the War when many U-boats were sunk in port.

Admiralty with invaluable information about departures and arrivals of U-boats, of losses and the growth and general disposition of the U-boat fleet,[29] just as had been possible from 1914 to 1918. Evasive routing of convoys was again only possible thanks to decrypting and literally thousands of tons of shipping were thereby saved at a time when shipping losses were exceeding new building. Despite the fact that the success of the German *B-Dienst* to some extent nullified this benefit (and in the first six months of 1943 came within an ace of entirely cancelling it), the somewhat belated measures to strengthen Anglo-American anti-submarine defences would indeed have been too late but for cryptanalysis. The Battle of the Atlantic would not have been won in May 1943, nor would Dönitz's attempt to renew the battle in October of that year have been defeated, if the Allies had had to rely only on the increased number of sea and air escorts and sophisticated anti-submarine weapons which were then provided. The battle would have been won in the end because of the superior resources of the Allies but, like the Zimmermann Telegram, the victory was important not only because it was a victory but even more so because of when it was won. No invasion of France would have been possible in 1944. American resources would have had to be diverted from the Pacific: might not Russia have made a compromise peace? And even if she had not done so, how many more years would it have needed to defeat the Axis? Professor Hinsley, and there can be no-one more qualified to express an opinion, has estimated that the war might have lasted twice as long but for British cryptanalysis. I agree with him. I am also certain that there would have been no Armistice in November, 1918, but for the work of Room 40.

The great contribution made by Room 40 to the success of the British mining campaign in 1917 and 1918 was repeated from 1941 onwards by OIC. Thanks to patient analysis of decrypts, German swept channels, convoy routes and movements in the Baltic as well as in the North Sea, Channel and Bay of Biscay were as well known to the British as to their enemy and compelled the German Navy to devote an ever-increasing effort to convoy protection and minesweeping.[30] The RAF's mining campaign, unpopular though it was with 'Bomber' Harris, was probably its most cost-effective operation.

I need not emphasise that cryptanalysis, no matter how complete and successful on one side, cannot alone ensure victory. It is only one among many weapons. Nor can the secrets which it reveals often lead to one quick and decisive coup: the Zimmerman Telegram is, I believe, the greatest, if not the only, example of its kind. In the naval war, and probably also in army, air force, economic and diplomatic fields, the acquisition of knowledge through cryptanalysis was the result of the patient accumulation of a mass of detail, of careful study of hundreds or even thousands of messages, individually of a routine and unimportant nature but which, when carefully analysed, revealed a great deal. This certainly was the case in the war at sea both between 1914 and 1918 and between 1939 and 1945. Looking at the individual decrypts for both periods now in the PRO one would, if one ignored the dates, be hard put to it to decide which period they belonged to, so similar in form and content are they—and in the type of information which they provided. Reports and instructions to minesweeper and patrol vessels, isolated information about individual warships, commissioning of fresh U-boats, reports from U-boats at sea of fuel and torpedoes remaining and weather conditions prevailing. One could multiply the list ad infinitum. The most important and vital differences between British Naval Intelligence in the two periods were the different ways in which information, and particularly operational intelligence, was handled and in the attitude of the leading members of the Naval Staff to those who produced and analysed that intelligence.

On 8 November 1914, Churchill wrote out in his own hand a 'charter' for Room 40.[31] He was very rightly concerned that no inkling of the British Intelligence success should leak back to the enemy, but the regulations which he laid down were far too restrictive and ignored the fact that a secret is not worth keeping if effective use cannot be made of it. Curiously, for so offensive-minded a man as Churchill, the emphasis was all on the defensive, not the aggressive use of intelligence, although perhaps he did not foresee the disadvantages of the rules which he laid down to deal with an unprecedented situation. The circulation of Room 40's decrypts was restricted to half a dozen most senior officers on the Naval Staff, of whom the most important, if not the most senior, was Oliver, Chief of the so-called War Staff. Oliver was an extemely able officer but he was a workaholic who was quite incapable of delegation. Until he was posted to sea in 1918 he hardly ever left the Admiralty, for more than a couple of hours, night or day. He drafted practically every single important signal himself in his own hand. He made little use of his own staff officers and he simply did not believe that the curious collection of amateurs in Room 40 could possibly come to understand the complexities of naval warfare and the true significance of the decrypts which they produced. He acted as his own analyst; he alone decided what information should be passed out to the Grand Fleet or other authorities, but, of course, he could not study the great volume of messages available and he did not ask for or welcome any opinions from the increasingly expert and knowledgeable staff of Room 40. I have seen no indication of his ever visiting the room or discussing matters with its staff. The results were predictable. No one man could possibly tackle the Intelligence job on his own, let alone deal with the hundred and one operational problems which were his main and vitally important responsibility. 'Intelligence of an important nature was either not forthcoming or was not available to the fullest extent in the right place at the right time.[32] I have already remarked that Room 40 deprived the *Hochseeflotte* of its advantages of surprise and also played an important part in the eleventh hour defeat of the U-boats. One must acknowledge that Oliver made a contribution to these successes, but the list of missed opportunities is endless. Jutland was the supreme example—if Jellicoe had been provided with all the information available in the Admiralty before, during and immediately after the battle, it should have been a second Trafalgar with results which I believe would have been of far greater significance to the future course of the war than is often alleged. It was not really until Oliver left the Admiralty early in 1918 that Room 40 ceased to be the Chief of War Staff's private cryptanalysis bureau and began, tentatively, to develop into a proper Intelligence Centre. It should not have taken more than three years of war for this to come about.

The situation in 1939 was very different. In 1937, Vice-Admiral 'Bubbles' James, Deputy Chief of Naval Staff, who had been Hall's deputy in charge of Room 40 in 1917 and 1918, gave instructions for the formation of an Operational Intelligence Centre in NID to collect, study, analyse and then promulgate to the Naval Staff information from every possible source about the location, movements and intentions of potential or actual enemy maritime forces.[33] He was not certain that much help could be expected from cryptanalysis, but thanks to the planning of the young Paymaster Lieutenant Commander Norman Denning and the vision and backing from 1939 onwards of the new DNI, Godfrey, the OIC was established and was equipped and authorised not only to fulfil its original remit but also to communicate direct with ships and authorities at sea and overseas and with other services. OIC was at first handicapped by the lack of first class sources—air reconnaissance, a fully developed direction finding organisation, reliable reports from the Secret Service and, above all, virtually nothing from Bletchley Park. But its status as *the* Intelligence Centre for maritime operational information was firmly established and, as gradually and despite initial mistakes, its expertise and the efficiency of its sources improved, it began to excercise an influence on maritime operations which Room 40, even at its best in 1918, had never been able to do. Even as early as 1940, it was in the OIC that more and more of the important operational decisions were being taken in the light of the information displayed on its charts and of the advice proffered by its experts. The old distrust of the senior and civilian background took time to dissipate but, by 1942, thanks to the supply of information form Bletchley and OIC's ability to marry this to information from all other sources, Operations were no longer dominating Intelligence: Intelligence was in practice if not in theory controlling Operations.

Nowhere was this more marked than in the OIC's Submarine Tracking Room. When Admiral Edelsten, Assistant Chief of Staff (U-boats and Trade) laid down that no convoy or independent ship was to be routed against the advice of the Tracking Room without his express and personal permission,[34] he was merely giving formal approval to a practice already generally applied by his subordinates. The allocation of anti-submarine forces between the various British and Allied Commands was based on the Tracking Room's estimation of the threat in the various areas affected. Admiral Sir Peter Gretton, a distinguished wartime Escort commander, has stated that, until he studied the secret records, he had always supposed that the second Battle of the Atlantic had been fought between Dönitz and Max Horton, Commander-in-Chief Western Approaches, but he had then concluded that in fact the two chief protagonists were Dönitz and Rodger Winn, the peacetime lawyer and temporary Commander RNVR who was head of the Tracking Room—or indeed in Winn's absence, his deputy or the junior watchkeeper on duty.[35] This may well be going a little too far, but it does demonstrate the immense change in attitude, organisation and practice which had taken place since the days of Room 40. From 1941 onwards (i.e. from the advent of Special Intelligence*) the information provided by Bletchley, combined with Direction Finding and all other sources, even allowing for delays, gaps and faulty appreciations, was so good that its vital importance could not be denied or ignored, and of all the sources available that derived from cryptanalysis was far and away the most reliable and useful.

Not only was there very close co-operation between OIC and Bletchley on the one hand but also between OIC, Western Approaches and all other naval commands and Coastal, Bomber and Fighter Commands of the RAF on the

---

* Information derived from decrypts is now erroneously if conveniently referred to as Ultra. The correct designation is Special Intelligence. Ultra was merely a security classification and followed a practice introduced by Hall in November, 1917. Godfrey had reinstituted this method in 1939 in anticipation that Bletchley would, sooner or later, again provide decrypts of enemy signals. On 13 May 1940, Godfrey signalled the C-in-C Home Fleet and others that the previous security classification Hydro was to be replaced by the word Ultra, the first use of this term that I have been able to trace.[36] The Royal Navy was well ahead of the other two Services in making provision for the prompt and effective dissemination of Special Intelligence.

other. The Tracking Room's day in fact started with a three way telephone conference between OIC, Western Approaches and Coastal Commands, which ensured a uniform presentation of the Intelligence situation to all concerned.[37] If, during the day or night any fresh information came in it was immediately discussed with these same authorities and the necessary action agreed. The excessive secrecy and overcentralisation which had prevented Room 40 realising its full potential were things of the past.

Nor, once America was forced into the war by Pearl Harbor, and, once, four months later, Winn had persuaded the US Navy to set up its own Tracking Room, was international co-operation any less intimate and close. The Naval Operational Intelligence Centres in London, Washington and Ottawa spoke with one voice so far as the Battle of the Atlantic was concerned—to such good effect that no cross-posting of staff was necessary: again a rather far cry from the days of Hall and Yardley. In America and in Canada, as in England, the operational authorities from the top down were in daily, even hourly, personal contact with the latest intelligence and with its interpretation by the experts. Although the cryptanalysts were no longer in the Admiralty (or Navy Department), doubtful points could be quickly elucidated by a telephone or telex call so that there was little danger of misinterpretation or misunderstanding. Moreover, the problem of balancing the need to protect the security of the source against the requirement to make the maximum practical use of secret information, which Room 40 was only tentatively beginning to solve in 1918, was admirably dealt with by the system of Ultra classified signals made with a one pad system to Flag Officers outside the Admiralty or at sea. Even those, such as commanders of escort groups, who were not indoctrinated, received the benefits of Special Intelligence at one remove by carefully phrased signals referring to information received from less secret sources such as direction finding or reports from our own ships or aircraft. There were, of course, delays and mistakes due to cryptanalytical difficulties and to faulty appreciations based on incomplete information, but the delay of eighteen hours in passing out vital intelligence which had occasioned the *Mary Rose* convoy disaster in 1917[38] was now inconceivable. Indeed, direction finding fixes would normally reach ships at sea within minutes of bearings being obtained and when, from mid-1943 onwards, Bletchley Park was often current in breaking Enigma, information was sometimes available to the Allies as quickly, sometimes more quickly, than it was to the German recipients. The system may not have been perfect, but it is hard to think, even in retrospect, of one which would have achieved better results.

The one great weakness between 1939 and 1943 was the failure of British codes and ciphers to withstand the attacks of the *XB Dienst*. The B Dienst's predecessor, the *E Dienst*, had also had its successes, but they had been on nothing like the scale that was achieved in the first five critical months of 1943 until, at last, this leak was virtually plugged. The German successes went a long way, while they lasted, to wipe out the advantages gained by Bletchley Park for OIC. The reasons for the British failure were complicated and numerous. They are admirably dealt with in Appendix 1 of Professor Hinsley's second volume.[39] Failure to foresee the vast increase in W/T traffic and a consequent overloading of codes such as the Convoy Code, misplaced confidence in the Long Subtractor system and in the improvements and changes made to it, combined with the Royal Navy's stupid refusal to adopt the Tupex system for use at sea, seem to me to be the main reasons. The potential weaknesses were recognised quite early on, but undue delay occurred in producing a new cipher, in part because the full extent to which the Convoy cipher was being penetrated could not be seen during the blackout in Atlantic U-boat traffic from February to December 1942. NID must take its share of the blame, but many other departments—BP and the Signal Division among others—were perhaps even more at fault and I believe that those who have held that the main responsibility should be laid on the DNI's shoulders are wrong and grossly unfair to Godfrey.[40]

To sum up briefly, I do not think it is unreasonable to claim that British Naval Intelligence made a most important contribution to the victories in 1918 and 1945 over its principal enemy, Germany. If, as Godfrey has written, 'the Hall tradition withered' between the wars, it did not die. There were too many direct links between the two NIDs in men, in ideas, in organisation and in sources. Godfrey himself admitted that 'when in doubt I often asked what Hall would have done'.[41] Hall's NID, it might almost be said, *was* British Intelligence, and in some ways its activities covered a much wider non-naval field than did Godfrey's, and, because his activities remained for so long secret, established a reputation for the Secret Service which it did not in fact deserve. By Godfrey's time the situation had changed, but NID's influence nevertheless continued to extend by example and precept far beyond the Admiralty, even affecting, for the better I would say, the development of the American Intelligence Services. On both occasions, NID's success was in very large measure due to the work of the cyptanalysts, a purely naval unit under Hall, and interservice and therefore better organisation in Godfrey's time. Hall was not able until 1918 to turn Room 40 into an effective Operational Intelligence Centre and its development as such was still incomplete at the Armistice. The attitude of the Naval Staff, personified by Admiral Oliver but initiated by Churchill, prevented the

Royal Navy from deriving the maximum advantage from Room 40's triumphs. OIC and NID in general benefited from a completely different atmosphere, a change which Godfrey did much to bring about. The Naval Staff came to recognise the vital importance of the weapon in their hands and the fact that civilians, whether temporarily in uniform or not, were perfectly capable, indeed better qualified, to interpret and disseminate Intelligence than those whose sole training had been designed to fit them for operations at sea. As a result, despite some mistakes and some weaknesses, NID was able to support, influence and, in effect, to decide operations at sea to an extent that had never previously been the case. I believe it was a factor of the greatest importance in the second Battle of the Atlantic.

Notes

1. Cf. J. H. Godfrey, Naval Memoirs, National Maritime Museum TS copy 74/96/1. Vol. V, p. 11.
2. Cf. W. James, *The Eyes of the Navy* (London, 1955), p. 8.
3. Cf. D. McLachlan, *Room 39. Naval Intelligence in Action* (London, 1968), p. 372.
4. Cf. P. Beesly, *Room 40. British Naval Intelligence 1914–18* (London, 1982).
5. Cf. W. James, op. cit., Chapter III.
6. Cf. D. McLachlan, op. cit., p. 382.
7. Cf. J. H. Godfrey, op. cit., V, Part I, p. 159.
8. Cf. W. James, op. cit., p. 84. See also the Hall Papers, Churchill College, Cambridge.
9. Cf. J. H. Godfrey, op. cit., VI, p. 226.
10. Cf. P. Beesly, op. cit. chapter IX.
11. Edward Bell Papers. Office of Counsellor Files. National Archives, Washington.
12. Ibid.
13. Cf. P. Beesly, *Very Special Admiral. The Life of Admiral J. H. Godfrey, CB* (London, 1980), pp. 127 ff. See also D. McLachlan, op. cit. pp. 129 ff.
14. Naval monographs *c.* 1949. Copy in author's possession.
15. Cf. J. H. Godfrey, op. cit., V, p. 349.
16. Cf. F. H. Hinsley, *British Intelligence in the Second World War*, I, (London, 1979). p. 29
17. Cf. J. R. Leutze, *Bargaining for Supremacy* (Chapel Hill , 1977), pp. 52–103; P. Beesly, *Very Special Admiral* pp. 172–184, and D. McLachlan, op. cit., chapter 10.
18. Edward Bell Papers.
19. Cf. J. H. Godfrey, op. cit, V, Part II, p. 135.
20. Cf. S. W. Roskill, *Churchill and the Admirals* (London, 1977), p. 144.
21. Cf. P. Beesly, *Very Special Admiral* p. 237.
22. Letter to author.
23. Cf. P. Beesly, *Room 40* op. cit. Chapters I and II.
24. Cf. F. H. Hinsley, op. cit. I, p. 337.
25. Cf. P. Beesly, *Very Special Intelligence, The Story of the Admiralty's Operational Centre 1939–1945* (London, 1977), Chapter V.
26. Cf. P. Beesly, *Room 40* p. 255.
27. Cf. R. M. Grant, *U-boats Destroyed* (London, 1964), p. 159.

28. Cf. D. W. Waters, The Science of Admiralty. Naval Review (private circulation).
29. Cf. P. Beesly, *Very Special Intelligence*, pp. 112 ff.
30. Ibid., p. 233.
31. Original in the Clarke Papers, Churchill College, Cambridge. Reproduced in P. Beesly, *Room 40*. p. 16.
32. Cf. Birch and Clarke, Contribution to the History of German Naval Warfare 1914-1918. Originally written, classified, in 1919-21. Now in MOD Naval Library, Earls Court, London.
33. Cf. P. Beesly, *Very Special Intelligence* p. 11.
34. Cf. D. McLachlan, op. cit. p. 118.
35. Letter to author.
36. Public Record Office, Ref. Adm 199/361. C-in-C Home Fleet War Diary.
37. Cf. P. Beesly, *Very Special Intelligence* p. 167.
38. Cf. P. Beesly, *Room 40*, p. 278.
39. See also P. Beesly, *Very Special Admiral* pp. 164–170.
40. Obituary in *The Times* 31 August 1971.
41. Cf. J. H. Godfrey, op. cit. VI, pp. 226 f.

The Operational Use of 'Ultra' in the Battle of the Atlantic

JÜRGEN ROHWER

To form a real understanding of the role played by radio-intelligence in the decision-making processes and in the conduct of operations during World War II, it seems appropriate to look at a concrete example of its use and consequences. Because of the relative completeness of the operational and intelligence documents available on both sides, the best example for the study of such problems appears to be the Battle of the Atlantic, in which radio-intelligence was of the first importance to both sides.

The Battle of the Atlantic was fought from the first to the last day of the war. For the Allies the objective was to secure the flow of shipping, transporting civilian and military supplies from all over the world, especially from the United States to Great Britain. The method used to defend this flow of shipping against attacks was the convoy system. The aim of the Axis powers was to sever the lines of communication by using aircraft, surface ships and especially U-boats to attack ships in convoys and to sink more vessels than the Allied shipbuilding yards could replace. Their method was to attack the convoys by groups or 'Wolf-Packs' of U-boats.

Of course there were periods in the Battle of the Atlantic when independently routed ships were the main targets of the Axis U-boats, especially in the distant areas of the oceans. But the decisive area was always the North Atlantic convoy-route and in these battles on the convoy-routes radio intelligence was of the greatest importance. After first describing the Allied convoy-system and the German U-boat group tactics and the communication systems used to make them operable, we shall elucidate the efforts of both sides to break into these communication systems and, finally, the effects of radio-intelligence on strategic decisions and operations on both sides.

THE ALLIED CONVOY SYSTEM

The British Admiralty started the war with a clear conception that the most effective defence against the U-boats was the convoying of transport ships.

Because the U-boats were at first limited by their range to operations up to a few hundred miles from Great Britain, it was not necessary to escort the convoys outside this range of the U-boats. Even if the ships coming from the west were organized into convoys on the western side of the Atlantic, they only received their anti-submarine escort when they arrived in the U-boats' operational zone. The westward bound convoys could be dispersed after passing this zone of operations.

From the summer of 1940 to June 1941, the extent of this anti-submarine escort had to be widened to the west and finally covered the whole North Atlantic route. Thus it seems appropriate to describe the convoy system as it was organized from mid-1941 onwards. As a first basis for planning, the Admiralty in London transmitted a route recommendation to all commands concerned about eight days before the convoy was to leave from Halifax, or from Sydney in Canada, or later from New York on the western side, or from Liverpool on the eastern side. It was based on an assessment of the enemy's situation and took into consideration the availability of the sea-and air-escort forces. This signal contained the following data:

1 The ocean route positions designated by letters.

2 The position and the date of the 'Ocean Meeting Point' (OMP), where the ocean escort groups relieved each other, at first in the area south of Iceland 'Mid-Ocean Meeting Point' [MOMP], and later on off New Foundland and the North Channel.

3 The standard route for the stragglers.

4 Some secret reference points designated by code words.

Two or three days later, after coordination with the other commands concerned, the route would be agreed and the routing signals sent to the commands concerned. While these instructions could be transmitted by cable or other wire communication networks, the port-director's sailing telegram was sent by radio at the time of the actual departure of the convoy, because by this time some of the forces concerned were already at sea and had to be informed. This sailing telegram contained the points 1 and 2 mentioned above, some information about the composition of the convoy, and details about the communication arrangements. The second part of this telegram contained complete lists of all the ships in the convoy, their nationality, position number, speed, cargo and destination.

Further radio communication was indispensable for effecting the filtering-in of feeder-convoys or for relieving the local escort groups by the ocean escort group. This was especially true when orders for a change of the route laid down had to be given, for example, because other convoys came too close, or because U-boats had been located near the route.

THE GERMAN 'WOLF-PACK' TACTICS

The German group—or 'Wolf-Pack'—tactics had been developed by the Commander of U-boats before the Second World War. The first test operation started in autumn 1939 and the first real 'Wolf-Pack' operations began in the summer of 1940. Initially, the operations were concentrated in the area off the Western Approaches to Great Britain, but with the rising number of U-boats and the increased range of the anti-U-boat aircraft in mid 1941, the operations began to cover the whole North Atlantic convoy route, From then on, the operations took place on the following pattern.

Approximately 10 or 15 U-boats, which had sailed from their Norwegian or French bases at short intervals of a few days, after reporting that they had passed the Iceland-Faroes-Gap or the area west of the Bay of Biscay, would receive orders to go for a heading point, designated by a square of the German naval grid map in an area in which the Commander U-boats intended to form a patrol-line. When most of the boats had reached the area, after five to seven days, the order for the formation of the patrol-line was given. The line was so positioned that the expected convoy would have to pass the line in daylight. If no convoy was picked up the patrol line was given a direction of advance and the day's run was fixed in such a way that the group could intercept the convoy on its assumed route before darkness.

Upon sighting a convoy, the U-boat making the first contact transmitted a signal and the Commander U-boats then ordered the submarines to concentrate on the convoy and attack. During the convoy operation, one of the U-boats had to operate as a contact holder, to send off contact signals every hour and to give bearing signals for the other boats of the group. If this boat had to dive, because the convoy-escort drove it off, another U-boat had to take over the task of contact-keeping. After the convoy operation the Commander U-boats would signal a new heading-point for those U-boats which had fuel and torpedoes left and order the other boats to return to base or to head for an U-boat-tanker. Very extensive radio traffic was necessary, for this kind of operational and tactical guidance of U-boat groups from the shore.

THE BRITISH CRYPTO-SYSTEMS AND THE GERMAN xB-DIENST

The unavoidable radio-traffic for the guidance of the convoys provided opportunities for the German radio-intelligence (*Funkbeobachtungsdienst* or *xB-Dienst*). Signal traffic analysis offered clues from which, for example, convoy schedules could be reconstructed by examining such external characteristics of the intercepted messages as the chosen frequencies and the addressees. Direction finding provided fewer opportunities for the German side because the basis for cross-bearings was too small and convoys only very rarely sent messages themselves. The Luftwaffe tracking stations, could often, however, give an indication of convoy positions by locating the signals of escorting planes.

The numerous signals necesssary for the simultaneous direction of the great number of convoys at sea offered a promising source of information for cryptanalysis the *xB-Dienst*, and the German Navy's *xB-Dienst* had been built up into a very efficient organization after the German Navy acquired knowledge of the successful cryptanalytical work of the Admiralty's 'Room 40' during the First World War.

Before the war, the Royal Navy used two main crypto-systems. There was a 'Naval Cipher' operated by officers solely for operational signals mainly concerning ships down only to destroyers. Secondly there was a 'Naval Code' operated by ratings and used first for administrative signals and messages concerning small ships and later on also for signals about ship movements. The first was based on a four-figure, the second on a five-figure code-book, and both were super-enciphered by long-subtractor-tables of 5000 groups each changing every month or two months.

The *xB-Dienst* had achieved the first breaks into the 'Naval Code' in peace time, when it was used partly without super-enciphering. By the end of 1939, a large part of the code-book had been reconstructed as had more and more parts of the long subtractor-tables. In April 1940, for instance, the *xB-Dienst* was able to decrypt some 30 to 50 per cent of the signals in the 'Naval Cipher' and could deliver to the German operational commands quite accurate estimates about the locations and the movements of the Home Fleet during the Norwegian operations. But it was never possible to penetrate the separate long subtractor-tables of the Commanders-in-Chief or the flag-officers. There was not enough signal material to work on and later these signals of the highest grade were enciphered in real one-time-pad ciphers. Because it was always a major logistical problem to change the code-books such changes could only be made at long intervals. Thus the German *xB-Dienst* could solve more and more code-groups when they were in use for extended periods.

On 20 August 1940 the British Admiralty distributed new code-books based on four-figure groups for both systems, in order to make the distinction more difficult. It also started to break down the cipher-networks into smaller ones and to change the long subtractor-tables sometimes two or three times a month. Nevertheless, by January 1941 the German *xB-Dienst* had reconstructed 19 per cent of the new code-book 'Köln', as the 'Naval Cipher No. 2' was called, and 26 per cent of 'München'—the 'Naval Code'—as well as a great part of the tables. Because of a cryptological mistake, the introduction of new indicator procedures for the long-subtractor-tables, on 1 September 1941, made the work of *xB-Dienst* easier than before. After 1 January 1942, when new code-books and tables again came into use and the number of networks with 'Köln' and 'München' was going up to 16 and 26, the results deteriorated a little, until 6 October 1942, when some code-books and a few tables were captured off Tobruk.

However, the *xB-Dienst* gradually transferred its main effort to the new 'Naval Cipher No. 3', which was introduced in June 1941 to carry the growing amount of radio traffic necessary for the routing and re-routing of the Allied convoy-system in the Atlantic. This was the case especially after the US Navy began to participate in the escort operations and took over operational control in the western part of the North Atlantic early in September 1941.

From the end of 1942, the German *xB-Dienst* could decrypt up to 80 per cent of the intercepted signals in this cipher-network. However, the extent of decrypting was variable and, most important, the time needed for decryption was much longer than at Bletchley Park as will become clear shortly. Only about 10 per cent of the intercepted and decrypted signals came in time to be used in actual operations. The other signals could only be used for background-information, like the reconstruction of convoy-timetables.

When, in Spring 1943, the Submarine Tracking Room of the Admiralty produced evidence that the Germans were successfully decrypting British signals, the whole cipher system was changed and from 10 June 1943, the new 'Naval Cipher No. 5' came into use which at first led to a complete blackout on the German side. However, it is not correct, as many historians believe, that the German *xB-Dienst* was unable from then on to decrypt Allied naval signals. Already in the Summer and Autumn of 1943 they were able once more to decrypt mainly the straggler route-signals. Even with the now longer time-lags, these decrypts sometimes continued to be of importance for operations, for as long as the Germans tried to attack the convoys in the North Atlantic.

THE GERMAN CRYPTO-SYSTEM AND BLETCHLEY PARK

In the same way, the extensive radio-traffic to and from the German U-boats provided many opportunities for Allied radio-intelligence. Bletchley Park at first had great difficulties with the German naval 'Enigma'-ciphers. The main problem was that the German naval 'Schlüssel M' used three rotors out of a stock of eight instead of a stock of five as used by the air-force and the army 'Enigma'.

The three additional cipher-rotors and their inner wirings could not be solved when the survivors of *U-33*, sunk on 12 February 1940, in shallow waters in the Clyde, produced only the wrong rotors. Thus, in spring 1941, the British forces at sea were ordered to spare no efforts to board sinking German ships or U-boats and capture cipher-machines or cipher-materials. On 3 March 1941, this was first successfully accomplished during the Lofoten-Raid, and Bletchley Park at last could start real work on the naval 'Enigma'. At the outset this proved very time-consuming and the results came too late to be of operational use. Only when, on 7 and 8 May, 1941, the British captured from the weather reporting ship *München* and from *U-110* an intact cipher machine, the short signal code-book, the naval grid-chart and other secret materials was it possible to prepare the decrypting machines or 'bombs' for the possible 336 rotor-sequences instead of the 60 used up to this time by the air-force 'Enigma'.

From the beginning of June 1941, the British could thus read the German naval signals of the network most commonly used ['Heimische Gewässer' later on called 'Hydra' or by Bletchley Park 'Dolphin'] by using the captured monthly programme for the cipher settings. A second operation against the weather reporting ship *Lauenburg* located by direction-finding at the end of June 1941, produced the cipher settings for the month of July. Because of the great danger of blowing the secrets of this British success, further operations of this kind were forbidden and so Bletchley Park had to count on real decryption from August 1941 onwards.

In the meantime the other two branches of radio-intelligence were used with some success. After the extension of the network of listening stations all around the Atlantic during Autumn 1940 and early in 1941, traffic analysis and direction-finding from the shore gave the Submarine Tracking Room precise and immediate information about the positions of individual U-boats every time they sent a signal and even indicated when U-boats had established contact with a convoy. Because there was some fear on the German side about the dangers of shore-based direction-finding, the U-boats used 'short-signals' based on a code-book, reducing all important terms, positions and the other necessary information to a few four-letter groups. These groups were super-enciphered by the daily key of the cipher-machine, 'Schlüssel M', and the enciphered short signals could then be sent off in a few seconds. German expectations that this time was too short for the enemy to get a good fix had at first been confirmed by the experience of the summer of 1940. But this changed when the British became able to use a cathode-ray direction-finder.

Since it was easy to pick out the contact signals, which were marked by two Greek letters at the beginning to silence all other radio stations on the frequency used, the Submarine Tracking Room could identify the threatened convoy and send a warning without knowing the content of the signal itself. By this combined method of direction-finding and traffic analysis it was possible, especially after the introduction of the shipboard high frequency direction-finding equipment, to divert convoys at the last minute and to avoid convoy battles and shipping losses. Moreover, these methods also gave the British considerable assistance in cracking the daily settings of the German cipher-machine. Because those concerned with traffic analysis knew a normal set-up of a contact-signal and could estimate from their own situation map the contents of such signals, they could feed the 'bombs' with a 'menu' of a possible clear-text and the actual enciphered text. Thus in order to find out the co-incidence between the enciphered and the clear-text, it was only necessary to make a few changes in the figures or terms of this possible clear-text. When 'Hut 8' at Bletchley Park received the daily key, it was possible to decipher all intercepted messages of the day in the same way as the German operator deciphered them in a few minutes. Everything depended on the time needed by the 'bombs' to crack the daily setting. But even when, as in 1941, the time needed was between two and four days average, it was often possible for the Submarine Tracking Room to re-route the convoy threatened by the German U-boat patrol-lines in time for it to get clear and avoid losses.

Beginning in June 1941, there was some anxiety within the German U-boat Command about a break in cipher-security. In consequence, some improvements were introduced: first, in September 1941, a random super-enciphering of the two grid letters for giving the positions and a new short-signal code-book came into use. In additon, the separation of the U-boat signals from the general naval cipher 'Heimische Gewässer' was prepared with a new cipher network 'Triton' for which the new four-rotor cipher-machine 'Schlüssel M-4' was introduced on 1 February, 1942. This led to a complete black-out for the decryption of the operational traffic of the U-boats for eleven months at Bletchley Park. It was then only possible to continue the decryption of the 'Heimische Gewässer' signals, which gave away some information on the departure or return of U-boats when the coastal escort vessels sent their mission-signals. After some time, Bletchley Park learned that the U-boats were using in their network 'Triton' a new four-rotor cipher-machine. However, because no preparations existed for such an eventuality the three-rotor-'bombs' used worked too slowly to check out the now raised cycle-length of the machine which had been increased from 16,900 digits to 440,000 digits. It took the three-rotor-'bombs' 26-times longer to go through a four-rotor signal than through a three-rotor signal. And, because the Germans had also changed their short signal code-books and their weather short signal-books, it was impossible to find the cipher/clear-text compromise as easily as before. Signals could be broken on the very few days when they could be identified as sent in a three-rotor cipher as well as in a four-rotor cipher. Only three such instances occurred in 1942.

However, after 30 October, 1942, when a boarding party captured the new weather code-book and some other cipher materials from *U-559* in the Mediterranean before it sank, it became possible to crack the 'Triton'-cipher, starting on 13 December 1942. To start with, there were some gaps and time-lags, but in mid-January 1943 and during February it was again possible to break the daily settings so fast that the convoys could be re-routed around the German U-boat lines. But then to improve cipher security again, the Commander U-boats introduced on 10 March 1943 a new weather code-book by giving a pre-arranged code-word. This weather code had become very important for finding the daily key and, when the code-word was decrypted at Bletchley Park, there was a great fear of a new black-out for 'Triton' or 'Shark', as the cipher was called at Bletchley Park. By concentrating all available means, including the use of some 'bombs' from the other services, the experts solved the problem in only nine days, because the very large number of contact signals from the big convoy battles of mid-March provided the necessary 'menus' for the 'bombs'.

On the German side, after Spring 1943 there was again some anxiety that cipher security had been compromised because the German decryption of the daily U-boat situation reports of the Admiralty seemed to be so exact that it was felt there must have been a leak. However, the investigation ordered by the Commander U-boats produced evidence that almost all the Allied U-boat positions could have been obtained by other means, and the experts came to the conclusion that the security of the 'Schlüssel M-4' was not in danger. Since the Commander U-boats remained suspicious, he ordered additional improvements to the machine and to the cipher-methods. First, a second 'Greek'-rotor for the fourth position was introduced in July. In August the departing U-boats received sealed envelopes with a list of secret reference points to designate the geographical positions by the direction and distance from such reference points instead of using the grid-positions.

As a result of this and other measures between June and September 1943, Bletchley Park had some difficulty in breaking the U-boat cipher. From 13 to 21 June, during the first three weeks of July, and the first ten days of August, the decrypts were all greatly delayed or completely blacked-out. In September, the normal delay with the decryption was about seven days for normal signals and up to fourteen days or more for the 'Officer'-setting. It was only from October 1943 onwards that the delays became shorter and the gaps vanished, so that from then until the end of the war the German U-boat signals could normally be read with only a few hours delay. On the German side, the development of a new and more elaborate cipher machine 'M-10' was not finished in time and the experimental machine-transmitter 'Kurier', which could send off 'short signals' in the space of a second, was never generally used.

THE INFLUENCE OF RADIO-INTELLIGENCE ON OPERATIONS

In the first phase of the Battle of the Atlantic, until June 1940, the German attempts to direct the 'Wolf-Pack'-operations from the shore headquarters failed on account of the insufficient number of U-boats available. The U-boats therefore operated individually against the Allied traffic, which at that time was only partly organized into convoys and more generally run by ships sailing independently. In the second phase, after the capture of bases in Norway and France, even if the U-boats had not yet increased in numbers, they could now be employed much more economically in groups against the convoy traffic concentrated off the North Channel. In this they were favoured by the weakening of the British convoy escorts, which were held back to deal with the expected German invasion (operation 'Sealion'). Thus, the U-boats achieved their highest successes per boat and day in the autumn of 1940 by sinking ships running in weakly escorted convoys. Radio-intelligence played only an insignificant role during this time.

The introduction of new codes and ciphers in Britain in August 1940 prevented the Germans for some time from using their current superiority in this field, whereas the British could not decrypt German naval signals at that time.

From the Spring of 1941, the reinforced air-and sea-patrols off the Western Approaches began to deflect the few U-boats into the open sea where they had greater problems in finding the convoys. In the third phase, from June to December 1941, the U-boat war probably experienced its decisive setback. Since the radio-directed group attacks of the U-boats depended on radio messages of U-boats concerning the enemy as well as on radio orders from the U-boat Command on shore, the breaking of the naval 'Enigma'-key by the British cryptanalysts at Bletchley Park proved disastrous, for it enabled the Submarine Tracking Room of the Admiralty to route the convoys so effectively around the German U-boat packs in the second half of 1941 that convoy battles only took place fortuitously. The Allied side was thus able to avoid shipping losses amounting from 1.5 to 2 million gross tons. This was not the only very important consequence of 'Ultra' for the Battle of the Atlantic during the second half of 1941. Since Hitler wanted to avoid war with the United States as long as he was fighting his war to conquer the European part of the Soviet Union, he several times ordered the Navy to avoid any incidents with the US Navy, notwithstanding the fact that the US Navy was obviously supporting the British and the Canadians to an increasing degree.

The decrypted radio signals to the U-boats containing such orders gave Churchill and Roosevelt clear evidence of Hitler's intentions. The President knew that he did not have to fear a German declaration of war when in the first days of Spetember, 1941, he ordered the US Atlantic Fleet secretly to start escort operations as early as possible. This was three months before Pearl Harbor. From this time on, operational control of all Atlantic convoy-operations, including Canadian and British escorted ships, west of 26° West lay with the Chief of Naval Operations in Washington.

At the same time, it was an indirect consequence of 'Ultra' that there were only three grave incidents between German U-boats and US naval ships, because the US escorted convoys were also re-routed around the German U-boat dispositions by signals from the British Submarine Tracking Room. Thus, more than eighty depth-charge attacks made by US escorts on suspected German U-boats in the three months before Pearl Harbor were almost all directed against false targets. It is tempting to speculate about what might have happened, had the break-down of the machinery of the German pocket-battleship *Admiral Scheer* not prevented a German-American naval battle in the Denmark-Strait on 5 November, 1941, for an American task group of two battleships, two heavy cruisers and three destroyers waited there to intercept the German ship having been alerted by the British decrypts of the German signals. It appears inconceivable that Hitler would not have been forced to declare war after the loss of so big a ship and possibly about 1000 sailors.

The big set-back to the German U-boat campaign in the second half of 1941 has been almost forgotten because in the fourth phase, during the first six months of 1942, the U-boats sank more shipping than in any other period. These were their 'happy days' off the US East coast. It is difficult to understand that it took the US Atlantic Fleet, which already had three months intensive experience in the command and protection of convoys on the North Atlantic-route, almost six months after the start of the improvised German U-boat offensive off the US East coast to adopt the convoy-system which had already proved so effective. This was without doubt one of the greatest mistakes in the Allied conduct of the Battle of the Atlantic. On the other hand, the association by many historians of the heavy Allied shipping losses until the middle of 1942 with the so-called 'big black-out' of 'Ultra' that lasted from 1 February to 13 December 1942 is also a mistake. Up to the start of American convoy-operations the German U-boats had no reason to operate in groups because they could find their targets easily enough by operating singly. The need to send operational or tactical radio-signals dropped off sharply and even with decrypting Bletchley Park could have done little to prevent the heavy shipping losses.

The cessation of sighting reports after the introduction of the convoy system forced the U-boat Command to shift its main effort in the fifth phase from July 1942 onwards once more to the 'Wolf-Pack'-tactics against the convoys sailing the North Atlantic. Now, without the decrypted 'Ultra'-signals, it was much more difficult for the Submarine Tracking Room to locate the German U-boat patrol-lines and evade them by re-routeing.

Sometimes the Allies could depend on another technique of radio intelligence to avoid heavy losses by the U-boat groups. Since the German convoy-operations depended to a great extent on the contact signals of the U-boats sighting a convoy, the Allied escort vessels now equipped with HF/DF, could take bearings on the signalling U-boats and run down the bearing line to force the U-boat to dive, while in the meantime the convoy took evasive action. Many contacts were lost after the first few sightings and no convoy-battle took place. With the rising losses of shipping even from the convoys in November 1942, the situation appeared to be becoming critical for the Allies. When the Allied leaders and their Combined Chiefs of Staff met in January 1943 at Casablanca, one of the most disturbing issues was the provision of the necessary mercantile tonnage for the build-up of the Allied armies for the invasion of fortress Europe: victory in the Battle of the Atlantic was consequently seen as a pre-requisite for any large-scale invasion and therefore had to be made the first priority of all Allied operations. However, it took time before the general decision at the top produced the required results. Notwithstanding the fact that already on 22 November 1942 the experts in the Admiralty had stated 'that the Battle of the Atlantic is the only one campaign in which the war can be lost', the American, British and Canadian delegations at the Atlantic Convoy Conference in early March

1943 had great difficulties in finding solutions for a revision of the operational control of the Atlantic convoys which was far too complicated, or for the provision and distribution of additional sea-and air-escort forces.

It is also difficult to understand how on the Allied side national and service rivalries, combined with ignorance, were permitted to prevent a timely concentration of available forces at the decisive spot. Before the support groups (withdrawn from the Home Fleet), and the escort carriers (which the US Navy believed it needed in the Pacific) and in particular the 'Very Long Range' (VLR) 'Liberators', (which had to be taken from the allocations for the bomber-offensive), began to come into operation, there was only one positive asset to influence the battle: Bletchley Park's success in breaking the Atlantic U-boat cipher 'Triton' again from 13 December 1942. First with some time-lags and gaps, then more and more consistently, it was now possible again to decrypt the radio-signals which the Commander U-boats used to order the movements of his U-boat groups. The Submarine Tracking Room and the Trade Division of the Admiralty could once again re-route their convoys as they had done so successfully in the second half of 1941 to evade the German U-boat patrol-lines. But this tactic was only really effective in January 1943. When in mid-February the violent storms abated and the number of U-boats operating on the convoy routes began to rise, it became more and more difficult to steer the convoys round the U-boats in accordance with the intelligence he received from his decryptian service, the *xB-Dienst*. In this period the *xB-Dienst* succeeded in decrypting not only a great part of the Allied routing and re-routing signals sent in the Naval Cipher No. 3 used to direct the convoys but also the U-boat situation reports sent daily by the Admiralty. Thus, the rate of convoys which were intercepted started to rise sharply and the situation appeared to become critical when, on 10 March 1943, the Germans changed their weather code-book. The old one had been captured together with the short signal code-book from *U-559* in the Mediterranean and proved to be the most important means to break the daily settings of the German four-rotor cipher-machine 'M-4', which had caused the big black-out at Bletchley Park on 1 February 1942. When the key-word ordering this change was decrypted at Bletchley Park on March 8th, the Director of Naval Intelligence reported 'that the Submarine Tracking Room will be blinded in regard to the U-boat movements for some considerable period possibly extending to several months'.

The anxiety that the consequences would be fatal was first underlined when, from 6 to 20 March, four eastward bound convoys in succession lost a total of 41 ships out of 202 in the convoys, a loss rate which could not be sustained over a lengthy period without catastrophic effects on the morale of the merchant ships' crews. Some leading figures came to doubt the effectiveness of the convoy system, the backbone of the Allied strategy in the decisive Battle of the Atlantic. However, by concentrating all its efforts, Bletchley Park was able to overcome this big cryptological problem in only nine days, because the Germans failed to change their short-signal code-book at the same time or to introduce new changes to the cipher-machine as was done in July. Thus the very large number of contact signals during the battle against the convoys HX. 229 and SC. 122, coded with the old short-signal code-book and enciphered with the version of the 'M-4'-machine used before, provided Bletchley Park with the means to crack the 'Triton' cipher, because the 'bombs' at Bletchley Park could easily find the clear-cipher-text compromise necessary to reconstruct the daily setting.

Now Rodger Winn and Patrick Beesly in the Submarine Tracking Room were once again able to follow the movements of the U-boat groups. And just at this moment the first two support groups—one of four destroyers from the Home Fleet, which had to cancel its North Russia convoys to provide these ships, and one of the first usable American escort carriers and two destroyers—became available, followed in the next weeks by three other similar groups. Also during this time, RAF coastal Command's squadrons 120 in Iceland and 86 in Northern Ireland, and the Canadian squadron 10 in Newfoundland were equipped with 15 VLR-'Liberators' each, of which between six and nine were operational per day under normal flying conditions. These new forces, meagre though they were, could now be used—and this was a very important change in tactics often overlooked—with optimum effect by sending them to support only those convoys in real danger and to support them through the U-boat lines.

Since battle was now no longer avoided as before, but rather sought, while the rate of those convoys reported remained at a level of about 60 per cent, the strengthened sea-and air-escorts fought off most of the U-boats and their sinkings declined decisively, whereas the U-boat losses in convoy attacks rose to an intolerable level: from 4 in March to 8 in April and 27 in May.

On 24 May, the Commander U-boats had to break off the convoy attacks in the North Atlantic. However, he regarded it as merely a lost battle and hoped to overcome the crisis in a short time. He ascribed the set-back chiefly to the very considerable increase of enemy air-cover in conjunction with a new locating device, which was apparently also being used by surface vessels. The gist of his assessment was: 'we have succumbed to a technical problem but we shall find a solution'.

IIR-K

The first question was about the nature of the new location device. Was it a new 9.7cm radar, an example of which was recovered from a bomber shot down near Rotterdam in the Spring of 1943? Or was it the radiation of the 'Metox'-radar-search-receiver, which a German investigation produced as a cause of the recent heavy losses, supported by the testimony of captured British air-crew members which was prepared—as we now know—on the basis of information from the 'Ultra' decrypts. By changing from the 'Metox' to a new radio-wave-indicator, 'Hagenuk-Wanz', it was hoped to neutralize the effects of radar. To fight off attacking airplanes, which seemed to be the most dangerous enemies, the U-boats had to be equipped with 20mm anti-aircrafts guns. And, as an effective counter against the destroyers and the escorts, the improved acoustic homing torpedo 'Zaunkönig' was to be introduced. With these new weapons at his disposal Dönitz looked forward confidently to being able to resume the battle against the convoys in late summer 1943. On the basis of the estimated gains or losses in the Allied shipping-pool, the Allies had—in Dönitz's opinion—a good deal of leeway to make up before they could carry out any large-scale amphibious operation. Any reasonable successes would thus delay the Allied invasion of Europe. In addition, a continuation of the U-boat war would tie down Allied naval, and especially air-forces which otherwise could be used in offensive operations against Europe and Germany.

When Dönitz decided to evacuate the North Atlantic convoy routes for the time being, he had left some U-boats to simulate big groups by sending radio-signals from changing positions and with different signatures and different frequencies. He hoped to surprise the Americans with his new group 'Trutz', secretly—as he thought—sent to the US–Gibraltar route.

Both hopes were frustrated by the continuing decryption of the U-boat cipher 'Triton'. This gave away his intentions to the British Submarine Tracking Room and its American counterpart Op20G, which now could count on its own decrypts which were always exchanged with the British. The American convoys evaded the U-boats in the Central Atlantic and in the North Atlantic British aircraft and support groups hunted down most of the U-boats there.

When, in July, Dönitz sent the U-boats once more into the distant areas—the weak spots of defence in his estimate—for a shorter time they had appreciable success before the gaps and delays in 'Ultra' were overcome thereby enabling the American carrier—'hunter-killer'—groups to break up the supply organization in the Central Atlantic.

Information about the evacuation of the North Atlantic by the U-boats allowed the British to relocate their air-squadrons and support groups. Some of the air-squadrons and most of the support groups were now transferred to the Bay offensive against the transit routes of the U-boats.

On 30 July, Rodger Winn in the Submarine Tracking Room prepared an appreciation of the U-boat situation which became the basis for the Most Secret appreciation by the Admiralty of 2 August. After describing the reasons for the withdrawal of the U-boats from the North Atlantic in May, Winn came to the following conclusion on the basis of his information from 'Ultra'.

> It is common knowledge both to ourselves and the enemy that the only vital issue in the U-boat war is whether or not we are able to bring to England such supplies of food, oil and raw materials and other necessaries as will enable us,
>
> (a) to survive and
>
> (b) to mount a military offensive adequate to crush enemy land-resistance.
>
> Knowing that this is so the enemy in withdrawing from the North Atlantic must have intended an ultimate return to this area so soon as he might be able by conceiving new measures or devising new techniques to resist the offensive we might be able to bring to bear upon him there.

Rodger Winn and the Admiralty paper were very confident that the new devices of the U-boats, such as the increased anti-aircraft armament and any new detector devices, had no chance against the Allied superiority in the air, even if the Germans were to try to swamp the convoy-routes with all the U-boats they could muster from France, Norway and the Baltic, a figure which might be as high as 150. Bletchley Park also obtained some information from Ultra on the most dangerous new weapon, the homing torpedo. Details of its technical performance were acquired through the effective interrogation of captured specialists.

Despite the fact that the Commander U-boats ordered very strict rules for secrecy in radio communications in order to achieve surprise in his new planned offensive in the North Atlantic, one of his own habits in leading his commanders had fatal consequences: his concluding messages or 'whip crack' signals, as his staff members called them, which were only intended as morale boosting measures and were totally unnecessary from an operational or tactical point of view.

The British only learned about the forthcoming operation with the new equipment a few days before it started because there were delays of one or even two weeks in the decryption process in early September 1943. For example, a signal which was sent only to the 'Zaunkönig'-boats and which gave away the tactical concept of the coming battle—already laid down in the written orders in the sealed envelopes—was decrypted only on 13 September after 11 days, as were other unnecessary but revealing signals.

When the first operation in September 1943 was over, the Commander U-boats could base his evaluation only on the radio-signals of the U-boats. Rodger Winn could not only use all the reports from the Allied sea- and air-forces, but he could compare these reports with the contents of the decrypted radio-traffic to and from the U-boats which was available a few days after the battle. Most important were the signals of the U-boats with all the details about their 'Zaunkönig'-attacks. Thus the British experts with information about the actual events on the Allied side could find out why each torpedo hit or missed, whether it was going off prematurely in the wake of an attacked ship or at the end of its run. This knowledge was of course very useful for the further development of counter-measures on the Allied side, whereas the Germans greatly over-estimated the hit-rate of this torpedo, which was in fact declining to 16.6 per cent after the introduction of the first couter-measures six weeks later.

While Dönitz tried to continue his offensive against the North Atlantic convoys after this first 'success', this was countered by rapid re-distribution of the Allied forces made possible by 'Ultra'. Air squadrons returned from Bay operations to the 15th Group in Northern Ireland and new squadrons were transferred to Iceland and Newfoundland. Also, the support groups were re-deployed from their Bay patrols to the support of the North Atlantic convoys as were new groups organized from the Home Fleet resources and the first two reconstructed escort carriers sent with them.

Since the 'Ultra'-decrypts now arrived with shorter delays, it was easier to send the available aircraft and support groups to cover the re-routed convoys near the U-boat patrol-lines, which the Commander U-boats tried to position according to the xB-Dienst decrypts of the Allied straggler routes. Thus on 7 November 1943, once again, after heavy losses, a disappointed Dönitz had to abandon his tactic of surface night attacks against convoys in the North Atlantic. This time his evaluation of the reasons for his defeat came much closer to reality, but missed 'Ultra'. The continuous air escort of the convoys by land- and carrier-based planes, using new location devices and more effective weapons, had frustrated all attempts by his U-boats to close in on a convoy and reach favourable attacking positions. Only U-boats able to operate submerged at high speed might be able to neutralize the superior air-power in the future and come in to the attack while submerged with new improved homing torpedoes. However, the new program which was ordered on the same 7 November to build hundreds of new revolutionary high speed

Diesel-type XXI U-boats, intended to be ready in the spring 1944, came too late.

In the meantime, the old type VII and IX U-boats had to operate a holding campaign to deny the Allies the use of their anti-submarine forces for offensive operations. At the same time they were ordered to acquire experience of the new techniques and tactics of the Allies and develop tactics for underwater attacks. However, although the old boats, re-equipped with the air-breathing device 'Schnorchel', achieved this goal to some degree, the new boats came too late to prevent the Allied operation 'Overlord' in June 1944. Some of the delays were also an indirect consequence of 'Ultra' decrypts, which gave away details about the new developments and so led to the bombing of construction yards and their associated industries.

To conclude, we are left with the question: Did the U-boats have a real chance of preventing the Allied counter-offensive which culminated in the decisive invasion of Europe?

In answering this question most historians see the spring of 1943 as the turning point of the Battle of the Atlantic when the tide turned from the sinking of merchant ships to the destruction of the U-boats. However, in my view we must pay more attention to the period June to December 1941, when the U-boats suffered their first big set-back. This has almost been forgotten owing to the great Allied shipping losses which they caused during their 'golden days' off the US east coast in 1942. During the second half of 1941, according to a very cautious estimate, the Submarine Tracking Room of the Admiralty, using 'Ultra'-decrypts, re-routed the convoys so cleverly around the German 'Wolf-Packs' that about 300 ships were saved by avoiding battles. This appears to me a more decisive contribution to the outcome of the battle than the U-boats sunk in the convoy battles of 1943 or in the Bay offensives. Without these 300 ships, probably augmented by about 100 more which would have been lost without 'Ultra'-based re-routing in the spring 1943, shipping and transport problems would have forced a postponement of 'Overlord' for months, perhaps to the spring of 1945. I am sceptical about the argument that if such a crisis had occurred early in 1942 it would have led to the re-allocation and re-distribution of resources thereby solving these problems in time for 'Overlord' in the summer of 1944. When such a crisis developed in January 1943 and the top Allied leaders placed victory in the Battle of the Atlantic at the top of the list of priorities, it took almost six months before the national and inter-service rivalries and the strategic and operational pre-occupations of many military leaders had been sufficiently overcome to enable the available resources to be concentrated at the right place.

There was of course never any doubt about the final outcome of the Battle of the Atlantic and of the Second World War as a whole. But the way in which it occurred and its timing might have been different. And while there were many factors which influenced the outcome of the decisive Battle of the Atlantic, I would place 'Ultra' at the top of this list of factors.

The Tottering Giant:
German Perceptions of Soviet Military and Economic Strength in Preparation for 'Operation Blau' (1942)*

BERND WEGNER

The history of German-Soviet relations has been to a great degree one of mutual misperception. The 12 years of National Socialist rule were in no way an exception: quite the contrary, in many respects these years represent a climax of self-deception regarding the respective opponents' goals, strategies and resources. In fact, it seems that both the severe crisis of Stalinism in 1941 and the final collapse of Nazism four years later were deeply rooted in those misperceptions.

As far as the German side is concerned, the most fatal consequence of this misjudgement was Hitler's decision in summer 1940 to invade Russia.[1] His hope for an easy victory, the basic assumption of German strategy, was shared to a greater or lesser extent by all his military advisers (as well as by many foreign observers). Field Marshal von Brauchitsch, for example, the Commander in Chief of the Army, expected a few weeks of fierce border battles then some more weeks of less intensive fighting.[2] In August 1941, his Chief of Staff, *Generaloberst* Halder, still regarded Hitler's amateurish interference in military operations as the only serious obstacle to beating the Russians before the onset of winter.[3] Such illusions were not only based on the myth of the *Wehrmacht*'s invincibility, but also on a failure to grasp the realities of Stalinist Russia. How then—and this is the underlying question

---

* Dedicated to Manfred Messerschmidt on the occasion of his 60th Birthday.

293

of my article—did the German military establishment respond to the immediate experience of Soviet reality? Did the Germans achieve a more realistic approach to the problem when in spring 1942 they began to prepare for yet another attempt to defeat Russia? However, before turning to these questions, to which historians have paid relatively little attention, I should like to stress some of the main difficulties with which German intelligence agencies were confronted in trying to establish a reliable and objective picture of Soviet military and economic capacities.

Before the launching of the German offensive, there was, for obvious reasons, comparatively little information available: no figures were published in Russian newspapers or specialist journals; espionage in the usual sense was utterly impossible; and reports by the few travellers allowed to visit Soviet Russia often proved unreliable and coloured by personal prejudice. Under these circumstances the experience of the First World War and the extensive postwar cooperation between the *Reichswehr* and the Red Army remained the primary sources of information on the Soviet Union's military-industrial complex. During the twenties and early thirties, many officers, some of whom were to become high-ranking military leaders in Hitler's *Wehrmacht* (e.g. Blomberg, Guderian, Manstein, Model and others), had visited the Soviet Union and attended Red Army manoeuvres. Many Soviet officers had, on the other hand, received specialised military training in Germany, and both armies had cooperated closely in the development and testing of tanks, aircraft and gas weapons.[4] Given the rapid changes which the Soviet economy and society were undergoing during the interwar period, much of this experience was, nevertheless, outdated by the time Hitler and the High Command began preparing for a war against Russia. The growing gaps in information were bridged by speculations concerning the innovative potential of the Bolshevist regime in general and the presumably disastrous consequences of the Red Army purges in 1937–38 in particular.[5] Regarding the latter point, special attention was given to the Red Army's performance in its winter campaign against Finland (1939–40) and in its occupation of the Baltic States and Poland's eastern territories following the Hitler-Stalin agreement. These events only served to strengthen the view of the German General Staff that the Red Army was temporarily incapable of carrying out large scale operations.[6] Interestingly enough, hardly anybody—with the exception of General Köstring, the German military attaché in Moscow—paid attention to the more successful Russian performance in the Manchurian conflict just one year earlier.

This leads me to my second point. A realistic assessment of Soviet strength was complicated not only by the lack of information but also by the observer's *ideological preconceptions*. Since Germany had joined the 'concert' of the Great European powers in the second half of the nineteenth century, the 'Russian threat' had become a constant feature of German self-evaluation—being both more mysterious than the 'arch enemy' France and more constant than 'perfidious Albion'. The Germans' image of Russia was nevertheless highly ambiguous: on the one hand there was the nightmare of a constantly growing Asian monster threatening occidental culture by a relentless drive towards the west; on the other hand, Russia appeared as a tottering giant verging on collapse because of its ethnic and social tensions and its cultural backwardness.[7] Contradictory as these two ideas may appear, they actually led to a similar conclusion by encouraging their protagonists to wage war against Russia either in order to gain an easy victory or in an attempt to prevent a further build-up of the Russian threat. This dualistic view gained further momentum following the Bolshevik take-over in 1917. Now both images—the 'optimistic' view of Russia as a tottering giant and the bolshevik threat as its 'pessimistic' counterpart—often merged into a single argument. In *Mein Kampf*, Hitler himself provided us with a good example of this. On the one hand he described Russian bolshevism as a most dangerous attempt 'undertaken by the Jews in the twentieth century to achieve world domination'. But in the same context he predicted the breakdown not only of 'Jewish Bolshevism' but also of the Russian state as such:

> Impossible as it is for the Russian by himself to shake off the yoke of the Jew by his own resources, it is equally impossible for the Jew to maintain the mighty empire forever. . . And the end of Jewish rule in Russia will also be the end of Russia as a state. We have been chosen by Fate as witnesses of a catastrophe which will be the mightiest confirmation of the soundness of the folkish theory.[8]

There were three ideological preconceptions inherent in Hitler's judgement: first, he identified Russia, Bolshevism and Judaism; second, he assumed any kind of peaceful coexistence with the USSR to be impossible in the long run; and finally, he was convinced that the cultural and racial inferiority of the Slavs would ensure his success in war. These ideas, consistently held by Hitler almost until his death more than two decades later, became after 1933 an increasingly common pattern of perception. They biased the evaluation of information, especially after the decision on the war against Russia, in the sense that too much attention was paid to the current weaknesses of the Soviet war machine, whereas its power was stressed only in terms of a potential threat in the future. Whether or not this kind of 'analysis' reflected

Soviet reality as it was, it helped at least to justify both the necessity and the opportunity of war in the East.

Apart from scarce information and ideological preconceptions, successful reconnaissance was also impeded by the *low priority* given to intelligence matters before and even during the war. Accustomed to look at war mainly in terms of combat, the German General Staff failed fully to recognize the importance of a systematic intelligence service. As far as the generals of the Army High Command were concerned, it was the appropriate operational approach which would decide the war in Russia rather than anything else. Intelligence (as well as economic and logistical matters) was regarded as just one of the many technical services which should assist operational planning. Intelligence experts of the so called 'Ic–Dienst' were considered as nothing but specialists, inferior to and sometimes even suspected by commanders and combat officers. It was the Chief of Staff or Chief Operations Officer (Ia), who still represented the ideal followed by the most gifted and ambitious junior officers. In contrast, the 'Ic' was, as an Allied report from 1946 rightly stated, 'a Cinderella, and his position was considered as little more than a preliminary to something better and more important.'[9] As a consequence of such disregard for intelligence matters, Ic-positions were among the first to be entrusted to reserve officers, when in the preparatory stage of 'Barbarossa' the growing lack of qualified general staff officers became more and more obvious.[10] In the final analysis, the personnel assigned to this kind of work were inadequate, both numerically and often as regards their qualifications.

A fourth factor characteristic of the operation of German intelligence was its fragmented organisation.[11] Not only did each of the three services—army, air force and navy—maintain an intelligence branch of its own; but within each service, intelligence was gathered and evaluated by several different agencies, most of which controlled field units of their own. Thus, for example, the Chief of the Army General Staff was provided with information not only by the two intelligence departments, *Fremde Heere Ost* (Foreign Armies East) and *Fremde Heere West* (Foreign Armies West), but also by the signals intelligence headquarters *Leitstelle für Nachrichtenaufklärung* and the attaché branch. Cooperation between these agencies was by and large fairly good; the same can be said regarding *Fremde Heere Ost* and its corresponding department in the Air Force High Command (*Fremde Luftwaffen Ost*), which delivered inter alia the findings of air reconnaissance. Of graver consequence was the fact that enonomic intelligence, as well as military espionage and counter espionage, were beyond the scope of the army intelligence branch. Instead, these functions were performed by the *Wehrwirtschafts- und*

Rüstungsamt (War Economy and Armaments Department) and by the *Abwehr* counter intelligence respectively, both of which formed part of the *Oberkommando der Wehrmacht* (Armed Forces High Command, abbr. OKW). Cooperation with Canaris's agency, the *Abwehr*, proved especially difficult. The *Fremde Heere Ost* experts often felt that the counter intelligence service tended to draw its own conclusions on the basis of isolated and unchecked reports and thus to present a false picture to the various High Command branches.[12] These problems were even more acute with respect to the intelligence department ('Amt VI') of the SS—*Reichssicherheitshauptamt* under the command of Walter Schellenberg.[13]

On the whole, one might say that there was, of course, some practical reason for dividing up the intelligence community according to its different fields and working methods. But since the whole apparatus lacked a mediating and coordinating agency—as existed in Britain with the 'Joint Intelligence Committee' system—the organizational fragmentation often led to difficulties in communication. These were not only due to the occasionally considerable physical distance between the agencies, but also to tensions within the polycratic German command structure, of which the organization of German intelligence was but a reflection *'en miniature'*.

Having sketched in more general terms the strains under which German intelligence on the USSR operated, we may now approach the central issue of this paper, i. e. the question of how far the experience of Soviet reality after June 1941, and especially the failure of the Blitzkrieg, challenged the traditional image of the Soviet Union and whether it led to a more realistic assessment. In other words, does the Stalingrad débâcle indicate that German intelligence experts had not learnt anything from previous failures? I shall deal with these questions by investigating two operations by German intelligence: the calculation of the Soviet manpower potential carried out by *Fremde Heere Ost* in spring and summer 1942; and the simultaneous attempts of both the *Fremde Heere Ost* and the War Economy Branch (of the *Wehrwirtschafts- und Rüstungsamt*) to estimate the output of the Soviet armaments industry.[14]

II

In Spring 1942, intelligence gathering on the Soviet Union was considerably extended and improved. Whereas up until then it had restricted itself mainly to assessing the enemy's short-term operational intentions and to collecting general information on the structure and fighting capacity of Red Army units, it now turned also to long-term prognoses. Studies of the strategic options of the Red Army as well as of its manpower and *matériel* potential were carried out, based on a systematic, and to some extent even scientific analysis of the available information. All these improvements are usually attributed to the personal contribution of Lt Col. Gehlen, who was appointed Head of the *Fremde Heere Ost* department in April 1942.[15] Compared to his predecessor, Colonel Kinzel, Gehlen was doubtless an exceptionally competent and resourceful officer, though he had no other qualification for intelligence work than the usual thorough General Staff Corps training and experience. Having served as chief of the Eastern Group of the Operation Branch, Gehlen was on very good terms with General Halder, the Chief of the General Staff, and knew very well how to influence the decision-making process inside the Army High Command. Nevertheless, the growing influence of the Intelligence Branch was not so much a result of Gehlen's personal abilities but rather the consequence of a fundamentally changed war situation. As long as the supposed invincibility of the *Wehrmacht*—apparently confirmed by the fall of France—had remained an unchallenged dogma, a detailed analysis of the Red Army's capacities was not seen as an indispensable requirement for operational planning. As long as the Blitzkrieg could be regarded as a reasonable concept for fighting the Russians, studies of the Soviet Union's manpower and industrial resources did not seem necessary. Instead, it was assumed that the Red Army would collapse before the main bulk of these resources could be mobilized. In any case, it was clear that an overall assessment of Soviet resources *before* the outbreak of hostilities would merely constitute a very rough estimation, for radio interception, which was then the most reliable source of intelligence, covered only the western areas of the Soviet Union. (Though intercept stations had been set up in almost all the European states along Russia's borders, their range was very limited because of insufficient personnel and inadequate equipment).[16]

By 1942, the situation had changed profoundly. Having occupied large stretches of Soviet territory the Germans had acquired a variety of new sources of intelligence, the most important of which were the regular reports of the combat troops, air reconnaissance, interrogations of deserters and prisoners of war, captured documents, as well as reports by agents. Even more important was the fact that by now intelligence had become a matter of the highest priority—far beyond the scope of short-term operational questions. Once the Blitzkrieg had failed and the General Staff had to face the inevitability of a long war, there was an urgent need to find out to what extent the enemy would be capable of mobilizing its economic resources and human reserves.

Systematic calculations with regard to the latter were started by *Fremde Heere Ost* in February 1942, i.e. before Gehlen took over.[17] On the basis of the Soviet census of January 1939, of observations by front line troops and of information obtained from prisoners, an attempt was made to estimate the number of combat formations which the Red Army would be able to raise during the months to come. Early in March, the initial findings could be reported to Halder, and, on 23 March 1942, a detailed study on the Soviet manpower potential was submitted.[18] By recapitulating the different stages of this evaluation, which remained of decisive influence until late Summer, one can achieve a clearer view of the difficulties involved (see Table 1 below).

The *Fremde Heere Ost* experts started out from the figure of 170.5 million people, which according to the Soviet census represented the country's total population in early 1939. To work out the corresponding figure for 1942,

Table 1:   German Estimation of the Soviet Manpower Potential in 1942.[19]

Soviet population according to the 1939 census		170,467,000
Population of areas occupied by the Soviet Union since	+	23,042,000
Birthrate 1939–1942	+	5,400,000
Estimated total population in January 1942		198,909,000
Population of areas occupied by Germany[20]	–	21,900,000
Basis for calculation	**ca.**	**177,000,000**
Males registered for the draft (age groups 1894–1923)		35,400,000
Unfit for military service	–	7,000,000
In a reserved occupation	–	11,400,000
		17,000,000
War casualties	–	7,230,000
Current strength of the Red Army (including air force and navy)	–	7,800,000
Theoretical manpower reserve		1,930,000[21]
Various other losses (sickness, exiles, minorities, etc.)	–	690,000
Remaining manpower reserve, 1 April 1942:		**1,240,000**
(correct for 1 May 1942:		1,000,000)
(correct for 1 June 1942:		750,000)

the average annual birthrate as well as the increase in population resulting from the annexation of the western Ukraine, Byelorussia, Moldavia and the Baltic states were taken into account. On the other hand, the losses due to the German occupation had to be subtracted. Estimating these losses was complicated by the fact that an unknown number of the able-bodied male population had been called up before the occupation, and nobody knew how many of them had been withdrawn in time. It was even more difficult to assess how many of the different age groups of the Russian male population had undergone medical examination and been found fit for military service, and what proportion of them had actually been called up. Lacking any concrete information *Fremde Heere Ost* took *German* regulations and practices as a model for answering all these questions. By applying those inadequate criteria, the German experts came up with a figure of roughly 17 million men. Having subtracted the casualties already inflicted and the current supposed strength of the Red Army, they calculated that the USSR had some 1.9 million men[22] remaining as a manpower reserve. In fact, this figure was seen as theoretical for it included members of home front units, casualties and convalescents, a few hundred thousand men from ethnic minorities regarded as unreliable (Germans, Poles, Caucasians etc.), as well as an unknown number of exiles. Taking all that into account, *Fremde Heere Ost* came to the conclusion that the Russian manpower potential was 'by no means inexhaustible', but rather almost completely drained:

> The manpower reserves available are sufficient to fill in the existing gaps, to make good the casualties expected during the next few months and to raise additional units on a much smaller scale than hitherto. Allowing for a further lowering of [the army's professional] qualities, the enemy will be able to maintain for some time this capacity by making use of extraordinary measures. Raising new units on a large scale seems possible only by encroaching on the core [of society]. Given the serious condition not only of the state apparatus but also of the food and armaments supply situation, it appears questionable whether such an encroach-ment is at all possible.[23]

Based upon this general judgement, the *Fremde Heere Ost* department could foresee no more than 60 new rifle divisions and an 'equivalent number' of cavalry and tank-units being deployed until the autumn mud period. From that point onwards, although the resources of Soviet manpower were not expected to dry up at once, they would definitely have passed their peak. With respect to the Germans' strategic objectives for 1942, this meant, as Gehlen himself pointed out, that henceforth heavy casualties such as those sustained in the previous year's battles of Bialystok, Vyasma or Bryansk would be unacceptable to the Russians. Nor would the enemy be able to keep back as large a reserve for the following winter campaign as they had managed to do in 1941.[24]

Though the Soviet Union was in fact confronted with severe manpower problems, German optimism proved, once again, to be illfounded. By the end of July at the latest, *Fremde Heere Ost* had to contend with the fact that its calculations had been upset by reality. For—according to German observations—the Red Army had by then already deployed at least nine new rifle divisions more than the 60 formations expected until the onset of winter; likewise, the number of new tank and rifles brigades far exceeded German estimations.[25] Moreover, *Fremde Heere Ost* was unable to demonstrate the general decline in the fighting capacity of the Soviet units, which it had predicted in the spring.[26]

Unlike the German army, whose manpower potential decreased despite the growing number of formations, the Red Army managed also to increase its overall numerical strength throughout that year. Only during the first months of 1943, after the battle of Stalingrad had entered its final stage, did the figures drop slightly and merely temporarily.[27] There was, in short, no question of a final exhaustion. Quite obviously *Fremde Heere Ost* had underestimated the scope and rigorousness of the Soviet mobilization policy. The Germans had, it seems, miscalculated on two counts in particular: the exploitation of female labour, which played a far greater role in Russia than in Germany; and the speed and extent to which the youngest male age group—i.e. those born in 1924—was called up. If only half of the approximately 1.4 million young men of that age group had been conscripted, they would have made it possible to establish a further 34 rifle divisions.[28] This example may serve to illustrate the dimension of any possible error. However, the continuous increase in the Red Army's strength was also due to something beyond the prognostic competence of Gehlen's department: in 1942 the Wehrmacht proved no longer able to inflict on the enemy such disastrous casualties as it had done previously.

There is still another point which should temper our criticism of the *Fremde Heere Ost* experts. Like many other contemporary documents, their prognoses could be understood in two different senses. On the one hand, they certainly stressed the optimistic view that not only Germany but also Russia was facing a growing manpower shortage, which would limit her operational options and restrict her to strategic defence. On this basis, it did not seem too far fetched to suggest, as Hitler indeed did, that achieving victory in the East was predominantly a matter of better nerves and endurance as well as of superior leadership. On the other hand, more sceptical observers could reach quite a different conclusion. For, despite its optimism, the *Fremde Heere Ost* study left little doubt that, for the time being, the manpower gap between the Germans and the Russians was widening in favour of the latter. Though in Germany too, the age groups of 1923 and 1924 were called up far earlier than initially intended, the combat strength of the German army in the East kept declining (except between April and July).[29] Against this background the increase in the Red Army's strength assumed an even more dangerous aspect. In fact, not only Halder's men in the Army General Staff but also Hitler's closest military advisers in the OKW were worried by this development. Their concern might have given reason enough to reconsider the far-reading military objectives of the 1942 summer campaign.

However, this was not done. Contrary to Halder's and others' claims after the war,[30] the Chief of the Army General Staff actually tried to avoid any major conflict with Hitler on this issue. Having accepted the inevitability of the Caucasian campaign, he seems to have adapted himself to the Führer's wishful interpretations of unpleasant facts: in April, after the final decisions on German strategy in the East had been made, it was he who reassured Hitler that the constant increase of Russian combat formations since November 1941 merely indicated the extent to which the enemy had already squandered its manpower resources.[31]

III

Theoretically, the question of how many formations an enemy state is capable of deploying can be answered either by calculating the output of its armaments industry or by estimating its manpower reserve. The German experts chose the latter approach because information on Russia's arms production was regarded as even less reliable than that on her population structure.[32]

By the 1941 winter crisis at the latest, there was a general agreement among German military leaders that not only had the steadfastness of the Red Army soldier been misjudged but that the Soviet armament situation had also been greatly underestimated. In a conversation with Finland's Marshal Mannerheim early in June 1942, Hitler himself admitted that in the preceding year he had been completely wrong in his assessment of the Soviet forces: if any of his generals had told him the truth about the number of tanks available to the Russians, he would have claimed it to be utter nonsense.[33] Ironically, while this remark was being made, the situation was well on its way to being repeated. Once more Hitler would not believe anybody who might have told him how many Soviet tanks, artillery pieces and aircraft the *Wehrmacht* would have to confront during the months to come. And again, as in 1941, nobody *did* actually tell him the real figures, for, as before, everybody underestimated them.

In order to find out to what extent the relevant calculations carried out by FHO and the War Economy Branch in Spring 1942 corresponded to reality, I have compared them with the figures given in recent Soviet historical literature[34] and, for additional scrutiny, with the data from German intelligence reports in 1943–44. Both methods are, of course, not completely satisfactory, nevertheless they allow one to draw some interesting conclusions. The most striking is the degree to which the output of Soviet industry was misperceived (see Table 2 below). With regard to tanks, for example, the real output figures for 1942 amounted to approximately double the FHO prognoses and to three and four times the *Wehrwirtschafts- und Rüstungsamt's* prediction. With the artillery sector the discrepancy was even greater. Though differences in the statistical definition of weapon systems make it difficult to verify the figures in detail, the output of guns and mortars (cal. 7.6cm and over) seems to have exceeded German estimates four to fivefold. Finally, Soviet aircraft production in 1942 was about three times higher than had been anticipated. Beyond these striking discrepancies, German intelligence agencies misjudged the general direction in which Soviet arms production was developing. While in spring 1942 the OKW War Economy Branch expected that the output of war matériel would continue to decline sharply[35] (as, in fact, it had done since Autumn 1941), productivity

Table 2:   Soviet Industrial Productivity 1942

		Estimations of the Wehrwirtschafts- und Rüstungsamt[36]	Official figures in Soviet postwar historiography[37]
(a)	*Raw material (in millions of tons)*		
	Petroleum	33	22
	Hard coal	95[38]	75.5
	Pig iron	7	4.8
	Steel (including rolled steel)	8	13.5
(b)	*Weapons (output in pieces)*		
	Aircraft (military)	6,600	21,500
	Tanks	6,000[39]	ca. 24,500
	Artillery (cal. 7.62 and over)	7,800	33,111[40]

actually recovered throughout the entire year in almost all sectors relevant to warfare (except motor vehicles)[41]. What were the reasons for an evaluation so totally out of touch with reality? Above all, we would do well to consider that predicting the development of a national economy is a hazardous undertaking even under peacetime conditions and with full knowledge of all the relevant data. It was that much more risky to forecast the performance of an economy shaken to its roots by war and devastation, occupation and mass evacuation. In the circumstances, the chances of an accurate prognosis were very slim indeed. Nevertheless, in this particular case, there were a number of concrete shortcomings, the accumulation of which led to the consequences detailed above. Let me indicate four main errors:

1. The rapid recovery of Soviet war industry was largely due to the fact that the thousands of industrial plants shifted to the East after the outbreak of hostilities resumed production within a few months.[42] Though in spring 1942 German observers were well aware of the fundamental importance of those transfers, they nevertheless continued to underestimate the rapidity of this process as well as the Russians' capacity for improvisation.

2. Calculations of industrial output were largely based on an estimation of the Russian raw material situation. Having realised the growing importance of the deposits in Western Siberia and the Urals, the German experts achieved, on the whole, quite a realistic assessment and even to some extent overrated the resources available. In one respect, however, they were wrong: the German occupation of the highly industrialized Donets basin was expected to cause a severe coal shortage, which would damage both the railway transport system and most industries in European Russia. In particular, the Germans hoped the reduction in coke production would seriously affect the Soviet iron- and steel industry.[43] But these hopes were not fulfilled. The railway system proved much more efficient in bridging long distances than the Germans had anticipated, and steel production in 1942 surpassed German estimates by more than 50 per cent. (see Table 2 on page 303).

3. A third error in German economic intelligence studies resulted from the fact that the experts failed to realise to what degree the Soviet economy had already adapted itself to the needs of total war.[44] Thus the amount of steel necessary for constructing locomotives, for example, was reduced by the use of concrete; in aircraft construction aluminium was partly replaced by plywood or other substitute materials. By contrast, German attempts to calculate the number of tanks, planes or locomotives were based on the

practices of *German* industrial processes, which until spring 1942, i.e. until Albert Speer was appointed Minister for Armaments and Munitions, remained geared more or less to peace-time standards.[45]

4. Finally, the implications of the Anglo-American Lend-Lease program on the Soviet war effort were not fully appreciated by the German intelligence agencies. They did point to the growing importance of the lend-lease deliveries, but they had no detailed knowledge of their quantities.[46] Moreover, their impact on the recovery of Soviet arms production was left out of consideration. Thus, for example, they did not realize that having been supplied with alloyed steel and other precious metals, of which the USSR was short, Russian industry was in a position to produce far more high quality weapons than it might have been able to do otherwise. To quote another example: the large number of motor vehicles delivered by the Allies enabled Soviet economic planners significantly to reduce the country's vehicle production in order to use the additional facilities for increased tank or artillery production.[47]

The view of Soviet war industry as presented by the War Economy Branch under General Thomas, and shared—on the whole—by *Fremde Heere Ost*, undoubtedly stimulated the deceptive optimism prevailing in the German High Command after the winter crisis had been overcome. However, much like the *Fremde Heere Ost* manpower study of 23 March 1942, the experts of the war economy memorandum submitted one week later also felt obliged to make—at least, implicitly—some alarming comments. The best example is the remarks on Soviet oil production. Without calling the German strategic objectives for the 1942 summer campaign into question, the War Economy Branch pointed out some unpleasant facts. By stressing the overwhelming importance of the Baku oil wells and refineries, it made clear that only by capturing this, the most distant of all the Caucasian oil fields, would the Wehrmacht be able to damage Soviet oil supplies effectively. However, as the experts pointed out, even in that case Russian resources would not completely dry up, as the Soviet Union could still rely on the growing share of non-Caucasian oil wells, which were supposed already to contribute almost one quarter of the annual production. In addition, overproduction in previous years was thought to have been exploited by the Russians to create large stocks of petroleum, the exact quantity of which remained unknown to the Germans.[48]

Having presented these disturbing arguments, the War Economy Branch was obviously at pains to play them down. It made an effort to retain the optimistic note of its reports as far as possible, while at the same time refraining from any unambitious prognosis. Scarcely five months earlier, things had been quite different: in October 1941 Thomas had dampened his comrades' optimism by predicting that the Soviet war economy would not collapse as long as the Urals' industrial centres remained undamaged.[49] Now, in spring 1942, he avoided any such clear-cut remarks. Rather like Gehlen's department, the War Economy Branch restricted itself to extremely vague conclusions: in view of the overburdening of the food and energy sectors in particular, as well as of the transport system, the Soviet economy would suffer in 1942 'further disadvantages'. In addition, the loss of industrial capacity, expected as a result of the German summer campaign, would 'accelerate' the destruction of the Soviet national economy, the first signs of which were already discernible.[50]

IV

The puzzling reluctance shown by Thomas's as well as Gehlen's agencies in dealing with the crucial question of the possible outcome of another German offensive in the East contrasts sharply with the very detailed and thorough— though not always correct—analysis of the Soviet Union's economic capacities and demographic structure. In order to explain this reluctance one could point to the failure of previous prognoses, which might have led to a more cautious attitude. But there is yet another more evident point. The *Fremde Heere Ost* manpower study was dated 23 March, the war economy memorandum 31 March. However, Hitler had made up his mind to launch an offensive towards the Volga and the Caucasus much earlier. As soon as the advance to Moscow turned out to be a lost cause Hitler decided to take up again what he had personally always advocated. As early as the beginning of January 1942, he outlined his plans to Japan's ambassador to Berlin, General Ōshima.[51] By mid-February, preparatory orders were given to Army Group 'South'.[52] The decisive meeting, at which the draft of 'Weisung 41'— Hitler's main directive for the 1942 summer campaign—was finally discussed, took place on 28 March, i.e. three days *before* the war economy memorandum was submitted. Moreover, it seems that Hitler actually read the report only *after* he had officially issued 'Weisung 41' on 5 April. In other words, the two most thoroughly researched intelligence assessments of Soviet manpower and economic questions did not play any role whatsoever in defining the strategic objectives for 1942. (Nor, for that matter, did the most important report on the fighting capacity of the *Wehrmacht*, submitted by the *Wehrmachtführungsstab* on 6 June, i.e. three weeks before the German main offensive was launched!).[53]

In short, the whole strategic decision-making process was reversed in a most peculiar manner. Instead of making a decision *after* having systematically analysed one's own as well as the enemy's situation, everything was done precisely the other way round. Without overstating the argument, one might say that *after* the decision had been made, the responsible staffs and agencies were expected to interpret reality according to the strategic requirements. Rooted in Hitler's inclination to decide matters by intuition rather than by knowledge, this procedure carried with it some grave consequences. Hitler himself found it now increasingly difficult to change his mind on matters of vital importance. When confronted with figures which did not fit into his own view of the situation, he either doubted their reliability or refused to accept any numerical comparison, claiming it to be inadequate for deciding the matter under discussion.[54]

Another result of this reversal of the decision-making process was that the evaluation of intelligence became strongly biased in view of the fact that the feasibility of German strategic intentions could not be questioned. Even when difficulties and obstacles were pointed out, they could in no way appear insurmountable. Compelled thereby to optimism, the intelligence experts usually refused to consider the worst case. I am not trying to suggest here that they made no real attempt to give a 'true' picture of Soviet reality. Naturally, they did, just as they were expected to do. But, as in this case truth was a question of interpretation rather than of undisputable knowledge, these officers preferred that interpretation of reality which was more or less in accord with the Führer's expectations. Otherwise they ran the risk of losing their influence on further decisions and of being branded 'defeatists'.[55] In spring 1942, General Thomas in particular had good reason to entertain that fear. By that time, both his personal position, as well as the role of the *Wehrwirtschafts- und Rüstungsamt*, which he headed, were seriously threatened by Albert Speer's advancement as Hitler's most influential adviser in all armaments' questions. Since early March, it had become evident that Speer was claiming to have a say also in matters which until then had been strictly the responsibility of Thomas's department.[56] If Thomas really wished to retain his chances in the race for Hitler's good will (and we know that he was determined to do so)[57] then he could not allow himself to disturb the dictator with memoranda which discredited the Führer's belief in the Soviet Union's imminent collapse.

A final point should be made in this context. As we know from his private notes, General Thomas did not personally share the official optimism to which his department contributed so much by its reports and memoranda.[58] The same is true with regard to many other officers, especially those within the Army General Staff. Well aware of the apparent weakness of the German forces in the East, which in spring 1942 were hardly more than a shadow of what they had been a year earlier, these officers were extremely sceptical about the prospect of success in 'Operation Blau'. Nevertheless, there was a wide consensus on the necessity of launching this campaign. Apart from the Naval War Command, which dreamed of a combined German-Japanese offensive on a global scale,[59] most members of the military élite agreed that there was just no alternative to the Caucasian operation. It was regarded as Germany's last opportunity to acquire the resources necessary for surviving the war against the Anglo-American naval powers.[60] The question was, however, whether this opportunity could be seized by an army of limited striking power. Any positive answer to this question obviously required the continued belief in Russia's military and economic weakness.

Thus the illusion persisted. Nevertheless, the misperceptions of 1942, some of which were illustrated in this paper, were somewhat different from the illusions entertained by the German military establishment in 1940 and 1941. At that time, the Germans entered into war against Russia because they actually believed in an easy victory. Now, in 1942, they felt compelled to believe in victory because they refused to think of any other way out of war.

Notes

I would like to thank my colleagues, Omer Bartov (Tel Aviv) and Thor Whitehead (Reykjavik), for having read through this paper and made some helpful remarks both in terms of content and structure.

1. See A. Hillgruber, *Hitlers Strategie. Politik und Kriegführung 1940–1941*. (Munich, 1982), pp. 207 ff.; J. Förster, 'Hitlers Entscheidung für den Krieg gegen die Sowjetunion', in: *Das Deutsche Reich und der Zweite Weltkrieg*, ed. Militärgeschichtliches Forschungsamt, 4 (Stuttgart, 1983), pp. 13 ff.

2. OKW/ WFSt/L IV/Qu., record of a meeting with Jodl on 30 April, 1941. (Bundesarchiv-Militärarchiv, abbr. BA-MA: RW 4/v. 575, p. 105).

3. Private letter to his wife from 23 August 1941, quoted in: H. Gräfin Schall-Riaucour, *Aufstand und Gehorsam. Offizierstum und Generalstab im Umbruch* (Wiesbaden, 1972), pp. 168 f.

4. See F. L. Carsten, *Reichswehr und Politik 1918–1933* (Cologne/Berlin, 1964), pp. 141 ff., 253 ff., 300 ff., and by the same author: Reports by two German Officers on the Red Army, in *The Slavonic and East European Review* 41 (1962), pp. 217–44. The economic side of German-Soviet military cooperation is thoroughly treated by R. D. Müller, *Das Tor zur Weltmacht. Die Bedeutung der Sowjetunion für die deutsche Wirtschafts- und Rüstungspolitik zwischen den Weltkriegen* (Boppard a.Rh., 1984), pp. 96 ff., 170 ff., 253 ff.

5. These efforts are reflected in a number of articles in the official 'Militärwochenblatt' (abbr. MWBl.); see 'Die Rote Armee nach den Säuberungsaktionen', in: MWBl. 123 (1938), pp. 614–17; 'Zu den neuen Verordnungen über den roten militärischen Führernachwuchs in der UdSSR', in: op. cit., pp. 19–22.

6. Fremde Heere Ost (abbr. FHO): 'Werturteil über die Rote Armee nach den Berichten über den Einmarsch in Polen, im Baltikum und in Finnland', 19.12.1939 (BA-MA: RH 2/ v. 2106); 'Erfahrungen aus dem finnisch-russischen Kriege', 2.10.1940 (BA-MA: RH 20-20/124). The negative assessment of the Red Army was shared also by General Köstring, the German military attaché to Moscow; see the collection of reports published by H. Teske, *General Ernst Köstring. Der militärische Mittler zwischen dem Deutschen Reich und der Sowjetunion, 1921–1941* (Frankfurt a.M., 1965), and the critical remarks by A. Hillgruber, (*Hitlers Strategie*, p. 218, n. 93).

7. A. Hillgruber, 'Das Rußland-Bild der führenden deutschen Militärs vor Beginn des Angriffs auf die Sowjetunion', in: *Rußland–Deutschland–Amerika. Festschrift für Fritz T. Epstein* (Wiesbaden, 1978), pp. 296–310.

8. A. Hitler, *Mein Kampf*. Translated by R. Manheim, II (Boston, 1943), pp. 661 and 655.

9. German Military Intelligence, 1939–1945, ed. Military Intelligence Division, US War Department (Frederick, Maryland, 1984), p. 273.

10. See E. Klink, 'Die militärische Konzeption des Krieges gegen die Sowjetunion', in: *Das Deutsche Reich und der Zweite Weltkrieg*, 4, p. 265.

11. A good guide through the polycratic structure of the German intelligence apparatus is D. Kahn, *Hitler's Spies. German Military Intelligence in World War II* (London, 1978), esp. pp. 42 ff.

12. G. Matzky/ L.Metz/ K. v.Tippelskirch, *Army High Command. Organization and Working Methods of the Intelligence Division*, p. 99 (US Army Europe, Historical Division, study MS # P 041 i); see also H. Höhne, *Canaris. Patriot im Zwielicht* (Munich, 1976), pp. 445 f., and R. Gehlen, *Der Dienst. Erinnerungen 1942–1971* (Mainz/Wiesbaden, 1971), pp. 50, 54 f.

13. See W. Schellenberg, *Memoiren* (Cologne, 1959), pp. 11 f., 182 ff.; D. Kahn, *Hitler's Spies*, pp. 255 ff.

14. Matters of operational intelligence are excluded here but will be treated by the author in a larger study: 'Der Krieg im Osten 1942/43', in: *Das Deutsche Reich und der Zweite Weltkrieg*, vol. 6 (in progress). See also H.-H. Wilhelm, 'Die Prognosen der Abteilung Fremde Heere Ost, 1942–1945', in: *Zwei Legenden aus dem Dritten Reich. Quellenkritische Studien von H.-H. Wilhelm und L. de Jong* (Stuttgart, 1974), pp. 43 ff.

15. See Gehlen, *Der Dienst*, p. 17.

16. See G. E. Blau, *The German Campaign in Russia. Planning and Operations (1940–1942)*. Department of the Army, (Washington DC, 1955), p. 42.

17. 'Vortragsnotiz' by Kinzel, 15.2.1942 (BA-MA: RH 2/ v. 2582).

18. FHO, 'Die personelle Wehrleistungsfähigkeit der UdSSR', 23.3.1942 (BA-MA: RH 2/ v. 1924).

19. The following calculations are based upon the FHO memorandum from 23 March (see note 18).

20. Excluding those conscripted by the Red Army prior to the German occupation.

21. A rather surprising miscalculation by FHO: the real figure ought to be 1,970,000.

22. In later calculations this figure was revised to between 1.2 and 1.7 million men.

23. See note 18: ibid., p. 6.

24. R. Gehlen, 'Rußlands Wehrkraft, Rüstungsumfang und Wehrmacht im Frühjahr 1942', lecture given at the 'Kriegsakademie', 9.6.1942 (BA-MA RH 2/ v. 2445, p. 24)

25. The deployment of another 30 rifle divisions was now seen as possible. See F. Halder, *Kriegstagebuch*, vol. III (Stuttgart, 1964), p. 497 (3.8.1942); FHO, 'Monatsübersicht Juni–Juli über den sowjetrussischen Kräfteeinsatz vor der deutschen Front, Stand: 31.7.1942' BA-MA: RH 2/ v. 2091).

26. Battle reports from front-line units sometimes even suggested the contrary. After the Kharkov battle, for example, the III Panzerkorps acknowledged a 'considerable improvement in the Red Army's fighting capacity'; see telex, 29.5.1942 (BA-MA: RH 20-17/ 125, p. 124).

27. For details see FHO, 'Bisherige Entwicklung des deutsch-sowjetischen Kräfteverhältnisses seit Kriegsbeginn und seine mögliche Weiterentwicklung bis Ende 1943', 17.10.1943 (BA-MA: RHD 18/249, p. 155).

28. See note 25.

29. 'Ubersicht über personelle Abgänge und Zugänge des Ostheeres ab 1.12.1941' (BA-MA: RH 2/ v. 1343).

30. See F. Halder, *Hitler als Feldherr* (Munich, 1949), pp. 48 f.; P. Bor, *Gespräche mit Halder* (Wiesbaden, 1950), p. 216; A. Heusinger, *Befehl im Widerstreit* (Tübingen/Stuttgart, 1950), pp. 176 ff. This view was later adopted by most German historians: see H. A. Jacobsen's remarks in Halder, *Kriegstagebuch*, vol. III, p. 401; Schall-Riaucour, *Aufstand und Gehorsam*, p. 174.

31. *Kriegstagebuch des OKW*, vol. II, p. 324 (19.4.1942).

32. See note 18 (BA-MA: RH 2/ v. 1924, p. 24).

33. Recording of a conversation between Hitler and Mannerheim, 4.6.1942 (in the author's possesion). Hitler admitted this fault even earlier in a talk with General Talvela, the Finnish liaison officer to the OKW; see P. Talvela, *Sotilaan Elämä. Muistelmat II* [A Soldier's Life. Memoirs II] (Jyväskylä, 1977), p. 131.

34. The main works consulted were: *Geschichte des Großen Vaterländischen Krieges der Sowjetunion*, 6 vol. (Berlin, 1962) (ff.); *Geschichte des Zweiten Weltkrieges*, 12 vol. (Berlin, 1975) (ff.); G. S. Kravchenko, *Voennaya Ekonomika SSSR 1941–1945* (Moscow, 1963); Ya. E. Chadaev, *Ekonomika SSSR v period Velikoi Otechestvennoi Voiny* (Moscow, 1965).

35. Wehrwirtschafts- und Rüstungsamt, 'Die wehrwirtschaftliche Lage der UdSSR Anfang des Jahres 1942', 31.3.1942, pp. 12 and 20 (BA-MA: Wi/ ID 138).

36. Projection of monthly production figures as given in the memorandum from 31 March, 1942 (see note 35).

37. See note 34.

38. In a FHO calculation from 25 September 1942 this figure was reduced to 70–80 mill. to. (BA-MA: RH 2/ v. 1924).

39. FHO was more pessimistic and calculated a tank production of about 900 per month; see 'Vortragsnotiz', 7.4.1942 (BA-MA: RH 2/ v. 1924, pp. 84 f.).

40. The figures given by Rokossovskii (Velikaya bitva na Volge. Moscow 1965, pp. 210 f.) and reproduced by J. Erickson, *The Road to Stalingrad* (London, 1983), p. 558 add up to 29,920 pieces.

41. Kravchenko, op. cit., pp. 197 (table 18).

42. See Chadaev, op. cit, pp. 171 ff.; Kravchenko, op. cit., pp. 85 ff., and the thorough analysis recently published by M. Harrison, *Soviet Planning in Peace and War, 1938–1945* (Cambridge, 1985), pp. 63 ff.

43. 'Die wehrwirtschaftliche Lage . . .', pp. 4 f. (see note 35); Wehrwirtschftsamt, Abt. Wi/Ia, 'Vermutetes derzeitiges Kriegspotential der UdSSR auf materiellem Gebiet', 3.6.1942 (BA-MA: RH 2/ v. 2578).

44. See M. Harrison, op. cit., pp. 81 ff.

45. B. A. Carroll, *Design for Total War. Arms and Economics in the Third Reich* (Den Haag, 1968), pp. 179 ff.; for details on the reorganization of the German war economy in spring 1942 see D. Eichholtz, *Geschichte der deutschen Kriegswirtschaft 1939–1945*, vol. II (Berlin, 1985), pp. 63 ff.

46. 'Russlands Wehrkraft, Rüstungsumfang und Wehrmacht . . .' pp. 40 ff. (see note 24).

47. R. H. Jones, *The Roads to Russia. United States Lend-Lease to the Soviet Union* (Norman, Oklahoma, 1969), pp. 229 f.; R. Munting, 'Lend-Lease and the Soviet War Effort', *Journal of Contemporary History*, 19 (1984), no. 3, pp. 495–510.

48. 'Die wehrwirtschaftliche Lage . . .', pp. 8 ff. (see note 35); 'Vermutetes derzeitiges Kriegspotential . . .' p. 13 (see note 43).

49. Wehrwirtschafts- und Rüstungsamt, 'Voraussichtliche Entwicklung der wehrwirtschaftlichen Lage Russlands mit Fortschreiten der Operationen nach Osten', 1.10.1941, p. 7 (BA-MA: Wi/ ID 73).

50. 'Die wehrwirtschaftliche Lage . . .', p. 21 (see note 35).

51. See A. Hillgruber (ed.), *Staatsmänner und Diplomaten bei Hitler*, vol. II (Frankfurt a.M., 1970), pp., 34 ff.

52. OKH, Generalstab des Heeres/Op.Abt. (Ia), Weisung für die Kampfführung im Osten nach Abschluß des Winters, 12.2.1942, publ. in: *Kriegstagebuch des OKW*, vol. I, pp. 1093 ff.

53. OKW/WFSt, 'Wehrkraft der Wehrmacht im Frühjahr 1942', 6.6.1942 (BA-MA: RM 7/ 395).

54. For an early example of this attitude see Halder, *Kriegstagebuch*, vol. III, p. 329 (6.12.1941).

55. That this fear was by no means merely theoretical is demonstrated by two diaries: *Goebbels Tagebücher*, ed. L. P. Lochner (Zürich, 1948), pp. 10 (24.1.1942) and 14 f. (25.1.1942); *Heeresadjutant bei Hitler, 1938–1943. Die Aufzeichnungen des Majors Engel*, ed. H. v. Kotze (Stuttgart, 1974), p. 119 (15.3.1942).

56. Wehrwirtschafts- und Rüstungsamt/Stab, Kriegstagebuch, 24.3.1942 (BA-MA: RW 19/ 166); see also G. Thomas, *Geschichte der deutschen Wehr- und Rüstungswirtschaft (1918–1943/ 45)*, ed. W. Birkenfeld (Boppard a.Rh., 1966), pp. 307 ff.

57. Wehrwirtschafts- und Rüstungsamt/Stab, Kriegstagebuch, ibid.

58. Private notes by General Thomas, May 1942 (Institut für Zeitgeschichte: ZS 310, vol. IIa).

59. See M. Salewski, *Die deutsche Seekriegsleitung, 1935–1945* (Munich, 1973–1975), vol. II, pp. 72 ff. and vol. III, pp. 262 ff.

60. 'Sollte es 1942 nicht gelingen, Russland endgültig zu schlagen oder wenigstens bis zum Kaukasus und zum Ural zu kommen, so muß die Kriegslage Deutschlands äußerst ungünstig, wenn nicht hoffnungslos beurteilt werden'; Thomas's private notes, pp. 35 f. (see note 58).

Notes on Contributors

Anthony Adamthwaite has taught at University College, Cardiff and at Bradford University. In 1978 he was appointed to the Foundation Chair of History at Loughborough University. He is the author of *France and the Coming of the Second World War* (1977) and *The Making of the Second World War* (1979).

Dr Christopher Andrew is Fellow and Senior Tutor of Corpus Christi College, Cambridge and Editor of *Intelligence and National Security*. He has written and broadcast widely on various aspects of modern history. His books on intelligence include *Secret Service: The Making of the British Intelligence Community* (1985).

The late Patrick Beesly served during the Second World War in the Admiralty's Operational Intelligence Centre, which formed the subject of his first book, *Very Special Intelligence* (1977). He subsequently published *Very Special Admiral* (1980), a biography of Rear-Admiral John Godfrey, wartime Director of Naval Intelligence and *Room 40* (1982), a study of the Admiralty's First World War signals intelligence unit.

Ralph Bennett retired four years ago as President of Magdalene College, Cambridge. He was a senior intelligence officer at Bletchley Park for most of the war, and published *Ultra in the West* in 1979. He has just completed a book on Ultra and Mediterranean Strategy.

Dr John W. M. Chapman lectures in International Relations in the School of African and Asian Studies at the University of Sussex. He spent most of 1986 as a Japan Foundation Fellow attached to the National Diet Library of Japan. He is co-author of *Japan's Quest for Comprehensive Security* (London and New York, 1983) and is completing a compilation of the war diary of the German Naval Attaché in Japan from 1939 to 1943, two volumes of which have already appeared as *The Price of Admiralty* (Ripe, Saltire Press, 1982–84). He has also served as editor of the *Proceedings of the British Association for Japanese Studies* since 1980.

Professor Sir Harry Hinsley, OBE MA FBA, is Master of St John's College, Cambridge, and Emeritus Professor of the History of International Relations. He is the author of *British Intelligence in the Second World War*.

Dr Keith Jeffery is a Senior Lecturer in History at the University of Ulster at Jordanstown and author of *States of Emergency, British Governments and Strike-breaking Since 1919* (with Peter Hennessy: 1983), *The British Army and the Crisis of Empire 1918–22* (1984) and editor of *The Military Correspondence of Field Marshal Sir Henry Wilson* (1985).

Dr Peter Morris lectures in modern history in the University of Exeter. His publications include *Eastern Europe since 1945* as well as articles on aspects of Middle Eastern history. He edited and contributed to the companion volume in this series *Africa, Asia and Central America*.

Ian Nish has taught at the London School of Economics since 1962. Since 1980 he has been Professor of International History in the University of London.

Dr Jeremy Noakes is Reader in Modern European History at the University of Exeter. He has written a number of books and articles on various aspects of Nazism and the Third Reich.

Richard Popplewell is a graduate of Corpus Christi College, Cambridge and is researching into police surveillance in India and Imperial Intelligence in Europe, America and the Far East in the first quarter of the twentieth century.

Professor Jürgen Rohwer is the director of the Bibliothek für Zeitgeschichte in Stuttgart. He is the author of numerous books and articles on German naval operations in World War II on which he is the leading authority.

Dr Alan Sharp is Lecturer in History at the University of Ulster. He is interested in British foreign policy after the First World War and particularly in the career of Lord Curzon. He is currently writing a history of the Versailles Settlement.

Jean Stengers is Professor of Contemporary History at the University of Brussels and a member of the Belgian Royal Academy. He has written extensively on Leopold II and the Congo, Belgian history and international relations. In the field of intelligence, he has contributed a chapter on 'Enigma, the French, the Poles and the British, 1931–1940' to *The Missing Dimension* (C. Andrew and D. Dilks ed.).

E. E. Thomas, OBE DSC, has been active in many branches of Intelligence 1940–1987. After grammar school, degrees (redbrick) in German and Music. Naval service 1940–1946 (including Staff Officer (Intelligence) Home Fleet in HMS *Duke of York*). Defence Intelligence 1946–68 (Singapore 1953–56: Fissistigma Thomasii 1956: qualified in Russian 1958). Cabinet Office 1968–87: co-author with Professor Sir Harry Hinsley of *British Intelligence in the Second World War*. Vice-President of Edward Thomas Association.

Dr Bernd Wegner was educated at the universities of Tübingen, Vienna and Hamburg, where he took his PhD in 1980. He was a Research Fellow at St Antony's College, Oxford, in 1979–80 and since then has been a member of the West German Militärgeschichtliches Forschungsamt. An English edition of his study *Hitlers Politische Soldaten: die Waffen-SS 1933–1945* is in preparation.